ERIN GO BRAGH

A Journey to Belfast and Beyond

Edmond Audubon

(**Note:** The text throughout this book refers to Republicans and Nationalists, Loyalists and Unionists using uppercase.)

This is a true story, although many of the characters' names have been changed and occasionally some minor details about their lives to conceal their identities. It's based almost entirely on the travel journal I kept while living for three months in Belfast in late 1992-93, during the final days of the Troubles.

Copyright © 2022, Edmond Audubon
First Edition

Without limiting the rights under copyright reserved above, no part of this publication may be reproduced,
stored in or introduced into a retrieval system,
or transmitted, in any form or by any means
(electronic, mechanical, photocopying, recording, or otherwise),
without the prior written permission of the copyright owner of this book.

Published by Aventine Press
55 East Emerson St.
Chula Vista CA, 91911
www.aventinepress.com

ISBN: 978-1-955162-19-7

ALL RIGHTS RESERVED

This book is dedicated to my Uncle Bob, who inspired me to write, and my good friend Dan Connolly, who encouraged me to finally complete my too long-neglected Irish memoir, and in memory of Mr. Tom O'Hanlon, who first introduced me to Ireland as a boy, long before my feet ever trod the Ould Sod.

It's for all the friends I had in Ireland too, especially for the fiery Irish rebel from Staten Island, who appears in these pages as Timothy J. Callaghan, without whom this book wouldn't have been written, for it was himself who had extended the invitation to me to cross the broad Atlantic and join him in Belfast. It's for the memory of my late, great friend, the witty Paddy Murphy, who kept me laughing and entertained as he toured me around his native city of Belfast and made sure my glass was never long empty; and for dear Geraldine McKeever, the gentle and kindhearted Belfast lass, who made me feel at home.

It's for the brave Irish patriots I knew, who fought to free their native land from British rule and received lengthy prison sentences.

It's for all those who so graciously welcomed me into their homes and for the young and charming colleen named Siobhán, who so sweetly sang an Irish song for me as we strolled through the green grassy fields of Donoughmore, County Cork.

The Minstrel-boy to the war is gone,
In the ranks of death you'll find him;
His father's sword he has girded on,
And his wild harp slung behind him –
"Land of song!" said the warrior-bard,
"Though all the world betrays thee,
One sword, at least, thy rights shall guard,
One faithful harp shall praise thee!"

The Minstrel fell! – but the foeman's chain
Could not bring his proud soul under;
The harp he loved ne'er spoke again,
For he tore its chords asunder;
And said, "No chains shall sully thee,
Thou soul of love and bravery!
Thy songs were made for the pure and free,
They shall never sound in slavery!"

Thomas Moore
1779-1852

CONTENTS

Chapter	Page
1. Callaghan	1
2. Irish Beginnings	5
3. From San Diego to Belfast	11
4. Welcome to the Falls Road	17
5. Tea with Mrs. Boyle	21
6. Callaghan's Girl	31
7. Dead Irish Patriots	39
8. Another Interrogation	43
9. Disco Night at Seán McDermott's	47
10. No Surrender: The War Cry of the Belfast Brigade	53
11. Legless in West Belfast	63
12. A Bit of Belfast History	73
13. The Men of Ardoyne	81
14. The Hills of Belfast	95
15. Strange Encounter on the Stranmillis Road	101
16. A Visit to County Tyrone	103
17. To Derry, Back to Tyrone & Return to Belfast	109
18. The Rocky Road to Dublin...and to Cork	119
19. Donoughmore, County Cork	125
20. A Night Out with the Boys of Donoughmore	131
21. Onward to Cork City	141
22. A Day in Cork City	157
23. Hitchhiking Back to Dublin	161
24. The Confrontation	167
25. Blown to Bits for Ireland	171
26. Clifton Street Cemetery	175
27. Long Kesh and Fergus Martin	181
28. Cider with Denis Irwin	189
29. Demonstration at James Murray's Betting Shop	193
30. Beechmount on a Sunday	197
31. Belfast Crown Court with the Casement Accused	201

32. The Killing of an I.R.A. Volunteer..................207
33. The Quinns & Sonny Boyle............................211
34. The Patriot Game......................................223
35. Portlaoise and Terry Quinn...........................233
36. In Dublin's Fair City..................................241
37. Return to the War Zone...............................253
38. The Party..261
39. Callaghan Leaves......................................267
40. Cathleen Ní Houlihan & The Giant's Ring..........271
41. Paddy Murphy...277
42. A Shamrock Tattoo....................................291
43. Whiskey Ye're the Devil..............................299
44. Geraldine McKeever...................................309
45. Paddy's Wee Tour of Ardoyne........................315
46. The Giant's Ring Revisited with Geraldine.........329
47. Cave Hill..335
48. As I Roved Out with Paddy..........................341
49. The Round Tower of Antrim.........................349
50. Christmas at Old St. Mary's.........................361
51. The Ghostly Mass at Friar's Bush...................367
52. The Parting Glass....................................373
53. Far Away O'er the Foam............................ ...385
    Epilogue..389
    Glossary..393

CHAPTER ONE
CALLAGHAN

Callaghan was in all of his glory that day, his flaming red hair blowing in the wind, waving his homemade green banner – "IRELAND FOR THE IRISH" – standing amid a small band of committed protesters outside the British Consulate. Many held up placards that demanded "BRITS OUT OF IRELAND!" Curious passersby paused to stare. Some offered words of support, and a few were openly hostile.

Southern California was as far removed from the Troubles of Northern Ireland as day is from night. But you wouldn't have known it on that warm and breezy morning, thirty years ago in downtown Los Angeles.

A stout, middle-aged man in a tan summer suit and a straw Panama hat stopped directly in front of Callaghan and fixed his eyes on him. His fleshy face was beet-red with anger.

"Murdering Fenian *bahstard*!" he exploded in an English accent.

"I never murdered anyone in my life," calmly declared Callaghan.

"But you support the Irish terrorists that do!" shouted back the Englishman.

"*Irish* terrorists, is it?!" shrieked an Irishwoman. "The real terrorists are those British soldiers shootin' dead Irish children in the streets of Belfast and Derry!"

The Englishman's fat face contorted with purple rage as he spewed out obscenities at the protesters. Big Donal from County Clare stepped forward. With his unkempt hair and bushy brown beard, he looked every bit the wild Irishman he was.

"On yer way!" roared Donal.

Furious, the Englishman glared at him a moment, then turned away and stomped off.

"Well," said Callaghan, now beside me, "looks like Big Donal took the wind outta his sails."

"I guess you can't please everybody," I replied.

"One man's terrorist is another man's freedom fighter," remarked Callaghan, repeating one of his favorite Irish Republican sayings, with a smile.

For Irish-Americans like Tim Callaghan and for Irishmen like Big Donal, there was a war going on in the northeast corner of Ireland, in the province of Ulster, and England was to blame. I didn't disagree with them.

It was my first time at a demonstration. But Callaghan had been to many of them. While not officially a member of NORAID, that is the Irish Northern Aid Committee, he often showed up for their demonstrations. That morning, I joined him, and we drove up together from San Diego.

Timothy J. Callaghan was obsessed with Ireland and everything that was Irish. And everything about Callaghan was Irish, from his flaming carrot-top to the green socks he always wore. His passionate love of his ancestral homeland was only matched by his deep hatred of England, as Ireland's oppressor, and all things British. Once he even threw out a pair of brand-new Reebok sneakers that his mother bought for him because they had tiny Union Jack flags on them.

We met a few months before the NORAID demonstration, at a performance of traditional Irish music on harp and uillean pipes in the back of a San Diego bookstore. When Callaghan heard my French surname, he repeated it awkwardly.

"You got a bit of frog in you?" he asked.

"Yeah, a bit. But mostly I'm Irish."

"Outstanding!" exclaimed Callaghan, extending his hand with a grin. "I'll shake whatever hand's got the most Irish in it."

We became immediate pals. At twenty-seven, he was a year older than I was. We were both a couple of New York boys living on the West Coast. Callaghan hailed from Staten Island. The son of a fireman and grandson of an Irish-born New York City subway digger, he was the first in his family to go to college. After graduation, he headed out to California and landed a job as a reporter for a small community newspaper. Five years later, Callaghan had grown weary of writing stories about the opening of new banks and the need to fill in potholes on residential streets.

A couple of months after the demonstration, Callaghan quit his job at the paper, shook the California sand from his shoes, and set off to fulfill his dream of living in Ireland. He went to Belfast in Northern Ireland to further his education with a master's degree from Queen's University. Of course, there were other universities in Ireland – in Dublin, Galway, and Cork, all far from the troubled North – but Callaghan picked Queen's in Belfast specifically because it was at the very center of the armed conflict.

He invited me to visit him there. Although not as intense as Callaghan's, I too had my Irish dreams.

CHAPTER TWO
IRISH BEGINNINGS

When I was a boy, I'd often dream of running through a green grassy field and leaping over a low stone wall, the kind seen all across the Irish countryside. Over a cliff was the sea below and a soft breeze carried the fresh sea air. Racing through another field and up a little hill, I'd stop a moment to catch my breath. Looking down at my clothing, I saw I was donned in 18th century attire: a white shirt with big billowy sleeves, knee-length brown breeches, white stockings, and black brogues with brass buckles. From the hilltop, I viewed the glen below. There was a tiny, lone, whitewashed cottage with a roof of thatch and a thin thread of smoke ascending from the chimney. I knew in my heart that was home, my true home. If only I could reach the red door of the cottage, I thought, as I tore down the hillside. But I'd always awake from my dream before I reached the cottage.

Today, hanging prominently on the wall above my apartment's fireplace is a painting of the beautifully wild and lush green coast of Ireland with the waves of the north Atlantic crashing against the rocky shore. It was painted by Edmund Sullivan, a fellow New Yorker and a proud Irish-American, whom I once had the pleasure to talk with on the phone. Many years later my cousin, Sister Marian, was one of the Dominican nuns who cared for him in a hospice before his death.

When I first saw Mr. Sullivan's painting of the magnificent Irish coast, I immediately recognized it as the place I so often visited in my boyhood dreams.

It was my boast to say I first saw the light of day on the Irish Riviera, as the Rockaway peninsula of Queens was once called when it was largely populated by working-class Irish immigrants and Irish-Americans and there was no shortage of Irish bars along the boulevard. A branch of my family – the Kanes – had lived in Far Rockaway since reaching American shores in the aftermath of the Great Irish Potato Famine of the 1840's. A hundred years later, people from all over New York City flocked to the Rockaways in the summer to rent bungalows and enjoy the beach and boardwalk. But even before I was born, large sections of the Rockaways had become Jewish and Italian, and black families had also moved in. The Rockaway Irish, though, retained a strong presence on parts of the peninsula.

The summer I turned thirteen, I went looking for work in nearby stores and shops. A vacuum cleaner repair business was too small to need any help, but the owner was a friendly old Irishman who invited me to have a seat with him in his empty shop. Giving me a can of soda, he reminisced about when he was a young lad like me seeking employment in his native County Monaghan. Tom O'Hanlon was a large, stout man in his late fifties with a big, beefy red face, blue eyes, and graying ginger hair. A lifelong bachelor, he came to America as a young man. I was eager to hear about his life in Ireland and he was more than glad to accommodate.

I eventually found work as a stock boy at a little grocery store. After I finished in the afternoons, I'd bike over to Mr. O'Hanlon's shop and spend a couple of hours listening to his Irish stories. When school began, I quit my summer job but continued to drop by Mr. O'Hanlon's in the afternoons.

I can still smell the sweet aroma of Mr. O'Hanlon's pipe as he prepared tea for us and vividly recall all the details of his workshop where I spent so many happy hours. Lined up against a wall were the broken vacuums people brought in to be repaired and on a workbench were his tools along with a hot plate and a kettle for tea. Above the bench, a large map of Ireland was tacked on the wall and beside it a little Irish tricolor flag on a stick. On another wall was a framed picture of the Sacred Heart of Jesus and from a nail beneath it hung a string of rosary beads.

"Remember lad," the old Irishman often told me, "God's help is nearer than the door."

Once the tea was ready and poured into cups, Mr. O'Hanlon would launch into one of his tales about the heroic deeds of the ancient warriors of Erin, or how Saint Patrick brought the light of Christianity to the pagan Irish and banished snakes from their green Emerald Isle, or how Saint Brendan the Navigator sailed from County Kerry to America nearly a thousand years before Christopher Columbus.

"Sure," he would say, "yer school history books probably make no mention of it, but 'tis as true as the fact that I'm sittin' right here before ye."

I first heard of Ireland's noble yet tragic history from Mr. O'Hanlon. He told me how marauding Norman knights from England invaded Ireland in the 12th century and how the Irish had been fighting the English ever since. I was fascinated by his accounts of battles fought, betrayals committed, ancient lands stolen, and innocents cut down by merciless English swords and guns. I learned how the Irish Gaelic language was forbidden, the Catholic faith of the people outlawed, their churches either destroyed or converted into Protestant churches, and their priests hunted down like wolves. But in each generation brave Irishmen arose to challenge the mighty Saxon foe, only to meet their deaths on bloody battlefields, or swinging from the ends of English ropes, or before firing squads.

Spellbound, I would sit on the edge of my seat as Mr. O'Hanlon recounted the dramatic events of the Easter Rising of 1916, when Irish patriots had seized Dublin's General Post Office to use as their headquarters. From its steps Pádraic Pearse read the now famous Proclamation: "Irishmen and Irishwomen: In the name of God and of the dead generations from which she receives her old traditions of nationhood, Ireland, through us, summons her children to her flag and strikes for her freedom…"

More than a thousand of Erin's sons and daughters boldly turned out with pikes and rifles and nothing more than their bare hands to take on the might of the British Empire with its machine guns and heavy artillery. The bloody week-long battle left hundreds dead and wounded and reduced much of the city center to rubble.

The Irish leaders surrendered to prevent further bloodshed and were executed by the British. Although the Rising failed, there were those who held the opinion that it was more glorious than many a victory. For it showed the world – and the Irish themselves – that Ireland still had men and women willing to fight and die so that she may be a free and independent nation. And, indeed, all of Ireland soon rose up against Britain. By 1922, three quarters of the country had gained partial independence. But the northeast corner, the larger part of province of Ulster, remained firmly in British hands.

My afternoon visits to the vacuum cleaner repair shop continued until the old Irishman died during my junior year of high school. Tom O'Hanlon had become like a second father to me. May God rest him.

As a boy, I also dreamed of strange and distant lands. I eagerly read *The Travels of Marco Polo, The Life and Adventures of Robinson Crusoe,* by Daniel Defoe, *King Solomon's Mines,* by H. Rider Haggard, along with the novels of Robert Louis Stevenson, Jules Verne, and Jack London. At the public library, I spent countless hours studying world atlases and maps, while planning out various travel routes. I saw myself paddling a canoe down the Amazon River, searching for lost Inca civilizations in Peru, going by dogsled across frozen Arctic wasteland, seeing the wonders of the Orient, gazing upon the Great Wall of China, discovering the mysteries of India, strolling along sandy beaches of exotic South Pacific islands, facing unknown perils in the dark jungles of Africa, standing amid the ruins of ancient Babylonia, traveling by camel in Egypt to view the pyramids, walking the Holy Land in the footsteps of Christ, touring the old cities of Europe and wandering through their great medieval castles and cathedrals, and, of course, rambling over the rolling hills and through the lush green glens of Mr. O'Hanlon's Ireland.

When I graduated from high school, in 1983, I set off to see some of the world. I made it to the Holy Land and traveled around with a pack on my back for nearly a year in Israel, visiting ancient cities and sacred places. I went on to Europe, worked in Amsterdam and London, and crossed the Irish Sea to Dublin. Strolling along O'Connell Street, I stood before the General Post Office and tried to imagine how it must have been during the Easter Rising of 1916. The din of battle, British heavy artillery leveling buildings, and through the smoke brave Irishmen fighting and dying to win their country's freedom.

A four-year hitch in the U.S. Navy brought me out to San Diego. By the time I was twenty-six, I was married with two little girls, living with my in-laws, and driving a truck up and down the freeways of Southern California making deliveries for a construction company.

When I wasn't working or being a family man, I entertained pipe dreams of becoming a professional photographer or a writer. Much of my leisure time was spent rambling around south of the border, down in Mexico, taking pictures with my new Nikon N4004s Autofocus camera, scribbling in notebooks, and drinking in *cantinas*.

CHAPTER THREE
FROM SAN DIEGO TO BELFAST

It was October, but it may as well have been the height of summer as the temperature was still in the upper 80's. I wiped the sweat from my brow and cursed the broken air-conditioner in the company truck as I lumbered down I-5. I dropped off my last load of plywood at a construction site in Vista and took the next freeway exit to Encinitas. I'd regularly stop at a bar there called Ireland's Own for a couple of pints of Guinness before heading home.

The place was like an Irish oasis in a Southern California wasteland of endless freeways, suburban sprawl, and perpetual sun. It reminded me of the Irish bars back in New York with signs outside for Guinness and Harp, the walls inside adorned with dartboards and travel posters of the lush green Irish countryside and framed corny sayings like: "God created Whiskey to keep the Irish from ruling the world" and "An Irishman is never drunk as long as he can hold onto one blade of grass to keep from falling off the earth."

Until recently, the Irish accents of many of its patrons and its bartender could regularly be heard at Ireland's Own. But the stage where Pat Hamill from County Tyrone once performed his repertoire of Irish drinking and rebel songs a few nights a week was now empty. Since Pat moved up to San Francisco and Danny the bartender returned home to County Westmeath, in the midlands of Ireland, there was less of an Irish crowd around.

On that particular afternoon, the only customer was an old man in a bright orange Hawaiian shirt nursing a beer at the far end of the bar. The new bartender was over at the sink washing glasses. He was a bronzed, lanky Californian named Jeff, who could talk non-stop about surfing if he had a semi-interested audience. Mercifully, he was without one that afternoon.

Downing my last swallow of Guinness, I ordered another pint. It had been eight years since I set foot on the Ould Sod and I fondly remembered my strolls down Dublin's O'Connell Street and along the River Liffey, ducking into one or another of the many little pubs for a jar of the black stuff.

The term *jar*, as a pint glass is alternatively known in Ireland, originated in Dublin, allegedly at a pub next to Glasnevin Cemetery commonly called The Gravediggers. The pub was actually built into the wall surrounding the graveyard and in the 19th century gravediggers used to take their porter through a hole in the cemetery wall. Taking a jar, rather than a glass, as ceramic jars were used, according to one venerable old Dubliner. His companion, another venerable old Dubliner, insisted it was due to a shortage of pint glasses during the First World War that forced barmen to use to jam jars, hence coining the term jar for a pint.

I took a generous sip of the fresh dark brew set before me. Unlike Callaghan, I reflected, who was still a bachelor with no one to care for save himself, I'd a family to think of. Still Ireland beckoned.

My wife, Beth, who hailed from the Philippines, on the far side of the world, never understood the pull Ireland had for me. But she didn't object when I suggested taking an unpaid, three-month leave of absence from work to visit Callaghan there. I had already bought my ticket and was to leave for Belfast in a few days.

"Erin go bragh," I said to myself, as I gulped down the last of my pint, and smiling lit one of my Camel cigarettes. Ireland forever!

I departed from San Diego on Thursday, October 15th, 1992. After a stopover at Newark, the Continental 747 jumbo jet flew over New York where I'd an excellent view of the Statue of Liberty in the harbor below. Leaning back in my seat, I lit a cigarette, looked out the window at the clouds and dreamed of Ireland.

As the early morning light filled the cabin, I wiped the sleep from my eyes and peered out the window to see we were flying over green patched fields. Ireland. Johnny Cash's "Forty Shades of Green" immediately came to mind. But I wasn't on my way to the beautiful Emerald Isle as pictured on so many travel posters. My destination was the war-torn city of Belfast. World news had long reported on the violence in Northern Ireland: British troops firing into crowds of unarmed protesters, I.R.A. bombs leaving people dead and maimed in city streets, the shootings of British soldiers, and sectarian strife. Belfast bore the brunt of it all.

I landed at London's Gatwick Airport and a minibus took me to the larger Heathrow Airport, where I transferred to a smaller British Midlands plane that brought me back across the Irish Sea. As we approached industrial Belfast, I saw the giant, twin yellow cranes of Harland and Wolff shipyard, where the ill-fated Titanic was built eighty years before.

Callaghan met me at the airport. He looked particularly Irish, I thought, in his bright Kelly-green sweater.

"*Céad míle fáilte!* he greeted me with a broad smile.

"That's very impressive," I replied. "Who would've thought you'd pick up a bit of Swahili in Ireland."

"It's Gaelic! Irish Gaelic! You ignoramus!" he shot back. "It means, 'A hundred thousand welcomes.'"

I just grinned at him.

"Ed Audubon, you haven't changed a bit." His smile reappeared as I warmly grasped his hand. "You always know how to annoy me."

"I didn't want to disappoint you, Callaghan."

We made our way to baggage claim and at the carousel I spied my battered green canvas bag.

"There's my old navy seabag," I said aloud.

A dark-haired girl nearby overheard and informed me in a low, somewhat ominous voice, "This is *Norn Iron,* mister. If ye were in the military, it would be best to keep that to yourself."

"Norn Iron" was how Northern Ireland was commonly rendered in the local accent.

An airport bus dropped us off at the Great Victoria Street Bus Station. From there we caught a black Austin taxi, and went past pubs and restaurants, steepled churches and Queen's University, to tree-lined Eglantine Avenue where Callaghan rented a studio apartment in one of the old three-story brick buildings. The front door was a bright yellow and a "97" was painted in white on the transom window.

As we climbed the stairs to the second floor (called the first floor in Ireland, while the first floor is known as the ground floor), I was again reminded that I couldn't smoke in Callaghan's flat. A nonsmoking teetotaler, he could be a be a real killjoy at times.

His furnished room, with a small kitchen and bathroom, had simply a card table, three folding metal chairs, a beat-up dresser, and a couple of twin beds. On the wall was a black and white poster of old Hollywood's favorite tough guy, Jimmy Cagney, in a fedora and double-breasted suit. He was also New York Irish and one of Callaghan's heroes.

Then I noticed by the window a big, magnificent antique wooden radio. I tossed my seabag onto one of the beds and went to take a closer look at it.

"Does it work?" I asked, running my hand along the polished walnut cabinet.

"Yeah, it works. I got it from Denis the super. He said it belonged to an old lady who lived in the building and died just before I moved in. Denis brought it up for me to use while I'm here. According to him, the thing's a McMurdo Silver and dates back to about 1938."

It was late in the afternoon, and I was anxious to look around before it got dark. So, Callaghan took me out for a walk along the Stranmillis Embankment beside the River Lagan. The sky was gray, and the brisk autumn wind was refreshing. A boat crew rowed by and along the towpath we were passed by joggers and groups of college students.

At a bridge we turned up the Lower Ormeau Road. The depressed, working-class Catholic enclave of small, red-brick rowhouses in south Belfast was a stone throw away, on the other side of the Ormeau Bridge, from the hostile, Protestant Loyalist Annadale Flats and Ballynafeigh with its Orange Hall on the Upper Ormeau Road. The local politics were obvious with Sinn Féin election posters plastered all around and graffiti on the walls proclaiming: "BRITS OUT! UP THE I.R.A.!" And, in Gaelic, the promise: *"Tiofaidh ár lá,"* Our day will come.

A bunch of young boys eyed us suspiciously from across the street. We were strangers on their turf. Then one boy suddenly ran across to us.

"Please, sirs, 20 pence…for Halloween."

The youngster must have been eight or nine years old. Reaching into my pocket, I produced a one-pound coin and gave it to him. He closed his fist tightly around it and hurried back across the street to join his pals.

We continued along the Lower Ormeau Road, passing Séan Graham's betting shop.

"There's where that massacre happened eight months ago," said Callaghan.

I read about it in *The Irish Echo*. Two Loyalist gunmen burst into the bookie's and shot dead four men and a fifteen-year-old boy just because they were Catholics. Then in July, there was the annual Orange parade on the Lower Ormeau Road and the Protestant marchers jeered Catholic bystanders at Séan Graham's and tauntingly waved five fingers at them to represent the five murder victims.

I stopped to light a cigarette and was approached by a middle-aged, unshaven man in a baggy old suit with a dirty cap pulled to one side. He smelled of liquor. When he asked for a cigarette, I handed him a couple from my pack. Then he demanded to know what our religion was.

"I'm a Catholic meself," he loudly declared. "What about yez? What are yez?"

People don't usually answer questions like that from strangers in sectarian Belfast, when the wrong answer could get you killed. But I reassured the old drunkard we shared his faith, and he staggered off.

I heard a few years before that a bishop told Catholics living in Northern Ireland to stop crossing themselves when passing Catholic churches, because the simple pious act identified them as Catholics and made them an easy target for Protestant Loyalists.

After dinner at a pub on the Malone Road, we returned to Callaghan's place on Eglantine Avenue in a jovial mood. As he turned on the old deluxe radio, I joked about Casey Kasem's Top Forty for Belfast being a mix of "A Nation Once Again" for Republicans and "The Sash Me

Father Wore" for Orangemen. But the evening news quickly brought us back to the reality of Belfast.

Sheena Campbell, a twenty-eight-year-old law student at Queen's University and a Sinn Féin activist, was shot dead by a lone Loyalist assassin from the Ulster Volunteer Force while she was sitting with friends at the York Hotel bar at nearby Botanic Avenue.

CHAPTER FOUR
WELCOME TO THE FALLS ROAD

In the morning, Callaghan and I left south Belfast's quiet, mixed Protestant and Catholic neighborhood around Queen's University to walk through the city center to the Catholic and staunchly Republican Falls Road district of west Belfast, which had long served as a battleground for the British Army and the I.R.A.

Turning onto Divis Street, we saw two army-green armored Land Rovers blocking off part of the street while soldiers checked vehicles leaving the area. To our left was the massive high-rise Divis Tower, the city's tallest residential building. The top two floors were occupied by the British Army who landed their helicopters on the roof. Across the street was the Morning Star House, a refuge for homeless men, with a large mural on its gable wall of the Blessed Virgin Mary holding the Baby Jesus, surrounded by blue sky and white clouds, over a blue sea – heavenly bliss in a war zone.

Divis Street turned into the Lower Falls Road. We walked by red-brick rowhouses, a blue community swimming pool building, and an old Victorian-era library. A Sinn Féin office had its windows bricked up and its caged doorway monitored by video-camera. A Green Cross bookshop, run by wives of Republican prisoners, was similarly fortified.

We ducked in and I picked up the latest copy of the Sinn Féin newspaper, *An Phoblacht/ Republican News*.

We then went into the nearby Sports Bar. I ordered a healthy pint of Guinness for myself and my teetotaling pal had a Coke. As we clicked our glasses, I noticed Callaghan had his trusty Pioneer pin with the image of the Sacred Heart in the lapel of his coat. He was seldom without it since he joined the Irish Catholic total abstinence association, after pledging to abstain for life from alcohol. Callaghan was embarrassed to talk about it, but his father's heavy drinking forced him into early retirement from the fire department.

There were only two other patrons seated at the bar, a big fellow with a shaved head in a Boston Celtics jacket and a skinny guy with long, thick sideburns in a checkered flannel shirt. The latter came over and informed us his name was Mickey McPeake. His broad smile revealed a mouthful of jagged, rotten teeth. Shaking our hands, he asked us where we were from. Mickey said he could tell straight off we were not locals, because he knew everyone in the Lower Falls and everyone in the Lower Falls knew him as he lived there his whole life.

"We're visiting from San Diego, California," I told him.

"I got an auntie livin' in Sah-crah-men-toe in California," said Mickey. "That's a lovely name for a place, d'ye not think? Aye, 'tis. Sah-crah-men-toe. Like the Blessed Sacrament in chapel. Me auntie married a Yank after the war and went over to live with him in Sah-crah-men-toe."

Mickey McPeake then wanted to know if perchance we knew his auntie and proceeded to give us her name and tell us the street she lived on. Callaghan explained that although Sacramento and San Diego were in the same state, the two cities were five hundred miles apart. Moreover, Sacramento had a population of nearly half a million people, almost the size of Belfast.

The big guy at the bar, with the shaved head and Boston Celtics jacket, had been listening to our conversation.

"What are yez doin' here?" he demanded to know, as he turned on his barstool to face us.

Before Callaghan or I could answer, Mickey leapt to our defense. "Sure, ye heard yerself, these boys are on their holiday. What are ye botherin' 'em for?"

"Yer gullible, Mickey boy. Soft in the head, like. Ye'd believe any-bloody-thing anybody tells ye. These two ye've been chattin' away with could be Brit agents for all ye know."

"Aw, give over," replied Mickey. "They are not spies! These lads are Yanks from San Diego, California."

The large, burly man eyed us threateningly.

"What's yer business here?" he persisted.

"None of your *damn* business!" suddenly snapped Callaghan.

Sweet suffering Jesus, I half prayed. Don't let Callaghan get us both massacred on my first day in Belfast. I noticed the guy's fists were the size of hams. There was a moment of tense silence, in which I stepped in front of Callaghan as he was at the greater risk of getting a face full of fist. The dreaded blow never came though, and the big fellow simply turned back to his pint on the bar.

I followed Callaghan and our new-found companion outside to the street. Mickey McPeake told us he knew just the place where we could enjoy a quiet pint. I was more than ready to go and promised him if he'd lead the way, his first pint was on me. But Callaghan, this time, was wiser than I was and said he was off to the barbershop to get a haircut.

Mickey brought me about half a block up the Lower Falls to the Seán McDermott Gaelic Athletic Club. The Republican drinking establishment was named after one of the martyred leaders of the 1916 Easter Rising. The doorway was caged and when Mickey pressed a buzzer, we were let in.

It was a packed crowd inside and he navigated us to a booth where five tough-looking guys sat behind pints smoking cigarettes. Mickey introduced me and one or two nodded but said nothing. One got up and offered me his seat. I hesitated a moment, then handed Mickey a ten-pound note for drinks and sat down beside a bald guy of about forty with a strong jaw and muscular, heavily tattooed arms. After taking a long drag on his cigarette, he introduced himself as Kevin.

"Better known as Kevin the Crippler," said one of the other men, with dark, sunken eyes and a menacing grin.

An uneasy, sinking feeling came over me. After several long, uncomfortable minutes of silence, it occurred to me that Mickey should have been back with our pints. I glanced over at the bar but there was no sign of him.

"Yer man won't be comin' back," said Kevin the Crippler.

"What do you mean, he won't be coming back?" I asked.

"We ask the questions here – not *you!*" barked one of the men.

Again, I was being interrogated. Who was I? What business did I have in Belfast and on the Falls Road? I answered the best I could. Nonetheless, I was yanked to my feet and searched. My wallet was gone through and tossed onto the table. The rolled-up copy of *An Phoblabht/Republican News* was found in my inside jacket pocket and the Crippler remarked that I had good taste in reading material.

"But that won't necessarily save ye," added the guy with the sunken eyes and menacing grin.

While all this was going on all chatter had ceased in the club, yet no one so much as glanced in our direction. The Crippler claimed they were members of the Provisional I.R.A. and, to dispel any doubt I may have had, he lifted his shirt to reveal a pistol tucked into his waistband.

"What, you gonna shoot me?" I asked, more annoyed than fearful.

"I haven't quite yet decided," he replied.

But Kevin the Crippler must have determined that I was all right, because he dismissed his brutish comrades, placed a strong hand on my shoulder, and asked me to sit back down. He apologized for troubling me. It was necessary, he explained, to fully check out any strangers who came into Republican clubs and pubs in the area. On a number of occasions, Loyalist paramilitaries sprayed patrons with bullets or tossed grenades into the premises. With that said, he bought me another pint of Guinness and we chatted amiably enough for a few minutes before he departed.

That evening I was exiled into the cold, drafty hallway as I had promised Callaghan I wouldn't smoke in his place. I pulled out one of his folding metal chairs, sat down, and opened my brand-new travel journal to write about my first day in Belfast.

Before I put pen to paper, though, I loaded up my briar pipe for a smoke. As an old Irish proverb says, "One may live without one's friends, but not without one's pipe."

CHAPTER FIVE
TEA WITH MRS. BOYLE

When I awoke the next morning, Callaghan had already left for Sunday Mass. Although I wasn't a regular churchgoer myself and I'd kid Callaghan about being a holy Joe, the truth was I respected him for it.

Since the apartment, or flat, as it's called in Ireland, didn't have a phone, I went to the phone booth out on Eglantine Avenue to call my wife to let her know that I'd arrived safely in Belfast. San Diego was eight hours behind the local time, so it was nearly midnight there. Beth was still awake when I rang, but the girls had long since gone to bed. She told me that afternoon our three-year-old Mary reminded her little two-year-old sister, Brigid (or Biddy, as we'd often call her), that Daddy had flown away in an airplane. The little one then kept crying "no more Daddy." God bless their tiny, precious hearts.

Once Callaghan returned from Mass, he wanted to head over to the Falls Road to visit the widowed mother of an acquaintance of his. He asked me if I'd like to go with him, and having nothing better to do, I tagged along.

As we walked, I asked Callaghan about this acquaintance of his. When he first arrived in Ireland, before he came to Belfast, he spent a month in Dublin. There he met Sonny Boyle, an I.R.A. veteran from west Belfast who served time in Long Kesh Prison. His widowed mother lived on Harrogate Street.

Leaving the main thoroughfare, we turned onto a residential street lined by 19th century brick rowhouses. An old woman wearing a kerchief hobbled by with a cane, as a group of young girls were singing and jumping rope. We paused to listen.

> *I'll tell me ma when I go home,*
> *The boys won't leave the girls alone.*
> *They pulled my hair, they stole my comb,*
> *but that's all right till I get home.*
> *She is handsome, she is pretty,*
> *She is the belle of Belfast City...*

We continued on and stopped to look at a mural painted on a brick wall. A black silhouette of an I.R.A. volunteer holding up a rifle against the national flag of green, white, and orange, with the words "Ireland unfree shall never be at peace," and the vow in Gaelic: *"Beidh ár lá againn."* We will have our day. Wandering around the narrow streets, trying to locate Harrogate, we saw the foundry and machine-building plant of James Mackie & Sons, its stacks belching out billows of smoke. Belfast was nicknamed "Old Smoke" in Queen Victoria's day, when the town was a teeming industrial city. But all the factories that once blackened the skies over Belfast have long disappeared, save Mackie's.

Harrogate Street was another narrow street packed with rowhouses. Callaghan knocked on Mrs. Boyle's door. A short, sturdy woman in her sixties, wearing a neat turquoise dress, opened the door.

"Sure, yez must be the two lads from America," she warmly greeted us. "Come in now, the pair of yez. I've been expectin' yez."

We were shown into the front room and directed to have a seat on a floral sofa, while our hostess went to the kitchen to fix us some tea. A picture of the Pope hung on the wall along with paintings of flowers and baskets of fruit. The room had a fireplace and, on the mantle, amid a clutter of framed family photographs, stood a two-foot-high wooden Celtic cross.

Mrs. Boyle returned with a tray loaded with a little teapot, dainty cups on saucers, sandwiches, and biscuits.

"Sonny made that for me when he was in Long Kesh, so he did," she said, indicating the Celtic cross. "Me other son, Eugene, made me a lovely wee harp when he was in. But the Brits smashed it to bits along with me beautiful German cuckoo in one of their pre-dawn raids."

She related how large bodies of heavily armed British soldiers and R.U.C. officers would pour into the little streets of west Belfast while it was still dark to invade Catholic homes.

"They'd break down our doors, then a bloody mob of 'em would rush in, wreckin' everything in sight – furniture, wee hand-carved harps, me beautiful cuckoo clock. That's me third picture of John Paul II. The Brits destroyed the other two when they smashed 'em with the butts of their rifles. They claimed to be searchin' for weapons, rippin' up me carpets and floorboards. I'll tell yez, they never found nothin'."

Mrs. Boyle poured us both another cup of tea and continued. "Dear God, but it was worse when Eugene and Sonny were livin' here. The Brits used to beat 'em bloody and drag 'em out of the house by their hair to be interrogated."

The old woman fell silent for a moment and her expression hardened at the bitter memories.

"Yez see," she went on, "I come from a well-known Republican family and both me boys were members of *Fianna Éireann.*"

Named for the Fianna warriors of ancient Ireland, the Republican youth organization was a sort of boy scouts for the I.R.A.

Mrs. Boyle then proudly recounted her family's long commitment to the cause of Irish freedom. Her great-grandfather had crossed the Atlantic and arrived in Boston just in time for the American Civil War. He served in Lincoln's army and after the war he sailed home a dedicated Fenian ready to drive the Saxon foe from his native land. Betrayed by an informer, he was captured by the British. Twenty years of solitude and torture in English prisons drove him insane. The unfortunate man's sons continued the fight to break Ireland's chains and sever their nation's connection to hated England. As Fenians they swore allegiance to the secret oath-bound Irish Republican Brotherhood.

Her mother, Mrs. Boyle told us, was a young Belfast mill worker when she met James Connolly. A Republican socialist, he was Ireland's greatest labor leader. In Belfast, he organized the dock workers and the mill girls.

"D'yez know, the Connolly family once lived in the Falls Road? Well, they did."

During the Easter Rising of 1916, James Connolly was Commandant of the Dublin Brigade. He was among the wounded and was taken prisoner when the Republican army surrendered. Shot in the leg, Connolly was unable to stand, and the British executed him by firing squad while he was tied to a chair.

"Me mother was there in Dublin that Easter week. She was in the *Cumann na mBan,* the women's auxiliary of the Volunteers, and she carried messages and tended to the wounded."

Mrs. Boyle's father and his brothers, all dock workers, were in the Irish Republican Brotherhood, and then the Irish Republican Army. They were members of the I.R.A.'s Belfast Brigade during the War of Independence and attacked British forces throughout the city while trying to defend Catholic areas.

But despite the efforts of the I.R.A. in Belfast, innocent Catholics often found themselves under attack by an onslaught of Protestant Loyalist gangs.

"The Orangies burnt thousands of Catholic homes, they murdered us in our own streets….and they massacred our *weans."*

One of the most savage atrocities of the time, Mrs. Boyle recalled, was when Loyalists threw a bomb into a group of Catholic children playing in Weaver Street, killing six of them.

Not only were the Belfast police of no help, but they were often Orange bigots themselves and in league with the Loyalist murder gangs. To reinforce the Royal Irish Constabulary in the North, the Ulster Special Constabulary was established. The B-Specials, as they were called, were quickly seen by the Catholic population as armed Protestant vigilantes.

"We had the Murder Gang comin' into our areas at night with blackin' on their faces to carry out raids and assassinations. Whenever someone caught sight of the gang the 'murder yell' was raised and everyone would join in the yell of 'M-U-R-DERR-EH!' as the people banged dustbin lids and pots and pans. The local I.R.A. on hearin' the din would come and drive 'em off.

"The Murder Gang committed the McMahon murders in broad daylight though. The I.R.A. had shot dead two of the B-men on patrol in Great Victoria Street and since they couldn't get the I.R.A., they picked a random Catholic family and murdered 'em instead. The killers broke into the McMahon house with a sledgehammer and shot dead four of their men and a young lad along with a man named McKinney, who was stayin' with the family. None of 'em was associated in any way with the I.R.A. or Sinn Féin. They were murdered simply because of their religion."

The War of Independence was brutal and bloody. England was a mighty foe, but little Ireland fought bravely.

To put an end to the conflict, the British government invited the Irish to negotiations in London. A deal was struck, and the Anglo-Irish Treaty was signed on December 6th, 1921. The Irish delegation obtained not the independent Irish Republic for which Republicans had fought and died, but something called an "Irish Free State." This new state was to be a self-governing dominion of the British Empire and members of the Irish parliament would need to swear an oath of allegiance to the Crown. Worse, by far, the Treaty allowed Ireland to be partitioned. Twenty-six counties in the overwhelmingly Catholic south and west became the Irish Free State, while the six counties in the northeast, in the province of Ulster, where Protestants loyal to the Crown were in the majority, remained within the United Kingdom as "Northern Ireland."

"Irish traitors bargained and sold our wee Six Counties," declared Mrs. Boyle.

The Treaty divided the Irish people as it did the country, she explained. The I.R.A. was split between anti-Treaty Republicans, who wanted to fight until all of Ireland was free, and pro-Treaty Free Staters, who were willing to settle for three-quarters of a semi-independent Ireland while the fourth quarter remained in bondage. By June 1922, Ireland had erupted into civil war. Former comrades were enemies and often brother fought against brother.

"Me father was a patriot, true to the Republican cause," said Mrs. Boyle proudly. "He went to Dublin with Joe McKelvey – the leader of the Belfast Brigade at the time – and fought at the Four Courts when the Free State Army shelled it with heavy artillery given to 'em by the Brits."

Republican troops had occupied Dublin's Four Courts in defiance of the new Free State government. When they refused to vacate the building, Free State forces bombarded the Four Courts until its garrison surrendered. This sparked the beginning of the Irish Civil War.

"I am ashamed to say," admitted Mrs. Boyle, "that two of me uncles were in the Free State Army."

After the surrender of the Four Courts, her father was arrested and held in Mountjoy Jail and the Curragh internment camp until the war ended in the spring of 1923.

Victory went to the better-armed Free Staters. But many Republicans kept the arms they had, waiting to fight another day. Meanwhile, Catholics living in the occupied six counties continued to be an oppressed minority under the heel of a sectarian Orange state. The Unionist Protestant majority knew exactly what kind of government they wanted. "A Protestant parliament for a Protestant people," proclaimed Lord Craigavon, the first prime minister of Northern Ireland, to his Orange brethren.

Rose Boyle was born and reared in the shadow of Clonard Monastery, off the Falls Road. As a child, she ran and played in the little streets lined by the old red-brick rowhouses of working-class Belfast. She lived in the "little India" area, where exotic street names - such as the Kashmir Road, Bombay Street, and Cawnpore Street – were drawn from the former "jewel of the Crown" of the British Empire.

When Rose was a young girl, she became acquainted with some of the leading figures in the Republican movement in Belfast.

"They were our friends and neighbors. Tom Williams lived at number 46 Bombay Street. Me sister was good friends with his girlfriend Nell Morgan."

I knew the story of Tom Williams. During an I.R.A. diversionary operation against the R.U.C. in 1942 a policeman was killed. The young volunteers of the I.R.A. unit involved in the shooting were captured on Cawnpore Street. Since it was uncertain who fired the fatal shot during the fray, all six of the I.R.A. men were convicted and sentenced to death for the murder of one R.U.C. man. While they awaited their executions, a campaign began to grant them clemency. It was supported by Pope Pius XII and the U.S. and southern Irish governments. However, Tom Williams, as leader of the I.R.A. unit, took full responsibility to save the lives of his men and their sentences were commuted. It was reported that Tom Williams, a lad of just nineteen, bravely held his head high as he walked to the scaffold in Belfast's Crumlin Road Jail.

Rose Boyle had four sisters. One became a nun and the others married into local Republican families. Her own husband, though, didn't come from a family with a strong Republican tradition.

"John – God rest him – wasn't what ye'd call politically minded," she explained. "But as a working-class Catholic from the Lower Falls, he was certainly a Nationalist."

Nationalists and Republicans – in Ireland's recent history, almost wholly Catholic in background if not always in practice – both wanted to see their country reunited and free of British rule. Their differences lay in how to reach these goals. Nationalists favored an independent, united Ireland achieved by non-violent, political means. Republicans generally accepted the use of violence as necessary to achieve this and therefore supported the armed struggle of the I.R.A. Republicans also tended to support the more radical politics of Sinn Féin, whose objective was to establish a socialist Irish Republic.

The Boyles had two sons and two daughters. John Boyle was a devoted family man who worked as a delivery driver for a local bakery and died of a heart attack at the age of forty-six.

"That was in 1967," said Mrs. Boyle, "before the current round of troubles started up in our wee occupied corner of Ireland."

As she refilled our teacups, the front door opened and an attractive young woman with long dark hair entered carrying a baby. Mrs. Boyle introduced us to her younger daughter, Patricia, and her granddaughter Róisín.

"Bout ye?" Patricia offered us the standard Belfast greeting, as she passed through the room on her way the kitchen.

We soon thanked Mrs. Boyle for her hospitality and were on our way. At the door, the old woman warned us to beware of the Brits and the R.U.C., "lurkin' around every corner."

"Drop by anytime now, boys," she called after us. "And mind yerselves. Cheerio!"

As we made our way back to Eglantine Avenue, Callaghan told me that Mrs. Boyle's daughter, Patricia, had served time in Armagh's women's jail due to her involvement, like her brothers, with the I.R.A.

Eglantine Avenue, Belfast

West Belfast with James Mackie & Sons, a foundry and factory, at the end of the street

Republican art in West & North Belfast

CHAPTER SIX
CALLAGHAN'S GIRL

Callaghan finally introduced me to the girl he had been seeing. Pretty and petite with shoulder-length straw-blonde hair, twenty-two-year-old Sandra Maginnis hailed from Banbridge in County Down. After working for three years over in England, she returned to Northern Ireland to study at Queen's University in Belfast.

For a couple of months, Callaghan and Sandra had been taking an Irish step-dancing class together on Wednesday evenings at the Crescent Art Centre and going to *céilí* dances on Monday evenings in the parish hall of St. Brigid's Church on Derryvolgie Avenue. It didn't take much coaxing from them for me to agree to accompany them to the *céilí* that night.

Historically, a *céilí* was a social gathering or party. Irish traditional music and dancing was often featured at the event and the word *céilí* in time was applied to just the dancing part.

After the English arrived in Ireland, they suppressed and outlawed all forms of Irish culture. But what the Irish couldn't openly practice – like their Catholic religion – they practiced in secret. On Sunday evenings in summer young people would meet on country roads to dance. Often, they would gather at the crossroads where it was easier to see approaching red-coated English soldiers. A fiddler would strike up a

31

lively tune and couples danced in a circle or a line. The Gaelic Revival in the late 19th century spread the popularity of Irish traditional music and folk dancing and the Gaelic League organized *céilí* dances at public dance halls throughout Ireland.

In the 1960's, rock-and-roll music began to be imported into Ireland and large ballrooms with showbands started to displace traditional music and *céilí* dancing for many in the younger generation. However, in Catholic areas in the North *céilí* dancing and the traditional tunes that went with it remained popular.

When we arrived, there was already a good turnout in the parish hall. Middle-aged couples wore their Sunday best, the men in jackets and ties and the women in attractive dresses or skirts. The younger crowd was more casually attired in blue jeans and sweaters. On stage was a band armed with an accordion, *bodhrán,* fiddle, flute, and keyboard. When they began to play Callaghan and Sandra joined other couples in a long line dance, while I sipped a cup of punch and looked on. The tune was a lively one and you could see the sheer joy on the smiling faces of the dancers.

Standing beside me were two girls who were also sipping punch and watching the dancers. We chatted for a few minutes, and I learned they were Theresa from Enniskillen, County Fermanagh, and Mairéad from a little town in County Cavan, and they were in Belfast as nursing students. While both said they did some step-dancing as little girls, neither felt comfortable enough to jump into the *céilí* dancing.

"And what about yourself?" asked an older, cheery-faced woman with her gray hair cut in the pixie style popularized by Audrey Hepburn.

She had been standing behind us and must have overheard our conversation. I told her that I wasn't familiar with the dance steps.

"Well, that can easily be remedied," she said brightly. "Because I've been *céilí* dancing before you were born, young man!"

She introduced herself as Mrs. O'Neill and proceeded to take my hand and lead me to the dance floor where a large circle was forming. Everyone joined hands as the music started and suddenly my feet started moving with everyone else's and around we went. I laughed with everyone else. It was great fun.

Although well into her fifties, Mrs. O'Neill was fit and energetic. A natural dancer, she guided me through the various steps. We lined up for "The Bridge of Athlone" and soon Mrs. O'Neill and I were galloping up the floor, joining both our hands in a raised position to form a bridge, for each couple to pass underneath. Then we joined three couples for the popular jig called the "Siege of Ennis," followed by the "Haymaker's Jig." Finally, "The Walls of Limerick" called for two couples. Mrs. O'Neill and I danced the reel with Callaghan and Sandra.

Afterward, I met Mr. O'Neill, who had been sitting with a group of men. He was a retired civil engineer. After living for the past twenty-five years in South Africa, the O'Neills had only recently returned home to Belfast. I thanked Mrs. O'Neill for all her patience and Mr. O'Neill for the loan of his dance partner.

"My dance partner?" he chuckled. "Och, no! I've been cursed with two left feet, lad."

The pair of them laughed and Mrs. O'Neill said she wouldn't want it any other way.

"That man can be brutal on a lady's toes!" she joked and gave her husband a quick peck on the cheek.

It was late when I left St. Brigid's parish hall with Callaghan and Sandra. We ducked into the Eglantine Inn for a nightcap. There was a large crowd for mid-week. Sandra remarked that it was the same every night and even more packed on weekends. Upstairs there was a disco. Most of the patrons were students from nearby Queen's University. The Botanic Inn, directly opposite the Eglantine Inn, was also jam-packed with students. The bars were affectionately referred to as the "Bot" and the "Eg."

We found a just vacated table by a window. I ordered a couple of pints of Guinness for Sandra Maginnis and myself and a glass of soda for the teetotaler among us. When our drinks arrived Sandra immediately took a long swallow of the rich, thick black stout, while Callaghan and I looked on and marveled how such a slip of a girl could chug it down. When she lowered her near-empty pint, a mustache of creamy foam remained on her upper lip. Sandra smiled broadly and then licked her lips as she ran a hand through her blonde hair.

"Great stuff, huh?" I queried.

"Oh, aye," she readily agreed. "Absolutely brilliant."

"Sláinte!" I said, raising my pint.

"Sláinte!" replied Sandra, before she swallowed what was left of her stout and remarked that Tim didn't know what he was missing.

"*Tim* knows exactly what he's missing," responded Callaghan in an irritated tone. "And I don't miss it."

"Guinness is good for you," she teased, quoting its famous advertising slogan.

"Yeah," I chimed in, "Guinness here is like apple pie in America."

"Are you saying you have to drink Guinness to be fully Irish?"

"Lighten up, Tim," said Sandra. "We're only slaggin' ye."

"Well, knock it off. You both know I don't drink, and I don't like bars."

Now it was Sandra's turn to get annoyed.

"If I can go with you to a Roman Catholic Mass, then you can accompany me to a pub."

The way she said a "Roman Catholic Mass" instead of just Mass, as any ordinary Catholic would, made me suspect she was a Protestant. Callaghan read my thoughts and confirmed it.

"But with a name like Maginnis?" I asked Sandra.

Although it doesn't hold true in every case, old Gaelic surnames are usually found among native Irish Catholics, while Irish Protestants tend to bear the English and Scottish surnames their ancestors brought over to Ireland with them.

Sandra enthusiastically related the ancient Ulster roots of Maginnis (more commonly spelled McGuinness).

"*Mac Aonghusa,* it would be in the Irish. The 'son of Angus.' The Maginnises were one of the leadin' septs in the province. The name actually originated in me own County Down."

"You're not a cousin of Martin McGuinness over in Derry?" I kidded her, referring to the Sinn Féin politician and former I.R.A. leader.

"Not *atoll*, and I wouldn't want to be either! As far as I'm concerned, he's a terrorist. And as you no doubt know, he's a Roman Catholic."

"That's the rumor," I replied, half in jest.

"Besides," Sandra went on, "Martin McGuinness spells his name like the stout, without the Mc. Mine is M-a-g-i-n-n-i-s. We spell it the same way as Ken Maginnis, the M.P. He's also a Protestant Maginnis, except he hails from County Tyrone."

"A Unionist politician," said Callaghan disdainfully. "Before he went into politics, the guy was a member of the murderous Ulster Defence Regiment."

"I suppose," reflected Sandra, ignoring Callaghan, "my people would have once been Roman Catholics, like the rest of the native Irish before they turned Protestant and intermarried with the Scots comin' over as planters in the 17th century. Aside from the Maginnis line, my father's entirely Ulster Scot with plenty of Campbells, McClintocks, and Stewarts up in the family tree. All good, solid Scottish Presbyterian names. My mum's pure English, though, from Yorkshire."

"Which proves a book can't always be judged by its cover," I offered for no particular reason.

"Right," agreed Sandra. "Just look at the likes of John Hume of the S.D.L.P and Sinn Féin's Gerry Adams. Both are Roman Catholics and very pro-Irish, yet their family names are totally English! The same with that I.R.A. hunger striker Bobby Sands. Then we had Terence O'Neill as prime minister of Northern Ireland. Sure, you'd think he was a Roman Catholic with a name like that. But you'd be wrong. O'Neill was of the old Anglo-Irish Ascendancy. Most O'Neills you'll run into here – and Ulster has more than her fair share of them – would be Roman Catholics though. Like that Mrs. O'Neill at the *céilí.*"

"How'd you know she was Catholic?" I asked.

"You know when you are born and bred in Ulster," declared Sandra. "For instance, those two girls you were chatting with were unmistakably Roman Catholic."

"They could hardly have been anything else with names like Theresa and Mairéad," I said.

"Absolutely," replied Sandra. "The Christian names of people here can often tell you what side of the sectarian divide they're on. Your Micks and Paddys, your Seáns and Kevins are all Roman Catholics, as are boys named Timothy, or Tadhg in Irish. Girls named Theresa, Bernadette, Siobhán, or Deirdre would be Roman Catholic. Protestants stay away from the more Irish names and your saint names. Your Billys and Sammys are usually Prods, as are girls with names like Victoria or Hope or Sandra."

"That's interesting," I said, with a grin Callaghan, who had a sour look on his mug.

"I don't recall," he remarked, "asking the opinion of the frog that hopped into the Irish stew. *Audubon.*"

"Ed, do you know what I call Tim?" asked Sandra with a mischievous smile.

"Please Sandra!" pleaded Callaghan.

"What?" I encouraged her, enjoying my friend's discomfort.

"Tadhg O'Callaghan!"

"I'll have to remember that!" I burst out laughing.

"But O'Callaghan *is* my family's real last name!" protested Callaghan. "My grandfather just dropped the O apostrophe somewhere in the ocean on his way over to America. We're the O'Callaghans of County Cork, descended from the great 10th century King of Munster, Ceallacháin of Cashel, known as a man of strife and contention."

"That's fascinating, Tim, really 'tis," said an amused Sandra.

"Well, Callaghan, with or without the 'O', if it makes you feel any better, you're certainly a man of strife and contention! There's no denying that!"

I ordered two more pints of Guinness and the old, celebrated master brewer, dead nearly two hundred years, became our next topic of conversation.

"You know, Arthur Guinness came from the Protestant Ascendancy," Sandra informed us. "Although oul Uncle Art is always associated with Dublin since his brewery was there, his people were actually from County Down."

A barmaid set our fresh pints down on the table and Callaghan eyed the creamy headed, dark stuff with an expression of distaste.

"Black Protestant Porter," he uttered contemptuously. "That's what Catholics and Nationalists called Guinness's brew when they boycotted it because he was supported British Protestant rule in Ireland. His four sons were founding members of the first Orange Lodge in Dublin."

"My goodness…my Guinness," I joked, quoting another of the stout's popular advertising slogans, with a wink at Sandra.

I thought about the old debate between the leading brands of Irish whiskey. Jameson was considered by many to be a Catholic whiskey, while Bushmills was considered a Protestant whiskey. Perhaps it was merely due to geography. Although John Jameson was a Scotsman and a Presbyterian, he set up his distillery in 1780 in Dublin – which, of course, later became the capital of the Irish Republic. Bushmills, on the other hand, had long been called a Protestant whiskey since it came from the so-called Black Protestant North and was distilled in the village of Bushmills, County Antrim, since 1608.

All these sectarian musings I kept to myself, however, so as not to ignite the spark that would set off a religious war between Callaghan and his girl.

"You know," said Sandra, after downing half her pint, "the Orange Order is not an evil organization. It's merely a fraternity and a great many decent Protestants belong to it."

"Like the ranks of the Ku Klux Klan in the American South are filled with good and decent, Christian white people," retorted Callaghan.

While the two angry lovebirds glared at one another from across Ireland's sectarian divide, I thought about my maternal grandfather. Davy Kirkpatrick was the son of a Papist-hating Orangeman from County Donegal. He was disowned when he converted to Catholicism to marry a local Catholic girl who became my grandmother. Years later, Granddad would turn out for St. Patrick's Day parades on Manhattan's Fifth Avenue wearing an orange necktie and would jokingly refer to himself as a Catholic Orangeman.

"Well," I finally broke the simmering silence between Callaghan and Sandra, "it has certainly been a pleasure, but I'm going to call it a night."

We waited outside in the cool night air for the taxi Callaghan called to take Sandra to east Belfast, where she lived with her married brother. Maybe it was the Guinness, or maybe the continued silence of my companions, but I felt like singing. I chose from my repertoire of Irish songs an old music hall ditty for Callaghan's benefit and burst out with: "If your name is Timothy or Pat, so long as you come from Ireland there's a welcome on the mat..."

Sandra joined in but changed the words to a version favored by Belfast Orangemen: "If your name is Timothy or Pat, you'll never get a job in the shipyards with a Fenian name like that."

It brought us a good laugh, even out of Callaghan, and we bid the pretty Sandra Maginnis a goodnight as she stepped into her taxi.

Before turning in for the night, I switched on the big, antique radio. A news report was talking about a British soldier in the newly formed Royal Irish Regiment who was shot dead in the village of Rasharkin, County Antrim, thirty miles northwest of Belfast. It was believed the I.R.A. was responsible.

CHAPTER SEVEN
DEAD IRISH PATRIOTS

Just down Eglantine Avenue, by the Lisburn Road, was the Mad Hatter Coffee Shop. I found it the perfect place to have a cup of coffee and a pipe smoke, and that's just what I was doing late that afternoon as I scribbled in my travel journal.

That morning I went with Callaghan to visit Milltown Cemetery at the top of the Falls Road. According to local tradition, there was once an old corn mill near the burial ground, from which it took its name Milltown. We entered the large graveyard through the Victorian stone arched gateway and looked out at a forest of Celtic and Roman crosses, and numerous statues of the Blessed Virgin Mary. I followed Callaghan as he eagerly made his way to the Republican Plot.

He stopped at the County Antrim Memorial. The large stone monument was inscribed with the names of Antrim's martyred dead from the Rising of 1798 to the present. Listed under the United Irishmen Roll of Honour were many of the heroes celebrated in song and story. At the top was William Orr of Farranshane, the first of the United men to be hanged by the British at Carrickfergus in 1797. Beneath his name was that of Henry Joy McCracken, who led his Green Company of the Belfast Regiment of Volunteers in an attack on Antrim town in the summer of 1798, and gallantly met his death on the gallows at the Corn

Market in Belfast. Further down the list was Roddy McCorley, who fought with "pike in hand" - as the Clancy Brothers and Tommy Makem tell us in their popular song - and was hanged by the British on the bridge of Toome.

The names of Fenians who died in lonely prison cells were found on another roll of honor. There was also Sir Roger Casement of Ballymena, the British diplomat turned Irish patriot, who was captured on the coast of Kerry attempting to smuggle German rifles into Ireland for the 1916 Easter Rising and was hanged for treason in London. The names of Antrim's patriot dead increased in number when it came to the War of Independence and the Civil War. But it was far surpassed by those killed after the latest round of Troubles began in the late 1960's.

Callaghan stood before a black headstone, inscribed: "This grave is reserved for the remains of Lieut. Tom Williams I.R.A. Hanged in Belfast Jail 2nd Sept. 1942 and still interred there." Fifty years after his death, there were fresh flowers on his empty grave, while his remains lay in the unhallowed ground of Crumlin Road Jail.

"Brave Tom Williams, we salute you," said Callaghan, quoting a line from a well-known ballad. He then uttered a short prayer for the repose of his soul.

Next, Callaghan was over at the New Republican Plot. I joined him at a flower-strewn grave where two hunger strikers from the H-Blocks of Long Kesh Prison were buried. One simple, flat, black headstone was shared by three I.R.A. volunteers: Terence O'Neill, Bobby Sands, and Joe McDonnell.

"Terence O'Neill wasn't one of the hunger strikers, was he?" I asked Callaghan, who was somewhat of an expert on Irish Republican history.

"No, O'Neill was killed on active service about a year earlier."

"There's no dates of birth or death inscribed on the headstone," I remarked.

"There's no need," replied my fervently Irish friend. "Their dates of death are seared forever into Irish hearts. Bobby Sands died on May 5th, 1981, aged twenty-seven, after being on hunger strike for a total of sixty-six days. Joe McDonnell died a couple of months later, on July 8th, at twenty-nine, after sixty-one days without food."

In the mid-1970's, the British government decided to abolish the political or special category status of imprisoned Irish Republicans and impose a new policy of criminalization. The British proclaimed there was no difference between Republican prisoners and common criminals. Republican P.O.W.s, however, strongly disagreed and refused to don the prison uniforms they were issued. As the popular H-Block song by Francie Brolly declared at the time: "I'll wear no convict's uniform nor meekly serve my time, that Britain might brand Ireland's fight, eight hundred years of crime."

Thus, the protest began. Denied their own clothes, naked Republican prisoners in the H-Blocks defiantly wrapped themselves in blankets. The prison guards abused the blanket men, as they were called, and tried in vain to beat them into submission. The attacks on the prisoners were vicious. But the prisoners fought back the best they could, and warders received their fair share of punches, kicks, and bites. As conditions went from bad to worse, the blanket protest escalated into the no-wash protest and the dirty protest, where prisoners smeared their excrement on cell walls. Finally, the decision was made to embark on a hunger strike to the death if the demand for political status was not granted. Bobby Sands, as the Provisional I.R.A. Officer Commanding in the prison, led the way and nine of his comrades followed him to the grave before the hunger strike ended.

I asked Callaghan if any of the other hunger strikers were buried in Milltown, and he pointed at Kieran Doherty's grave.

"Sands, McDonnell, and Doherty were Belfast men. Of all the hunger strikers, Kieran Doherty, aged twenty-five, lasted the longest at seventy-three days. They all died slow and agonizing deaths defending their status as prisoners of war and demanding to be treated with human dignity."

The wind carried to our ears the sound of mocking laughter. We turned to see, some distance away, about half a dozen British soldiers trampling over graves. I could feel my own anger rising.

"They don't even respect the dead," I remarked.

"Why should they?" replied Callaghan bitterly. "The graves are Irish ones."

The laughter of the British soldiers grew louder as they drew nearer to us. Callaghan glared fiercely at them.

"Bastards," he muttered.

"C'mon, pal," I said, "let's get out of here."

As we left the cemetery, Callaghan quoted from Pádraic Pearse's famous graveside oration at the funeral of the unconquerable Fenian leader Jeremiah O'Donovan Rossa in 1915: "The fools, the fools, the fools! - they have left us our Fenian dead and while Ireland holds these graves, Ireland unfree shall never be at peace."

"You know," said Callaghan, "O'Donovan Rossa actually died in Staten Island at the ripe old age of eighty-three and his body was sent back to Ireland."

"Rossa sounds like an Italian name," I commented.

"He was a Cork man, through and through. Rossa was a sort of nickname, added on to O'Donovan, from his family's connection to Rossmore townland in West Cork. He was a Fenian before there were Fenians, before the Irish Republican Brotherhood was established in 1858. He was sentenced to penal servitude for life in England for plotting a Fenian rising and only released as part of a general amnesty of Irish political prisoners on the condition that he wouldn't return to Ireland. He agreed to live in exile New York and settled with his family in Staten Island.

"From America, O'Donovan Rossa became one of the main organizers of the Dynamite Campaign to bomb strategic and economic targets in England during the 1880's. The Fenians struck at the merciless heart of the British Empire, primarily London, to try to drive the Brits out of Ireland. It's the same tactics used by the I.R.A. today in the bombing campaign in England."

As Callaghan spoke, I heard the passion in his voice and caught a glimpse of the fanaticism in his eyes.

CHAPTER EIGHT
ANOTHER INTERROGATION

Callaghan had gone out with Sandra, and I was alone in his flat. Seated at the card table with my open travel journal, dated Thursday, October 22nd, I tried to collect my thoughts about the day's events. I glanced over at the radiator by the wall where my wallet and its contents were drying out from the wetting they got earlier that afternoon.

As Callaghan didn't have any classes that day, he joined me on a walk around west Belfast. Along the Falls Road, young mothers pushed strollers and old people stopped to chat with one another as black taxis and delivery trucks drove by. A gray armored R.U.C. Land Rover slowly rolled by on patrol with a dark green British Army Land Rover following close behind it.

"So, what do you think of Sandra?" asked Callaghan, as we turned onto a side street.

I lit a cigarette before answering. "Well, there's no denyin' she's a handsome lass, a real charmer," I said in my best Irish brogue. "But I fear ye'll never make a Fenian outta that one."

"I'd be happy just to have her a Catholic," replied Callaghan earnestly.

It was obvious their religious differences were troubling him. He didn't need my jokes. We continued down the street in silence as it began to drizzle.

The neighborhood had a number of abandoned rowhouses with their windows and doors bricked up and marked by graffiti. The street was littered with broken bottles and a child's bicycle that was crushed as if it was run over by a car or a Land Rover. A feeling of depression and despair hung in the air.

As we made our way on Beechmount Pass, three armored Land Rovers crept towards us. Callaghan and I were alone on the deserted street. There were stories of people in similar situations who were set upon by Crown forces and beaten senseless. We began moving in the direction of some nearby houses where we hoped the presence of other people would provide us with some safety. But we had already been targeted.

A voice over a loudspeaker ordered us to stop where we were. The gray Land Rover in the lead came to a halt a short distance away and out of the rear jumped two R.U.C. men. The two green Land Rovers of the British Army continued a little farther down the street before they too came to a stop. The soldiers however remained inside their vehicles.

There was something ominous in the slow and steady walk of the approaching R.U.C. men. Heavily armed, they were clad in bottle-green uniforms and flak jackets. The shorter of the two had sandy-colored hair covered by a peaked cap. His partner, a big ape in a helmet, gripping an automatic weapon, stood beside him. The first one questioned Callaghan. What was his name? Where was he from? What business did he have in the Beechmount area?

On his peaked cap was the crowned harp insignia. The harp – the beloved ancient symbol of Ireland – surmounted by the hated imperial crown dated back to the days of King Henry VIII. No Irish patriot could look upon it without feelings of anger and bitterness.

Seemingly satisfied with Callaghan's answers, the policeman turned his attention with an arrogant sneer to me.

"Where were ye born?" he demanded.

"New York," I replied.

"How long have ye been in the province or in the Republic of Ireland?"

I knew by "province" he meant the British-held six counties of Ulster, not the entire nine counties of the province, as three Ulster counties were actually located in the Republic of Ireland. I told him what he wanted to know and informed him I was just there as a tourist and produced my Nikon camera from under my jacket as proof.

"A tourist, are ye?" said the R.U.C. man with a malicious grin.

"Yeah, just on vacation."

"Well, then…how's yer holiday been thus far?"

"Great!" responded Callaghan, before I could answer. "His *holiday* has been great, up until the two of you came along!"

"Is that right, Ginger?" said the R.U.C. man, eyeing Callaghan. "Take off yer fuckin' shoes, the both of yez!"

We complied and stood in the cold wet street in our socks. Our wallets were then demanded from us and everything in them was removed and dropped onto the wet pavement.

"I thought ye were from New York," said the smirking constable. He had seen my California driver's license.

"I live in San Diego, California, but I'm originally from New York."

The R.U.C. man who did all the talking then tossed my empty wallet and Callaghan's into a dirty puddle and marched off with his helmeted, ape-like comrade to their waiting gray armored vehicle. We watched as they drove away, followed by their British Army escorts in their green Land Rovers. When they were out of sight, Callaghan and I fished our wallets out of the puddle, gathered up their wet contents off the ground, and put our shoes back on.

I wanted a drink to wash out the bitter taste I had in my mouth. We found a tiny pub nearby that wasn't much bigger than a walk-in closet.

The darkened hole stunk of stale beer and cigarettes. Three old men in caps were lined up on barstools staring up at a small black and white TV set on a corner shelf. Behind the bar stood an old gent in an apron smoking a pipe. I had a double Bushmills, neat, while Callaghan asked for a cup of tea. Neither of us spoke. Downing my drink, I called for a second double with a Guinness chaser. I noticed Callaghan hadn't touched his tea.

"Do you remember Phil Connors?" he suddenly asked. "He used to be a regular at Ireland's Own in Encinitas."

"Phil from Philly? The used car salesman?"

"Yeah, that's the guy. You know he spent twelve years in the Marine Corps and lost a brother in Vietnam. Once he told me that he got out of the service because he felt like a mercenary fighting for a cause that wasn't his own. As Phil saw it, he wasn't defending the United States of America but being used to protect and further corporate America's oil interests in the Persian Gulf and in toppling dictatorships that were no longer to our government's liking, like those in Grenada and Panama. He said he'd sooner fight and die for a free and united Ireland. Something he believed in."

"And you feel the same," I said.

"You're damn right I do," replied Callaghan.

We left the hole in the wall of a pub and made our way back to the busy Falls Road. The drizzle had stopped, and the sun was shining. People were going in and out of shops and happily chatting together. We passed a group of kids in their Catholic school uniforms gaily laughing and filled with the joy of childhood. A coal truck rattled by, followed by three armored Land Rovers.

"You think they're the same bunch?" asked Callaghan.

"I don't know. Just keep walking and don't look at them."

Then we heard our names broadcast over the gray Rover's loudspeaker. When the speaker was certain he had everyone's attention, he continued: "We would like to thank yez for the valuable information yez provided today."

"We're being set up," I said, as we picked up our pace.

But the people of the Falls Road had seen and heard it all before, and the incident the R.U.C. hoped to provoke never materialized. The forces of the Crown continued on their way, to look elsewhere for potential victims.

CHAPTER NINE
DISCO NIGHT AT SEÁN McDERMOTT'S

Thursday night was disco night at the Seán McDermott Gaelic Athletic Club on the Lower Falls Road, and they opened the hall adjacent to the bar for dancing. Callaghan had gone out with Sandra, so I was on my own at Seán McD's. The place was packed. Drinking Guinness as disco diva Donna Summer sang "Hot Stuff," I felt I was no longer in Belfast, or in Ireland for that matter.

I knocked back the last of my pint and stood up to go. Surely, the Falls Road as a self-proclaimed bastion of Irish Republicanism had pubs with more of an Irish atmosphere. With any luck, I could find one where I could hear some good Irish music.

As I made my way through the crowd, a guy limping and stumbling between two girls caught my attention. His hair was in disarray, his shirt half unbuttoned and hanging out of his trousers, and he was drunkenly singing something about the I.R.A. blowing up all the discos in Ireland. No doubt a song of his own creation. Then he burst forth with a different ditty.

"Oh! There were ninety-nine Brits on the wall. If the I.R.A. should shoot one of 'em off, there'd be ninety-eight Brits on the wall!"

Seemingly, an Irish Republican version of "Ninety-nine Bottles of Beer."

The girls he was with tried to quiet him down, but to no avail. The guy began to spin around until he crashed into a table and collapsed in a heap on the floor. Everyone laughed, including the drunk himself along with his female companions. I went over to lend the fellow a hand getting to his feet. He accepted my help to a nearby chair and once he was seated, he dismissed me with a curse.

"Ah, don't ye mind Lame Liam," said the chubby brunette in her early twenties, standing at his side. "His bark is worse than his bite, so 'tis."

"Sure, he's tame Lame Liam," added the other girl, a slender, slightly older, bleached blonde with crimson red lipstick.

I soon found myself seated at a table, clinking glasses with the trio. The brunette introduced herself as DeDe and the bleached blonde said her name was Maeve. DeDe was Lame Liam's girlfriend and Maeve was married to an imprisoned I.R.A. man. I learned only DeDe had a job and she worked at the Seán Graham's betting shop on the Lower Ormeau Road. She was there on the day of the massacre when two masked members of the Loyalist Ulster Freedom Fighters – the death squad of the Ulster Defence Association – sprayed the packed bookie's with assault rifles, leaving five dead and nine wounded.

"It was absolutely horrific," said DeDe. "There was blood everywhere."

"I heard the place was like a butcher's shop," remarked Maeve.

"Aye...'twas. When they finished shootin' the killers fled. People were on the floor screamin', groanin' in agony and cryin', like. I just laid there in a pool of blood thankin' God it wasn't me own."

"February was a brutal enough month," offered Lame Liam.

Nodding in agreement, Maeve lit a cigarette, inhaled deeply, and slowly exhaled, before speaking.

"The slaughter at Seán Graham's came in the wake of the previous day's murderous rampage by a deranged R.U.C. man at our Sinn Féin office at Sevastopol Street. Three men were shot dead, one in front of his wee two-and-a-half-year-old son, and another man and a woman were seriously wounded. Then to bring the bloody month to an end there was the gruesome sectarian killin' of Anne Marie Smyth, a young Catholic mother of two. Loyalists strangled the poor woman and cut her throat, after she was lured to a house party in east Belfast."

Sickened by what I heard; I hardly touched my pint. But my three companions quickly moved on to more pleasant conversation and were happily knocking back their pints and sharing a laugh. One of the girls asked if I was contemplating turning teetotaler.

"Not tonight," I replied.

"Then bevvy up!" cried Lame Liam.

"As they say," added Maeve, "eat, drink, and be merry for tomorrow we die!"

"Feckin' speak for yerself!" exclaimed DeDe.

"*Sláinte!*" Lame Liam toasted our health.

"Oh aye, cheers!" answered the girls.

I noticed that DeDe and Lame Liam kept bringing their pint glasses under the table and when their pints reappeared, they were filled to the brim. Maeve then slid her half-empty pint across to DeDe and indicated I should do likewise.

"The gin's quite dear here," she explained. "Therefore, we always bring our own."

My pint disappeared under the table, then Maeve's, to be topped off with gin from a bottle DeDe had stashed in her oversized handbag. I joked about the national drink of Ireland being contaminated by limey swill.

"English?" questioned DeDe. "Ah, not *atoll.* I'll have ye know, 'tis one hundred percent Cork Dry Gin ye're drinkin'. Distilled in our very own County Cork."

We had another round of Guinness, followed by a third round, and a fourth, and a fifth until I lost count. All the while generous pourings of gin were added to the black stuff, lightening its dark hue. Lame Liam sat in a drunken stupor while the girls, smoking a steady stream of cigarettes, matched me pint for pint and questioned me about America.

Maeve asked why the American government kept bullying the small nations of the world and supported Israel's oppression of the Palestinian people. DeDe wanted to know, since I lived in California, did I run into a lot of movie stars.

As her boyfriend slept in his chair, with his chin on his chest, DeDe told me how he came to be called "Lame" Liam. As a teenager, she said, he was "a bit of a hood," stealing from local shops.

"He was warned by the I.R.A. more than once to cease his antisocial behavior. But Liam didn't and to learn him a lesson, like, they gave him a kneecappin'."

"Kneecapping?" I was unfamiliar with the term.

"Aye, some of our bold Provie boyos got a hold of him, held him face down in a back entry with a gun to his head and feckin' blasted away his right kneecap."

"A punishment shootin', they call it," said Maeve.

"Liam was but sixteen years of age at the time," continued DeDe. "The surgeons at the Royal Vic did what they could for him, but he's been left a bloody cripple for life. Everyone calls him Lame Liam now cause of the way he limps when he walks."

"We're all Republicans here," added Maeve. "Me husband's in Long Kesh and one of DeDe's brothers died fightin' for Ireland, but that doesn't mean we agree with all the actions of the I.R.A."

It was closing time and Donna Summer was belting out her "Last Dance." Maeve flipped back her bleached blonde hair and flashed a red-lipped grin, before bidding us a goodnight. I finished off what was left of my G&G – as the girls called their mixture of Guinness & gin – and helped DeDe roust her boyfriend and get him to his feet.

Lame Liam's legs were like a couple of wet noodles and we both had to throw one of his arms over our shoulders to get him out of Seán McD's. Once outside he fell onto all fours.

"Look at him," said an amused DeDe. "He's absolutely poleaxed!"

After he vomited on the sidewalk, Lame Liam was able to stand on his own. At least for a while. When he started to sway again, he draped an arm back over DeDe. I agreed to see them up the road to a taxi office as there were none out driving around at that hour. Not a single car drove by as we walked along the dark and deserted Falls Road.

DeDe still had some gin left in the bottle in her handbag and passed it to her boyfriend. He immediately drained its contents and hurled the empty bottle. It hit the road and smashed to bits, just as Lame Liam hit the pavement and passed out.

DeDe knelt down and tried to revive her man, as I smoked a cigarette. We were in front of St. Paul's Church. It was a red-brick edifice, built in the Gothic Revival style of the 19th century. Behind a decorative iron fence, in the church's front garden, was a life-sized white crucifix with an all-white corpus, flanked by white statues of the Blessed Virgin Mary and St. John the Evangelist.

When I turned from the crucifixion scene, a foot patrol of eight British soldiers were stealthily advancing up the road in our direction. Armed with assault rifles, they wore camouflage uniforms and flak jackets with berets. DeDe stood up to face them as they silently passed by while Lame Liam remained unconsciousness, belly up on the pavement.

A sense of uneasiness hung heavily in the night air. Then one of the last two soldiers walking backwards to cover the rear of the patrol broke the silence.

"Whit, anither brae Fenian whose fa'en in th' fray?" he cracked in a thick Scots accent. "Or is auld Paddy blooter'd again?"

"Shut yer gob, ye Scotchie hun!" shrieked DeDe. "'Tis only a matter of time before the I.R.A. will take care of yez!"

Again, I envisioned being beaten senseless by Crown forces and left for dead in the street, along with DeDe. But the Scottish soldier merely laughed at us and continued his backward walk at the tail end of the patrol.

DeDe's outburst woke Lame Liam, and he rolled over on his stomach and lifted his head from the pavement to watch the soldiers turn down a side street.

"Up the Ra!" he suddenly shouted at them. "Up the Ra!!"

I deposited the two of them at the Falls Road taxi office and made my way back to south Belfast and Eglantine Avenue.

CHAPTER TEN
"NO SURRENDER" THE WAR CRY OF THE BELFAST BRIGADE

"There are those who will say the Troubles began in 1969. But the truth is our troubles with the English began back in 1169, when Strongbow and his men first crossed the Irish Sea. Eight hundred years of murderin', pillagin' and plunderin', oppression and religious persecution, mass starvation and forced evictions followed. Have another cup of *tay,* boys?"

"Thanks, Mrs. Boyle," we replied in unison, "that would be great."

Callaghan and I were again seated on Mrs. Boyle's floral sofa in her rowhouse on Harrogate Street, sipping tea and munching on blueberry scones, while she continued to lead us on a tour through Irish Republican history.

"After the Irish Free State was set-up in the twenty-six counties, the Republican movement became increasingly left-wing. Some I.R.A. men were outright communists, wantin' to turn this country of ours into another Soviet Russia. Thanks be to God; we were spared that fate. We're Irish. We're green, not red!

"Then we had Irishmen in the '30's runnin' off to Spain to fight Franco whilst their own country was unfree. Now I ask ye, boys, what the hell did all that carry-on over in Spain have to do with us? If ye ask me, as much as the price of *tay* in China.

"Meanwhile, Catholics were still gettin' slaughtered in the streets of Belfast. And when we defended ourselves, we had the likes of Peadar O'Donnell sayin', 'we don't have an I.R.A. battalion in Belfast, we have a battalion of armed Catholics.'

"Sure, some of Ireland's most gallant sons fought in the Belfast Brigade. When I was a wee girl, ye'd hear people sing –

> *Craigavon sent the Specials out to shoot the people down,*
> *He thought the I.R.A. were dead in dear ould Belfast town,*
> *But he got a rude awakenin' with the rifle and grenade,*
> *When he met the First Battalion of the Belfast Brigade.*

> *Glory, glory to ould Ireland, glory, glory to this island,*
> *Glory to the memory of the men who fought and died,*
> *'No surrender' is the war cry of the Belfast Brigade.*

> *We have no ammunition, or no armored tanks to show,*
> *But we're ready to defend ourselves no matter where we go,*
> *We're out for our Republic and to hell with your Free State,*
> *'No surrender' is the war cry of the Belfast Brigade.*

"The sacrifice made by brave Tom Williams is well remembered, and the darin' exploits of Jimmy Steele haven't been forgotten. Them and their kind were the cream of Irish manhood.

"I first laid me eyes on Jimmy Steele when I was fourteen years of age. A few months earlier, himself and Hugh McAteer, along with two other lads, had escaped over the wall of Crumlin Road Jail. I was at the Broadway Cinema on Holy Saturday afternoon in 1943 when more than a dozen armed volunteers strolled in, seized the cinema, and stopped the film. We only learnt what was goin' on when a slide appeared on the screen sayin' the cinema had been commandeered by the Irish Republican Army for the purpose of holdin' an Easter Commemoration for those who died for Ireland. Yer man Jimmy then gets up on stage and reads out the 1916 Proclamation. McAteer was up next with a statement from the I.R.A., followed by a minute of silence for our patriot dead.

"The peelers weren't long in recapturin' Jimmy Steele. Hugh McAteer managed to stay out of their grasp a little longer. I was there the day they arrested him some months later as he was leavin' St. Paul's after Mass."

Belfast played no significant role in the I.R.A.'s 1956-62 Border Campaign. The campaign lacked support from ordinary Nationalists on either side of the border and was officially called off by the leadership of the I.R.A.

The I.R.A. then took a leftward turn again. Cathal Goulding became chief of staff in 1962 and tried to steer the I.R.A. away from the armed struggle for a free and united, thirty-two county Irish Republic and towards a Marxist revolutionary philosophy. Many of the physical force men were dismissed from the ranks of the I.R.A., while many others resigned in disgust. Jimmy Steele said at the time, "One is now expected to be more conversant with the thoughts of Chairman Mao than those of our dead patriots."

"Goulding even went so far as to sell I.R.A. arms to Welsh separatists," said Mrs. Boyle contemptuously. Then added, "Though we would certainly support the Welsh in their fight for independence, our first priority should be Irish freedom."

In the late 1960's, a radical wave of rebellion swept across the world. Around the globe there was political and social upheaval, violence, and bloodshed. Across Europe and the United States there were demonstrations and riots, as college students protested against the war in Vietnam and embraced left-wing social causes.

The black civil rights movement in America inspired the rise of the civil rights movement in Northern Ireland. One sought to end racial discrimination, the other religious discrimination. Peaceful protest marches, on both sides of the Atlantic, provoked a violent backlash from authorities.

The Northern Ireland Civil Rights Association demanded fair elections, equal access to housing for Catholics, an end to discrimination in employment, and the repeal of repressive legislation.

"In other words," said Mrs. Boyle, "this new breed of leftist, university educated civil righters merely wanted to reform the rotten sectarian character of the Orange statelet. They were perfectly content to remain British subjects so long as they got equal treatment as Catholics under the law. They had no notion in their heads of a united Ireland *atoll.*"

But the Unionist government at Stormont wasn't ready to concede an inch. Civil rights demonstrations were banned. The N.I.C.R.A., however, defied the ban and marched in Derry City on October 5th, 1968. They were met by baton-wielding Royal Ulster Constabulary and beaten viciously in the streets. A television cameraman filmed the bloody assault, and the images were beamed around the world. There was widespread anger across Ireland and two days of rioting in Derry between Catholics and the R.U.C.

"After the batterin' they received," remarked Mrs. Boyle, "more than a few civil righters became Republicans – though of a red hue."

Within days of the initial attack, a new civil rights group emerged from Queen's University, in Belfast, calling itself People's Democracy. The student leaders included the radical firebrand Bernadette Devlin. The organization advocated a socialist Republic for all of Ireland.

On New Year's Day 1969, members of People's Democracy set out from Belfast on a four-day anti-government march to Derry. The march began with about forty participants and grew to about 150 student protestors. Along the route, the marchers repeatedly met counter-demonstrations by militant Protestant Loyalists. At Burntollet bridge, five miles outside of Derry, they were ambushed by hundreds of Loyalist thugs, including many off-duty B-Specials, armed with stones and spiked cudgels, while the R.U.C. stood idly by.

When Nationalists learned of the Burntollet attack, rioting again broke out in Derry. The R.U.C. then went on a rampage through the city's Catholic working-class Bogside district, smashing windows and breaking down doors, beating rioters and non-rioters alike.

Civil unrest escalated during the summer marching season as Orangemen and like-minded Protestant groups paraded provocatively through Catholic quarters throughout the North to commemorate Protestant William of Orange's victory over Catholic King James II at the Battle of the Boyne in 1690. On August 12th, 1969, thousands of Loyalist Apprentice Boys marched through Derry City and as they passed the Bogside, they exchanged taunts and insults with residents, followed by stone throwing. The intervention of the Royal Ulster

Constabulary sparked off a fierce, full-scale, three-day riot, which came to be known as the Battle of the Bogside.

The Bogsiders erected barricades and hurled stones and petrol bombs at police. The R.U.C. responded by firing over a thousand canisters of CS gas, choking the Bogsiders. The hated B-Specials were called up to Derry to assist the R.U.C. Among Catholics, there was a genuine fear that the Bogsiders would be massacred.

The Northern Ireland Civil Rights Association made an appeal for demonstrations across the Six Counties to take the pressure off the Bogside. Huge crowds took to the streets in support of the Bogsiders in Belfast, and there were protests in Dungannon and Coalisland in County Tyrone, Dungiven in County Derry, Armagh City and Crossmaglen in south County Armagh, and in Newry, straddling Counties Down and Armagh.

Meanwhile, the *Taoiseach* of Ireland, Jack Lynch, addressed the nation in a televised broadcast, stating: "It is evident that the Stormont government is no longer in control of the situation. Indeed, the present situation is the evitable outcome of the politics pursued for decades by successive Stormont governments. It is clear also that the Irish government can no longer stand by and see innocent people injured and perhaps worse…"

However, that was exactly what the Irish government did. Mr. Lynch's speech not only gave besieged Catholics in the North a false hope, but Protestants took it as a warning and rumors started that Southern troops from the Irish Republic were preparing to invade British-held Ulster.

In sectarian Belfast, tension was at fever pitch. Throngs of Catholics marched along the Falls Road and Divis Street in support of the Bogsiders and protests outside of a R.U.C. barracks turned into a riot. An enraged Orange mob, which included armed B-Specials, from the Protestant Shankill Road invaded the Lower Falls and attacked residents and petrol bombed Catholic houses, beating up and shooting their fleeing occupants. Following the Orange mob, more R.U.C. came into the area in their Shorland armored cars mounted with heavy caliber Browning machine guns. Stones and petrol bombs rained down on the invader from the rooftop of the twenty-story Divis Tower.

"It was absolute mayhem that night," declared Mrs. Boyle. "As houses burned in Percy, Beverly, and Dover Streets, the peelers fired their machine guns indiscriminately into Divis flats. Walls offered ye scant protection from high velocity bullets. One that pierced the bedroom wall of a frightened nine-year-old boy killed him instantly as his poor father held him in his arms. Patrick Rooney was the first child to die in the present Troubles. Later that night, Hugh McCabe, a local man, home on leave from the British Army, was shot dead whilst pullin' a wounded man off the roof of the Whitehall building.

"Thanks to Goulding and others of his ilk, the I.R.A. in Belfast had dwindled away to almost nothin', maybe thirty volunteers, a dozen women in the *Cumann na mBan,* and forty-odd Fianna boys. Amongst 'em were me boys, Eugene and Sonny. They were called up to defend Catholic streets.

"Rumor had it the local I.R.A.'s arsenal was reduced to just one rifle, two submachine guns and nine handguns. Badly outnumbered and outgunned, the I.R.A. were a bit like the wee Dutch boy with his finger pluggin' the hole in the dyke. Only our brave boys couldn't hold back the ragin' Orange sea."

In the early morning hours of August 15th – Feast of Our Lady's Assumption for Catholics – the Orange horde broke through the Conway Street barricades and burned down most of the houses on the street.

"The peelers held the people back at gunpoint," recalled Mrs. Boyle, "whilst their fellow Prods set their homes alight."

Many families fled to the perceived safety of Catholic Andersonstown, on the edge of west Belfast. Others, in streets not yet affected, braced themselves for the coming onslaught.

In Mrs. Boyle's Clonard district, Catholics feared for the monastery as well as their homes. As a Loyalist attack appeared imminent the most vulnerable streets were evacuated. Mrs. Boyle and her two daughters joined hundreds of other refugees at St. Paul's parish hall. Her teenage sons, Eugene and Sonny, remained behind with other members of *Fianna Éireann* and local able-bodied men to try to defend their district the best they could.

When Clonard was attacked that afternoon, priests at the monastery called the police for assistance. But none came.

As Catholic Bombay Street was aflame, a fifteen-year-old Fianna boy, Gerald McAuley, helping people flee their homes, was shot dead by a Loyalist sniper. Father Egan, who had been watching the wanton destruction all around him from an upstairs window of the monastery, rushed out into the fray to anoint the youth.

"Me Sonny and Gerald McAuley were the same age," said Mrs. Boyle, pouring us more tea. "We had a handful of I.R.A. men takin' pot shots at the Orangies and B-Specials with .22 rifles from houses in Kashmir Road. They may as well been armed with bloody pea-shooters! For they were unable to get the sniper who murdered young McAuley or stop people's houses from bein' set ablaze."

The Loyalist mob burned nearly every house on Bombay Street to the ground, along with many Catholic homes on Kashmir Road, Clonard Gardens, and Cupar Street. While no military intervention came from the Irish government in Dublin, the British government deployed troops to Derry and Belfast to keep order.

"We watched in disbelief from our wee gutted street, still smolderin' from all the fires, as British soldiers with bayonets fixed marched by us. I am tellin' yez, 'twas a sight to behold. We hadn't seen the like of it in Ireland for fifty years, since the country was partitioned. It made the hair stand up on the back of me neck, so it did.

"Over the years, much has been said about some of the Catholics here welcomin' the bloody Brits as saviors with applause and cheerin' and housewives greetin' the squaddies with plates of biscuits and cups of *tay*. Thank God, none of mine were with that lot.

"It soon became clear to everyone that the British Army weren't here to save us from the Orangies and the peelers, but to protect the sectarian Northern State.

"There were those who blamed the I.R.A. for not adequately defendin' Catholic areas, and 'I.R.A. = I Ran Away' was seen painted on walls. Most anger, though, was rightfully directed at the Dublin-based I.R.A. leadership and at Billy McMillen – the commander of the Belfast Brigade – for lack of weapons and bein' militarily unprepared for the attack. Mind, people stood one hundred percent behind those local volunteers who bravely fought the invader."

The following month, Belfast I.R.A. veterans Billy McKee and Joe Cahill led a group of I.R.A. men into a meeting called by McMillen and informed him in no uncertain terms that they would no longer be taking orders from him or his fellow Marxist Cathal Goulding in Dublin.

As 1969 came to a close, the Irish Republican Army split into two factions; the Marxist enthusiasts became the Official I.R.A. under Cathal Goulding and the traditional physical force Republicans emerged as the Provisional I.R.A. with Londoner Seán MacStiofáin as chief of staff. In Belfast, hardened fighting men like Jimmy Steele, Billy McKee, Joe Cahill, and Séamus Twomey wasted no time declaring their allegiance to the Provisionals. A total of nine out of thirteen I.R.A. units in the city did the same. Billy McKee became the first Officer Commanding of the Belfast Brigade of the Provisional I.R.A. While Billy McMillen, remaining loyal to Goulding, was Officer Commanding of the rival Belfast Brigade of the Official I.R.A.

The Provisionals immediately began planning to go on the offensive against the British. But first, they were called to defend a vulnerable Catholic enclave from another sectarian attack.

The district of Short Strand is a small Catholic island of green, surrounded by an angry Orange sea, in Protestant east Belfast. In late June 1970, Orangemen and Loyalists returning from a parade threatened to burn down St. Matthew's Church and the Catholic homes of Short Strand. Billy McKee and his men took up positions around the chapel and nearby streets, and the ensuing gun battle raged throughout the night. Finally, by morning the Loyalists retreated. The clash left three men dead, two Protestants and one Catholic. McKee was among the dozens wounded. He had been shot five times but remained conscious. Although the British Army and the R.U.C. were in the area that night, they declined in intervene.

"Sure," said Mrs. Boyle, "if it hadn't been for the Provisional I.R.A. there would have been a Loyalist pogrom and Short Strand would have been razed."

Her eldest son, Eugene, was with McKee's men at the Battle of St. Matthew's. It was the first major engagement of the newly formed Provisionals. Their success in defending the church and Short Strand won them the respect and support of ordinary Catholics. No one could again say that the I.R.A. stood for "I Ran Away."

Short Strand ended the British Army's so-called honeymoon in occupied Ireland. A week later, when troops from the Black Watch and Life Guards regiments began searching a house in the Lower Falls for I.R.A. weapons they found themselves facing an angry crowd which refused to move. The army fired canisters of CS gas to disperse the crowd and violence ensued. Crown forces found themselves embroiled in a pitched gun battle with both factions of the I.R.A. as hundreds of local youth hurled stones and petrol bombs at them.

The British Army imposed a thirty-six-hour curfew on the area. Then the "Rape of the Lower Falls" began. The Army fired 1,600 canisters of CS gas into the Falls Road and its densely populated narrow side streets. Canisters sometimes went directly through people's windows. The entire area was saturated with gas and residents – including many young children – coughed, choked, and nearly suffocated to death.

Three thousand British troops overran the Catholic district as military armored vehicles lined the streets and helicopters hovered overhead. Hundreds of homes were utterly wrecked by soldiers making a house-to-house search for weapons. Front doors were broken down, windows smashed, floorboards ripped up, and walls punched in with rifle butts. Furniture was destroyed, clothes scattered on the floor, and plaster statues of the Blessed Mother and saints were smashed to bits.

"Cromwell's men had returned to poor ould Ireland," declared Mrs. Boyle.

Hundreds of people in the Lower Falls were arrested and many were injured. Four innocent men were killed by the British Army. Charles O'Neill, a thirty-six-year-old Catholic and an invalided ex-serviceman, was deliberately run down by a British Saracen. William Burns, a fifty-four-year-old Catholic bachelor, was shot dead two hours before curfew as he stood on the front step of his home on the Falls Road. Patrick Elliman, a sixty-two-year-old Catholic and retired boot repairer, who in his youth was a goalkeeper with the Antrim hurling team, was shot in the head and later died of his wounds. Zbigniew Uglik, a twenty-three-year-old Polish national living in England, who was a postman and amateur photographer, was shot dead as he tried to take photographs.

"I'll tell yez," said Mrs. Boyle, "after the Rape of the Lower Falls the world and his brother wanted to join the I.R.A. Me Sonny had just turned eighteen when he joined Eugene in the Provos."

> *We have no ammunition, or no armored tanks to show,*
> *But we're ready to defend ourselves no matter where we go,*
> *We're out for our Republic and to hell with your Free State,*
> *'No surrender' is the war cry of the Belfast Brigade.*

CHAPTER ELEVEN
LEGLESS IN WEST BELFAST

I awoke to find myself lying on an unfamiliar carpeted floor, zipped up in a sleeping bag. Looking around the room, I tried to remember where I was and how I got there.

The drinking spree from the night before took me from pubs on the Lower Ormeau Road to pubs and Republican clubs along the Lower Falls Road. At closing time, I departed whatever drinking establishment I was at completely *legless* – one of the local, colorful terms for being three sheets to the wind, or bloody well drunk.

A group of teenage boys were hanging out on a street corner, smoking cigarettes, and I asked them if they knew of any clubs or pubs still open. The boys said that everything in the area had closed up for the night and politely pointed out, since I was already wavering on my feet, I that should go home. But as I recalled, they had some concern about how I'd safely navigate my way back to Eglantine Avenue through the Brit-infested streets of west Belfast.

Beside the sleeping bag that I found myself in was a bed with one of the teenage boys, I met the night before, sleeping in it. On the wall, above the bed, hung a crucifix. On another wall was a large, framed picture of the Sacred Heart of Jesus. Then I noticed the posters on the wall above my head. One had the familiar faces of the ten hunger strikers who chose to sacrifice their lives in the H-Blocks of Long Kesh than to forsake their principles. Another poster had three men in dark green balaclavas and black berets holding up automatic rifles under the caption: "Support your local I.R.A."

There was a stack of *An Phoblacht/ Republican News* papers on the floor and I started looking through them. Soon there was a stirring in the bed and I became reacquainted with my young host.

Sitting up in bed, Hughie McGowan cracked a few good-natured jokes about the terrible state I was in when we met. He was an amiable, slightly built, nineteen-year-old with large blue eyes and close-cropped sandy hair.

We chatted about life in west Belfast and Hughie McGowan wanted to know what Americans thought of the armed struggle against the British in the Six Counties. The sad truth, I told him, was that many Americans weren't even aware that there was a Northern Ireland, let alone what "the Troubles" are all about. And those Americans who were aware of the conflict often viewed it through the pro-British news media, giving them the impression that it was all about two warring tribes – Irish Catholics against Irish Protestants – kept apart for their own good by an impartial British Army.

"Och, nothin' could be further from the truth," replied Hughie. "This isn't about religion *atoll*. Republicans are engaged in a war to liberate our country and reunite the Irish nation."

A committed Republican, young Hughie was a member of Sinn Féin. When he wasn't working as a clerk in a department store in the city center, he was selling copies of *An Phoblacht/ Republican News* in west Belfast.

There was a light knock at the bedroom door and Hughie's father entered. He was a small, bald man with black-framed glasses, wearing a dark suit and tie. It occurred to me that he was probably in his Sunday best and as it was already late morning, he must have just come from Mass.

"Good mornin' lads," Mr. McGowan greeted us, as he seated himself on the edge of his son's bed.

I awkwardly introduced myself and offered Mr. McGowan my hand. He shook it with an amused expression on his face.

"Sure, we met last night," he said. "But ye were in yer cups, so ye were."

More than a little embarrassed and ashamed of myself, I apologized for arriving at his house in such a state.

"Arrah, ye're all right, son," said Mr. McGowan. "Ye got a good night's sleep anyway."

I noticed the little Sacred Heart pin in the lapel of his coat, like Callaghan's, which indicated that he was a member of the Pioneer Total Abstinence Association and had taken a pledge to abstain for life from alcohol to atone for the excessive drinking of others.

Mr. McGowan removed a pack of cigarettes from his coat pocket, took one for himself and tossed another to his son. He also offered me a cigarette and I accepted it and a lighter was passed around.

"Has Hughie converted ye yet?" he asked.

I wasn't entirely sure what Mr. McGowan meant.

"Me da means," explained Hughie, "have I made a committed Republican out of ye."

It was obvious that father and son didn't agree on politics. The elder man didn't approve of Sinn Féin.

"Thou shalt not kill," declared Mr. McGowan. "That is God's law. I don't support those who condone violence any more than I support those who commit it. Sure, I'd like to see Ireland reunited and for the British to leave the country, aye, but I'm not goin' to kill for it."

Mr. McGowan excused himself as Hughie and I got dressed. By the time we arrived downstairs in the kitchen, he had hot tea, toast, boiled eggs, and Irish sausages waiting for us. We sat down at the table, and I followed Hughie in blessing myself and saying grace before digging into a welcome breakfast.

When Mr. McGowan stepped out of the kitchen, Hughie explained in a lowered voice that his father did most of the cooking as his mother was ill and had been bedridden for years. Hughie was the youngest in the family and the only boy. His two eldest sisters had married men who took them away from the Troubles in Belfast. One lived over in London and the other had recently wed a farmer in County Longford in the south. Only his sister closest to him in age remained at home to help their father care for their sick mother and do household chores. Hughie, as a store clerk, was the sole breadwinner of the family.

Mr. McGowan returned and handed me a brown scapular. I hadn't seen a scapular in a while. The two small squares of woolen cloth, a bit bigger than a postage stamp, held together by two cords, had been worn as a sort of necklace by devout Catholics for centuries. Its name derived from the Latin for shoulders, as it hung from the shoulders, typically underneath one's clothing. I put the scapular over my head, with one woolen square on my chest and the other on my back and slipped it under my shirt.

"Ah, that's grand," said Mr. McGowan. "Our Lady of Mount Carmel appeared to Saint Simon Stock in 1251 and holdin' the scapular before him, she told him, 'Whosoever dies wearin' it shall not suffer eternal fire.' 'Tis our Blessed Mother's promise of salvation to those who'd seize it."

"Me ma makes scapulars," said Hughie, "and me da gives 'em out."

Hughie then invited me to attend a commemoration ceremony that morning at Milltown Cemetery for the fallen I.R.A. volunteers of the Lower Falls.

We left the McGowans' red-brick rowhouse on Cairns Street, hopped into a blue Ford Cortina that Hughie had parked by the curb, and sped just around the corner to Leeson Street where he stopped in front of a red-brick rowhouse identical to his own. We were to pick up a friend of his named Aidan. The door of the house immediately flung open and out ran a slender boy of eighteen or nineteen with pale skin and a shock of jet-black hair.

Aidan got into the back of the sedan and greeted me in typical Belfast fashion, "Bout ye?" As Hughie put the car into gear and turned onto the Falls Road, he casually introduced me as, "This is Ed from America."

At Milltown Cemetery, just inside the stone arched gateway, about a hundred people had gathered for the event. It was a cold and windy day, and the mood was somber. Hughie and Aidan were part of the color party bearing the national flag of Ireland, the four Irish provincial flags, the Starry Plough flag (first used by James Connolly's Citizen Army), and the Sunburst flag of *Fianna Éireann.* Everyone followed silently behind the color party through the cemetery to the Republican Plot, where the flags were lowered. I looked at the set, determined faces of those around me there to honor their Republican dead. They were a proud, unbowed people.

An old man removed his cap, revealing a head of snow-white hair, and recited a decade of the rosary in Gaelic, beginning with the Apostles' Creed.

Creidim i nDia, an tAthair Uilechumhachtach, Cruthaitheoir Nimhe agus Talún, agus i nÍosa Críost a Aonmhac san ár dTiarna…

Next, someone made a brief speech and read out the names, ages, and dates of death of the fallen Provisional Volunteers of "D" Company, 2nd Battalion, Belfast Brigade, *Óglaigh na hÉireann.*

Volunteer Charles Hughes, aged 26,	8th March 1971
Volunteer James Quigley, aged 17,	29th September 1972
Volunteer Daniel McAreavey, aged 21,	6th October 1972
Volunteer Paddy Maguire, aged 24,	10th October 1972
Volunteer John Donaghy, aged 18,	10th October 1972
Volunteer Joseph McKinney, aged 17,	10th October 1972
Volunteer Eddie "Mundo" O'Rawe, aged 27,	27th April 1973
Fian Michael Marley, aged 17,	24th November 1973
Volunteer Teddy Campbell, aged 54,	3rd May 1974
Volunteer Martin Skillen, aged 20,	3rd August 1974
Volunteer John "Bap" Kelly, aged 28,	21st January 1975
Volunteer Billy Carson, aged 32,	25th April 1979

They were killed in gun battles with the British Army, accidentally by their own bombs, in Loyalist attacks, in the feud with the Officials, and the oldest among them died in Long Kesh Prison.

Also mentioned were Sinn Féin members Pat McBride, aged forty, and Paddy Loughran, aged sixty-one, who were shot dead in February by a crazed R.U.C. man during a lone attack on the Lower Falls Sinn Féin office.

Since 1969, over three hundred members of the I.R.A. and Sinn Féin had lost their lives in the armed struggle. More than one hundred were from the Belfast Brigade.

The Provisional Irish Republican Army, or *Óglaigh na hÉireann* (Volunteers of Ireland), was divided into a Northern Command and a Southern Command. The former operated in the nine counties of Ulster as well as in the border counties of Leitrim and Louth, and the latter operated around the rest of Ireland. The I.R.A. had at least five brigades within the northern "war-zone." By far the largest of these was the Belfast Brigade, followed by the Derry Brigade, the Tyrone Brigade, the South Armagh Brigade, and the Donegal Brigade. Then there were the smaller Active Service Units of the I.R.A., not attached to the Brigades, that were spread across the North.

"The Belfast Brigade is organized into three battalions," explained Hughie McGowan, as he drove me back to Callaghan's flat on Eglantine Avenue after the commemoration was over. The First Battalion covered the suburbs of Andersonstown, Lenadoon, and Twinbrook in southwest Belfast. The Second Battalion covered the Falls Road, Clonard, and Ballymurphy districts in west Belfast. The Third Battalion covered different Nationalist areas of the city: Ardoyne, New Lodge, and Ligoniel in the north; the Markets and Lower Ormeau in the south; and Short Strand in the east.

The next day I spent wandering around the back streets of west Belfast with my camera. Despite the rainy drizzle, I took a number of photos of wall murals in Ballymurphy and the Lower Falls.

Ballymurphy was a grim cluster of housing estates built after the Second World War at the foot of Divis and Black Mountains. The solidly working-class, Catholic community with strong Republican sympathies had been one of the hardest hit areas during the Troubles.

In 1971, there was the Ballymurphy Massacre in which the 1st Battalion, Parachute Regiment of the British Army murdered eleven civilians. Among the dead was a priest, Father Hugh Mullan, killed in the street by a sniper while giving Last Rites to a man who was shot as he was trying to get children to safety. At the time, Father Mullan was waving a white cloth. Another victim was a forty-four-year-old mother of eight named Joan Connolly. She was shot dead while going to the aid of a wounded teenager.

The Springhill Massacre occurred a year later, in 1972, when British Army snipers shot dead five civilians in Springhill housing estate in Ballymurphy. Three of the dead were teenagers. The youngest was a thirteen-year-old girl. A second priest, Father Noel Fitzpatrick, administering Last Rites to the dying was killed as he rushed to the girl. The bullet passed through him and also killed a local man accompanying the priest. A fifteen-year-old boy was then shot dead as he tried to pull the priest to his feet.

Greater Ballymurphy, approximately one square mile in size, had more than its fair share of violent deaths. According to one count, seventy-two civilians and thirty-two Republican volunteers had been killed in the area. In addition, at least twenty-seven members of the British forces had met their deaths in Ballymurphy.

On Whiterock Road, I stopped to take a picture of a brightly colored mural on a gable wall. Beneath a rising phoenix were the Starry Plough and Sunburst flags. "Who fears to speak of Easter Week," it declared and in Gaelic, *"Éirí amach na Cásca 1916-1991."* Included in the mural were the signatories of the Irish Proclamation along with Countess Markievicz.

An interesting woman, the Countess was born into the Anglo-Irish Protestant Ascendancy, married a Polish count, took part in the Easter Rising, and fought on the Republican side during the Irish Civil War. She was the first woman to be elected to the British House of Commons, but refused to take her seat, in line with Sinn Féin abstentionist policy, and later served in the *Dáil Éireann,* the lower house of the Irish parliament. Countess Markievicz became a Catholic and after giving away the last of her wealth died among the poor of Dublin at the age of fifty-nine in 1927.

Another mural I came across covered the gable wall of a two-story apartment building. It was a copy of a mythological Celtic painting by the renowned Dublin artist Jim Fitzpatrick, beautifully enlarged to mural size by Belfast man Gerry Kelly. A helmeted, mighty warrior-king of the Tuatha Dé Danann was pictured brandishing a sword. The Tuatha Dé Danann were the people of the goddess Danu. Skilled in magical and powerful arts, they came from the "northern islands of the world" and ruled ancient Ireland until they were defeated by the Gaelic-speaking Milesian invaders from Spain, a thousand or more years before Christ. The Tuatha Dé Danann were said to have withdrawn to Ireland's hills and the underworld and became known as the Fairy Folk. The Milesians became the ancestors of the modern Irish people.

I continued to walk and turned onto the Falls Road. Ballymurphy and Whiterock have been called the Republican heart of west Belfast and the Falls Road has been called its Republican backbone.

Wandering down back streets lined with old brick rowhouses, I saw and photographed more wall murals and Republican slogans. *"Tiofaidh ár lá"* – Our day will come. In bold letters, *"SAOIRSE"* – Freedom – and the Irish tricolor flag and beneath it, *Óglaigh na hÉireann.*

Off Beechmount Avenue was Amcomri Street. One would be tempted to think the odd-sounding name was Gaelic, but it was actually an acronym for the **AM**erican **COM**mittee for the **R**elief of **I**reland. The committee was set up for Catholics who were burnt out of their homes during the troubles of 1921-22. Enough money was raised in America for the White Cross Fund to rebuild homes for displaced residents.

On Locan Street, I chanced to meet Mr. Gerald McCann. I was cleaning my camera lens when he stumbled along in my direction and stopped to introduce himself. The short, red-faced old man, in the need of a shave, looked like he had long ago lost the battle with drink. His open overcoat was stained and perched on his head was a worn plaid cap. Pulling a half-pint bottle of whiskey from his pocket, he took a quick swig, placed it back into his pocket, and told me he was a Belfast hard man.

"Would ye like to take me picture?" he asked cheerfully, as a coal truck stopped at the curb. "Just for the hell of it, like."

"Why not?" I replied, snapping a couple of pictures of Mr. McCann before leaving him on Locan Street.

As I headed down the Lower Falls Road and Divis Street, the R.U.C. and British Army were stopping and checking vehicles leaving the area. I walked by the checkpoint unchallenged. From a safe distance, I took my Nikon out of its camera case, attached a zoom lens onto it, then focused on the checkpoint and snapped a picture of a truck driver being questioned. Through the zoom lens, I could see a R.U.C. man pointing at me and soldiers turning to look in my direction. That was my cue to scram, and I took off as fast as possible without breaking into an actual run.

But I wasn't fast enough. A gray Land Rover hastily sped after me and I was quickly overtaken. The dour-faced R.U.C. man's eyes narrowed under the shiny black visor of his peaked cap as he questioned why I was photographing a vehicle checkpoint.

"It's just that in American cities we don't normally have military or police checkpoints," I answered.

"Right," replied the constable. "Well, if ye're caught again takin' pictures of members of the security forces ye'll find yerself without a camera. Now, what's yer name?"

I gave him my name.

"Right," he said again. "Now, be on yer way."

It was still lightly drizzling as I began to walk away and the R.U.C. man remarked, "Rotten weather we're havin' here. Big difference from sunny San Diego, eh?"

I half-shrugged in agreement. It was only after I had gone half a block that I realized I never mentioned San Diego or even living in California. Obviously, when I was stopped by the R.U.C. four days earlier with Callaghan, my name and San Diego address had been noted.

CHAPTER TWELVE
A BIT OF BELFAST HISTORY

Belfast City Hall dominates Donegall Square in the city center. Built in the Baroque Revival style at the turn of the 19th century, the exterior is mainly of Portland stone. The impressive edifice is capped with a green copper dome and has a tower at each of its corners. On the grounds are various monuments and statues, including one of Sir Edward Harland, the city's leading shipbuilder and one-time Lord Mayor of Belfast. At the main entrance, an enormous marble statue of sour-faced Queen Victoria looks down on passersby as a Union Jack flaps in the wind behind her. Known in Ireland as the Famine Queen, her government exported under armed guard food grown in Ireland while half her Irish subjects starved to death or were forced to emigrate during the so-called "Potato Famine" of 1845-49. As John Mitchel, an Irish Protestant Nationalist and journalist, wrote a few years later, "The Almighty, indeed, sent the potato blight, but the English created the Famine."

Across from City Hall is Belfast's oldest library. Founded in 1788 as the Belfast Reading Society and renamed the Belfast Society for Promoting Knowledge in 1792, the library originally occupied the site of the present City Hall. Thomas Russell once served as its librarian. A Cork man, he was called "The Man from God Knows Where." He was among the founders and leaders of the Society of United Irishmen, who boldly vowed to "break the connection with England." Before the Rising of 1798, Thomas Russell traveled the North as an organizer and emissary for the United Irishmen. He was arrested, hanged, and beheaded in Downpatrick Jail in 1803.

But to return to Belfast's oldest library. In 1802, it was granted a place in White Linen Hall, from which the library took its name. Ninety years later, as preparations were underway to build the new City Hall, the library was transferred to its present building, a former linen warehouse on Donegall Square North.

I crossed the street over to the Linen Hall Library. A yellow-gray brick building, above its arched doorway was draped linen in stone with the Red Hand of Ulster.

Although widely regarded as a Loyalist symbol, the Red Hand of Ulster has absolutely no historical connection to Britain. Its roots are purely Irish. The ancient symbol of the northern province can be traced back to medieval Ireland. There are various stories told about its origin. The one most often heard is of two Gaelic chieftains claiming the throne of Ulster, having agreed to a boat race and that "whoever's hand is the first to touch the shore of Ulster, so shall he be made the king." Their longboats cut through the water as fast as their oarsmen could row. As they neared land, the losing chieftain pulled out his sword and chopped off his hand and threw it, red with blood, onto the shore ahead of his rival's boat, thus winning the kingship of Ulster.

It's said that the chieftain who cut off his hand was from the Uí Neíll clan and the red hand became the official emblem of the O'Neills. In time, the bloody hand was associated with all of Ulster.

I strolled through the wooden double doors of the Linen Hall Library and spent an enjoyable afternoon immersed in books about Belfast history.

The name Belfast is the anglicized version of the Gaelic *Béal Feirste,* which means "mouth of the sandbank." It refers to the sandy ford at the point where the River Farset (from the Gaelic *fearsad* for sandbank) enters the River Lagan and flows into Belfast Lough. The old Celts used this sandbank as a river crossing place and in time a cluster of forts were built to guard the ford.

In the early Christian era, eastern Ulster was ruled by the Ulaid, the Celtic people who gave their name to the modern province of Ulster. But most of the inhabitants of the region belonged to the Cruthin, a rival tribe of Celts. The Annals of Tighernach recorded a battle between the Ulaid and Cruthin fought at the "Fearsat" in A.D. 667.

A small chapel was built at the marshy ford for pilgrims crossing the waters and a Papal Taxation Roll of 1306 refers to "the chapel of the Ford."

When the Normans arrived in the 12th century, they built strong stone castles all over Ireland to protect themselves as they attacked Irish chieftains and took three quarters of the country. Belfast's first castle was probably built by the powerful Anglo-Norman knight John de Courcy in 1177, who farther up the Antrim coast constructed Carrickfergus Castle.

In 1210, King John of England marched his army through *Béal Feirste*. A little over a hundred years later, in 1316, the forces of Edward Bruce, the younger brother of Scotland's famous Robert the Bruce, King of Scots, destroyed Belfast Castle and the tiny hamlet around it. Subsequently, it was rebuilt under the O'Neills.

For nearly two centuries, the mighty clan held Belfast and the surrounding countryside, until the Earl of Kildare, Gerald Mór FitzGerald, twice took the town and demolished the castle in 1503 and 1512. The O'Neills regained and repaired the castle.

In the 16th century, Ulster was the most Gaelic part of Ireland and the only province still outside of English control. It was therefore in Ulster that Celtic Catholic Ireland made her last stand against Protestant England.

The English first invaded Ulster in 1571. The forces of Queen Elizabeth I were initially repulsed from the province by the chieftain of the O'Neills of Clanaboy, Sir Brian MacPhelim O'Neill. But two years later the English returned under the 1st Earl of Essex, Walter Devereux, and defeated the chieftain at Ballymacarett (located now in east Belfast). Essex occupied Belfast Castle and built a fort at the Ford. In 1574, Essex persuaded O'Neill to attend a feast in the Castle where he treacherously seized O'Neill and his wife and brother, and after massacring two hundred of his clansmen, had them executed in Dublin for treason.

Brian MacPhelim O'Neill's kinsman, Hugh O'Neill, the Earl of Tyrone, known as The Great O'Neill, along with Red Hugh O'Donnell, the Lord of Tyrconnell (which later became County Donegal), carried on Ireland's fight against the foreign invader. But the Nine Years' War, from 1593 to 1603, ended with the defeat of the great Gaelic chieftains. They were forced to flee into permanent exile in continental Europe, accompanied by about ninety of their followers. Their departure, called the Flight of the Earls, marked the end of the ancient Gaelic order in Ulster, and Ireland's fourth green field joined the other three in bondage.

Once Irish resistance was crushed in Ulster, lands long occupied by Gaelic clans were confiscated by the English Crown and the organized colonization of the northern province began. Ulster Catholics, like their coreligionists across Ireland, were driven into the hills and bogs, where their enemies hoped that they would die of starvation, while their lands were given to Protestant planters (colonists) imported from England and Scotland.

In 1603, King James I (who authorized the Protestant version of the Bible bearing his name), gave a large portion of the southern part of County Antrim, including Belfast Castle, to Sir Arthur Chichester (who scorched the Ulster countryside during the Nine Years' War with genocidal intent and later oversaw the plantation of the province). Chichester rebuilt and strengthened the Castle, and a small town grew up around it.

Belfast in the early 17th century was an entirely Protestant town of about a thousand inhabitants. Its English and Scottish settlers made early Belfast a thriving market and trading center. They were joined by an influx of French Huguenots (Protestants) fleeing Catholic France, who established a prosperous linen industry.

Across the water, a Catholic ascended the English throne. Irish Catholics dared to hope that James II would restore their lands to them. But Protestant England wouldn't suffer a Catholic king and a Dutch Protestant prince, William of Orange, was invited to rule in his place. King James II, however, refused to give up his throne. The War of the Two Kings was fought in Ireland, 1689-91. Irish Catholics supported James and Protestants in Ireland backed William.

Belfast was occupied by the troops of King James, then by the Williamite army. King William III himself visited Belfast and issued a royal proclamation prohibiting plundering by his Protestant army.

James's defeated Catholic army surrendered at Limerick in 1691. Before the ink on the Treaty had dried, though, a lot more Catholic land was confiscated, and the promises William made to Catholics guaranteeing them religious tolerance were broken. A series of new harsher penal laws were enacted.

The Penal Laws forbade an Irish Catholic to bear arms and barred him from public office. He couldn't vote, practice law, serve in the army or the navy, act as a sheriff or a constable. He couldn't engage in trade or commerce, live in the larger corporate towns, or own a horse worth more than five pounds. A Catholic was forbidden to purchase land or inherit land from a Protestant and he couldn't lease land for longer than thirty-one years. A Catholic was forbidden to marry a Protestant and a Protestant was forbidden to convert to Roman Catholicism. Catholic teachers in Ireland were outlawed. A Catholic couldn't receive an education or educate his child, and it was forbidden for a Catholic to go overseas to be educated. No Catholic could be guardian to a child, or when dying could a Catholic leave his young children under Catholic guardianship.

The Irish Catholic was forbidden the exercise of his religion and he saw his churches destroyed or turned into Protestant churches. Catholic clergy were outlawed and expelled en mass from Irish shores. The priests who remained faced imprisonment and death. They hid themselves and said Mass by stealth with faithful Catholics gathered around them at Mass rocks on lonely hillsides, deep in the woods, and in old, ruined abbeys.

The Penal Laws also discriminated against Presbyterians and Quakers and other Protestant Dissenters, who didn't belong to the established Anglican Church. Dissenters were no longer allowed to hold public office and Belfast saw its entire town council of Presbyterians thrown out of office. (The Presbyterians of Ulster were almost solidly Scots, while most of the English settlers were members of the Established Church.) But Presbyterians and their fellow Dissenters suffered far less persecution than Catholics, and they were able to keep the land they had taken away from the native Irish.

In 1708, the year Belfast Castle burned down, the town's Protestant population was about 2,500, and reportedly there were a mere seven Catholics living in Belfast.

As the century progressed so did the views of many Protestants in Ireland towards Catholics, and some of the Penal Laws began to be repealed.

Across the Atlantic, the American War of Independence was being fought. When British troops were sent to fight in the American colonies, a volunteer militia – almost wholly Presbyterian – was raised in Belfast in 1778 to guard against foreign invasion and to keep law and order.

By 1782, the census reported that Belfast had about 13,000 inhabitants, 365 of whom were Catholics. The town's enlightened Presbyterian and Anglican (Church of Ireland) population took up a special collection and generously donated the money to build Belfast's first Catholic church – St. Mary's in Chapel Lane.

In Dublin, a young Protestant barrister named Theobald Wolfe Tone published an influential pamphlet called *An Argument on Behalf of the Catholics of Ireland,* in which he asserted the political interests of uniting the whole people of Ireland against their one common enemy. He sought to substitute the common name of Irishman in place of Protestant, Catholic, and Dissenter; and "to break the connection with England, the never-failing source of all our political evil."

Wolfe Tone was invited to Belfast by his friend Thomas Russell – "The Man From God Knows Where" – and some like-minded, predominately middle-class Presbyterians to found the Society of United Irishmen in October 1791. A month later, a branch was established in Dublin. The society was inspired by the American and especially French Revolutions. Initially, the organization called for parliamentary reform but soon demanded nothing less than an independent Irish Republic.

In addition to Russell, founders and prominent members of the Belfast United Irishmen included: Henry Joy McCracken, Samuel McTier, Samuel Neilson, William Drennan, Henry Haslett, William Tennant, brothers Robert and William Simms, Reverend William Steel Dickson, Thomas McCabe, and James "Jemmy" Hope. Along with Tone and Russell, McCracken nobly gave his life for Ireland.

If Ireland had Protestants who so loved her, and fought and died to make her free, she also had Protestants who sought to forever keep her firmly under British control. In 1795, four years after the founding of the United Irishmen, Protestants loyal to the Crown formed the Orange Order in Loughgall, County Armagh, to combat the rise of Irish Republicanism, support the monarchy, and uphold the Protestant Ascendancy. From the start, Orangemen were known for their violent sectarianism. Large numbers of armed Orangemen wrecked and burned in Armagh thousands of Catholic cottages and chapels.

After the United Irishmen rebellion of 1798 was ruthlessly crushed, the British and Irish Parliaments passed the Act of Union. Under this Act, Ireland became part of the United Kingdom of Great Britain and Ireland in 1801, and the Irish Parliament was abolished.

In the 19th century, Belfast grew rapidly as it emerged as Ireland's second-most important industrial city, after Dublin, and became renowned worldwide for its shipbuilding. In 1802, Belfast had about 19,000 inhabitants. By 1841, the population had climbed to 70,447, and by 1861 had soared to 207,671.

By the 1850's, Catholics made up one third of the inhabitants. But their increase in numbers only increased sectarian attacks. Protestants felt that Catholics from the surrounding countryside were coming to Belfast to take their jobs. Often Protestant preachers, like Hugh "Roaring" Hanna, fanned the flames of hatred by bigoted speeches from the pulpit that incited Orange mobs to violently attack Catholics. Throughout the 19th century, there were bloody sectarian riots in Belfast and the city became segregated into Catholic areas and Protestant areas.

Little had changed in Belfast, I reflected. As Maurice James Craig wrote in his oft-quoted poem, "May the Lord in His mercy be kind to Belfast."

CHAPTER THIRTEEN
THE MEN OF ARDOYNE

It was late morning when I opened my travel journal at a table at the Mad Hatter Coffee Shop. Lighting my pipe, I leaned back in my chair and slowly savored the sweet tobacco smoke as I tried to recall all the events of the previous day.

In the afternoon, I had strolled up past Carlisle Circus, a roundabout north of the city center, and onto the busy Antrim Road and the New Lodge Road. The area had a number of interfaces where segregated communities of Catholics and Protestants met and were flashpoints for sectarian violence. Along the Antrim Road, from New Lodge to the Newington district, so many Catholics had been killed by Loyalist paramilitaries that it was dubbed "murder mile" by locals. The most dangerous spot to stand in Ireland, they said, was at the corner of the Antrim Road and the New Lodge Road.

I wandered around the New Lodge district, down streets lined with century-old red-brick rowhouses and past large, modern apartment towers. Republican murals were everywhere. I had my camera and started taking pictures. On a rowhouse gable wall was a huge Celtic cross with the words: "A Tribute to the Heroes of 1916." Painted on a brick wall, beside a gate, was a black masked Provo beneath the initials P.I.R.A. – Provisional Irish Republican Army. Nearby, across a Tricolor

81

flag mural was written: "The support of our people is obvious in that we could not survive or increase our operations without it. With our support, our weaponry and the calibre of our volunteers and activists, we will win and are set firmly on the task of achieving Victory."

On another wall was a skeleton wrapped in a Union Jack and holding a smoking gun next to the word 'MURDERERS' – the larger letters, UDR, for the infamous Ulster Defence Regiment. A locally recruited and almost entirely Protestant regiment of the British Army, the U.D.R. replaced the hated Ulster Special Constabulary (B-Specials) in 1970. Since its formation, the U.D.R. was linked with Loyalist murder gangs and sectarian attacks and killings of Catholic civilians. The discredited U.D.R. merged with the Royal Irish Rangers a few months earlier to become the Royal Irish Regiment. But a new name and a change of uniform did not fool anyone.

Further along the road, by a group of little children taking turns pushing a toddler on a tricycle, was the smiling face of Joe Doherty covering an entire gable wall. Callaghan used to have on his old Datsun coupe a bumper sticker that read: "Free Irish P.O.W. Joe Doherty in U.S. Jail."

An I.R.A. volunteer from the New Lodge, Doherty and three of his comrades were involved in a shootout with eight members of the elite S.A.S. (Special Air Service) in 1980 and a British commando was killed. When more security forces arrived at the scene, the I.R.A. unit was trapped and had no choice but to surrender. A year later, Doherty was one of eight Republican prisoners who escaped in a hail of gunfire from Crumlin Road Jail. Doherty made his way to America using a fake passport. He was arrested in 1983 by the F.B.I. at Clancy's Bar in Manhattan where he was working as a bartender. For nine years he fought a legal battle against extradition and deportation from his jail cell in Manhattan. His struggle attracted wide support, including from New York City Mayor David Dinkins and the Archbishop of New York, John Cardinal O'Connor. Although U.S. courts ruled in Doherty's favor, in the end politics prevailed and the American government returned him to the British to serve a life sentence in the H-Blocks of Long Kesh Prison.

Doherty was seen by many as a soldier who killed an enemy soldier in battle. U.S. Attorney General Ramsey Clark asked: "What did Joe Doherty do that George Washington, Alexander Hamilton, or Tom Paine wouldn't have done?"

Like so many Republican murals in Belfast, Doherty's was splattered with paint. It was said that British soldiers went around at night shooting paint bombs at them.

The kids and the toddler on the tricycle were gone and groups of heavily armed Brits began to emerge from alleys behind houses and fill the street. It was obvious that they were looking for someone. I made my way back to the Antrim Road and down to Carlisle Circus and then up the Crumlin Road.

The Lower Crumlin Road took me past the Mater Infirmorum (Mother of the Sick) Hospital. The handsome, red-brick, 19th century building with a statue of Our Lady in a niche under a cross, high above its main entrance, was opened in 1883 by the Sisters of Mercy. The good nuns treated all patients regardless of class or creed.

A block up from the Mater was the notorious Belfast Prison, better known as Crumlin Road Jail. Solidly constructed of black basalt rock, it held many an Irish patriot as well as some of the worst criminals and murderers. When the jail first opened in 1846, during the Famine, the inmates included men, women, and children. Often, they came from the poorest of the poor – especially the children – and were imprisoned for stealing a bit of food or clothing. The president of the Irish Republic, Éamon de Valera, was once locked up for a month in Crumlin Road Jail in the 1920's for "illegally" entering the Northern state. Seventeen men were hanged on the prison gallows and buried within its walls, before the British abolished capital punishment. The most well-known execution, of course, was that of the nineteen-year-old Republican prisoner Tom Williams in 1942.

Although security was always tight at the prison, known as Europe's Alcatraz, over the years there were several jailbreaks. These escapes were made almost entirely by Republican prisoners in the Crum. In 1943, four Republican prisoners, including Hugh McAteer, the I.R.A.'s chief of staff, and Jimmy Steele, who later became a founding member of the Provisionals, clambered over the wall.

In 1971, nine Republican prisoners hopped the wall while their comrades distracted the warders with a soccer match in one of the exercise yards. The escapees were soon called the Crumlin Kangaroos. Two weeks later, despite increased security measures, local I.R.A. commander Martin Meehan and Anthony "Dutch" Doherty, both from

Ardoyne in north Belfast, along with another Republican prisoner, hid themselves under the cover of darkness and fog and scaled the wall to a waiting car.

And, as was already mentioned, the most dramatic escape occurred in 1981, when Joe Doherty and seven other Republican prisoners shot their way to freedom and exited the Crum, not over the wall but through the main gate.

Across the road, facing the prison, was the equally notorious Crumlin Road Courthouse. Built during the same early Victorian era, the courthouse was ironically topped by the statue of Justice - the Roman goddess Justitia.

Farther up the road, I became aware that I was in a Protestant area. Graffiti spray-painted on the side of a rowhouse proclaimed "Kill All Taigs" (Taigs being a derogatory term for Catholics). On gable walls were Loyalist paramilitary murals. One depicted masked gunmen with assault weapons and included the Ulster Banner, or flag, with a red hand inside a white six-pointed star, surmounted by the imperial Crown, and flanked by the Union Jack and St. Andrew's Cross, the national flag of Scotland. The mural also had a red clenched fist and the initials U.F.F. – for the Ulster Freedom Fighters (a Loyalist murder gang). Another mural had more Ulster and British flags and the initials U.V.F. – for the Ulster Volunteer Force (a rival Loyalist murder gang). Another had a red hand wrapped in barbed wire beneath L.P.O.W. (Loyalist Prisoners of War).

Looking over my shoulder to see if anyone was watching, I took my camera out from under my jacket and snapped a couple of pictures. But I didn't linger long. Although an American, I was still aware of being a hated *Taig* in enemy territory.

Continuing up the Crumlin Road, I took a right turn onto Flax Street, which ran alongside an old mill, and into the Republican stronghold of Ardoyne. Covering a gable wall was a mural of rural bliss in old Ireland. A couple dancing in a green field by a low stone wall while a fiddler and fluter played Irish tunes. Over the idyllic scene was painted in ornate Celtic lettering: *Ardoyne Fleadh Cheoil* (Music Festival). *Maireann An Spiorad Go Fóill* (The Spirit Still Lives). As I drew closer to the mural, I saw the dancers' faces had been splattered by a paint bomb.

In the early 17th century, Ardoyne was a village set on a grassy hill overlooking Belfast Lough. Its name was derived from the Irish Gaelic *Ard Eoin,* meaning Eoin's Height, after a member of the O'Neill clan.

On my right was a green painted building – The Shamrock Bar. After such a long walk, I was thirsty and stepped in for a jar. As the barman pulled a Guinness for me, I noticed all eyes in the place were looking at me – the stranger. A group of men began to surround me. I suspected I was heading for another interrogation.

A balding, middle-aged man in a black leather jacket, with tattoos on the backs of his hands, broke into a smile as he pointed to my camera, hanging from a shoulder strap under my open jacket.

"Arrah now! He's a tourist, so he is."

"Where ye from?" asked another man.

"What brings ye up to Ardoyne?" queried a third.

The older, balding man took a seat on the barstool beside me and introduced himself as Danny, as he firmly shook my hand. I soon learned he was born and reared in Ardoyne, had served in the I.R.A. but was retired after a ten-year-stretch in Long Kesh. Noticing my new companion was without a pint, I ordered him a Guinness along with another one for myself.

When the pints arrived, a smiling man wearing a green Boston Celtics sweatshirt slapped a five pound note down on the bar. "Welcome to Ardoyne, Yank! The pints are on me."

He was in his early thirties, of average height and built, and had a mustache and dark hair.

"I'm Seán Moore," he declared, "and this here's Seán Less."

The guy standing next to him gave a nod. He was a slightly chubby fellow in a worn brown leather jacket. Despite his ginger mustache, he had a boyish face, but he must have been about thirty.

"It is McCand*less*. "Me name's Seán McCandless."

"Arrah, Seánie, ye'll always be *Less* to us!" said a grinning Seán Moore.

Fresh pints were set before us and lifting one to his lips, Seán Moore exclaimed, "Drink up, boys!"

"Sláinte!" we responded.

Over a couple of more pints, I learned that Seán Moore and Seán Less, or McCandless, like Danny the former I.R.A. man, were Ardoyne born and bred. They were both married men with a few kids. Seán Moore had only recently returned home from Toronto, Canada, where he spent two years working as a construction worker. An unemployed chef, Seán Less had traveled no farther than Dublin and asked a number of questions about life in America. The other Seán mentioned that Seán Less had spent four years in Long Kesh after he was caught in the possession of a few handguns.

"Seánie Less was holding 'em for the I.R.A.," added Danny.

Another round of pints was called for and Seán Moore excused himself to step into a back room. He returned a few moments later with a green and white striped Celtic Football Club jersey. Presenting it to me, he loudly declared: "This is a gift from the men of Ardoyne – wear it with pride!"

"We're all Celtic fans here," said Seán Less, "but Seán Moore is totally mad for 'em."

I held the jersey up, before removing my jacket and pulling it over my sweatshirt. Across the front of the jersey was the name of the sponsor, CR Smith, and, on the left breast, the club's four-leafed shamrock badge with 1888, the year their first game was played.

The Scottish football (that is, soccer) club was established in Glasgow by an Irish Marist Brother to raise money for the impoverished Irish who had fled a starving country and found refuge in the teeming industrial city. As Catholics, however, the Irish were unwelcome in Protestant Scotland. Fierce competition for jobs added to the tensions between Protestants and Catholics, and Glasgow often saw sectarian strife that rivaled 19th century Belfast.

In recent decades, however, the chosen battlefield in Scotland had been the sports field. Glasgow boasted two football teams – Celtic and Rangers. Celtic fans were mainly Scots of Irish Catholic descent and Catholics living in Ireland, and overwhelmingly their sympathies were with the Republican armed struggle (although Celtic had always allowed Protestant members). The Rangers were a Protestant only club and supported British Unionism.

At Celtic and Rangers matches, fans taunted and jeered each other and belted out sectarian or Republican songs. The bitter hatred between the fans often erupted into violence with opposing sides furiously charging onto the playing field to bash each other senseless.

"Sure," said a beaming Seán Moore, "it's the streets of Belfast within a stadium."

I reached into my jacket pocket and pulled out my pack of Camel cigarettes for a smoke.

"Jaysus!" exclaimed Seán Less. "American cigarettes."

I passed out Camels to my new companions.

Lifting my expensive camera from where I had placed it on the bar, Seán Moore carefully examined it and asked if I'd like to take a few pictures of the boys there at the Shamrock. I took one of the two Seáns with Danny, and another of Seán Moore with a sort of devil-may-care look and a lit cigarette dangling out of one of his nostrils as a grinning Seán Less held up two fingers, like a couple of horns, over his head.

I was then off with the two Seáns to see a local memorial on nearby Berwick Road.

Behind a low stone wall with a wrought iron gate emblazoned with a harp on top, was Ardoyne's Garden of Remembrance. Mounted on a white gable wall was a black plaque depicting a phoenix rising from the flames and engraved: "Freedom hath arisen, oft from prison bars, oft from battle flashes, oft from heroes' lips, oftenest from the ashes."

Beneath this was a long list of names which included fallen volunteers of the I.R.A. and Fianna Éireann and civilian casualties from the area. To the right of the plaque was a tall, beautiful Celtic cross, dedicated: "In loving memory of all from the Ardoyne, Bone and Ligoniel who died because of Ireland's Troubles."

"Our Garden of Remembrance," said Seán Moore, "was unveiled at Eastertime in 1976 by none other than Nora Connolly O'Brien."

"She was the daughter of the Irish rebel James Connolly of 1916 fame," added Seán Less.

"Irish *patriot,* not rebel," corrected Seán Moore.

"Aye," agreed Seán Less, "a true son of Ireland."

I stepped across the road to take a picture and Seán Moore offered to take one of me in front of the memorial. I briefly explained how my Nikon worked, then handed him the camera and went back to stand by the garden gate. He snapped a picture and called out that he'd take another for good measure.

But Seán Moore saw what was coming down the road and I didn't. As he took another shot, two British Army Land Rovers and a R.U.C. Land Rover slowly rolled between us. They didn't stop, though, and we watched as they disappeared around the corner. I joined Seán Moore and Seán Less, and we hastily made our way down a long alley that cut between rowhouses.

But when we reached the end of the alley, we found the Brits and the R.U.C. waiting for us on Balholm Drive. First, the two Seáns were briefly questioned by a R.U.C. man, who apparently knew them. Then it was my turn. The policeman's questions appeared to be routine: my name, where was I from, what was I doing in Belfast, my local address.

Seán Moore still had my camera and while I was being questioned, he raised it as if to take a picture of the constable.

"Ah, now," said Seán Moore cheerily, "wouldn't this make a lovely picture for the visitin' Yank to stick in his picture album of Belfast?"

The R.U.C. man wasn't amused, and neither were the two heavily armed British soldiers standing only a few feet away.

"Knock it off, Seán," I said, not wanting to see my $500 camera confiscated or thrown to the pavement to be smashed to bits.

But the forces of the Crown departed peacefully enough in their Land Rovers, and Seán Moore returned my camera undamaged to me with a smile.

"Arrah," he said dismissively, "those bastards wouldn't have wrecked yer camera. Ye're an American tourist!"

I was about to say something when Seán Less spoke up.

"C'mon, let's go in for a couple of jars at the Star."

We were standing directly in front of the Crumlin Star Social Club. Inside the place was packed. Seán Moore took me around, introducing me to various people, including the proprietor, an elderly gentleman in a gray suit named Frank Murphy. Someone was good enough to put a pint of Guinness in my hand, as Seán Moore continued to lead me through the crowd to meet more people.

Eventually, I was introduced to an old fellow named Joe Parker. He was a short, stout man with balding silver hair wearing a cardigan sweater under a brown suit jacket. Mr. Parker was a former Republican prisoner recently released from Portlaoise Prison in the Irish Republic in the South. We shared a pint as Seán Moore related to him the tale of our run-in with the R.U.C.

When Mr. Parker learned I had a camera, he asked if I wouldn't mind taking a few pictures of the youngsters in the band and sending them to him once they were developed. I readily agreed, though I had no idea what band and youngsters he was talking about.

Joe Parker then led us into a large room where a group of teenage boys and girls with flutes and drums were practicing marching tunes. On a big drum was printed, "Bone & Ardoyne Martyrs Flute Band."

Known locally as "The Bone," the small Marrowbone district, next to Ardoyne, along with the small suburb of Ligoniel, farther out towards Wolf Hill, had much in common. The three north Belfast working-class communities were almost entirely Catholic and largely Republican in their sympathies. Surrounded by Loyalist districts, they had long suffered violence and a record number of murders by Loyalist paramilitaries.

Mr. Parker introduced me to the kids in the marching band as Seán Moore clicked away with my camera. We were soon joined by Seán Less and Danny from the Shamrock Bar.

Flags were unfurled and Seán Moore proudly held up a corner of the Tricolor and snapped to attention as the band struck up a patriotic tune. I immediately recognized it as one written by Thomas Davis, the chief organizer and poet of the Young Ireland movement of the 1840's. Enthusiastically, I sang along with my companions.

When boyhood's fire was in my blood
I read of ancient freemen,
For Greece and Rome who bravely stood,
Three hundred men and three men;
And then I prayed I yet might see
Our fetters rent in twain,
And Ireland, long a province, be
A Nation once again!

A Nation once again,
A Nation once again,
And Ireland, long a province, be
A Nation once again!

And from that time, through wildest woe,
That hope has shone a far light,
Nor could love's brightest summer glow

> *Outshine that solemn starlight;*
> *It seemed to watch above my head*
> *In forum, field and fane,*
> *Its angel voice sang round my bed,*
> *A Nation once again!*
> *A Nation once again,*
> *A Nation once again,*
> *And Ireland, long a province, be*
> *A Nation once again!*
>
> *It whisper'd too, that freedom's ark*
> *And service high and holy,*
> *Would be profaned by feelings dark*
> *And passions vain or lowly;*
> *For, Freedom comes from God's right hand,*
> *And needs a godly train;*
> *And righteous men must make our land*
> *A Nation once again!*
>
> *A Nation once again,*
> *A Nation once again,*
> *And Ireland, long a province, be*
> *A Nation once again!*
>
> *So, as I grew from boy to man,*
> *I bent me to that bidding*
> *My spirit of each selfish plan*
> *And cruel passion ridding;*
> *For, thus I hoped some day to aid,*
> *Oh, can such hope be vain?*
> *When my dear country shall be made*
> *A Nation once again!*

Someone brought me a tumbler of whiskey and I bought everyone a round of Guinness. After the band played a few more lively tunes and a few more rousing songs were sung, it was time for me to call it a night. Seán Less offered to call me a taxi, but I was low on cash and told him not to bother. I arrived in Ardoyne on foot and figured I'd hoof it back to south Belfast.

"No!" Seán Moore almost shouted. "I'll not allow it."

"Ye'd be takin' yer life in yer hands," said Mr. Parker, "leavin' Ardoyne after dark and steppin' into bloody Loyalist territory."

"They'd murder ye," agreed Seán Less.

"If it's a matter of a few quid for a taxi," said Seán Moore, in a lower voice, "ye needn't worry about that. The men of Ardoyne will get ye safely home."

With some embarrassment, but with only a few pence in my pocket, I accepted the generous offer and thanked "the men of Ardoyne" as several pound coins were pressed into my hand.

"Aye, now ye're being a sensible lad," said Mr. Parker, shaking my hand.

"Mind yerself," a couple of others told me, as I shook everyone's hand and wished them good night.

Seán Less accompanied me outside to await the taxi. As we shared a smoke, he told me how Seán Moore's father was murdered by a Loyalist death squad simply because he was a Catholic and his own father was killed by Crown forces.

Such is life in Ardoyne. But long will I remember the warm welcome I received on my first visit to Ardoyne.

New Lodge Road, Belfast

Edmond Audubon

Loyalist art on the Crumlin Road, Belfast

The author at Ardoyne's Garden of Remembrance, Belfast

CHAPTER FOURTEEN
THE HILLS OF BELFAST

I set out with Callaghan for a hike in the Belfast Hills. Located just outside the city, the series of basaltic and limestone hills are part of the southeastern edge of the Antrim Plateau formed millions of years ago by an outpouring of lava. The Belfast Hills include Divis Mountain, Black Mountain, Cave Hill, and Wolf Hill – where the last wolf in Ireland was reportedly killed in the late 17th century.

Callaghan had a backpack and carried two, about four-foot-long, metal pipes that he had duct-taped together. When I questioned him about it, he'd only say that I would have to wait and see.

After a great deal of walking that took us along the Upper Springfield Road and up a street lined by neat brick houses – a number of them flying Union Jacks – we found ourselves on a part of Ballygomartin Road with overgrown hedges and shrubs. There were no longer any houses, and all was quiet around us. It was the peace and quiet of the countryside.

We were at the base of Black Mountain, and looking for a way to the top, we turned onto an ascending little dirt road. In the distance, we saw two or three small farms with cows, goats, and sheep. We passed a sign saying "Quaker Cottage," and we noticed a white house perched high on the hillside.

"Quakers, huh?" said Callaghan, somewhat surprised, as I was, to find the religious sect there.

"Quakers have been in Ireland since the 17th century," I remarked, pleased to show my Ireland-obsessed friend that I knew a fact or two about Irish history that he didn't. "The Quakers fed the starving Irish during the Potato Famine."

"They fed those who took the soup anyway," answered Callaghan.

He was referring to the Protestant proselytizers who set up soup kitchens during the Famine and would only offer a sip of their soup to the Irish hungry and desperate enough to renounce their faith. Most Irish were devout Catholics, though, and would sooner starve to death rather than forfeit their immortal souls. The few who "took the soup" were derisively called "soupers" and often regarded as traitors by their coreligionist countrymen.

While the Quakers established soup kitchens, unlike other Protestant denominations, they never required the starving Irish to convert to be fed.

"No," I corrected him, "the Quakers weren't among those trying to convert the starving. They only wanted to help ease the suffering at the time in Ireland."

As we were looking up at the mountain trying to locate a path to the top, we heard the barking of dogs. Coming down the pathway was an old man carrying a pail. Two dogs ran ahead of him, their tails wagging.

"Good afternoon, lads!" the old fellow called out as he approached. We waved back a greeting.

He appeared to be a farmer with his knee-high Wellington boots, tweed cap, and worn red sweater. His weathered face was welcoming, and he seemed glad to take a break from his daily routine to chat with a couple of strangers. He shook our hands and said his name was Richard Bell.

According to Mr. Bell, the "Quaker Cottage" facility, run by the Religious Society of Friends, provided childcare and practical support services for disadvantaged families from both the city's Catholic and Protestant communities. As Mr. Bell was telling us about the Quakers' charitable works, his five-year-old grandson came running down the pathway to join him. Lifting the little boy up in his arms, he said that the boy's parents were killed a year earlier when a drunk driver crashed head-on into their car.

Mr. Bell told us that there was no really easy way up the mountainside from where we stood. He pointed out a narrow path, however, made through the dense shrubs by roaming goats, and said that would be the best route. Together with Mr. Bell, we stared in silence up at the mountain. I was looking at a little stream running down the side of it when I heard Callaghan cry out.

We were suddenly surrounded by several huge, hairy pigs; grunting, snorting and rooting around in the dirt at our feet. Callaghan and I were city boys and knew nothing about pigs, though we both noticed they had teeth on them – some long and sharp. Callaghan asked if pigs bite when a six-hundred-pounder pushed its snout against his leg, nearly knocking him over. Callaghan let out a startled yelp as he steadied himself.

"Ah, ye needn't fear Betsy," laughed Mr. Bell. "She'll do ye no harm."

We bid farewell to Mr. Bell and his little grandson and turned toward the goat path up Black Mountain. The steep trail was narrow and muddy and there were thickets all around us. Mr. Bell was right about it not being an easy climb. The mountainside was already slippery from the mud and then we began to come across piles of goat droppings. They were everywhere and mixed in the mud. Callaghan used his pipes duct-taped together as a walking stick, but it didn't prevent him from slipping and diving into a mound of dung.

Sprawled out in the muck, Callaghan angrily struggled to get to his feet. Laughing, I gave him a hand. He got up with his blue jeans and jacket soiled and with pieces of dung in his mop of flaming red hair. I continued to find my friend's discomfit amusing until I slipped into a heap of it myself. But at least I didn't go headlong into the muck and only got some of the stuff on my trousers. Thankfully, I managed to keep my Nikon camera out of it.

As we gained elevation the trail became steeper and narrower. The thorny thickets cut our hands as we grabbed at them to avoid slipping again in the goat excrement as we continued to scramble upward. In spots the muck was ankle-deep and soon our shoes were completely covered in it. Amid the dense shrubbery were goats grazing on patches of grass.

Callaghan stopped to look at a brownish bird emerging from some bushes. About a foot in length, it made a loud, rasping *krek-krek-krek* sound with its beak wide open as it walked. Then turning to face us, it stared at us with beady black eyes.

"What kind of a bird is that?" asked Callaghan.

"Hell, if I know." I replied. "An Irish one!"

"And you call yourself an Audubon!" he said in feigned disgust.

Our laughter startled the bird, and it flew off.

Later I learned the bird was most likely a rare corncrake. Once widespread across the Irish countryside, corncrakes have sadly been in steady decline for some time.

Finally, we reached the top of Black Mountain. According to my guidebook, it reaches a height of 1,275 feet. Callaghan and I stood just gazing down at the city of Belfast and the Lough beyond without saying a word for a full five minutes as a gentle wind blew across our faces.

Then Callaghan remarked, "There's a poem called 'Flying to Belfast' by Craig Raine that talks about the city from above looking like 'a radio with its back ripped off.' And it really does!"

We both laughed again and reveled in the sheer joy of our surroundings. At that moment, I couldn't have been more carefree and happy.

Before I ran out of camera film, we snapped a few pictures of ourselves overlooking the city. As breathtaking as the view was, our attention was distracted by the imposing guyed steel mast of a transmitting station.

"It has to be a good seven, eight hundred feet tall," said Callaghan.

"At least," I agreed, although I really couldn't venture a guess as to the height of the lattice mast. We were both convinced, though, it belonged to the British Army.

"I've heard the Brits do training up here," said Callaghan. "That's why I brought this." He indicated his duct-taped together pipes.

Taking a small pen knife from his pocket, he cut them apart and proceeded to fit one into the other, making an eight-foot pole out of the metal pipes. Then, removing his backpack, he pulled out an Irish tricolor flag – about three-foot by five-foot in size – and put pieces of cord he had already cut through the metal rings in the flag's corners and tied it tightly to the pole. Next, he pulled out a smaller American flag and attached it beneath the national flag of Ireland.

"Just to let the limey bastards know this was the work of a couple of crazy Irish Yanks," explained Callaghan. He then rammed the flagpole into the earth. There was a satisfied smile on my friend's face as the flags began to flap in the wind.

"Well done, Tim Callaghan! Well done!"

"ERIN GO BRAGH!!" he shouted at the top of his lungs. *"ERIN GO BRAGH!!!* IRELAND FOREVER!!!" Then, wild-eyed, he just screamed out, long and hard, into the wind: "Irrrelaaand!! *My* Irrrelaaand!!!"

As the wind continued to blow, we both loudly sang out with gusto–

> *A Nation once again,*
> *A Nation once again,*
> *And Ireland, long a province, be*
> *A Nation once again!!!*

By now it was already late in the afternoon, and it would soon be dusk. Once the sun set, we would never be able to find our way down the mountainside in the dark, so after Callaghan saluted his fluttering flags, we headed back to Eglantine Avenue.

The author on Black Mountain overlooking Belfast

CHAPTER FIFTEEN
STRANGE ENCOUNTER ON THE STRANMILLIS ROAD

It was after midnight on Halloween night, and I sat alone in Callaghan's flat. He still hadn't returned from when he went out earlier with Sandra. I arrived back at the flat only a few minutes earlier. Sitting at the card table with my open travel journal before me, I tried to compose my thoughts well enough to relate what occurred less than an hour before.

After going out for a couple of jars at a local pub, I found myself walking along nearby Stranmillis Road. I passed the Ulster Museum, on the side of the darkened, empty road lined by old brick rowhouses across from the high stone wall of Friar's Bush Graveyard. It was Belfast's oldest burial ground, I read in my guidebook, but had been long closed to the public.

My shoelace had become undone, so I bent down to retie it. When I stood back up again, there just a few feet in front of me was standing a young woman, or a teenage girl, wearing a long, dark hooded cloak.

I was surprised to say the very least, stunned was more like it, as she hadn't been there just a moment before and no one else was around. Then there was her unnatural appearance. Her pretty but expressionless face, framed by the hood of her cloak, had large, unblinking eyes and was as white as porcelain.

Was this some sort of a Halloween joke? Or was the girl coming from a costume party? Before I could utter a word, though, she spoke in a clear, soft voice, "For pity's sake, good sir…pray for me."

My heart nearly stopped as her dark eyes peered deeply into my own. Her speech sounded old, or archaic, like it was from another time. I couldn't speak, maybe I nodded, but I can't be sure. I remained frozen, watching her walk on and disappear down the Stranmillis Road, past the graveyard gatehouse. I was convinced I had seen a ghost.

Then I remembered her desperate plea for help, from purgatory perhaps? I blessed myself on the empty, darkened sidewalk and offered up the best prayer I could come up with.

"O my Jesus, forgive us our sins and save us from the fires of hell. Lead all souls to heaven, especially those in most need of Thy mercy. Amen."

CHAPTER SIXTEEN
A VISIT TO COUNTY TYRONE

Before I joined him across the great pond, Callaghan had already gone a couple of times out to County Tyrone. There he was welcomed by the family of our mutual friend Pat Hamill, who sang rebel and drinking songs back at the bar Ireland's Own in Encinitas. Callaghan and I bought round-trip Ulsterbus tickets in Belfast, for £9.10 apiece, for Strabane in West Tyrone.

Looking out the bus window, I saw the countryside's lush green hills and fields covered with grazing sheep and cows. Ah, the real picture-postcard Ireland! Truly God's country. I opened my guidebook to Tyrone and began to read.

Ulster's County Tyrone derived its name from the Gaelic *Tír Eoghain,* "land of Eoghan." This Eoghan was one of the sons of the legendary fifth century A.D. High King of Ireland, Niall of the Nine Hostages, so named because he led raids across Ireland, into Britain and Gaul (today's France), and took hostages from opposing royal families to guarantee their support. Saint Patrick was said to have been kidnapped in one of Niall's incursions in Britain and taken as a slave to Ireland.

The O'Neills and other prominent Irish families trace their ancestry to the royal line of Niall of the Nine Hostages.

Tyrone is O'Neill country. The sons of the mighty monarch became powerful chieftains of Ulster and made Tyrone their stronghold from where they led Irish resistance to English rule. As I've already mentioned, the Great Hugh O'Neill, the Earl of Tyrone, and his steadfast ally and son-in-law Red Hugh O'Donnell, the Lord of Tyrconnell (Donegal), were the last great Gaelic chieftains to fight against the Saxon invader during the Nine Years' War (1593-1603).

The bus pulled into the town of Strabane just after 11 a.m. and we were met by Pat Hamill's elder brother, Maurice. A solidly built man of forty-two in a blue turtleneck and denim jean jacket, he was the spitting image of Pat, with a well-trimmed mustache and dark, longish hair graying at the temples.

Maurice Hamill grasped our hands warmly and greeted us in his broad Tyrone accent. He explained as we walked that while he was on the wagon himself, and he knew Callaghan was a committed teetotaler, he wanted to at least buy me a pint and get us all a bite to eat. With that goal in mind, he led us into a nearby pub. I had my usual Guinness, of course, while Callaghan and Maurice each had a Coke, and we all had sandwiches.

Then Maurice took us on a brief tour of the small town, pointing out various landmarks of the Troubles. The local I.R.A. was a force to be reckoned with, he said, and gave Strabane the dubious distinction of being the most bombed town in Northern Ireland.

"Yez see that field over there?" asked Maurice. "That's where the Brits shot dead three Republican boys a few years back."

We turned onto a street on which there were a number of Republican wall murals. A masked man was pictured firing an assault rifle beside the words: "There Can Never Be Peace In Ireland Until The Foreign, Oppressive British Presence Is Removed. Provisional I.R.A."

On Fountain Street, Maurice pointed out a memorial plaque. It read: "This Marks The Spot Where Éamonn McDevitt, Deaf Mute, Aged 28 Years, Was Murdered By Royal Marine Commandos, 18th August 1971. May He Rest In Peace."

Lighting a cigarette, Maurice said, "Éamonn was guilty of nothin' more than bein' a Catholic. Bein' deaf and dumb he couldn't hear the soldier's command to stop. His parents sadly died of broken hearts shortly afterwards."

Callaghan and I followed Maurice up a grassy hill and down through a cemetery overlooking the River Mourne. I had brought my camera along and began snapping a few pictures. In the distance was a massive old stone bridge with arches over the river. Beyond that were the green hills of County Donegal, from where my mother's people – the Kirkpatricks and McLaughlins – hailed from.

I stopped to look at one of the many gravestones in the cemetery. A Celtic cross with two crossed rifles on it had the inscription: "In Proud And Loving Memory Of Vol. Charles Breslin, West Tyrone Command, *Óglaigh na hÉireann,* Killed On Active Service, 23rd February 1985, Aged 20 Years." Fresh wreaths of flowers covered his grave.

Maurice took us back to the town center and to what was his favorite watering hole, or at least it was until he decided to walk on the dry side for a while.

We entered Felix's Bar, owned by one Felix O'Neill. It was a nice, homey establishment with little tables and a fire going in the fireplace. Maurice introduced us to a couple of guys he knew standing at the bar. A pudgy man in his fifties with shaggy gray hair and a drooping mustache was called Spud Gallagher. The guy beside him, in a red and blue striped sweater, around the same age as Callaghan and me, was Tommy Leeds.

"But Leeds is not me proper name," he said. "People just call me that as I was born across the water in the city of Leeds. Me ma and da, though, are both from Strabane and I've been here all but the first few months of me life."

A short and stout middle-aged man in a tweed cap and glasses came over from farther down the bar. Maurice introduced him as Busty Buchanan and told us he had served fifteen years in English prisons as an Irish Republican Prisoner of War.

Callaghan and Maurice joined Busty in a game of darts, while I joined Spud Gallagher and Tommy Leeds for a pint at the bar. As so often happens, one pint led to another. Soon Spud stood swaying back and forth, pint in hand, demanding a song.

"A song! A song!" he hollered. "Whose gonna sing us a song?!" As there were no offers, Spud burst out with "The Flower of Sweet Strabane."

If I were King of Ireland and all things at my will
I'd roam through all creation, new comforts to find still
And the comfort I would seek the most as you might understand
Is to win the heart of Martha, the Flower of Sweet Strabane.
Her cheeks they are a rosy red, her...her hair a...a...

Spud began to sputter when he could no longer recall the words. His brain too soaked in Guinness.

"Arrrrah!!" spat Spud with a curse. "I can't bloody remember! C'mon, somebody else give us a song!"

Callaghan, Maurice, and Busty had finished their dart game, and my pal and flatmate declared he'd attempt a song.

"C'mon Yank, sing us Yankee Doodle!" someone called out.

"No," said Callaghan. "I'm in Ireland and it'll be an Irish song. 'The Dying Rebel.'"

The night was dark, and the fight was over,
The moon shone down O'Connell Street,
I stood alone, where brave men perished
Those men have gone, their God to meet.

My only son was shot in Dublin,
Fighting for his country bold,
He fought for Ireland, and Ireland only,
The Harp and Shamrock, Green, White and Gold.

The first I met was a grey-haired father
Searching for his only son,
I said, "Old man, there's no use searching
For up to heaven, your son has gone."

The old man cried out broken hearted,
Bending o'er I heard him say:
"I knew my son was too kind hearted,
I knew my son would never yield."

> *The last I met was a dying rebel,*
> *Bending low I heard him say:*
> *"God bless my home in dear Cork City,*
> *God bless the cause for which I die."*

Callaghan gave an excellent rendition of the song, and he received a round of applause by everyone – except Spud.

"Och, that's about a Cork man," he said dismissively. "We're all Ulstermen here. Men of Tyrone."

"Aw, g'wan, Spud," said Maurice, "'tis a grand Republican ballad. Good on ye, Tim! Pay no mind to oul Spud."

Someone bought me another pint of Guinness, while Callaghan and Maurice stepped out to order some late-night dinner at the Chinese takeout next-door. They then returned to the bar to wait for their order to be ready.

Meanwhile, Tommy Leeds was on his feet, though he needed to steady himself by holding tightly onto the back of a chair otherwise he'd fall over. Much to everyone's annoyance, he was bellowing out an overly emotional rendition of the irritatingly emotional song "Feelings."

> *Feeelings, nothing more than feeelings!*
> *Whoa! whoa! whoa!....feeelings!!*
> *Whoa, ohhh, ohhh, feel it again in me arms...*

"Arrah, Tommy boy, shut yer gob!" yelled the barman.

"Give it a rest, will ye!" shouted someone else.

No one noticed when Spud slipped out of the pub. But when Callaghan and Maurice went to pick up their orders just before the Chinese takeout closed, they discovered that Spud had already been there and had disappeared with both their already paid for boxed dinners.

Callaghan was red-faced and fuming when they returned. "That greedy old rat bastard stole our grub!"

"Bloody blackguard!" said Maurice.

Someone joked about Sesame Street having its Cookie Monster and Strabane having its Spud Gallagher. But neither of the injured – and hungry – parties found it amusing.

"And there's no more food to be had because the damn joint's closing up," continued an angry Callaghan.

"Aye, 'twas bad enough luck yez had," someone said.

"Bad luck me arse!" countered Maurice. "Spud's a bloody thief!"

"Arrah, oul Spud's a *dacent* enough skin," said Busty Buchanan, "when he wants to be."

While my two companions may have been hungry, I was quite full. As it's said, Guinness is a meal in a glass, and I had enough to equal a lavish twenty-one course dinner!

Callaghan and I followed Maurice back to the pub we were at earlier so we could retrieve our luggage that we left in the care of the barkeep. Then we walked through the darkened streets of Strabane to his house.

Maurice explained his domestic situation to us. He was a married man with five children, but his wife had taken the kids and moved out a few months earlier due to his heavy drinking. It's what finally put him on the wagon, he said, and he even started making a daily novena at the Church of the Immaculate Conception to be reconciled with his family.

Once we arrived at Maurice's place, he made us cups of tea and he and Callaghan devoured an entire loaf of bread. As he was out of butter and jam, they just ate it plain right out of the bag. Maurice then switched on the TV for the late-night news, and we learned back in America the Democratic candidate Bill Clinton had been elected president of the United States.

CHAPTER SEVENTEEN
TO DERRY, BACK TO TYRONE & RETURN TO BELFAST

Derry City in County Derry is situated about fourteen miles northeast of Strabane, on the River Foyle, near the border with County Donegal. Callaghan and I took an Ulsterbus to visit the historic city for the day.

It's said, Derry was a city when Belfast was a swamp. People have lived there since the Iron Age. Derry was originally called *Daire Calgaich* – the oak grove of Calgach, an ancient warrior who claimed the territory as his own. A monastery was founded there in the sixth century by Saint Columba, or – to use his Gaelic name – Colum Cille, meaning "dove of the church." Later settlers renamed the spot *Daire Columcille,* after their saintly patron.

Ten centuries after the holy abbot, Ireland was tightly in England's grip and with that came the Protestant colonization, or plantation, of Ulster. Derry was built up as a city by wealthy guilds in London and by 1613 was renamed Londonderry. While most Protestants insist on using the official name of Londonderry, Catholics continue to call the city and county Derry.

In the 17th century, Derry was a Protestant town. Great, thick, high walls were constructed around it to protect the planter inhabitants from

England and Scotland from the hostile native Irish who opposed their lands being taken away. Derry was besieged many times, but its walls were never breached, and it came to be called the "Maiden City." Derry is the last remaining completely walled city in Ireland and its citadel walls are among the best preserved in Europe.

The place was absolutely packed with history, and Callaghan and I walked around taking it all in. We passed the neo-Gothic red sandstone Guildhall with its large clock tower and visited the O'Doherty Tower Museum by the Magazine Gate, which was only completed in 1986 and modeled on the medieval castle built by the O'Dohertys that once stood nearby. We made our way past The Diamond and numerous Georgian, Victorian, and Edwardian-era buildings to the spired St. Columb's Cathedral. Constructed in the early 17th century "Planter's Gothic" style, it was the first non-Roman Catholic cathedral built by the Anglican Church after the Reformation.

I had never been in a Protestant church before in Ireland. We strolled in to have a look around and we both agreed that St. Columb's looked similar to so many large Catholic cathedrals we had seen, with plenty of pews, pillars with arches, and stained-glass windows. Similar but not quite the same. Maybe it was all the Union Jacks and regimental flags hanging high on the walls – very British, very Protestant.

Callaghan wanted us to head over to the Bogside outside of the city walls. The Catholic, working-class district had long been a Republican stronghold. In fact, the Troubles started there in August 1969 when disaffected residents clashed with local Protestant Loyalists and the Royal Ulster Constabulary. The three days of violent rioting came to be called the Battle of the Bogside. As angry Catholics threw bricks and home-made petrol bombs, police shot rubber bullets and tear gas canisters into the crowds. Barricades were put up as Bogsiders feared they were on the verge of being massacred. But they continued to fight with a fierce determination. British troops were finally brought in to restore order and separate the largely Protestant police force and the Catholic Bogsiders.

The Bogside was declared "Free Derry," and was a Republican no-go area for the British Army and the R.U.C., policed and defended by members of both the Official and Provisional I.R.A. On a gable wall, at the time, someone had painted: "YOU ARE NOW ENTERING

FREE DERRY." Although the house was later demolished, that wall was retained. Located in the middle of three street junctions, the freestanding wall became a well-known landmark. Callaghan and I took snapshots of one another posing beside it.

The self-declared autonomous area in the Bogside existed until 1972 when the British Army came with tanks converted into bulldozers to smash through the barricades. The year 1972 also brought the infamous "Bloody Sunday" massacre, when British paratroopers murdered fourteen unarmed civilians during a peaceful civil rights march in the Bogside. The same Parachute Regiment was responsible for the Ballymurphy Massacre in Belfast.

We made it back to Strabane by 7 p.m. When we arrived, Maurice Hamill told us that he just learned his uncle Eddie over in Liverpool had died. We joined him at his kitchen table. Noticing the overflowing ashtray, beside an empty teacup and an empty pack of John Player's cigarettes, I offered Maurice one of my Camels. He took it, lit up, and inhaled deeply.

We heard how Uncle Eddie had been across the water for the past forty years, was married and had children in Liverpool, and was to be buried there. As the eldest son of the Hamill clan, Maurice felt it was his duty to accompany his parents over to England. But like too many of his countrymen, Maurice was "on the *bru*." That was, he was unemployed and just living on meager government benefits. He couldn't afford the travel expense to attend the funeral and he was obviously busted up about it.

Callaghan and I gave one another a look and agreed, without exchanging a word, that we'd help him out. Maurice told us, when asked, that a round trip ticket on the ferry to Liverpool would run him £30. We both pulled 15 quid apiece from our wallets and placed it on the table. A look of relief suddenly passed over Maurice's face and he shook our hands in gratitude.

Although his parents were grieving the loss of his father's brother, Maurice insisted we visit them before we left Tyrone.

"Me ma wouldn't forgive me if I let yez go without yez droppin' by, yez bein' friends of Pat's."

Maurice called a taxi in the morning and the three of us were off to the little village of Clady, four miles outside of Strabane, where Maurice and his eleven siblings were all born and reared. We soon arrived at the Hamills' small, white stucco rowhouse.

We were warmly greeted by the family matron, Mrs. Mary Hamill, who ushered us into the front room to be seated on a sofa by the window. She was a small woman in her mid-sixties with a bouffant hairdo, wearing a light floral blouse and blue skirt. Mr. Hamill, gray and balding, in a worn cardigan sweater, sat smoking a cigarette and reading a newspaper in a nearby chair.

As Mrs. Hamill fixed us all a hearty lunch, I stood up to look at the various watercolors that hung on the walls. Maurice said the local landscapes were painted by his brother Jim, who occasionally made "a few bob" selling one. Maurice then pointed out one particular picture of beautiful, gentle rolling hills and lush green fields divided by old stone walls.

"That once belonged to our family," he said. "It's just up the road from here. We were evicted from our land three hundred years ago because we were of the wrong religion and the land was given to a Scottish Presbyterian family. They hold it to this day."

"Aye, that's true enough," affirmed Mr. Hamill, from behind his newspaper.

I heard the story before and others from Pat over numerous pints at Ireland's Own. He reminisced more than once about the time he was arrested as a boy with his father, a couple of his brothers, and his old grandfather for illegally fishing in a lake that was on their forefathers' land. Later as a teenager, Pat would go sheep rustling with his brothers. They would go at night and lift a few lambs from one of the wealthier Protestant farmers.

"Ye could run well enough with wee lambs on yer shoulders," explained Pat.

They would then take the lambs across the border to sell in Donegal.

As we ate lunch, Mrs. Hamill repeatedly asked questions about how Pat was getting on in America, how his American wife and their two "wee daughters" were, and was Pat working steady and steering clear of the drink?

Callaghan and I were both at a loss as what to say, and it must have showed on our faces.

"'Tis all right, lads," said Mrs. Hamill reassuringly, before either of us could answer. "Pat's me son and I know his ways. Ye needn't tell us the word of a lie. He's been takin' more than the odd drop now, hasn't he?"

"Yes, Mrs. Hamill," admitted Callaghan, "he has…on occasion."

"I thought as much and no doubt those occasions are frequent enough too."

Mercifully, Callaghan didn't elaborate any further. There was no point in bringing more grief to the old lady by giving her details about her son's alcoholic exploits.

Pat was drunk almost as often as he was sober. He was quick to throw punches in bars and had been hauled off to jail on numerous occasions for fighting, disorderly conduct, and public intoxication. Once when he was on a week-long bender, he was pulled over by a California Highway Patrol cop on a motorcycle. Pat attacked the cop, threw him down the grassy slope beside the highway, kicked his bike down after him, and sped off.

I raised my teacup and took a long, slow sip to hide the slight smile forming on my lips, as I remembered the last time I went out drinking with Pat. It was just before he moved to San Francisco. Callaghan had already left for Ireland by then.

Usually I drove, but that night Pat was behind the wheel of his old, beat-up Buick. He knew of an English pub just north of San Diego. After getting drunk enough there to get us both thrown out of the place, Pat decided to take his jalopy, throw it into reverse, and plow into the large lit-up Union Jack sign in the parking lot, smashing it to bits. Absolutely out of his mind from drink, Pat cursed England as he drove his car again through what was left of the sign. Then he madly raced down the dark street, as I held on for dear life in the passenger seat.

"ARRRAH!!" he maniacally shouted, *"Tiocfaidh ár lá!* Another blow for ould Ireland!"

Maurice called us a taxi and we said our goodbyes to the senior Hamills. We ducked into Kelly's Pub in Strabane for a quick drink – Guinness for me and Cokes for my teetotaling companions – before Callaghan and I boarded our Ulsterbus back to Belfast.

A letter from my wife awaited me at Eglantine Avenue. Dated November 1st, Beth wrote about our little girls' Halloween. She had bought them identical pumpkin costumes and took them around the neighborhood trick-or-treating. When they arrived home, Mary and Biddy wanted their mother to carve the big orange pumpkin that was set out on the front porch. But Beth told them they would need to wait until Daddy returned home, as I was the family jack-o'-lantern carver.

Beth also added that all the goldfish I had in my aquarium had died a few days earlier. Apparently, Mary and Biddy thought the fish must be tired of just drinking water, so they poured soda into the tank. Unfortunately, the poor fish didn't survive their ordeal.

Edmond Audubon

Republican murals in Strabane, County Tyrone

The River Mourne in Strabane

Strabane

The author on the Derry's Bogside

CHAPTER EIGHTEEN

THE ROCKY ROAD TO DUBLIN ...AND TO CORK

One, two, three, four, five
Hunt the hare and turn her down the rocky road
And all the ways to Dublin, Whack fol-lol-de-rah!

A night in Belfast and then in the morning we set out to make our way down Cork - Ireland's largest and southernmost county - to the small village of Donoughmore, where Callaghan had relations. We journeyed to Dublin on an Ulsterbus, at a cost of £12 each for a round-trip ticket. From the nation's capital, we planned to hitchhike the remainder of the way to Cork. Unlike in America, where fear of crime had made hitchhiking all but disappear, or in the sectarian-ridden North, where there was an understandable distrust of strangers, hitchhiking was still quite popular in southern Ireland.

In Dublin, we made our way up Abbey Street to a Bank of Ireland to withdraw a bit of cash in Irish punts, as all we had on us were the British pound banknotes used in Northern Ireland. We then navigated our way through the hustle and bustle of the crowds on O'Connell Street, the city's main thoroughfare, past the statue of the Liberator, Ireland's Great Emancipator, Daniel O'Connell, who campaigned for

119

Catholic emancipation in the 19th century, and over the bridge named for him above the River Liffey. Ah, to be strolling in fair Dublin town once again was a marvelous feeling!

Merchants lined the bridge hawking everything from socks, sweaters, and underwear to cassette tapes and pocket lighters. Seated on the ground, amid the street vendors, were tinkers – as of late called travellers. They were mostly desperate-looking women wrapped in old shawls or blankets, together with unkempt small children in dirty clothes, begging with cups held out for passersby to toss coins into. Callaghan and I dropped in whatever coins we had in our pockets.

"Thank yez, kind sirs, God bless yez," said one tinker woman.

Callaghan was more familiar with Dublin than I was and led the way to a street where a line of green, double-decker buses awaited passengers. We took a bus across town to the Naas Road.

The Naas Road was a part of the major highway that passes through the Irish midlands to the counties farther south. It was also the best place, we were told, to hitch a ride. I had brought a piece of cardboard along and a black marker, and as Callaghan attempted to thumb a lift, I wrote in big bold letters "CORK" across the cardboard. Standing beside him, I held up the sign.

It was a busy divided highway, or dual carriageway, as it's called in Ireland, and as it was already mid-afternoon on a Friday, traffic was especially heavy. Everyone was rushing to get home for the weekend. Besides us, there were other hitchhikers waiting to be picked up. We walked down the road a bit, passing a young man with his own cardboard sign with "CARLOW" on it.

We positioned ourselves a little farther on and waited for a ride. Then we watched in horror as a terrible scene unfolded before our eyes. A teenage girl ran across the highway and a car struck her with enough force to send her catapulting through the air.

"Holy Mother of God," uttered Callaghan, in disbelief.

The poor girl came crashing down hard in the middle of the road. All traffic had stopped, and we raced with the other hitchhikers and people from their cars to the injured girl. A circle was formed around her twisted body, but everyone was afraid to move her as she may had broken her back or neck. She was twitching and making gurgling noises.

Her face was covered by her blood-soaked sweater, and a pool of blood was quickly forming under her head.

"Merciful Jesus!" shrieked a woman. "Oh, please somebody do something!"

An Irish soldier in a green beret stepped forward and knelt down by the girl. Taking a knife from his pocket, he carefully cut through the sweater to reveal her bloodied face. Her pale blue eyes stared blankly in shock.

I said a silent prayer for the girl. Then I helped direct traffic around her until the Gardaí – the Irish police – arrived followed by an ambulance. I watched as the unfortunate teenager was lifted onto a gurney, her face in agony. As the ambulance drove off, I looked at the car that hit her, its windshield was completely broken in. Nearby the driver was being questioned by two gardaí.

Shortly after the accident, we were picked up by a guy in a white Vauxhall Belmont on his way to Portlaoise. A middle-aged Dubliner named Bertie; he was a traveling salesman with a car phone.

After the initial introductions, he launched into a long, boring account of how successful he had been selling computer parts all over Ireland. Grateful for the lift, we listened with feigned interest. But our thoughts were still very much of the tragic scene we had just witnessed.

Upon entering the town of Portlaoise, the salesman pointed out the old 19th century prison.

"That's the Republic's top security jail, where we lock up our I.R.A. terrorists. A murderous lot to be sure."

I glanced over at Callaghan. He was staring out the window, but his jaw was clenched tight, and a muscle was working in his cheek. He was listening intently to the salesman and trying to control his anger. Portlaoise Prison was where members of the I.R.A. and other illegal paramilitary groups were interned by the government of southern Ireland. Callaghan corresponded with an I.R.A. man named Terry Quinn in the prison and had stayed with his family near Dublin on a few occasions.

Bertie the salesman dropped us off by the road that would take us to Cork. As we got out of the Belmont, I thanked him for the lift but Callaghan slammed the door hard behind him. After the car pulled away, I eyed my scowling Fenian friend.

"You ought to be more grateful for favors rendered," I remarked. "The guy was good enough to give us a lift."

Within minutes a red Volkswagen Passat stopped for us, and we made the acquaintance of Mr. and Mrs. Mulcahy. They were a nice, older couple on their way home to Blackpool, a suburb of Cork City. Mr. Mulcahy was a sales representative for a paint company. As we motored along, they told us about their recent trip over to America, to visit relatives in Massachusetts and about the sights they saw there.

The drive took us nearly two hours. At Blackpool, Callaghan rang his relations from an old green and white phone booth outside of a pub. Called phone boxes in Ireland, above the door was the Gaelic word *Telefón* – telephone.

After he made the call, we went into the pub to wait for our ride to arrive. The distance between Donoughmore, the small village where Callaghan's kin lived, and Blackpool was around twenty miles, so there was enough time for me to quench my thirst with a welcome pint of the black stuff, while my pal sipped a cup of tea.

When my pint was set before me, I soon recognized it wasn't my regular pint of stout. Although the same black hue, it was something entirely different. Its head was foamier, its body thicker and creamier, and it was much sweeter than the bittersweet Guinness Stout with which I was so familiar.

I queried the bartender and was told I was savoring the delights of Cork's very own Murphy's Stout. Apparently, in Cork it surpassed the national drink of Guinness to such a degree that very often Cork pubs didn't even offer Guinness.

"In CAWWWRRRK," as the barman pronounced his native county, "you simply do not order a Guinness, boy. 'Tis a Dublin stout, and bad manners to ask for here. Murphy's and Beamish Stouts are both proudly brewed here in CAWWWRRRK."

As I enjoyed my first pint of Murphy's Stout, Callaghan filled me in a bit more on his family history and his connection to his Cork cousins.

He began with his grandfather and namesake, Timothy O'Callaghan, who was born in Donoughmore at the close of the 19th century. He came from a large farming family. Like millions of his impoverished countrymen and women, he crossed the ocean to America as a young man seeking a better life. According to family lore, he dropped the O apostrophe from his surname in the voyage and arrived in New York as Timothy Callaghan. He married, settled in the Bronx, reared six children, and drilled and sweated as a "sandhog," that is, a tunnel laborer, for more than forty years, digging the city's subway system. It was a typical Irish immigrant's experience in old New York. A brother of his, who joined him as a digger, was crushed to death in a tunnel collapse in the 1920's.

Meanwhile, another younger brother called John Pat remained in Donoughmore. As he came of age, Ireland was aflame with rebellion. Irishmen fought the ancient Saxon foe once more. John Pat joined Irish forces in the War of Independence. Then in the Civil War that followed, he was on the Republican side against the Free State. After the fighting was over, he returned to Donoughmore and a peaceful life of farming. He married and had eight children. Most still lived and farmed around Donoughmore. A nonagenarian widower, John Pat O'Callaghan was the last of his siblings, either in Ireland or abroad, still living. It was one of his married daughters who was coming to pick us up.

Soon, we were on our way to Donoughmore with Callaghan's cousin, Anne Daly, behind the wheel of an older gray Ford Orion. An attractive middle-aged woman with auburn hair pulled back into a bun, she was the mother of seven sons.

Listening to her welcome us and ask us how our trip down to Cork was, I was struck by the sing-songy sound of her high-pitched accent. It was the same as the bartender back in the pub. The unmistakable, sweet, musical lilt of Cork. Words rolled off their tongues so quickly that my American ears needed to listen carefully to understand what was being said. I was more familiar with harsh Belfast accents, with their heavy Scottish undertone due to the old Planters' influence, and the working-class brogues of Dublin, than the mellifluous voices of Cork.

It was late by the time we arrived in Donoughmore. Anne Daly was good enough to fix us a couple of sandwiches. As we ate, she switched on the small TV set on the kitchen counter, and we heard on the news that the young girl who was hit on the Naas Road died en route to the hospital.

"Jesus, have mercy on that poor girl's soul," declared Mrs. Daly, as she made the sign of the cross. Callaghan and I did likewise.

We went to turn in for the night in the room she had prepared for us. But my heart felt like a stone in my chest. I laid in bed and saw the girl's pale blue eyes staring blankly in shock and her bloodied face. I prayed that she'd rest in God's mercy and peace, and that He would bring comfort to her family.

CHAPTER NINETEEN
DONOUGHMORE, COUNTY CORK

The day begins early on a farm, but it didn't for Callaghan and me. It was after 8 o'clock in the morning when we presented ourselves for breakfast. The Daly men were all seated at the long table finishing their morning meal, though they had been up and working since before dawn.

Anne Daly came from the kitchen, wiping her hands on her apron, and introduced me to her husband, Jim, and their sons, from the oldest down to the youngest. There was twenty-four-year-old Vincent, Gerard, James, Dominic, Patrick, Seán, and sixteen-year-old Kevin.

As we sat down for a hearty Irish breakfast, the Daly boys and their father began to get up to return to work. The woman of the house set before us heaping plates of bacon and sausages, fried eggs and tomatoes, potatoes cut into cubes, soda bread, black and white puddings, and enough tea to wash it all down.

I learned from Mrs. Daly that the family had a total of eighty-four cows on their dairy farm. It was considered an average-sized herd in Cork.

As for Donoughmore itself – or to give the place its Gaelic name, *Domhnach Mór* – the parish contained nearly two thousand inhabitants.

After breakfast, Callaghan led the way a mile down the road to his other cousins' farm – that of the O'Callaghans. We were greeted by a barking black and white spotted dog, appropriately called Spots. Callaghan's cousin, Michael O'Callaghan, was loading up a work truck with one of his sons in front of the house. They both gave us a wave, as Mrs. O'Callaghan stepped out of the house to ask us to come in.

Inside, by the fireplace was the old gentleman himself, Callaghan's ninety-four-year-old granduncle, John Pat O'Callaghan, seated in a chair, smoking a pipe in his knee-high, rubber Wellington boots and wearing an old, battered fedora.

"Good mornin', lads," he said, removing the pipe from his mouth. "Grand day to be young and alive."

We wholeheartedly agreed and went over to shake the old fellow's hand. Seeing that I was a stranger, he inquired if I was a Yank, like his grandnephew Tim. I replied that I was and sat in the empty chair beside him.

The three O'Callaghan boys were out working on the farm, while the two younger girls were somewhere off playing. Mrs. O'Callaghan went to prepare us tea, then turned to ask if we wouldn't perhaps prefer something a bit stronger. I readily agreed, adding if it wasn't too much trouble. My teetotaling friend stuck with his tea. After bringing him a cup, she returned to the kitchen to make glasses of hot whiskey for her father-in-law and me.

I tagged along to see how she prepared it. Mrs. O'Callaghan was a dark-haired woman in her early forties, with a ready smile, in a neat, pink plaid house dress. From a cabinet, she brought out three thick glasses with handles.

"I'll join ye," she explained in her pleasant Cork lilt, "as I got meself a bit of the sniffles and this is the best cure for that."

I paid careful attention, watching as she swished warm water around in each of the glasses at the sink, emptying each in turn. Then she put into each glass two teaspoons of brown sugar, followed by a generous shot Paddy's Irish Whiskey. She stirred each glass a bit. Sliced a lemon and added some cloves into the fruit, then dropped a lemon slice into each glass.

Finally, she placed a spoon into the first glass and poured boiling water onto it from a kettle, as "ye wouldn't want to be scaldin' and crackin' the poor glasses by pourin' directly into 'em." After stirring again, she handed it to me and said, "Enjoy!" I raised up my glass and replied, "*Sláinte!*"

I took my hot whiskey back to the living room. Callaghan was seated beside the old man talking animatedly with him. I noticed hanging on the wall, beside a picture of the Pope, was a picture of President John F. Kennedy.

"Me mam thinks he's kin of ours," said a lanky teenage boy, who had just walked into the room and was standing behind me. There was some amusement in his voice.

"I think no such thing!" answered Mrs. O'Callaghan, coming in from the kitchen with the other two hot whiskeys. "True, I was born Eileen Kennedy, but me people were Cork Kennedys. Yer late, great president was of the Wexford Kennedys."

Mrs. O'Callaghan introduced me to her smiling fifteen-year-old son, Ollie, "short for Oliver." He was her third-born, she explained, after Conor and Patrick. The family also included two daughters, Siobhán, "that's the Irish for Joan," aged twelve, and Máire, "the Irish for Mary," aged six.

As if on cue, as soon as their names were spoken, the girls entered the room. The older girl had long, light brown hair, while the younger one's long hair was more of a golden brown. The fresh, rosy-cheeked sisters had fair Irish skin, wide blue eyes, and wore matching striped blouses and jeans.

Apparently, the hot whiskey had agreed with the old man, and he proposed we go out to a local pub. Mrs. O'Callaghan loaded up the family car with her father-in-law, the girls, Callaghan, and me, and drove us the few odd miles down the road to Regan's Pub. There she dropped us all off and continued on her way to visit her sister.

It was already late in the morning, but only the bartender was in the pub. The girls stayed outside to play. I bought us a couple of pints of Murphy's Stout and a glass of Coke. We seated ourselves on three barstools, and old Mr. John Pat O'Callaghan told us about his experiences in the war.

"The cursed Black and Tans were a vicious, murderous bunch," he said. "English killers, they were, set loose in Ireland by Churchill to rob, torture, and destroy us Irish. By God, we drove 'em out of Cork and out most of Ireland."

"Up rebel Cork!" exclaimed his grandnephew.

Winston Churchill, as the British Secretary of War, sent the Black and Tans into Ireland in early 1920 to bolster the Royal Irish Constabulary during the War of Independence. The paramilitary police auxiliary force was overwhelmingly recruited from British veterans of the First World War. They were nicknamed the Black and Tans due to their improvised uniforms initially being a mix of police dark green (which appeared black) and British Army khaki. The Black and Tans were responsible for some of the worst atrocities and retribution attacks during the war in Ireland.

Mr. O'Callaghan had forgotten to bring his pipe along, so I gave him one of my Camel cigarettes. After lighting it for him, I lit one for myself. He then set a bony old finger on Callaghan's notebook on the bar, and tapping it with a smile, he asked what it was. The old fellow knew very well what it was, as I did. Callaghan had been carrying the notebook around with him all morning, and eagerly opened it and explained how he was jotting down notes about his family history. As he turned the pages, I saw various hand-drawn pedigrees of O'Callaghans and Sheehans and O'Sullivans. All branches of his deeply rooted family tree in Cork.

Six-year-old Máire wandered into the pub, followed by her big sister Siobhán. It was obvious the girls had grown bored with playing outside. Callaghan bought them chocolate bars and I placed little Máire up on the barstool beside her grandfather. I had my camera with me and snapped a picture of them together.

Mrs. O'Callaghan returned to drive us back to their house. Siobhán was seated next to me and asked if she could see my camera. I removed my Nikon from its case and told her to be careful with it.

"I will indeed," said the twelve-year-old girl, gingerly examining the camera. "I received a Pentax for me last birthday. But sure, it's not as dear as this. I've been learnin' all about different cameras."

"Our Siobhán," chimed in her mother, from behind the wheel, "is thinkin' she'd fancy bein' a photographer one day."

"Perhaps for a magazine," said the girl.

"Why not!" I replied enthusiastically, flashing Siobhán a smile.

It was a clear, beautiful day. I mentioned how I hoped to walk around Donoughmore and take some pictures. Siobhán immediately asked her mother if she could accompany me. Mrs. O'Callaghan consented and pulled over by an old graveyard, surrounded by a low stone wall. The two of us got out and they drove off. We entered the cemetery and walked around amid the numerous Celtic crosses and statues of the Blessed Virgin.

Siobhán pointed out the grave of her grandmother, who died only the year before. She then blessed herself and softly sang "Ave Maria" in Latin. I stood a few feet off and listened. She had a sweet, angelic voice.

"Nana loved that," she said, when she finished. "I was just learnin' it in the Latin when she died."

There were inviting green grassy fields beyond the graveyard, and we easily climbed over the low stone wall. Siobhán said she sang in her church choir. As we walked, she began to sing.

You may travel far, far from your own native home,
Far away o'er the mountains, far a-way o'er the foam,
But of all the fine places that I've ever seen,
Sure, there's none can compare with the cliffs of Dooneen.

Although I didn't have the voice to sing along with such a sweet-sounding girl, I found myself doing just that.

Take a view o'er the mountains, fine sights you'll see there,
You'll see the high rocky mountains o'er the west coast of Clare,
Oh, the towns of Kilkee and Kilrush can be seen,
From the high rocky slopes round the cliffs of Dooneen.
It's a nice place to be on a fine summer's day,
Watching all the wild flowers that ne'er do decay,
Oh, the hares and lofty pheasants are plain to be seen,
Making homes for their young, round the cliffs of Dooneen.

Fare thee well to Dooneen, fare thee well for a while,
And to all the kind people I'm leaving behind,
To the streams and the meadows where late I have been,
And the high rocky slopes round the cliffs of Dooneen.

When the song was finished, young Siobhán turned to me and smiled with her blue eyes shining brightly.

"Sure, we make a brilliant duet!"

"What, are you kidding, girl?" I replied, laughing. "You gotta voice like an angel while I got one like a toad!"

She laughed too, putting a hand over her mouth.

"You know I'm right, then!"

"I know no such thing," she declared, but kept laughing all the same.

Siobhán went on to tell me how she especially loved how the "Cliffs of Dooneen" was sung by Christy Moore, and said her parents went to see the popular singer in concert when he was last in Cork.

I couldn't have been happier. I felt like a carefree kid myself in this young girl's company. In her I saw my own little daughters in ten years. From a small grassy hill, we observed two brown horses grazing in a field beyond another low stone wall. I showed Siobhán how to use the camera's autofocus and let her zoom in to take a couple of pictures of the horses.

It was a delightful afternoon that I wouldn't forget, nor would I forget the delightful young Cork colleen named Siobhán O'Callaghan.

CHAPTER TWENTY

A NIGHT OUT WITH THE BOYS OF DONOUGHMORE

That evening two of the Daly brothers brought Callaghan and me, along with their cousin Conor O'Callaghan, out to a more than two-hundred-year-old public house in the countryside. It was dark when we arrived. The five of us entered through a low door, which we had to duck down to go through. One of the Daly boys said something about how men were a lot shorter back when the pub was built.

"Bloody leprechauns," cracked another of the Donoughmore cousins.

Inside the place was bursting at the seams. A heavy cloud of cigarette smoke hung over the crowd, and people laughed and chatted away. Although men predominated, there were also a number of women drinking at tables and at the bar. What struck me most was the authenticity of the place. It was just the sort of an Irish pub you would see in old Hollywood movies about Ireland – something out of *The Quiet Man* with John Wayne and Maureen O'Hara.

Well, almost authentic, I reflected, if not for the female presence, as traditionally ladies didn't frequent pubs. But Ireland's fairer sex would no longer be denied their glasses of stout and their odd drop of the craythur.

Vincent Daly waved us over to a table in the far corner. There we joined a friend of his. He introduced the sandy-haired young man, in a dark turtleneck sweater, as Jerome. Vincent's brother, Gerard, bought us our first round of pints.

"I heard ye boys are the Yanks stayin' up in Belfast," said Jerome, in a high-pitched accent.

Callaghan told him that he was studying at Queen's and that I was over in Ireland on a visit.

"Sure, they're all feckin' mad up in the Black North, warring tribes slaughterin' one another," remarked Jerome.

Callaghan glared at him.

"But as Irishmen," said Vincent Daly, "we must not forget 'tis the British who are ultimately responsible for the mess they created up in Northern Ireland."

I was about to toss in my two pence worth, when our pints of Murphy's Stout were brought over by a striking barmaid. Her shoulder-length raven black hair framed an ivory-skinned, beautiful heart-shaped face. Clad in blue jeans and a purple sweater, with its sleeves pushed up to her elbows, she wore a little gold Celtic cross on a chain around her neck.

"Are ye well, Nora?" asked Conor O'Callaghan, from across the table. "Coz ye're certainly lookin' *very* well."

"Ah, away with ye!" exclaimed the barmaid, with an amused chuckle, as she walked back to the bar.

We all took generous swallows from our pints, and a couple of the guys lit up cigarettes.

"An entirely different country up there, so 'tis," declared Jerome, picking up where he seemingly left off. "Northern Ireland is British."

"Ah, no, not *atoll*," contradicted a dark-haired young man, with intense brown eyes behind wire-rimmed glasses, seated at the adjacent table. "Ulster is not British. Not geographically, historically, nor legally. As 'tis said, 'Ireland was Ireland when England was a pup, and Ireland will be Ireland when England is buggered up.' Remember that, boy!"

"Nicely put," I said.

"*Erin go bragh!*" exclaimed Callaghan, raising his glass of Coke. "A nation once again!"

"*Sláinte*, lads," said the young man, draining what was left of his pint. "And please God, 'twill be sooner rather than later that our fourth green field shall be in bondage no more!"

We all shook hands with the well-spoken young man – with the notable exception of Jerome – and someone called for another pint for him. He wasn't known by any of Callaghan's local relations.

"Name's Owney Ó Riain," he said.

"Well, Owney Ó Riain, have you not heard?" replied Jerome sourly. "Romantic Ireland's dead and gone, sure, it's with O'Leary in the grave."

He was quoting a well-known line from the country's national poet, William Butler Yeats.

"Shut yer gob, Jerome," said Vincent.

"Go 'way, you langer ye," added his brother. "Are ye not an Irishman *atoll*?"

"Whisht!" hissed Conor, looking over in the direction of Nora the barmaid.

All eyes had turned to the gorgeous dark-haired, fair-skinned colleen, who stood in the center of the pub. Conversations were put on hold and chatter ceased, as she began to sing in the most extraordinary soprano voice. Her singing, and the song itself, transported me back to a time long ago.

> *When I was a maiden fair and young,*
> *On the pleasant banks of Lee,*
> *No bird that in the greenwood sung,*
> *Was half so blithe and free.*
> *My heart ne'er beat with flying feet,*
> *No love sang me his queen,*
> *Till down the glen rode Sarsfield's men,*
> *And they wore the jackets green.*
>
> *Young Donal sat on his gallant grey*
> *Like a king on a royal seat,*
> *And my heart leaped out on his regal way*
> *To worship at his feet.*
> *O Love, had you come in those colours dressed,*
> *And wooed with a soldier's mein*
> *I'd have laid my head on your throbbing breast*
> *For the sake of your jacket green.*

No hoarded wealth did my love own,
Save the good sword that he bore;
But I loved him for himself alone
And the colour bright he wore.
For had he come in England's red
To make me England's queen,
I've rove the high green hills instead
For the sake of the Irish green.

When William stormed with shot and shell
At the walls of Garryowen,
In the breach of death my Donal fell,
And he sleeps near the Treaty Stone.
That breach the foeman never crossed
While he swung his broadsword keen;
But I do not weep my darling lost,
For he fell in his jacket green.

When Sarsfield sailed away I wept
As I heard the wild ochone.
I felt, then dead as the men who slept
'Neath the fields of Garryowen.
While Ireland held my Donal blessed,
No wild sea rolled between,
Till I would fold him to my breast
All robed in his Irish green.

The old ballad told of the days when two foreign kings fought on Irish ground for the English crown. Catholic King James was backed by French and Irish Catholic troops, while Protestant King William of Orange was backed by an army of his coreligionists.

Owney Ó Riain brought his pint over to our table, took a seat beside Callaghan, and recounted Sarsfield's epic tale.

Patrick Sarsfield was a daring and courageous commander in the Jacobite Irish Royal Army. He heroically defended the city of Limerick, even after his cowardly king had deserted his troops at the Battle of the Boyne and fled Ireland for the safety of France. Sarsfield fought on until the heavy losses and suffering of his men made him recognize the futility of a long siege. The enemy permitted Sarsfield to lead thousands of Irish soldiers, accompanied by their families, into exile in France. Their departure from Ireland, in 1691, became known as the Flight of the Wild Geese.

In France, the Irish troops continued to serve their deposed King James. After a planned invasion of England by France's Louis XIV had to be abandoned, and James's army was disbanded, Sarsfield became a general in the French army. He gallantly fought for France in Flanders and was fatally wounded at the Battle of Landen in 1693.

"As he watched his life blood flow out of him," concluded Owney dramatically, putting down his empty pint glass, "the noble Sarsfield gasped with his dying breath, 'Oh, that this were for Ireland.'"

Patrick Sarsfield was remembered in Ireland with affection. King James, on the other hand, was referred to with contempt as *Séamus an Chaca*, or James the Shit.

I sprang for the next round of pints for everyone at the table.

"Give us another one, Nora!" shouted someone at the bar. "A song in the Irish."

"Nora's a native Irish-speaker from the Dingle," said Conor.

"That's the Dingle Peninsula in County Kerry," remarked Jerome, obviously for the benefit of us ignorant Yanks.

Callaghan was talking with Owney and hadn't heard Jerome. If he had, he'd be quick to answer, and no doubt a bit testily, that though from America we were both well-acquainted with Ireland's geography.

The Dingle is in the Gaeltacht, one of regions of the country which are still largely Gaelic-speaking. These areas are mostly in the western counties of Donegal, Mayo, Galway, and Kerry, with smaller pockets in Cork and Waterford.

The raven-haired beauty from the Dingle looked over at us and smiled.

"Owney Ó Riain," she called out to him, "this is for ye."

A fat, red-faced, middle-aged man wearing a large sweater with a plaid cap, a couple of sizes too small for him, and muddy green Wellington boots, stood up by the bar holding a flute. When all was quiet, he lifted the flute to his lips and began to play a tune. The barmaid then sung in a hauntingly beautiful Gaelic.

Cé hé sin amuigh a bhfuil faobhar ar a ghuth
Ag réabadh mo dhorais dúnta?
Mise Éamonn an Chnoic atá báite fuar fliuch
Ó shíorshiúl sléibhte is gleannta.

The mournful ballad continued as everyone sat in silence and focused their attention on the singer. It wasn't the first time that I wished I knew Gaelic, the mother tongue of my Irish ancestors. I once took an evening class to learn the ancient language at the House of Ireland in San Diego's Balboa Park, but I didn't make much progress aside from a few basic phrases and words.

It should be noted, the Irish in Ireland usually call Gaelic simply "Irish," though Irish-Americans generally refer to the language as "Gaelic." But whatever it's called, only a very small percentage of Ireland's population can fluently speak it. None of Callaghan's Cork relations, for instance, could actually hold a conservation in the first official language of the Irish Republic.

Callaghan was also curious about the mysterious ballad and asked if anyone knew what it meant.

"I haven't a clue," said Vincent, "but 'tis a lovely oul ballad all the same."

"More's the pity," replied Owney. "The ballad's called 'Éamonn an Chnoic' and concerns a distant relation of mine, from me own County of Tipperary, one Éamonn Ó Riain, or as he's known in English, Edmond O'Ryan."

Éamonn an Chnoic, or Ned of the Hill, was of the old Gaelic aristocracy and was born about year 1670 at Knockmeoll Castle, which was situated on the hill of that name, near Atshanboy, County Tipperary. No trace of the Castle now remains where he first saw the light of day, but a green patch on the hillside marks the site. His epithet, very likely, derived from his birthplace on the hill, *cnoc* in Gaelic.

As Catholics, his family were dispossessed of much of their lands after the Cromwellian conquest.

The young Éamonn first heard the call of religion and went to France to study for the priesthood. But when his father became ill, he returned home. While there, he intervened when a tax collector seized the only cow of a poor neighboring widow who couldn't pay her rent. A struggle ensued and Éamonn an Chnoic shot and killed the tax collector.

"After that," continued Owney, "me kinsman was forced to take to the hills, where he hid in the many woods of his native county and began his career as a highwayman. He became a local Robin Hood-like figure, robbin' from the rich to give to the poor."

Our hero and his band of fellow outlaws fought as rapparees, or irregular soldiers, under the banner of King James. Éamonn an Chnoic was at the Battle of the Boyne and at Aughrim, and he and his men joined ranks with Patrick Sarsfield as he attacked Williamite forces on their march to Limerick.

When the Jacobite army were defeated at Limerick, and Sarsfield and the Wild Geese sailed away to the continent to serve in foreign armies of Catholic monarchs, rapparees like Éamonn an Chnoic and Galloping Hogan and others remained behind to spoil the spoilers, and plunder the plunderers, of their native isle.

Many a wealthy Saxon landowner traveling on a dark and lonely road suddenly found himself facing Éamonn an Chnoic, with his pistol pointing at his breast, and the greeting of "stand and deliver" ringing in his ears. Relieved of his gold and silver, the trembling landowner watched in the moonlight as the highwayman galloped away on his steed.

It's told when a new agent was appointed over some property near the Tipperary townland of Rossmore, with the tenants who presented themselves to pay their rents also came Éamonn an Chnoic. Having noticed that Éamonn made no move to pay rent, the agent finally asked him why he didn't tender his rent. In reply, Éamonn produced his blunderbuss and commanded the agent to give back all the money he received and to sign a receipt in full for all the tenants in acquittal of their rents. The agent had no choice and did as he was told. Éamonn returned to each tenant his own part, and said, "Poor fellows, you may want some of this to buy a pig or a something which may be of service to yourself and your family." He then departed and wished the agent farewell and a safe journey.

The bold tales told about Éamonn an Chnoic were abundant. But he also led a desperate enough existence on the run. It was said, he was proclaimed an outlaw in 1702 and a reward of £200 was offered for his capture.

"As for the ballad," said Owney, "there's more than one version of it, in the Irish as well as in English."

Our companion then recited one in English where the hunted outlaw takes shelter with a girlfriend, a lass named Mary Leahy.

> *"O who is without*
> *That with passionate shout*
> *Keeps beating my bolted door?"*
> *"I am Ned of the Hill,*
> *Forspent wet and chill*
> *From long trudging marsh and moor."*
> *"My love fond and true,*
> *What else could I do*
> *But shield you from wind and from weather?*
> *When the shots fall like hail*
> *They us both shall assail,*
> *And mayhap we shall die together!"*
> *"Through frost and through snow*
> *Tired and hunted I go,*
> *In fear both from friend and from neighbour,*
> *My horses run wild,*
> *My acres untilled,*
> *And they all of them lost to my labour,*
> *But it grieves me far more*
> *Than the loss of my store*
> *That there's none who would shield me from danger;*
> *So my fate it must be*
> *To fare eastward o'er sea,*
> *And languish amid the stranger!"*

But it wasn't to be the fate of Éamonn an Chnoic to flee to foreign shores. It was said, he moved farther into the hills and sought shelter from a relative of his named O'Dwyer. While poor Éamonn lay sleeping, his kinsman, hoping to obtain the reward being offered, chopped off his head with a hatchet. Then...

"Ancient Irish history!" interrupted Jerome, scornfully. "Ye are livin' in the past."

"Och, look about ye, boy!" said Nora with a laugh, as she set down another round of pints for us. "In Ireland, the past isn't dead, 'tis not even the past. Sure, the past is always present here."

"True enough," added Vincent, "just look at the never-ending Battle of the Boyne bein' fought up in the North."

"What do any of ye know about the North?" asked an irritated Jerome. "Barring these two Yanks, have any of you even been up there?"

"I've been up to Bundoran on holiday once," declared Gerard Daly, lighting a cigarette.

"Eejit!" slagged his brother. "Geography was never his best subject. Bundoran's in Donegal!"

"Well, Donegal is part of Ulster," replied Gerard.

"Indeed 'tis, but Donegal's in the Republic, boy!"

When twenty-six of Ireland's thirty-two counties gained partial independence from Britain, to form the Irish Free State in 1922, the other six counties in the northeast corner of the island remained under British rule. Ulster, one of the four historical provinces of Ireland, was composed of nine counties. When Ireland was partitioned, six Ulster counties (Antrim, Armagh, Derry, Down, Fermanagh, and Tyrone) became the political entity of Northern Ireland, while three counties in Ulster (Cavan, Donegal, and Monaghan) became part of the Irish Free State, which later became known as the Republic of Ireland, or simply Éire.

"I've been in the occupied Six Counties," said Owney Ó Riain.

"Have you now?" queried Jerome.

"Indeed, I have," he answered. "And what I have seen in the North is that brave Irishmen and Irishwomen there are engaged in an armed struggle. As the oul song says about the boys of Wexford, they fight with heart and hand to break in twain the galling chain to free our native land."

"I suppose then that would be a fight ye'd be willin' to join in?"

"How do you know I haven't already?" replied Owney.

"Ye're absolutely feckin' mad!" exclaimed Jerome.

"Sure, I've been called worse," said Owney, with a slight smile and a determined look on his handsome face.

Downing the last of his stout, he placed a tweed cap squarely on his head and stood up to leave.

Callaghan firmly shook the young patriot's hand, as I did, along with Conor and the Daly brothers. Jerome took the opportunity to visit the toilet, and we saw no more of him.

"All the best, lads," said Owney Ó Riain. Then fixing his brown eyes on Callaghan and me, he added, "and a safe voyage across the broad Atlantic and back home to the two of ye."

Watching him walk away with his head held high, I couldn't help thinking he seemed taller than he actually was.

Alas, it was growing late, and the time had come for us to depart too. As we left that age-old pub set out in the Cork countryside, I knew I'd long remember it, and the evening I spent there, as an authentic bit of dear ould Ireland as ever there was.

CHAPTER TWENTY-ONE
ONWARD TO CORK CITY

In the morning, I attended Sunday Mass with Callaghan and his relations. Afterwards, I went out to take a few more pictures despite the rainy drizzle. I got a few nice shots of cows grazing in a field and in another field a very large, dangerous-looking bull.

By the time I returned to the O'Callaghan farm the rain had let up, and young Siobhán was waiting for me. She wanted to take me to see an old holy well named after the seventh century patron of the parish, Saint Lachteen. But I needed to first check with Callaghan, as he said something earlier about leaving Donoughmore that afternoon or the following morning. Siobhán told me I'd find him down by the pigsty some distance from the house.

As I walked across the yard, I could see a small, dilapidated stone building with a rusty tin roof. A neat low stone wall encircled it, and just outside was Callaghan in his bright Kelly-green sweater seated on a pile of rocks. Drawing closer, I saw several pigs in the enclosed area and Callaghan was just sitting there, his head hanging down with his chin on his chest. He lifted his head as I approached, but he didn't turn to face me. I could see my friend's cheeks were streaked with tears.

"That was once a whitewashed cottage with thatch on the roof," he said, staring painfully at the crumbling hovel. "My grandfather was born on its dirt floor, as was my granduncle, John Pat, and the rest of their generation. Now pigs fill it with their shit."

There was no door on the old cottage and the pigs freely roamed in and out. I stood beside him, not knowing quite what to say. Callaghan's Irish roots were stronger and deeper than my own.

While my maternal family tree had more recent Irish roots, my paternal side was more firmly planted in American soil. My five-times-great-grandfather was a swashbuckling French sea captain and privateer in the service of Louis XVI, when France came to the aid of the American colonists in our Revolutionary War against England. He was my first ancestor to arrive in America, and he came to New York as a prisoner of war of the British in 1779. His only son became the celebrated naturalist and wildlife artist John James Audubon, who established my family in New York City by the middle of the 19th century. The Audubons later married into the English and Irish branches of my family tree.

"I'm leaving early tomorrow morning," Callaghan finally said. "Conor's going up to Dublin and can give me a lift. From there I'll get over to Offaly."

I knew he had some relations on his mother's side named Fallon whom he hadn't met yet in County Offaly.

"Well, like I said, I want to see a bit of Cork City before returning to the war zone in the Black North."

We agreed to meet up on Tuesday, at three o'clock in the afternoon, at the O'Connell Monument in Dublin.

It was still early in the afternoon, and I figured I had enough time to hitch a ride to Cork City if I left then. So, without further delay, I said my farewells, especially to Siobhán, who I told to keep singing and giving the angels in heaven something to envy, and not to give up on her dream of becoming a photographer or whatever else she may set her heart on.

After standing by the roadside for a while and trying unsuccessfully to hitch a ride from several passing cars, I began to suspect the twenty-odd-mile journey to Cork City might take longer than I anticipated.

I began to walk with my duffle bag over my shoulder, and soon encountered a group of men in their Sunday best, wearing suits and ties and caps. They were throwing a shot ball – a 28-ounce solid iron cannonball, the size of a tennis ball, called a "bowl" or a "bullet" –

down the road. It's a popular sport in Cork called road bowling. The bowlers greeted me and I gave them a wave.

Approaching a long stone wall by a field, I turned to face an oncoming car. It stopped and the driver of an older Ford sedan indicated I should get in. Behind the wheel was a grizzled, middle-aged man with a bushy mustache, wearing an old tweed jacket and a greasy brown cap. As he put the car into motion, I asked if he was going as far as Cork City.

"Ah, no," he replied, with what seemed like a chuckle, "not as far as all that."

"Well, at least you'll get me somewhat closer. How far you going?"

"Not far *atoll*, boy. Just to the end of this wall here."

And with that he came to an abrupt stop to let me out before he turned down a dirt lane. I thanked him for the ride of less than a hundred yards and stepped back out onto the road.

Lighting a cigarette, I began to walk again as the drizzle resumed. As I trudged along, I kept looking over my shoulder in case another car came along going my way that might be willing to give me a lift.

I had no sooner finished my smoke than I got picked up by a blue Renault. A dark-haired, dapper young man of about twenty-five, attired in a gray suit, white dress shirt, and a narrow burgundy tie, introduced himself as Raymond O'Donovan. He said he was from a village near Donoughmore, and while he couldn't give me a lift all the way to Cork City, he could at least get me three-odd miles closer. And so, he did. I thanked him and hopped back out onto the road again.

The drizzle had turned into a steady downpour which soon soaked my corduroy jacket and tweed cap and caused my sopping wet trousers to cling to my legs. More than two hours must have elapsed as I plodded through puddles, my feet sloshing in my waterlogged shoes. At least the duffle bag thrown over my shoulder was waterproof, so I'd have some dry clothes to put on later. Fortunately, I also packed an extra pair of loafers.

I came to a small cluster of whitewashed houses. A sign pointed the way in English and Gaelic to Cork, or *Corcaigh*, and another the road to take to the village of Blarney, or *an Bhlarna*. There, of course, was the famous Blarney Castle with its Blarney Stone, promising to impart to all who kiss it the gift of the gab; that is, great eloquence in speech. Callaghan paid a visit to Blarney Castle on one of his previous trips down to Cork, but he never mentioned whether or not he puckered up to kiss the ould stone.

I was standing in the deluge of rain, soaked to my skin, staring down the road to Blarney, when suddenly a battered old white van pulled up beside me and the passenger door flung open.

"Wanta c'mon in outa the rain?" asked the driver.

I gladly climbed in and was pleased to make the acquaintance of Cormac Twomey. He was a big, smiling, beefy fellow in his early thirties, with a shock of curly, bright red hair, in a dingy white sweater with blue sleeves. Reaching behind him, he tossed me a towel and I removed my dripping wet cap and wiped my face and head. He poured me a cup of hot tea from his thermos.

"There ye go, boy," he said, handing it to me. "Put that in ye before ye catch a death of cold."

When Cormac Twomey heard my destination was Cork City, he insisted on taking me the remaining six or so miles himself.

"Sure," explained the Cork man, "I know what 'tis like to be hoofin' it down some road and the divil a one roarin' by Christian enough to stop and give ye a lift. So, I says to meself, Cormac, whenever ye're blessed with an automobile of yer own, ye're gonna help out the poor soul who's still awalkin'. Besides, I'm in no rush, like. Sure, I'm only on me way to me work, and God knows I'm in no great hurry for that!"

I learned as he drove that Cormac was a bachelor and employed as a night watchman guarding a fenced-in yard containing farm machinery.

He went on to relate how once during a bus strike he loaded up his van with schoolchildren but "the guards" (i.e., the *gardaí*, or *An Garda Siochána*, the Republic's police force) pulled him over and ticketed him for lacking the necessary insurance to carry so many passengers.

It was late in the afternoon when we entered Cork City, the country's third largest city, after Dublin and Belfast. Built on an island between the two main channels of the River Lee, Cork was founded by Saint Finbarr in the seventh century as a monastic settlement. Then came the Vikings, and later came the English. What became a town expanded into a city.

The rain had stopped. We drove along the River Lee, which was crisscrossed with picturesque bridges, and lined by tall and elegant

Georgian houses and buildings, some brightly painted, but more of redbrick or painted gray or white.

Cormac Twomey said he'd take me to the Lower Glanmire Road where there were "B&B's galore." Bed and breakfast guesthouses were very popular throughout Ireland and were usually inexpensive, family-run accommodations. He pulled up to the Rendezvous B&B.

I wanted to buy Cormac a pint at a local pub, however, he declined the invitation.

"Ah, no. If I'm late again I'll be sacked from me work. But here, boy, hold on a minute."

Then he pulled out from under his seat a large flask and removed its metal top cup.

"A partin' drop of a craythur," he said with a smile, pouring me a good three fingers of whiskey.

"*Sláinte.*"

"Cheers, boy."

Cormac then took a swig of the flask himself and smiled more broadly than before. I shook his big hand and thanked him before stepping out of his van.

"Ah, sure, 'tis nothin' *atoll,*" he said. "Oul Cormac's always willin' if he's able to do the good turn for a fellow traveler in this world."

I strolled up to the Rendezvous B&B and was met at the door by a Mrs. O'Connell, the proprietress of the house. She was a short and sturdy woman, in her early sixties, wearing a conservative blue dress. She was also the spit and image of Mrs. Boyle of Harrogate Street in Belfast.

Although there was a single room available for the night and I was welcome to it for 12 Irish punts, I would need to find other lodgings in the morning as Mrs. O'Connell said she was expecting several German university students to arrive for a week's stay. I readily agreed as I wanted to get into some dry clothes and out to explore Cork City before sunset.

I was soon walking along the River Lee, pausing at quays and crossing bridges to take pictures. It was a wonderfully charming city with fine Georgian houses and grand neoclassical buildings on either side of the river and church spires in the distance. I meandered through narrow 18th and 19th century residential streets and lanes and went by more recently constructed houses and apartment buildings.

Out of Camel cigarettes, I ducked into a small newsagent's shop. Behind the counter there were plenty of brands to choose from: Benson & Hedges, John Player, Dunhill, Major, Carrolls, Silk Cut, Rothmans. I wasn't overly familiar, though, with Irish or British cigarettes. Remembering Maurice Hamill smoked Player's, I bought a pack.

As dusk fell, I found myself facing a two-story, white-painted public house called the Glenryan Tavern, situated on the Glen Ryan Road, off Blarney Street. I happily stepped inside for a jar.

There were a fair number of patrons, all of them chatting away, but the place wasn't packed. It was a comfortable atmosphere with typical dark-wood decor and familiar Irish knick-knacks adorning the walls above nicely upholstered and cushioned seats. I made my way straight to the bar with its large selection of whiskeys, gins, brandies, cognacs, and other spirits on display.

I had become accustomed to Murphy's Stout and ordered a pint without even looking to see if Guinness was available. Murphy's smooth, creamy brew certainly rivaled Guinness, though I hadn't determined which I preferred. Then there was also Beamish Stout, another Cork brew, which I hadn't even tasted yet.

There were two men working behind the bar. My pint was brought over by a distinguished, middle-aged chap with a beard named Chris Kendellan. He was the owner of the establishment. After I introduced myself and took a long, welcome sip of my Murphy's, we discussed and weighed the merits of Ireland's three stouts.

"Bass is yer only man," said a guy sitting a couple of barstools down.

He was a balding, serious-looking man, around forty years old, in a blue zip-up jacket.

"What's that?" I asked.

"I prefer Bass," he replied.

I realized that he was talking about the English ale and eyed the amber-colored pint before him on the bar.

"John's a loyal Bass man," said an amused Mr. Kendellan.

"Indeed, I am," answered John, most earnestly.

The publican asked where in America I hailed from. When I told him New York but was then living in California, he questioned me about the differences between the East Coast and West Coast.

"All of America's bloody barbaric," muttered John into his pint of Bass, but loud enough for us to hear him.

"Now John," began Mr. Kendellan.

"It's all right," I interrupted, "let him speak."

"I'm just sayin'," he went on, without pausing to draw breath, "if ye look at the history of yer country from the enslavement of the black people, to the annihilation of the Indians and the stealin' of their lands, to the hundreds of thousands of Japanese people mercilessly incinerated in Hiroshima and Nagasaki when you Yanks dropped yer atomic bombs on 'em, to America's brutal war against the Vietnamese people, and more recently yer country's dirty tricks in Central America, 'tis a bloody barbaric nation. And then within the borders of the high-and-mighty U.S. of A., ye got the evil of abortion, yer slaughter of helpless innocents in their mother's wombs. Sufferin' Jaysus! Not to mention, ye still got the draconic death penalty over there."

When Bass John finished his tirade, he fell silent. His accusations couldn't be denied.

"That was an earful," I finally replied, "but all true."

"But here," objected Mr. Kendellan, seemingly concerned I might be offended, as he set down a fresh pint on the house for me, "you cannot blame this man for all that."

"Ah, no, indeed, I do not," replied John. "Even Satan himself couldn't be capable of all that evil on his own."

I was relieved to hear that I wasn't being held solely to blame for all the evils committed by America, either domestically or internationally.

Down at the end of the bar was an old man in a tattered cap and frayed coat. He had been rolling a cigarette, but it was obvious he was listening.

"Och, enough of that!" he suddenly scoffed. The three of us turned to look at him.

"Now, I will tell ye," he began. "In '39, I was amongst the countless young Irish navvies over in London laborin' on the roads. I was there for the Blitz, when the German Luftwaffe were tryin' to bomb us all to hell. Like so many of our Irish lads here and across the water, I donned a British uniform, for at the time there was no greater evil in the world than Hitler's war machine. Whilst the R.A.F. won the Battle of Britain, 'twas when America joined the fight that the tide really changed. The Yanks beat back the Jerries and saved Europe from Nazi domination."

"Quite right," agreed Mr. Kendellan, "and for that America is owed a debt of gratitude."

I walked over and shook the old veteran's hand and asked for a whiskey for him with a pint of stout to wash it down.

"Thank ye, lad. But, sure, the whiskey will do."

"And another Bass for our friend, John, here," I called to Mr. Kendellan, "and another Murphy's for me."

When I asked the old fellow his name, he told me it was William Driscoll.

A few more jars followed, and a whiskey or two, before closing time at the Glenryan Tavern.

The wind was blowing as I stepped out into the chilly night air, and I zipped up my corduroy jacket and pulled my cap more snugly down on my head. I walked towards Blarney Street, past a row of little one-story brick houses with chimneys, and an old stone wall with a wrought-iron gate, and past a row of three-story gray houses. No one else was around. A light shone through a window's lace curtains, and as I wandered along, I caught a whiff of the sweet smell of turf smoke.

I made my way towards the River Lee. I knew from there, I just needed to get to Bridge Street and turn onto MacCurtain Street, which would become the Lower Glanmire Road, where my bed and breakfast was located. What was it called again? The Au Revoir B&B? No, it was the Rendezvous. I laughed aloud, maybe I was a little drunker than I thought.

Reaching the river, I stopped to light a cigarette and take in the beauty of the night. I looked at the wonderful old buildings lining the Lee and the glistening reflection of the yellow streetlights on the water. A couple strolling hand in hand paused on a quay to embrace. I took a deep drag on my Player's cigarette and walked on.

Staggering along the riverside towards me was a guy swinging what looked like a bottle of whiskey by its neck.

"Fine evenin'," he called out jovially, as we approached one another. I replied in kind.

He was a young man, a small fellow, maybe just five-foot-two or three, in a black leather jacket with jeans and white sneakers. His dark hair was slicked back. He was very drunk.

"You gotta fag?" he asked.

I handed him one of my John Player's and lit it for him. He thanked me and said his name was Pio McGreevy.

I likewise introduced myself and asked him if he was named for Padre Pio, the Italian stigmatist and mystic.

"None other," he replied with a grin. "Pio Francesco McGreevy. Me ma and da are powerful Catholics. Great believers, they are. Daily communicants and 'twas the rosary every night for us. I've a brother named Ignatius and a sister Scholastica. Even meself, I never go anywhere without this –"

From under his shirt, he pulled out on a chain a Miraculous Medal of Our Lady along with a smaller medal of Saint Brendan the Navigator.

"Good oul Brendan made many an ocean voyage," said Pio McGreevy, looking down at the little medal of the Irish seafaring abbot. "You know, he's a patron saint of sailors."

He told me he was a sailor himself in the Irish navy. Twenty-two years old and from landlocked County Roscommon, he was an able seaman stationed at Haulbowline, an island in Cork Harbour.

When I said I had been a sailor in the U.S. Navy, McGreevy merrily suggested we should then have a drink together and held up the bottle of booze he had been swinging back and forth. A half bottle of Hennessy cognac.

"Excellent!" I declared.

"Ah, 'tis not Jameson, but sure it will do," he replied.

McGreevy uncorked the Hennessy and took a swallow. Then handing me the bottle, I did likewise. I lit us up a couple of smokes and we continued to pass the bottle between us as we slowly meandered along the Lee.

"Jaysus!" he exclaimed. "An American navy man...you got a terrible amount of ships in yer navy, haven't ye?"

"Yeah, we've quite a few." I took another swig of Hennessy.

"Not the Irish bloody navy!" McGreevy roared with laughter, throwing back his head. "We're got bloody few!" Then he burst out into a song.

> *The Clíona, the Meabh and the Mucha*
> *The pride of the Irish navy.*
> *When the Captain he blows on his whistle*
> *All the sailors go home for their tea...*

It was a little ditty performed by The Dubliners.

> *We are a seafaring nation,*
> *Defence of our land is a right,*
> *We'd fight like the devil all morning*
> *Provided we're home by the night...*

The liquor continued to flow, and we both laughed drunkenly. We sat together on the quayside wall. I held the near empty bottle and reflected how Hennessy was from the Cognac region of southwest France yet bore a fine Irish name. I knew the story behind it and began to relate it to my drinking buddy.

"Ever heard of Richard Hennessy?"

"Ah, sure, you mean Mr. and Mrs. Hennessy's boy?" asked a grinning McGreevy.

"The guy who founded the Hennessy Cognac Distillery back in 1765." I took another swallow from the bottle. Great stuff.

"He was a Cork man," I continued, "born into the native Catholic gentry in the little village of Killavullen. Richard Hennessy was among the 'Wild Geese' who left for France in the 18th century to serve as an officer in the Irish Brigade in the French army. He later settled in the Cognac area, where he took to distilling wine to make brandy. And brandy made there, unlike brandy made anywhere else in the world, is called cognac."

"Is it now?" replied Pio McGreevy, uninterestedly. "Well, I know nothin' about all that."

I realized not everyone was that enthused about these obscure tidbits of Irish history. Where was my pal Callaghan when I needed him? He would have been delighted to discuss Ireland's "Wild Geese." But then again, as a teetotaler, he wouldn't have been overly interested in a guy who brought another brand of booze into the world; or as an Irish-American patriot, an Irishman who forsook dear ould Erin's isle for France.

As I was sitting on the quayside wall, watching the gentle flowing waters of the River Lee, McGreevy stood up and knocked back the last of the cognac. Then he hurled the empty bottle as far as he could out into the river and started stumbling around on the quay. He began to sing again. This time an old sea shanty.

> *What do you do with a drunken sailor?*
> *What do you do with a drunken sailor?*
> *What do you do with a drunken sailor?*
> *Early in the mornin'!*

I got up from the wall and joined in.

> *Way hey, up she rises*
> *Way hey, up she rises*
> *Way hey, up she rises*
> *Early in the mornin'!*

> *Put him in a long boat 'til he's sober*
> *Put him in a long boat 'til he's sober*
> *Put him in a long boat 'til he's sober*
> *Early in the mornin'!*

> *Way hey, up she rises*
> *Way hey, up she rises*
> *Way hey, up she rises*
> *Early in the mornin'!*

> *Put him in the bed with the captain's daughter*
> *Put him in the bed with the captain's daughter*
> *Put him in the bed with the captain's daughter*
> *Early in the mornin'!*

"That's what we do with drunken sailors...early in the mornin'!" sang a young woman, standing but a few yards away from us. "Sure, I wish I had whatever ye lads had tonight," she said, with a wide grin.

A slender, petite girl with dark shoulder-length hair, wet from the earlier rain, she wore a pink jacket and blue jeans. But it was the black-and-blue bruises around her eyes and cheekbones that got your attention.

She answered our stares. "A couple of days ago, 'twas much worse," she said, in a low voice. "I couldn't even open me eyes."

"Who gave ye the shiners?" asked Pio McGreevy.

"Me husband. He was rotten with drink when he took a couple of pokes at me."

"You should've ducked," I said, stupidly.

"Indeed, I should have," she replied, with a weak smile.

I remembered an old joke that ran: What do you tell a woman with two black eyes? Answer: Nothing, she's already been told twice. But such brutality towards a woman was no laughing matter.

"We've been married for seven years," she said sadly. "'Twas not always like this."

Lorraine Deasy told us she lived her entire life on the city's northside and had never been outside of County Cork. We were soon strolling down the Lee together, making occasional stops so Able Seaman McGreevy could vomit over the quay wall. I lit a cigarette for myself and one for Lorraine, as we waited for the sailor boy to finish his puking. When he was done, we walked on.

We left the river and wandered through the old and narrow, deserted streets and lanes. All was quiet and windows at that hour were all dark. Again, there was the sweet aroma of turf smoke wafting from chimneys. Lorraine was becoming more comfortable as she spoke and her accent was becoming a bit thicker and more melodic. When I commented on it, she insisted my own accent also had "a touch of the Irish to it."

"Like ye were born here but been off in America for many years."

I assured her I was born and raised in New York but was then living in California and temporarily staying in Belfast.

"Belfast!" she exclaimed. "You must be jokin' me. 'Tis a mad place up there. Ah, but California, that's the feckin' place to be! Sun, beaches, and film stars everywhere. G'wan, ye're havin' me on, like! Do you really live in California?"

I pulled out my wallet and showed her my California driver's license as proof.

"Jaysus, that's brilliant," said Lorraine, with a sense of amazement.

Pointing to my birthdate on the license, she told me that we were both twenty-seven years old and her birthday was only a week after my own.

It began to rain again as we accompanied Lorraine to her mother's house, where she had been staying since she walked out on her husband.

It hadn't been the first time she had suffered his abuse, she said. Her blackened eyes filled with tears as she spoke. Maybe it was because she failed to give him any children, she suggested.

"That's no excuse," I said. "No woman deserves that kind of treatment."

"I know," she replied, fighting back a sob with a sniffle and a forced smile.

Turning onto another old narrow street, Lorraine Deasy stopped in front of a run-down, two-story gray rowhouse. Giving us both a quick hug, she thanked us for the walk home. We watched as she opened the door to disappear into the darkened house. I was left with a feeling of pity and a sorrow for her.

It was already after 4 o'clock in the morning, and Pio McGreevy and I were sobering up. We shook hands, wished one another well, and went our separate ways.

The River Lee in Cork City

The Glenryan Tavern, Cork City

Cork City's St. Fin Barre's Cathedral

CHAPTER TWENTY-TWO
A DAY IN CORK CITY

By the time I woke up in the bed I had at the Rendezvous B&B, none the worse for wear, breakfast was over. I had hardly stepped into my trousers, when Mrs. O'Connell came urgently knocking at my door to remind me that I had to leave immediately as she needed my room for her soon-to-arrive German university students, and crossly added that she was none too pleased at the hour at which I arrived back at her B&B. I duly apologized and packed up my duffle bag.

A little farther down the road was the three-story Moynihan's Bar and B&B, opposite the entrance to Kent Railway Station. I stopped in and ordered a pint of Murphy's Stout for breakfast. As it's said, a meal in a glass. A big, white-haired gentleman in an apron behind the bar told me I could have a room upstairs for 12 Irish punt. I agreed and he set before me a fresh pint on the house.

I spent the afternoon taking more pictures of bridges over the River Lee and quaint old pubs I came across and then, after I made my way down Sharman Crawford Street, on the southside of the city, St. Fin Barre's Cathedral.

The imposing Gothic Revival three-spire Church of Ireland cathedral was completed in 1879. Dedicated to Saint Finbarr, the patron of Cork's name was alternatively spelled Fin Barre. (There is also a Catholic St.

Finbarr's Church in Cork City, which predates the Protestant cathedral by a hundred years.)

The heavy, ornate doors of the grand limestone edifice were locked, but above the doors was a beautiful carving of the Last Judgment. Flanking the sets of double doors were statues of the Apostles, along with saints and virgins. I took several pictures. The cathedral seemed more Catholic than Protestant. But then many Anglican churches can appear very Catholic with their highly ornamental architecture and exquisite artwork on their interior walls, unlike the simpler Protestant churches of Presbyterians and other non-conformists.

The Anglican Church was once the established Church in Ireland, and was called the Church of Ireland, equivalent to the Church of England, or to the Episcopal Church in America. In 1869, the British Parliament disestablished the Church of Ireland, dissolving its union with the Church of England. The Act also repealed the unjust law that required Ireland's Catholic majority and other non-Anglican Protestants to pay tithes to the Anglican Church of Ireland.

The Church of Ireland, however, remained part of the Anglican Communion and is the second largest church on the island after the Catholic Church.

According to the 1991 census, while Protestants made up 58% of the population in Northern Ireland, in the South – in the Republic of Ireland – they were just a mere 3%. A hundred years earlier, the twenty-six counties, which became the Republic, had a 10% Protestant population, indicating a 70% decline.

My grandfather, Davy Kirkpatrick, who was a Catholic convert, came from a Church of Ireland family, of Scottish descent, in County Donegal.

Callaghan told me to be sure to visit the public museum in Fitzgerald's Park while in Cork City. As I made my way back towards the river, I flagged down a passing taxi to take me to the park.

The museum was in an old white Georgian house. There were exhibits relating to the ancient Celts and their early settlement of Cork. The Republican section of the museum was also impressive, from the Fenian Rising of 1867 to the Easter Rising of 1916 and the War of Independence and Civil War which followed.

The Rebel County, as Cork had long been called, was in the forefront of the fight for Irish freedom. Cork men proved capable and heroic leaders. There was Tom Barry, the commander of the famed flying column of the Irish Republican Army's Third West Cork Brigade; Liam Lynch, who commanded the Second Cork Brigade, which won a series of victories during the Tan War, and was the chief of staff of the I.R.A. during the Civil War; Michael Collins, Director of Intelligence for the I.R.A., who operated in Dublin an elaborate spy network and band of ruthless assassins called "The Squad," and during the Civil War became the Free State's commander in chief of the National Army; and there were many others.

Two Lord Mayors of Cork lost their lives during Ireland's struggle for freedom. Tomás MacCurtain, an I.R.A. commander and the city's first Republican Lord Mayor, was shot dead in March 1920, in front of his wife and young son, by police with blackened faces when they burst into his home.

Terence MacSwiney, one of the founders of the Cork Brigade of the Irish Volunteers – a forerunner of the Irish Republican Army – and president of the Cork branch of Sinn Féin, was elected Lord Mayor after the murder of his close friend and comrade Tomás MacCurtain. In August 1920, MacSwiney was arrested for possession of seditious materials and after a summary trial was sentenced to two years' imprisonment at Brixton Prison in England. He immediately commenced a hunger strike in protest. Despite gaining worldwide attention and support, MacSwiney breathed his last seventy-four days later. His body was returned to Cork City, where tens of thousands attended his funeral.

In a graveside oration, Arthur Griffith, who founded Sinn Féin, said of Terence MacSwiney: "He laid down his life to consolidate the establishment of the Irish Republic, willed by the vote of the people of Ireland. His heroic sacrifice has made him in death the victor over the enemies of his country's independence. He has won over them, because he has gained by his death for Ireland the support and sympathy of all that is humane, noble, and generous in the world."

MacSwiney's own words are well-remembered and often quoted: "It is not those who can inflict the most, but those who can suffer the most who shall conqueror."

I left the museum and strolled down the tree-lined footpath along the River Lee. Fitzgerald's Park had a tranquil atmosphere with its lush lawns, beautiful gardens, and fountains. My thoughts were of the two martyred Lord Mayors, especially the latter. I recalled the popular song about him, "Shall My Soul Pass Through Old Ireland."

In a dreary British prison where an Irish rebel lay.
By his side a priest waits standing were his soul to pass away.
As he gently murmurs father, the priest takes him by the hand.
Father tell me if I die shall my soul pass through Ireland.

Shall my soul pass through old Ireland pass through Cork city grand.
Shall I see the old Cathedral where Saint Patrick made his stand.
Shall I see the little chapel where I placed my heart in hand.
Father tell me when I die shall my soul pass through Ireland.

Was for loving dear old Ireland in this prison cell I lie.
Was for loving dear old Ireland in this foreign land I die.
When you see my little daughter won't you make her understand.
Father tell me if I die shall my soul pass through Ireland.

With his soul pure as a lily and his body sanctified.
In that dreary British prison our brave Irish rebel died.
Prayed the priest his wish was granted as his blessing he did give.
Father grant this brave man's wish may his soul pass through Ireland.

CHAPTER TWENTY-THREE
HITCHHIKING BACK TO DUBLIN

After breakfast at Moynihan's Bar and B&B, and a couple of pints of Murphy's to wash it down with, I put on my jacket and cap, picked up my duffle bag, and headed down the Lower Glanmire Road. I already had my cardboard sign prepared with "DUBLIN" printed boldly across it and stood where the Lower Glanmire continued out of the city as the N8 road to Fermoy and Dublin.

I lit a cigarette and waited. It was morning rush hour traffic, but nearly an hour passed, and no one had stopped to give me a lift. I was beginning to think I might need to shell out the cash for a bus ticket.

Then finally a beige minivan stopped up the road for me. I ran up and got in. The driver was a chubby Englishman in his mid-forties. I shook the hand he offered me and introduced myself. He told me his name was Gavin Falk. I learned he was the London-born son of a German Jewish father and a French Catholic mother and had lived in Ireland for the past twenty years with his Irish wife. Together they operated a bed and breakfast called the Westropp House in the Cork village of Innishannon.

As we made our way northward to Cashel town in County Tipperary, where Mr. Falk was going on business, he pointed out various landmarks, an old castle here, a road leading to a particular town there.

"You see," he explained, "I might be an Englishman but I've a great love for this land and I've read up on this part of it quite a lot over the years. I probably know Cork better than my native London."

I thanked Mr. Falk for the lift along with the guided tour, and he dropped me off on the outskirts of Cashel town where he said I'd have the best chance of catching another ride.

I didn't have long to wait for another lift. Tipperary man Dan Hayes, a mustached civil engineer in his early forties, wearing a white shirt and tie, took me as far as County Kilkenny.

Where exactly I had been set down in Kilkenny, I wasn't sure. But there were rolling green hills on either side of the road where I stood. There were no cars passing by though. I looked down the empty road, waiting with my cardboard sign with "DUBLIN" written on it. At least it was a clear fall day with just a gentle breeze blowing.

About thirty minutes later, a silver Ford Sierra came down the road and gave me a lift. The man behind the wheel was Tony Bishop. A big, well-built twenty-eight-year-old, the sleeves of his dark blue shirt were rolled up to his elbows, revealing strong, muscular forearms. I learned he had been a heavyweight boxer and still played soccer, along with the traditional Irish sports of Gaelic football and hurling. But he possessed a Cockney accent. He was a Londoner, he explained, and came over to his parents' native Ireland at the age of nineteen. His father was a Cork man, and his mother was from County Wicklow.

Tony Bishop said he sometimes received "a bit of stick," as it's said, over his accent.

"Y'know, 'ye Brit bastard, ye' or some bloke tellin' me to fuck off back home to England, all that sort of shit, y'know? I just let it roll off my back, mate, coz I know I'm Irish and I got an Irish passport to prove it. So, fuck 'em. Just because one is born in a stable doesn't make one a bloody horse."

Tony Bishop was more or less quoting the Duke of Wellington, who had said over a hundred years earlier the same about his own birth in Dublin. The famous British soldier and prime minister rejected the idea that his accidental birth in Ireland made him any less an Englishman.

After passing through Counties Laois and Kildare, we entered Dublin. The London Irishman dropped me off on the city's Naas Road, where only four days before I had witnessed the terrible death of that young girl. From the Naas Road, I took one of Dublin's green double-decker buses to O'Connell Street to meet Callaghan at Daniel O'Connell's statue.

Around the hundred-year-old monument, with the great Catholic Emancipator high up on his pedestal, were over thirty bronze figures representing various people from Irish society, with the Maid of Erin in the center pointing up at old Dan. Below, on the lower tier's limestone base were the four-winged Victories representing Courage, Eloquence, Fidelity, and Patriotism.

Seated on the monument's steps and benches were an assortment of those who had no other place to go. Poor wrinkled old men and old women in shabby clothes smoking cigarettes to their of butts and feeding breadcrumbs to the many pigeons gathered around them. An old tinker woman, wrapped in a dirty shawl, sat puffing a pipe. Nearby stood an elderly priest chatting with two nuns in brown habits. A couple of black-leather-clad punkers with matching neon blue mohawks passed by. Then I spied Callaghan with his mop of flaming red hair, crossing the street towards me. Sporting a new cream-colored Aran sweater, he looked as Irish as Paddy's pig.

It was three in the afternoon, and we had some time before we'd take a bus back to Belfast. Callaghan suggested a walk to see an important historical landmark. We headed down Bachelor's Walk by the Liffey and crossed over the cast iron, pedestrian Ha'penny Bridge – as it was commonly called because it once cost a ha'penny, or halfpenny, to cross it.

Callaghan told me as we walked about his trip to County Offaly to meet his distant Fallon kin. The only remnants of his family left there were an elderly bachelor cousin and his spinster sister who lived together in the little cottage in which they were both born. All the other Fallons had long ago departed for the teeming cities of industrial Britain and the farthest reaches of the English-speaking world.

We continued to make our way down the south side of the River Liffey, along Wellington Quay, past the green metal Grattan Bridge with its beautifully ornate lampposts adorned by seahorses, along Essex and Wood Quays, past O'Donovan Rossa Bridge, with the domed Four Courts, rebuilt after being destroyed in the Civil War, across the Liffey, then along Merchant's Quay, turning down Lower Bridge Street.

We were walking through the Liberties, one of Dublin's oldest working-class neighborhoods, past numerous brick apartment buildings, finally to Callaghan's destination on Thomas Street.

It was an old Georgian Church of Ireland, built of granite stone, with four Doric semi-columns supporting a pediment, and had a tower with a non-working clock. I later learned, St. Catherine's Church, like so many of the Protestant churches throughout the South, when the number of its parishioners dwindled, closed in the 1960's and fell into disrepair.

But Callaghan didn't bring me all that way to admire the architecture of a long-ago abandoned Protestant church.

"It was here that bold Robert Emmet was martyred for Ireland," he declared.

I knew the story of the celebrated Irish patriot, but I didn't know that was the spot where he bravely met his fate.

Robert Emmet came from a wealthy Church of Ireland family in Dublin. His family sympathized with the plight of Catholics and Protestant Dissenters, as they did with the rebel American colonists across the Atlantic. When the United Irishmen were defeated in 1798, young Emmet led a short-lived rebellion against British rule in 1803. But his plan to seize Dublin Castle and proclaim an Irish Republic failed, and the insurrection amounted to little more than a riot of two to three hundred of his supporters on Thomas Street.

When Emmet witnessed a dragoon pulled from his horse and brutally killed with a pike, he called off the rising to avoid further bloodshed. But his followers no longer heeded him. They were mad for blood. Lord Kilwarden, the Lord Chief Justice of Ireland, and his nephew were dragged from their carriage and repeatedly stabbed with pikes. Emmet was horrified by their murders. Lord Kilwarden's daughter, who was with them in the carriage, was mercifully allowed to escape the attack unharmed by the rebels.

Emmet, too, escaped and went into hiding. However, he was captured by British soldiers when he tried to see his fiancée. Put on trial for treason, twenty-five-year-old Robert Emmet was sentenced to be hung, drawn, and quartered.

From the dock, he delivered a powerful, moving speech, with the closing words: "I am here ready to die. I am not allowed to vindicate my character; no man shall dare to vindicate my character; and when I am prevented from vindicating myself, let no man dare calumniate me. Let my character and my motives repose in obscurity and peace, till other times and other men can do them justice. Then shall my character be vindicated; then may my epitaph be written."

On September 20th, 1803, his public execution was carried out on Thomas Street, in front of St. Catherine's Church. Emmet was hanged and beheaded once dead.

The struggle is over, the boys are defeated,
Old Ireland's surrounded with sadness and gloom,
We are defeated and shamefully treated,
And I, Robert Emmet, awaiting my doom.
Hung, drawn and quartered, sure that was my sentence,
But soon I will show them no coward am I.
My crime is the love of the land I was born in,
A hero I have lived and a hero I'll die.

Bold Robert Emmet, the darling of Erin,
Bold Robert Emmet will die with a smile,
Farewell, companions both loyal and daring,
I'll lay down my life for the Emerald Isle.

The barque lay at anchor awaiting to bring me
Over the billows to the land of the free;
But I must see my sweetheart for I know she will cheer me,
And with her I will sail far over the sea.
But I was arrested and cast into prison,
Tried as a traitor, a rebel, a spy;
But no man can call me a knave or a coward
A hero I lived and a hero I'll die.

Hark! The bell's tolling, I well know the meaning,
My poor heart tells me it is my death knell;
In come the clergy, the warder is leading,
I have no friends here to bid me farewell.
Goodbye, old Ireland, my parents and sweetheart
Companions in arms, to forget you must try;
I am proud of the honour, it was only my duty –
A hero I lived and a hero I'll die.

I remember fondly when I first learned the words to "Bold Robert Emmet." It was the summer that I turned twenty and was living in Brooklyn. Late in the afternoons, I used to sit outside on the fire escape of my studio apartment with my two closest friends, Andy Breen and Nicky Ciancaglini. We would drink beer and smoke cigarettes, or Nicky's cigars, as we laughed at one another's stupid jokes and shared our dreams for the future. As the beer flowed, Andy – whose family, like Callaghan's, hailed from County Cork – often led us in Irish songs. Sometimes I'd bring out my cassette player so we could listen to one of his tapes of the Clancy Brothers and Tommy Makem, or The Dubliners, or the Irish Rovers, or the Wolfe Tones. We were especially partial to the rebel songs, and "Bold Robert Emmet" was a favorite.

We arrived back in Belfast that night. In the morning, Callaghan went out to meet up with Sandra and I made my way down Eglantine Avenue to the Mad Hatter Coffee Shop for some breakfast and to scribble away in my travel journal.

CHAPTER TWENTY-FOUR
THE CONFRONTATION

The previous night, the I.R.A. set off a huge bomb in a parked van in the town of Coleraine, County Derry. The blast caused extensive damage to surrounding commercial buildings and the town hall. But thankfully it was reported that no one was killed or hurt.

"Expertly done!" declared an enthused Callaghan, as we walked together on the Antrim Road. "As usual, the I.R.A. issued a warning to the media and the area was successfully evacuated before the explosion. A superb job."

"Glad you think so," I answered, annoyed at his constant I.R.A. cheerleading. "The Provies weren't such experts, though, when they detonated that bomb outside the Baltic Exchange killing three innocent people and injuring scores of others."

"Casualties of war," said Callaghan, a little too flippantly.

"Is that right?" I demanded, my voice rising in anger. "Same as the bombing in Enniskillen that left eleven dead and a multiple of injured, and that Harrods department store in London a few years before, and the Brighton hotel – how many innocent 'casualties of war' were killed in those bombings?"

I had listed the worst of the I.R.A. atrocities that occurred over the past decade. Callaghan didn't answer and I said nothing more.

We continued in bitter silence walking along the Antrim Road and onto Clifton Street. We didn't have any particular destination in mind, and after our confrontation we both became absorbed in our own thoughts.

While I supported the idea of a free and united Ireland, and believed the Irish people had every right to fight the occupying British forces, I didn't agree with the I.R.A.'s bombing campaign, in which hundreds of innocent civilians were killed. Callaghan, on the other hand, unequivocally supported any action undertaken by the freedom fighters of the I.R.A.

I knew Callaghan was an extremist and a fanatic. He was blinded by his hatred for England and anything English. Although I didn't share his views, I fully understood them in the light of all the wrongs that England had inflicted on Ireland over the past eight hundred years.

However, Tim Callaghan was my best friend. Since he left California, I had literally counted the days until I could join him on the Ould Sod. I dreamed of rambling over Erin's green hills and strolling through her lush glens with my pal, and of course treading the mean, grim streets of Belfast together with him.

But friction quickly developed between us. At first, it was over my smoking in the flat we shared. So, I did my smoking either out in the chilly hallway or down the street at the Mad Hatter Coffee Shop. Then different opinions about the armed struggle divided us and often our conversations became strained and tense.

That evening Callaghan cooked us dinner and we ate without exchanging more than a few words. Afterwards, I switched on the old McMurdo Silver radio, and we listened to the news.

Earlier that afternoon, two Loyalist gunmen burst into James Murray's betting shop, frequented by Catholics, on the Oldpark Road in the Bone district of north Belfast, and sprayed the crowd with an assault rifle and tossed a grenade into the place, shouting "Yez deserve it, yez Fenian bastards!" Francis Burns and Peter Orderly, two middle-aged Catholic men, were killed outright and a number of others were severely injured.

The next day it was reported a third man, John Lovettt, a seventy-two-year-old Catholic, succumbed to his injuries in the hospital. He was a World War II veteran who served with the R.A.F. during the Battle of

Britain and was then shipped to India and Burma, where he was captured by the Japanese and tortured in a prisoner of war camp.

Mr. Lovett made me think of another old Irishman – Mr. Driscoll at the Glenryan Tavern in Cork City – who fought for Britain in her greatest hour of need.

CHAPTER TWENTY-FIVE
BLOWN TO BITS FOR IRELAND

At Milltown Cemetery that afternoon there was a commemoration ceremony for the first anniversary of the deaths of I.R.A. Volunteers Frankie Ryan and Patricia Black. Both were killed when the bomb they intended to set off at a British military band concert in St. Albans, England, exploded prematurely. Frankie Ryan was twenty-five years old and Patricia Black was just eighteen. They came from Belfast to take the war to England, as Callaghan said.

"They made a heroic sacrifice," he insisted, "and they paid the ultimate price in the struggle for a free and united Ireland."

Of course, Callaghan wanted to attend the commemoration ceremony, and I went with him.

Although the commemoration was similar to that of the fallen I.R.A. men of "D" Company, I had gone to, there was a much larger crowd and the cemetery was swarming with R.U.C. men and their gray armored Land Rovers, along with a number of British Army Land Rovers, going up and down the narrow walkways.

There was a fear among those attending such events of another attack, like the one in 1988 at the funeral of the three I.R.A. volunteers killed in Gibraltar, when Loyalist Michael Stone, of the Ulster Defence Association, went on a deadly rampage against mourners with an automatic pistol and hand grenades. Three people were killed then and more than sixty others were wounded.

Stone was a callous killer, a terrorist. The definition of a terrorist is a person who uses violence, especially against civilians, to create fear in a population to achieve a political objective. Stone's objective, as a British Loyalist, was to keep Northern Ireland within the United Kingdom by whatever means he could. Including the slaughtering of innocent people.

Frankie Ryan and Patricia Black's objective, as members of the I.R.A., was to force the British out of Ireland and see the reunification of their country. But the I.R.A. wasn't averse to the killing of innocent people to achieve this. If Frankie and Patricia had succeeded in their mission, army bandsmen along with an untold number of civilians who came to attend the charity concert could have been horribly torn apart by their seven-pound Semtex bomb. It would have been a terrible massacre. Like the rest of the humane and civilized world, I could not accept such ruthless tactics as legitimate warfare.

Such were my thoughts as I followed, beside Callaghan, the procession led by a lone piper to Patricia Black's grave for the dedication of a new headstone. At her graveside, the rosary was recited. Then a speech was given by a popular Sinn Féin councillor, the bearded Francie Molloy from County Tyrone. As R.U.C. men looked on, the councillor denounced Britain and called on her to withdraw from "that part of Ireland she still holds in her bloody grasp."

As Mr. Molloy spoke, Callaghan pointed out in the crowd Gerry Adams, the M.P. for West Belfast and president of Sinn Féin. He was easy enough to spot at over six feet tall. I immediately recognized him, with his dark brown beard and glasses, from pictures I had seen over the years in Irish papers. He wore a tweed cap, similar to my own.

After the ceremony, Callaghan brought me over to meet him. He introduced us, saying we were both over from America.

"Well, yez are most welcome here," said Gerry Adams, as he firmly shook our hands.

When the crowd slowly began to drift away, I followed Callaghan to the other side of the cemetery, to the New Republican Plot. We walked behind two middle-aged women in raincoats with kerchiefs over their heads. Although they were talking in lowered voices, we overheard their conversation.

"I'm tellin' ye," said one, "they wasted their young lives, so they did."

"Not here, Phyllis," said the other, in an anxious tone. "Somebody will hear ye."

"I don't bloody well care!" Phyllis replied angrily. "Blown to bits for Ireland, they were. What kind of sick and twisted people have we become?"

"At least they only killed themselves and no innocent lives were lost," said the other.

When we were out of earshot, Callaghan admitted even the family of Patricia Black didn't support the armed struggle. We found Frankie Ryan's flower-strewn grave near those of the H-Block hunger strikers and the Gibraltar Three.

It was Sunday, November 15th. The date marked one month since I had left San Diego. It was also my mother's birthday. My parents lived in Florida, and I rang up Mom to wish her a happy birthday from the phone booth on Eglantine Avenue.

CHAPTER TWENTY-SIX
CLIFTON STREET CEMETERY

Since I was a kid, I enjoyed wandering around and exploring in cemeteries. Reading inscriptions on old tombstones and monuments was like glimpsing into the past. So, I readily accepted Callaghan's invitation to accompany him and Sandra to the old Clifton Street Cemetery.

I also liked Sandra Maginnis and was glad to see her again. She offered some relief from Callaghan's intensity.

We strolled up north Belfast's Clifton Street towards Carlisle Circus. It was a Protestant, Loyalist working-class neighborhood. On the corner stood the long-abandoned and deteriorated Carlisle Memorial Methodist Church, built in the Victorian Gothic Revival style of the late 19th century with a tall bell tower, its windows bricked and boarded up. Nearby was a three-story Orange Hall, dating back to the same period. On its roof was an equestrian bronze statue of King William of Orange with a raised sword.

Since we weren't sure about the graveyard's exact location, Sandra stopped to ask directions from a kerchiefed old woman carrying grocery bags. She pointed across the street to a smaller side street called Henry

Place. Passing red-brick buildings, we came to an open wrought iron gate in the high, thick stone wall that surrounded the old Protestant burying ground.

The Clifton Street Cemetery was established at the end of the 18th century by the Belfast Charitable Society and contains the graves of many of the city's most distinguished Presbyterians, including industrialists, shipbuilders, newspapermen, ministers, social reformers, Unionist politicians, and United Irishmen. We were on a pilgrimage to the grave of one of those United Irishmen.

The gallant Henry Joy McCracken led the Rising of 1798 in Ulster with an attack on Antrim town. But after a desperate struggle the United Irishmen were overpowered by Crown forces. McCracken fled to the Belfast Hills and his sister, Mary Ann, arranged his passage to America. However, he was captured on his way to the ship. Although McCracken was offered clemency at his trial if he testified against his fellow United men, he refused to turn informer. Thirty-year-old Henry Joy McCracken was hanged on July 17th, 1798, at Belfast's Corn Market where a scaffold had been erected outside the Market House at the corner of High Street.

The cemetery appeared deserted, except for a lone caretaker removing dried-up bouquets of shriveled flowers from graves. Although many of the ancient tombstones were cracked and leaned this way or that way, the graveyard was generally kept up. There were no recent burials, however, and the burying ground was no longer in use.

We asked the caretaker about the location of McCracken's grave. He was a chubby little man of about thirty-five with a round face in the need of a shave, wearing a checkered cap and a dirty jacket zipped up to his chin.

"Ah, now the brave, noble-hearted Henry Joy," he said, rubbing the stubble on his cheeks as his pale blue eyes met ours. "An Ulsterman I am proud to be," he uttered. It was the first line from the popular song about the celebrated patriot.

"At the beat of a drum the great man was brought out as the redcoats mustered there," the caretaker continued. "Henry Joy kissed his weeping sister goodbye and manfully climbed the gallows high…

"Mary Ann McCracken was a grand girl herself, y'know – one of Belfast's finest daughters, so she was. She never married but dedicated her life to the poor and forsaken. She campaigned for the welfare of women and children, for improvement of conditions for factory workers, and for prison and social reform. Miss McCracken spoke out against slavery and could be seen at the ripe old age of eighty-eight handing out abolitionist leaflets on the docks to emigrants bound to America, where the diabolical system of buyin' and sellin' fellow human beings was still practiced. Aye, she was a remarkable woman."

The caretaker led us over to her grave by an ivy-covered wall beside a mausoleum. Sandra read aloud what was inscribed on the tombstone.

> *Mary Ann McCracken*
> *the beloved sister of*
> *Henry Joy McCracken*
> *born 8th July 1770*
> *wept by her brother's scaffold*
> *17th July 1798*
> *died 26th July 1866*
> *DILEAS GO h-EAG*

"Faithful until death," Callaghan translated the Gaelic words.

Surrounding the plot was a stone grave curb with the following inscription:

> *In This Grave*
> *Rest Remains Believed To Be Those Of*
> *Henry Joy McCracken*
> *Born 31st August 1767. Executed 17th July 1798.*

We heard from the caretaker how McCracken was first laid to rest at the Parish Church of St. George at High Street, where his ancestors were buried, but years later his grave was disturbed when the churchyard was cleared away. McCracken's remains were then reinterred in Clifton Street Cemetery along those with his sister, Mary Ann, by the local historian Francis Joseph Bigger in 1909.

Their maternal grandfather, Francis Joy, was a printer and paper manufacturer who established the *Belfast News Letter,* the world's oldest English language general daily newspaper still in publication.

"The Joy family were descended from French Huguenot Protestants," said Sandra. "Their surname was originally Joyeuse. I once wrote a paper in school on Huguenot settlement in Ulster during their great exodus to escape religious persecution in Roman Catholic France in the 17th century."

Callaghan had walked away and was standing before a white tombstone. We went over to join him.

William Drennan M.D.
Born May 23rd 1754 Died Feb. 5th 1820

Pure, just, benign thus filial love would trace
The virtues harrowing this narrow space
The Emerald Isle may grant a wider claim
And link the Patriot with his Country's name

"Dr. Drennan was one of the principal founders of the Society of United Irishmen," remarked Callaghan. "He was also a poet. The good doctor is credited as the first to have referred in print to Ireland as the Emerald Isle."

Callaghan then quoted the opening lines from Drennan's "When Erin First Rose."

When Erin first rose from the dark swelling flood,
God bless'd the green island and saw it was good;
The em'rald of Europe, it sparkled and shone,
In the ring of the world the most precious stone.

"'Tis a romantic ye are, dear Tim," said Sandra, accentuating her accent.

"United Irishmen – like yer man Drennan – were radical idealists," she went on. "They were men of all creeds. In the South, many were Roman Catholics. Agrarian rebels in places such as County Wexford, following the likes of Father Murphy. But in Ulster, the United Irishmen were predominately Presbyterians, ardent Republicans aflame with the ideas of the French Revolution."

Callaghan was no longer paying attention to her and appeared to be absorbed in his own thoughts. Sandra turned towards the caretaker and me but continued to address Callaghan.

"In time, Willie Drennan saw the error of his ways and withdrew from the United Irishmen and became a good Unionist. In fact, many of the United men in Ulster and their descendants became the most loyal supporters of the Union with Britain," she said, a bit triumphantly. "Mr. Timothy J. Callaghan is not the only student of Irish history."

Sandra's lips had curled into a mischievous smile, which quickly faded as her boyfriend again wandered off by himself.

"Well, I know nothin' about any of that," replied the caretaker, removing his cap and running his hand through his thick, brown hair.

"All I can say is Dr. Drennan was a true born Irishman, who loved his native land and hadn't a sectarian bone in his body. He campaigned for Catholic emancipation. Before he died, he requested that six poor Protestants and six poor Catholics receive a guinea apiece to carry his coffin to his grave, and he asked to have a Dissenting clergyman and a priest in attendance. Aye, that was the man. That was Dr. William Drennan."

The caretaker told us that the cemetery had the graves of other patriots from 1798. There was the Reverend William Steel Dickson, a radical Presbyterian minister and commander of the United men in County Down. Thomas McCabe was buried there too. A goldsmith, watchmaker, and cotton manufacturer, McCabe was a founding member of the Society of United Irishmen and one of the founders of the Belfast Charitable Society. McCabe was also a leading abolitionist in the city and prevented a slave trading company from being established in Belfast, declaring: "May God eternally damn the soul of the man who subscribes the first guinea."

Other prominent men who were laid to rest in Clifton Street Cemetery included William Ritchie, a Scottish shipbuilder, and John Templeton, a local naturalist who helped establish Botanic Gardens. The Dunville family, who distilled whiskey, were buried there too.

Callaghan was still brooding by himself, as Sandra and I walked among the graves with the caretaker. We passed by a tombstone against a wall, inscribed simply:

YOUNG!
moulders here
1829

The caretaker informed us, he was John Young, Professor of Moral Philosophy at the Royal Belfast Academical Institution.

But as our guide went on to say, not only were the wealthy and well-known patriots interred there. The Belfast Charitable Society helped many poor people and set aside a portion of land in the graveyard known as the "Strangers Ground," for those who couldn't afford to pay for burials. A great number included inmates from the Poor House, paupers and beggars, victims of the 1832 cholera epidemic and the Famine that followed more than a decade later. Approximately seven thousand souls were buried in a mass grave.

Callaghan hailed a taxi on Clifton Street to take Sandra back to her brother's place in east Belfast. There was a noticeable coolness between them as they parted.

As Callaghan wasn't in the mood for talking as we walked, I let his thoughts keep him company. Then as we made our way along Carrick Hill, past red-brick rowhouses, he finally spoke.

"For those who believe, no explanation is necessary. For those who do not believe, no explanation is possible."

My well-read friend was paraphrasing a line from a popular old novel, *The Song of Bernadette,* by Franz Werfel, made famous by the classic movie of the same title. I saw it more than once as a kid. But Callaghan wasn't referring to the French peasant girl, Saint Bernadette, or Our Lady of Lourdes. He meant the long-sought-after thirty-two county Irish Republic.

"And obviously Sandra doesn't believe," I said.

"Yeah, we see things very differently," he answered bitterly.

"I suppose, as Rudyard Kipling said, 'and never the twain shall meet.'"

"Kipling was pro-Unionist," replied Callaghan.

"Does it never stop with you?" I asked, annoyed. "Does everything got to be green or orange?"

"Yeah, here it does!" he shot back.

I gave up trying to talk with Callaghan. He had the one-track mind of a fanatic.

CHAPTER TWENTY-SEVEN
LONG KESH AND FERGUS MARTIN

I went with Callaghan to visit one of his pen pals incarcerated in the H-Blocks of Long Kesh Prison. We walked in the morning through Belfast's downtown to the Lower Falls Road Sinn Féin office and boarded a Sinn Féin minibus, which made the ten-mile trip daily down the M1 motorway to the prison.

With the exception of one other guy in his mid-to-late twenties, in a black Adidas tracksuit and white sneakers, the minibus was packed with women – mothers, wives, girlfriends, sisters, and even two little girls of maybe five or six years old. They were all Irish and judging by the local accents of the females chattering away around us, they were all from Belfast.

The minibus pulled directly into the prison yard through the main gates. As we entered, I looked up at the 20-foot walls of sheer metal, topped with billows of barbed wire. Not only was it the highest security prison in Ireland or Britain, but in all of Europe.

Commonly called Long Kesh, from when a disused R.A.F. airfield located in the small village of Long Kesh, on the outskirts of Lisburn, was turned into the Long Kesh Detention Centre in the early 1970's, it was built to hold the hundreds of Republican paramilitary suspects – along with some Loyalist ones – then being interned by British authorities. In 1976, the internment camp was officially renamed H.M. Prison Maze and prisoners were moved from large Nissen huts into eight newly constructed prison blocks built to a uniform H-shaped plan.

The minibus came to a stop, and everyone got out. We "queued up" with our visitor permits in hand to be checked at the door by a guard, or "screw" in prison slang. Into a waiting room we all went and then we were called separately by name into a back room. There we were searched by two screws and everything in our pockets was removed – my wallet, comb, pen, lighter, keys, even my handkerchief were all put into a large envelope which I was told I'd receive back when leaving the prison. I was able to keep my pack of Player's though.

A screw ushered us into the visitors' room. There were about twenty cubicles in the room, each containing a table with benches on either side, and in the center of the table was a battered old ashtray. The cubicles were numbered. Callaghan and I were to meet his friend at cubicle eleven.

We didn't have long to wait until a door at the opposite end of the room opened and prisoners filed in and made their way to their assigned cubicles. It was significant that the prisoners all wore their own clothes.

Just over a decade earlier, ten men starved themselves to death to preserve that right as Republican prisoners of war – one of the five demands over which the hunger strike was waged. (The four other demands were: the right not to do prison work; the right of free association with other prisoners, and to organize educational and recreational pursuits; the right to one visit, one letter and one parcel per week; and full restoration of remission lost through the protest.)

Fergus Martin wore blue jeans, a gray sweatshirt, and a light blue windbreaker. He was of medium height and built, had short brown hair, a brown mustache similar to my own, and brown eyes.

"So, ye finally made it back," said the young Belfast man to Callaghan, grasping his hand.

"Fergus," he said, introducing himself to me as he firmly shook my hand.

Sliding onto the bench beside me and across from Callaghan, Fergus Martin placed the plastic bag he brought with him on the table and took out three cans of soda for us and tossed us each a bag of potato chips (or "crisps" as the Irish call them).

Callaghan and Fergus spent a few minutes catching up since his last visit. I opened my Coke, took a sip, and listened as the convicted I.R.A. volunteer spoke in the thick accent of working-class Belfast. Callaghan had mentioned earlier that Fergus was from Ardoyne. He was from a prominent Republican family and his father was a leading I.R.A. man. In his twenty-four years, Fergus Martin had experienced a lot of pain and violence, and it showed on his hardened face. I noticed there were already traces of gray in his brown hair.

I had heard from Callaghan some of Fergus's story. His mother died of cancer when he was fourteen, while his father was locked up in prison. Friends he grew up with were murdered and his brother-in-law was killed by the Loyalist Ulster Volunteer Force. Fergus himself was shot by the British Army and nearly died. His baby daughter died a crib death and his wife divorced him after he was arrested and given a lengthy prison sentence. Tattooed across his right hand was the name "Maureen." By its brightness and sharp color, it had to be fairly recent. No doubt it was his ex-wife's name. On his left hand was another tattoo that read "Mum."

After Fergus finished his bag of chips, he lit up a cigarette, took a deep drag, and told us what he could about his Republican activities. His manner was friendly but direct.

"When I was eighteen years of age, I got a job as a roofer and met a local girl in Ardoyne whom I later married. But comin' from a well-known Republican family, I was constantly harassed, arrested, and beaten, which put a considerable strain on me life and eventually I was sacked from me job.

"When I looked about me, I realized me personal struggle was part of the larger struggle to free this wee corner of Ireland from a foreign occupying force. Like me father before me, I became involved in the Republican movement at this time. I knew sooner or later, I would be killed or imprisoned for me point of view. But I was only twenty-one and I carried on, not thinkin' about the odds."

Fergus paused, drank what was left of his Coke and lit another cigarette. I lit one too.

"In the three years leading up to me last arrest," he continued, "we moved into a house in Ardoyne and a year later me daughter was born. Two months later, British soldiers smashed their way into our home and in front of me wife shot me at point-blank range with a plastic bullet in the abdomen. Me heart stopped and I was given the Last Rites by a priest."

"Jaysus," uttered Callaghan, in an accent as if he were born and bred in Ireland.

"Sometime later," Fergus went on, "I was arrested in possession of an AK-47 after three separate gun attacks on the R.U.C. Now yez must understand, I must be mindful of how I tell this."

We were aware of the two screws, who periodically passed by the cubicles eavesdropping on conversations.

"A house was commandeered by the I.R.A. in the New Lodge area of north Belfast," continued Fergus. "The house was secured, and the family's car was taken to enable volunteers to bomb an R.U.C. barracks. The car was stopped, and the driver apprehended before its target was reached. A cordon was thrown around the area and a bomb disposal unit sent for. Whilst this was happening another house in the Oldpark district was taken by volunteers and another car to ensure the I.R.A. withdrew safely from the area and back to base.

"Well boys, in this house were a number of men. I was later convicted of being in this house with a rifle to fire on Crown force personnel manning the cordon. A total of seventeen shots were fired, with no injuries inflicted.

"The I.R.A. volunteers drove away in the car and were chased by an R.U.C. jeep, and a number of shots were discharged from the car which struck the jeep. Yet again, I was convicted of being in the car. According to the judge, I was the gunman on both occasions. A few streets away the same car was stopped, and I was given the rifle, the judge said.

"I had no mask on and it was just gettin' dark when another R.U.C. jeep came on the scene, spotted me, and challenged me to drop the weapon. I fired a total of ten shots at the enemy who were inside the jeep, to enable the men in the car a safe escape and in order so as I could escape and get to safety also.

"I then ran down a street but unlucky for me it was a cul-de-sac, and I was arrested as I had no bullets left! Ha ha ha!!

It was the first time we heard him laugh. Fergus then gave us an account of what happened after his arrest.

"I was taken to the notorious Castlereagh Interrogation Centre, questioned and held for five days. Durin' me questionin' I was asked who me associates were, et cetera. I used me right to silence – which durin' yer trial, the judge takes into consideration as the I.R.A. train their members for interrogation.

"Anyway, after this I was remanded to Crumlin Road Jail where the conditions are poor as it was built at the middle of the 19th century. As we are integrated with Loyalists down in the Crum, there was a lot of fightin' between both different political affiliations and this came to a climax last October when a bomb exploded in the canteen, killin' a U.V.F. man."

Fergus lit another cigarette, closed his eyes, and deeply inhaled the smoke before he slowly exhaled it. Then he continued.

"Shortly after I was lifted – or arrested – me wee baby daughter died of sudden infant death syndrome. She was just five months of age. As yez can imagine this wrecked me. I was given seven hours compassionate bail to bury her, and this helped a little.

"Four days later me trial started. It lasted a fortnight, and I was given twelve years with another seven to serve. A week later, me wife informed me that she couldn't wait that long and said she was leavin' me!

"So, all in all, boys, these last two years haven't been great but me commitment to the struggle for Irish freedom is stronger, me morale good, and I'm fortunate enough to get support from me comrades and friends both inside and outside, includin' those from across the great pond."

"You can count on us," declared Callaghan enthusiastically. "We're with you."

The conversation turned to more current events, and we talked about the sectarian attack three days earlier at James Murray's betting shop. While condemning the ruthless murders committed by the Loyalist death squad, Fergus admitted that even the Republican movement had been plagued by sectarianism.

"One of the worst purely sectarian attacks committed by Republicans, that comes to mind, was the Kingsmill Massacre in 1976. In retaliation for a string of Loyalist attacks against Catholics, a group callin' itself the South Armagh Republican Action Force stopped a minibus carrying a dozen workmen home from a textile factory.

"They were lined up alongside the vehicle and asked to state their religion. There was one Catholic amongst 'em. He was sent down the road and told not to look back. Then the eleven Protestant workers were cut down in a hail of gunfire. One man survived, despite bein' shot eighteen times."

Fergus's story confirmed my feeling that the conflict was often as much about old hatreds and sectarianism, as it was about driving out the Brits.

"But that's not what Republicanism is all about," said Fergus. "The movement itself is a hundred percent against sectarianism."

"To unite Protestant, Catholic, and Dissenter under the common name of Irishmen," offered Callaghan, "in order to break the connection with England, the never-failing source of all our political evils."

He was quoting the words of the father of Irish Republicanism, the great Wolfe Tone.

"Aye Tim, that's right," replied Fergus, with a smile.

He then related the events surrounding the much-publicized I.R.A. bombing of Enniskillen in 1987, in which ten civilians were killed along with one R.U.C. officer. Among the victims were three married couples and several elderly pensioners. Sixty-three people were injured, including thirteen children. All of the victims were Protestants. It was reported that the I.R.A. unit responsible shot their guns into the air afterwards in celebration.

"True Republicans don't glorify killin'," said the imprisoned volunteer, "even if it was deemed necessary."

"Was what happened in Enniskillen deemed necessary?" I asked.

"No," answered Fergus. "It was a massacre. A total atrocity. Afterwards, that particular unit was disbanded."

But it was a war the I.R.A. were fighting and Fergus made this point more than clear. He held that the bombing campaign was an important component of the guerrilla war the I.R.A. were engaged in.

"It's the aim of the I.R.A. to make it financially, militarily, and politically unacceptable for Britain to continue to keep the Six Counties in her dark clutches," he said. "By specifically bombin' London, as the I.R.A. has been doin' more and more frequently, the I.R.A. hopes to bring the war 'home' to the Brits by strikin' at the very heart of the British establishment."

The cities of Northern Ireland were still getting more than their share of horrific bombings though.

Fergus mentioned the massive bomb that ripped through downtown Coleraine the previous Friday, which miraculously avoided casualties but caused millions of pounds worth of damage to the town's commercial center. Like Callaghan, he was exuberant about the results of the operation. It was in line with the I.R.A.'s "hit them where it hurts the most" strategy – in their pocketbooks. In other words, make the Six Counties such a financial liability for the British to continue to occupy that they would finally leave Irish shores.

Another reason, Fergus explained, that the I.R.A. hit towns like Coleraine was because they *were* predominantly Protestant and Loyalist, and would therefore bring the British Army and R.U.C. out of the heavily Catholic and Nationalist areas.

"It makes Crown forces place more of their personnel in what they previously regarded as 'safe' areas, and it gets the Brits a bit off the backs of Nationalists – at least for a while."

Grinding out his cigarette in the ashtray, Fergus gave us a slight smile, indicating it was time to move on to pleasanter topics.

"So how yez enjoyin' yer stay in Ireland?" he asked, his face losing some of its seriousness.

We spoke briefly of our trip to Strabane and down to Cork, and of the run-ins we had with the R.U.C. in Belfast, before our hour and a half visit came to an end. We stood up and shook hands and watched as Fergus Martin was led out the door he had come through with the other prisoners. Callaghan and I then followed the other visitors out the door we entered through and, after we received back our personal belongings, we loaded back into the minibus that would return us to Belfast.

CHAPTER TWENTY-EIGHT
CIDER WITH DENIS IRWIN

The old three-story brick building at 97 Eglantine Avenue didn't have proper mailboxes. Instead, letters were just tossed onto a little, narrow table in the lobby, where any passerby could walk off with them. Sometimes, I saw envelopes torn open on the table or cast on the floor, so I made a point of looking through whatever mail there was for letters addressed to me or Callaghan.

As I sifted through the day's mail, the door of the flat behind me opened and out peeked a thin, pale woman wearing thick glasses. She uttered an awkward hello, and I returned her greeting, as I picked up a letter I saw from my wife.

Opening the letter in our flat, I saw it was dated November 14th, five days earlier. I could hear Beth's Filipino accent through her written words.

Well, Mary and Biddy are okay. They both play a lot together and sometimes ends in fight. They like teasing each other. They are still asking on you. Biddy was talking to her doll this morning and I heard her saying to the doll, "Dolly, sometimes daddy leave me," over and over again.

I'm going to walk Mary to shopping mall to see those Christmas decorations. I want to bring them both but I couldn't handle them. We'll see if my mother come with me.

Sometime Mary sleep with me, especially during my days off. The problem now when I come back from work she doesn't want to sleep on their room. She sleep downstairs on your rocking chair and wait for me to come home.

Love,
Beth

Late that afternoon, I sat out in the drafty hallway, enjoying a pipe smoke as I flipped through Jonathan Bardon's *Belfast: An Illustrated History*, which Callaghan had checked out from Queen's University library. He had left an hour earlier to have dinner with Sandra, with the parting reminder not to smoke in his flat and stink up the place. Personally, I always liked the smell of a good smoke-filled room.

As I was sitting in the hallway, Denis the building super came down the stairs wearing white coveralls and carrying a paint can. The upstairs flat was vacant, and he was repainting it. He stopped to ask me what I was reading and to chat a bit.

The super, or caretaker, as he called himself, was a slight, short man, maybe five-foot-five, in his mid-thirties, with short brown hair, neatly parted on the side. He had an easy smile and friendly eyes.

"How's the McMurdo Silver?" he asked.

"The old-time radio? Oh, it works great," I replied.

"Ah, that's grand."

Denis headed downstairs with his can of paint. I just relit my pipe and reopened the book, when he came back up with a bottle of Bulmers cider.

"Sort of a wee welcome gift to Belfast," he said, smiling. "Hope ye fancy cider."

I thanked him and we were soon chatting down in his flat, where I was permitted to smoke.

"Now, I don't smoke meself," he said, "but I'd not deny a man a puff, if he's so inclined."

Seated in one of his two comfortable cushioned chairs, I watched my host pour the Bulmers cider into a tall glass. His flat was simply furnished. A couple of landscape paintings hung on the walls, and there was a large TV set on a stand across from a well-maintained 1960's-era wooden stereo console.

Denis Irwin – for that was his surname – then poured a cider into a tall glass for himself. He told me that he had only moved back to Belfast a year earlier after living for twelve years down in Dundalk, in the Republic's County Louth, just on the other side of the border. In addition to being the building's super, I learned, he was a part-time orderly at Royal Victoria Hospital.

Although Denis was a chatty fellow, there was a timidness about him. It seemed he was trying too hard to please me – offering me potato chips, some stew he had on the stove, another cider, and reminding me again that I was free to light up my pipe. He was also overly open about himself, as if his life were an open book that he wanted to share with me.

I heard how Denis Irwin was raised in an orphanage on the Antrim Road. His mother was a Catholic girl in her teens when her Protestant boyfriend left her pregnant, saying he could never marry a Catholic. Her parents, understandably ashamed of her condition, placed her in a home for unwed mothers on the Cliftonville Road.

For years he periodically looked at the Irwins listed in the Northern Ireland telephone directory. Denis never doubted that he must be related to at least one of them. But it wasn't until he was thirty-one years old that he mustered up enough courage to start making phone calls. He was soon speaking to his mother's brother. His uncle put him in touch with his mother.

She was a middle-aged, happily married woman living in west Belfast's Andersonstown, and she welcomed Denis into her home, and he became part of the family. It was a wonderful story and I told him so.

"Indeed, 'tis," he replied, with a smile.

Opening another bottle of cider, he refilled my glass and brought out a large photo album. He turned the pages to show me pictures of his mother and her husband and a couple of his half-sisters. Then Denis flipped to the back pages of the album to show me the trip he took that summer to County Mayo.

"I went with me mum and her husband to the wee village of Cong to see where *The Quiet Man* film was made in 1952, starring Maureen O'Hara and John Wayne and Victor McLaglen and Barry Fitzgerald. Ah, Cong was a lovely place, so 'twas. Real picture-postcard Ireland."

I relit my pipe as Denis chatted on.

"Next we went over to Knock to see where Our Blessed Mother appeared more than a hundred years ago."

I was familiar with the story. One rainy evening in 1879, villagers in Knock saw on the exterior gable wall of the parish church an apparition of Our Lady, Saint Joseph, Saint John the Evangelist, and a Lamb standing on an altar before a cross surrounded by angels. The villagers knelt and recited the rosary in the rain as they stared at the vision. The heavenly visitors didn't say anything; however, no rain fell where they were. Our Lady didn't give any predictions or warnings as she usually did when she appeared, but the humble villagers understood her message. In their poverty and suffering, she was with them.

Over the years, Knock became a place of pilgrimage. Faithful Catholics who visited the shrine had their prayers answered and others had serious diseases cured.

"I got that wee Lady of Knock there," said Denis, indicating a small white statue of the Blessed Virgin on an end table, beside the stereo console.

"Mary, Queen of Ireland," I remarked, finishing my third tall glass of cider.

"Aye, true enough," said my host. "Are ye a Catholic yerself?"

"Yeah, I am," I answered. "But not a very good one."

"Ah, sure, none of us are," replied Denis.

Later that night, I put on the McMurdo Silver radio for the news and heard about a U.V.F. attack in the small village of Kilcoo, County Down. The Loyalist death squad burst into a pub and fired indiscriminately, murdering Peter McCormack, a local forty-two-year-old farmer, who was once a schoolteacher, and injuring an eighteen-year-old boy, a thirty-three-year-old man, and a sixty-nine-year-old blind man. All were guilty of simply being Catholics.

CHAPTER TWENTY-NINE
DEMONSTRATION AT JAMES MURRAY'S BETTING SHOP

That evening, Callaghan and I went to attend a demonstration in the Bone district of north Belfast, in front of James Murray's betting shop on the Oldpark Road, where Loyalist gunmen had recently murdered three men in a gun and grenade attack. Local residents had been protesting the past few nights over the lack of security in the area.

The Marrowbone, or simply "The Bone," was a small working-class, Catholic, and overwhelmingly Republican community, located between Ardoyne on its west and the Cliftonville area on its east. The Bone was bordered by the Protestant and Loyalist Torrens community to its north and the Protestant, Loyalist Lower Oldpark district to its south. The Oldpark Road went through the center of the Bone.

Belfast neighborhoods were mostly divided along religious and political lines, and in many parts of the city there were so-called "peace walls" separating Catholic Republican or Nationalist areas from Protestant Loyalist or Unionist ones. There were also a number of interfaces in Belfast; that is points where streets from the segregated communities met. These interfaces often became flashpoints of sectarian violence. The Oldpark Road had long been such a flashpoint.

Local residents wanted barriers placed across their road after sunset, citing the fact that they lived in an area especially vulnerable to Loyalist attacks. In the past two years, we heard, six people were murdered by Loyalist paramilitaries in the Rosapenna Street – Oldpark Road area.

The turnout for the demonstration was smaller than we expected though, possibly due to the rain. Callaghan and I signed our names to a petition being passed through the crowd asking the R.U.C. for barriers to be erected.

The betting shop's corrugated metal shutters were rolled down over the window and entrance, and bouquets of flowers leaned against it. The sign above the betting shop read: James Murray Bookmakers – Est. 1928. Other businesses in the brick building were likewise closed with their shutters down.

I lit a cigarette and took in the scene around me. It was already dark, and the rain had stopped. Nearby there were several parked gray armored Land Rovers, a lot of R.U.C. men in full riot gear with helmets, holding batons and plexiglass shields. Beyond them was a green tank-like British Army armored personnel carrier and a number of soldiers, also in riot gear. I overheard snippets of conversations from people around me.

"These Loyalist scum are gettin' away with murderin' us and we're left undefended," said a man.

"All rotten Orange Prods, the lot of 'em, like these ones!" yelled a woman, pointing at the nearby police.

"We have been under bloody siege for twenty-five years," complained another woman. "Loyalists are petrol-bombin' our houses, smashin' bricks through our windows, and killin' innocent Catholics."

There was some commotion in the crowd, some muffled shouts. I couldn't see what was going on, but I noticed the row of R.U.C. men were all looking intensely in that direction as several began to menacingly swing their batons. An ominous feeling hung in the air and I felt a sudden chill.

"Let me go!" cried a man.

I saw him through the crowd. A middle-aged man with a cap pushed back on his head, in a baggy suit, staggering in the street. Two guys tried to grab a hold of him. He pulled away and stumbled but didn't fall. It was obvious he was drunk. He stopped and faced the police and soldiers.

"Baaastards!!!" he screamed. "Yez killed me son...yez...yezz... fuckin' murderers!!"

Most of the R.U.C. men had their batons out and had tightened their grips on them.

"Ohh, Gawwd!" he wailed, his voice cracking. "Me boy!!"

The poor guy's knees buckled, and he fell to the road. Smirking R.U.C. men and sneering soldiers looked on as the broken-hearted father was lifted up by two of his friends and led away. It was a pathetic scene.

"C'mon," I said to Callaghan, "let's get out of here."

We walked away from the demonstration and found a taxi. We decided to get off in downtown Belfast, along Great Victoria Street, and walk the rest of the way back to the flat.

The taxi dropped us off across from the Grand Opera House, a majestic century-old building with an ornate façade of white cast stone and red-brick, designed in an oriental style, evoking the days of the British Empire in India.

It felt like we were suddenly a world away from the Troubles, from deadly sectarian hatreds, and the occupying British Army. The city center was bustling with young people out for a few drinks and a good time on a Saturday night. We passed the Europa, a modern high-rise hotel popular with visiting dignitaries and foreign correspondents, and with the dubious distinction of being the most bombed hotel in the world. A group of university students were laughing and chatting together outside the Crown Bar, a lavish Victorian-era saloon.

But our thoughts were still very much occupied by what we had witnessed at the demonstration.

"A couple of months before you arrived here," said Callaghan, "Trevor Hinton was convicted along with another Loyalist psycho of attacking a drunk Catholic man with a hammer and hatchet on a north Belfast street."

I admitted I wasn't familiar with the case and had never heard of Hinton.

"He's one evil and depraved son of a bitch," said Callaghan, lowering his voice, so that people wouldn't overhear our conversation as we walked through Shaftesbury Square.

"In the early '70's, this maniac Hinton was one of the four U.D.A. killers who broke into the home of Sarah McClenaghan. A widowed mother, she lived with her mentally retarded fourteen-year-old son. They were the only Catholics living on their street in the Oldpark Road area.

"The killers demanded to know the poor woman's religion. There was a Protestant man living as a lodger with them and he tried to intervene, saying they were all Protestants. He was brought upstairs, where he was beaten and tortured. But he managed to escape.

"The McClenaghans weren't as fortunate. The disabled boy – who had the mind of a small child – was ordered by Hinton to bring him his mother's prayerbook. The terrified kid brought him her Catholic missal and rosary beads. They brutally raped the mother in front of her son."

Callaghan stopped and looked away from me. I knew he was trying to control his rage before he continued. He took a deep breath.

"Mrs. McClenaghan begged and pleaded with these sadistic animals not to hurt her son. Hinton shot the boy in the head and killed him. His mother was also shot, but she survived to tell her horrific ordeal in court.

"Although Hinton was given a life sentence, he spent just sixteen years behind bars and then strolled out of prison."

As we turned onto Eglantine Avenue, I thought how in Ireland the past was always so painfully present.

CHAPTER THIRTY
BEECHMOUNT ON A SUNDAY

During the year that Callaghan was in Belfast, he had taken to attending Catholic Mass at different churches to better acquaint himself with different communities in the city. While I didn't practice my religion as faithfully as Callaghan did, I was still a Catholic and decided to join him. That Sunday morning, we went to Mass at St. Paul's on the Falls Road.

We walked up to Divis Street and the Lower Falls Road to the Beechmount district. It was a chilly morning and we both zipped our jackets all the way up to our collars. Callaghan, as usual, went hatless, and, as usual, I wore my tweed cap.

The familiar brick neo-Gothic church, which celebrated its first Mass in 1887, was situated across from Royal Victoria Hospital. The life-sized white statues of the crucifixion scene stood out prominently in the church garden. The entrance was on Cavendish Street, and we passed through the main doors, beneath a large statue of Saint Paul with a long beard and holding a sword. The church was full, and the Mass had already started, but we were able to squeeze into a back pew.

After Mass, Callaghan headed down the Grosvenor Road to meet Sandra in the city center and I wandered down the little streets around

St. Paul's, by Victorian-era two-story brick and white stucco rowhouses. I passed a newsagent's shop and a group of giggling adolescent girls. As I walked by Mrs. Boyle's Harrogate Street, an elderly couple bundled up in overcoats greeted me with a slight nod of their heads.

The Beechmount district received its name from the Beechmount House, the 18th century family home and estate of local gentry, which was situated atop a hill surrounded by beech trees. By the early 1930's, the grand house and property was bought by the Catholic bishop of Down and Connor and given to the Sisters of Mercy, who turned it into Our Lady's Hospital.

Meanwhile, the population of Beechmount grew rapidly from the 19th century as Belfast became more industrialized as linen mills and factories sprang up throughout the city. The Falls Road – once a quiet country lane – became the main road through west Belfast and passed through Beechmount. Like most of west Belfast, the area was working-class and Catholic and largely Republican. When the Troubles began, Beechmount was in the thick of the violent conflict.

I turned onto a grim street littered with debris. There was an old burnt tire laying in the middle of the street and a couple of broken wooden chairs. Old red-brick rowhouses had their windows and doors bricked up and were covered by graffiti. I realized I was near to the spot where, a month before, Callaghan and I were stopped and interrogated by Crown forces. I lit a cigarette and looked around. The street was deserted, like it was then.

Suddenly, I heard a barking dog. Some distance behind me was a big, black and tan shepherd, followed by a dark-haired girl in a bulky, oversized denim jacket and jeans. The dog ran up to me, tail wagging.

"He'll do ye not a bit of harm," the girl called out.

"Sure," she added, as she drew closer, "me doggy wouldn't hurt a fly, so he wouldn't. Barrin' the peelers and the Brits – with 'em he can be quite fierce. He may be black and tan but he's Irish through and through. He knows who the enemy is."

I patted the friendly shepherd's head and walked for a while with the girl and her Republican canine.

She was a plumpish girl, with shoulder-length black hair and a turned-up nose, named Doreen. She told me she was born twenty-three years ago, in 1969, when the Troubles erupted.

"I first saw the light of day at the Royal Vic, but a stone's throw from here," she said.

Doreen meant Royal Victoria Hospital. She went on to say how she spent her entire life in Beechmount. After inquiring about what sort of work I did in America, she told me she once had a job as a shop girl for nearly a year. But she had been unemployed for the past three years.

"Like most of us here, I've been livin' on the *bru,* so I have," declared Doreen.

In Northern Ireland, the *bru,* also known as the dole, was a government unemployment benefit. It was a mispronunciation of *bureau,* as in the "welfare bureau."

"There's nothin' here for us Catholics in Belfast, God help us," she continued. "We don't really live as normal people do in normal places in the world – we just exist here."

She echoed what I saw stray painted on a crumbling gable wall in west Belfast: "Is there life before death?"

I bid farewell to Doreen and her dog and made my way back to the Falls Road. I was feeling parched and needed a pint of the black stuff.

The first public house I came to was called the Beehive. When safely behind a creamy Guinness, I pondered how a Belfast pub came to be known as the Beehive.

I asked the pimply-faced boy, in a white shirt and black bowtie, tending the bar. Before replying he carefully folded the towel, he was using to dry pint glasses, and placed it on the bar.

"Ah...well, sure, I haven't a clue," he finally said.

"I can answer yer question, Yank," said a fellow, sitting a few barstools away.

He was a middle-aged man with thick, wavy, fiery red hair, sporting a wild, untamed mustache. Smiling, he removed the cigarette from his mouth.

"This here drinkin' establishment was built a hundred odd years ago by a Dutchman. Yer man kept bees for honey in the back garden and that's how the bar came to be called the Beehive. 'Tis an old and historic place."

The flaming-headed man finished his pint, and I bought him another, as well as another for myself. After we both lit cigarettes, he continued.

"Robert Baden-Powell, who started the Boy Scouts, was a major in the British Army's 13th Hussars cavalry regiment when he would occasionally ride into the Beehive on horseback, order a drink, and down it without ever leavin' his saddle."

"Is that right?" I asked skeptically.

"True as God," affirmed the man with a wink, clinking his pint glass to mine. "Sure, I witnessed it meself."

It may very well have been true, though if it was, it would have occurred long before his lifetime, as Robert Baden-Powell was stationed at nearby Willowbank Barracks on the Falls Road at the turn of the 19th century.

CHAPTER THIRTY-ONE
BELFAST CROWN COURT WITH THE CASEMENT ACCUSED

When taking a black taxi on the Falls Road a week earlier, Callaghan got to chatting with the driver and learned he was the father of one of the Casement Accused. He invited Callaghan to attend the ongoing trial to witness what he called British injustice for himself, and Callaghan invited me to accompany him.

We hoofed it in the morning from Eglantine Avenue to the courthouse on the Crumlin Road and discussed the case as we made our way through the city streets. I was familiar with the tragic events. All the major U.S. newspapers at the time carried the story and Irish-American publications like *The Irish Echo,* which I had a subscription to, provided even more coverage.

It began in early March 1988, when three unarmed members of the I.R.A. were shot dead in Gibraltar by undercover soldiers of the S.A.S. (Special Air Service), an elite unit of the British Army. The Gibraltar Three – as they came to be known – were allegedly there to bomb a British military band. The trio – Seán Savage, Dan McCann, and Mairéad Farrell - were from west Belfast and their bodies were returned home for burial. Thousands of mourners came to their funeral at Milltown

Cemetery, during which the Loyalist Michael Stone launched his gun and grenade attack, killing three mourners and wounding more than sixty others.

One of the dead was I.R.A. Volunteer Caoimhín MacBrádaigh (also known as Kevin Brady, the anglicized version of his name), who with other brave, unarmed young men tried to stop the attack by pursuing Stone.

Three days later, MacBrádaigh's funeral cortège was making its way along the Andersonstown Road towards Milltown Cemetery. Again, there was a huge turnout of mourners, including a large number of I.R.A. men. According to witnesses, the atmosphere was extremely tense as people were fearful of another attack.

Then suddenly an unknown car sped towards the funeral procession. The crowd panicked, convinced that it was another Loyalist attack. The car was quickly surrounded, and its escape route was blocked by a black taxi.

An enraged mob attacked the vehicle and smashed the windows to get at the two men inside. One of the men produced a handgun and attempted to drive back the mob by firing a shot into the air. But the men were soon dragged from the car, disarmed, and viciously beaten.

Taken to waste ground close to Casement Park, their beating by dozens of men continued. They were stripped to their undershorts and searched. They had been dressed in plain clothing, but documents found in their pockets identified them as British soldiers.

A Redemptorist priest who was present tried to intervene and begged people to call an ambulance. But Father Alec Reid was ordered not to interfere and was forcibly hauled away. The I.R.A. then executed the soldiers. It was later determined that Corporal Derek Wood was shot six times, twice in his head and four times in his chest. Corporal David Howes was shot five times, once in his head and four times in his body. Both had multiple other injuries, including stab wounds.

The violently brutal murders of the corporals was witnessed by journalists and captured on film by news crews and a British Army helicopter circling overhead.

After the executions, the crowd near Casement Park vanished. On the ground remained the soldiers' bloody and battered bodies. Father Reid returned to the horrific scene and found Corporal Wood seemingly dead and Corporal Howes breathing his last. An English photographer snapped a picture of the stunned priest kneeling down by the latter soldier and giving him Last Rites. That picture was seen around the world, on television, in newspapers and magazines.

I remembered an interview I read in which Father Reid said after he was done anointing him, he went to anoint the other soldier, a few yards away. "Then two women came along with a coat and put it over his head and said, 'he was somebody's son'." As Father Reid remarked about the barbaric killings, "this shouldn't be happening in a civilized society."

Over the next four years, more than two hundred people were arrested in connection with the murder of the corporals. Forty-two were charged with crimes which included murder, attempted murder, conspiracy to murder, and causing grievous bodily harm. The first of the so-called Casement Trials ended quickly with two I.R.A. men being found guilty of murder and sentenced to life imprisonment, though neither had actually fired shots into the soldiers. Three more men were convicted, under the doctrine of "common purpose," and given life sentences in 1990. As the trials continued many were based on weaker evidence, but the accused were likewise determined guilty through common purpose.

Belfast Crown Court, on the Crumlin Road, was surrounded by a high fence of corrugated wrought iron railings topped by barbed wire. Directly across the road was the infamous Crumlin Road Jail. They were connected by an underground tunnel to bring prisoners from jail to court, and back to jail if convicted.

We were stopped at the gate by two green-uniformed, flak-jacketed R.U.C. men, patted down, asked for our identifications, and the reason for our visit. Beyond the heavy security fence was the cream-colored, neoclassical courthouse with eight Corinthian columns and a pediment above, built in 1850.

We entered the building's high-ceilinged central hall, and, amid more armed R.U.C. men and black-robed and bewigged barristers, Callaghan located the taxi driver he met a week before. A big, mustached, bear of a man, Jim Kelly greeted us both with a firm handshake and a smile.

"Hell of a place to spend any of yer holiday time," he said, glancing around us.

Mr. Kelly's twenty-three-year-old son, Seán, one of the Accused dubbed the Casement Three, was sent to prison for life in 1990 for kidnapping, causing grievous bodily harm, and aiding and abetting in the murders of the British corporals.

As we followed Mr. Kelly into the courtroom, he explained the court that day would be hearing the case against the next of the defendants. Patrick Doherty, aged twenty-three, had been charged with causing grievous bodily harm and false imprisonment.

We took seats beside Mr. Kelly in the gallery with other visitors. As usual in cases deemed political offences or terrorist acts in Northern Ireland, it was a Diplock court – that is a trial without a jury, only a judge.

I took it all in as the proceedings began. The appearance of the courtroom was very different than what we had in the States. The presiding Judge MacDermott (addressed as "my lord") donned a red robe and a long white wig – attire carried over from the 18th century. Likewise, barristers in the courtroom had black robes and shorter white wigs. And because this was a British court in Northern Ireland, there were plenty of uniformed R.U.C. men present.

It was difficult to follow the proceedings as the trial had begun over a week before. Mr. Kelly tried to bring us up to date. The court had already reviewed film coverage to prove Patrick Doherty, and six others on trial at the time, acted with common purpose in the corporals' murders.

As a journalist, Callaghan attempted to take notes in a pocket-sized notebook he had brought with him, but a R.U.C. man quickly stepped over to tell him to put it away. All notetaking was strictly prohibited.

Soon there was a cry of "God Save the Queen" and court was adjourned for lunch. Mr. Kelly departed as he needed to go to work. Callaghan wanted to sit in on the rest of the day's proceedings, but I had seen enough. Mr. Kelly was right; Belfast Crown Court was a hell of a place to spend my holiday.

Callaghan walked me to the gate. Entering the gate was the well-known priest and community activist, Father Des Wilson. I recognized him from his picture included with his weekly column in NORAID's *Irish People* newspaper. He was an old man, with black framed glasses, and fluffy tufts of white hair around his bald crown. His clerical collar could be seen underneath his heavy beige coat.

Father Wilson had long spoken out against the British occupation of the Six Counties, and the violence and injustices inflicted on Nationalist Catholics. Although he was a pacifist, the priest refused to condemn the I.R.A. in their armed struggle. Father Wilson promoted community development through adult education to open new career paths for often unemployed, working-class people. He was instrumental in establishing the Conway Mill Education Centre in an old disused spinning and weaving mill in the Lower Falls Road area.

Callaghan went over to meet him and shake his hand, and I followed. The old priest was friendly and chatty. He repeated our names a couple of times as if he was trying to lock them away in his memory.

"Drop by the Conway Mill anytime and we'll chew the fat a bit," he told us, before we parted company.

CHAPTER THIRTY-TWO
THE KILLING OF AN I.R.A. VOLUNTEER

Callaghan set out again in the morning to take in more of the Casement Accused trial. I chose to spend my day out walking to see some parts of Belfast I hadn't seen yet. I accompanied Callaghan up to Carrick Hill and as he continued on to the Crumlin Road and the courthouse, I turned onto Peter's Hill. I decided to venture up the staunchly Protestant Loyalist Shankill Road, to see what I would see.

I strayed into a small street off Boundary Street. There were the same red-brick rowhouses that could be seen in all the working-class districts of Belfast. But this was an entirely different neighborhood. Union Jacks flew from flagpoles and hung in windows, along with Red Hand of Ulster flags, and curbstones were patriotically painted British red, white, and blue. Not a single Irish tricolor in sight.

As I walked, I came across on a rowhouse gable wall a huge mural of King William of Orange on his white horse defeating the Irish at the Battle of the Boyne in 1690. Everywhere on brick walls were painted slogans representing the views of the residents: "No Surrender," "Ulster, Scotland – United We Stand," "Ulster Still Says No," "We Will Never Accept a United Ireland," "One Faith – One Crown," and, of course, "Kill All Taigs."

Like at the courthouse, I had seen enough and moved on. By late afternoon, I found myself dandering along the Upper Falls Road by Belfast City Cemetery. It was rush hour with bumper-to-bumper traffic on the four-lane road. I had just passed a primary school and was approaching St. John's Catholic Church. There was some commotion up ahead with cars honking. At first, I figured it was just a minor fender-bender. But it was quickly evident that this was something more serious.

I only learned the details later from news reports. At a quarter after five in the afternoon, twenty-two-year-old I.R.A. Volunteer Pearse Jordan, from Ballymurphy, was driving towards the city center in a stolen red Ford Orion when he was deliberately rammed by two unmarked police cars, forcing him onto the sidewalk. Uniformed R.U.C. men leaped from the vehicles, as a shaken Jordan stumbled away from the car he was in.

Witnesses, closer to the scene than I was, reported there was no shout to halt, and no warning issued by any R.U.C. man.

A man, who had been walking home from work, was quoted in the following day's newspaper as saying the police simply "let rip with a Heckler and Koch."

I heard the loud burst of gunfire and saw from a distance Pearse Jordan stagger and turn to face his foes and fall to the street.

"Jaaaysus!" screamed a woman.

"You bastards!" yelled a man, from the small crowd of onlookers.

As I draw closer, I saw the R.U.C. man who shot the unarmed I.R.A. volunteer three times in his back looking satisfied and composed, as he lowered his gun. Then, with his three colleagues, he was standing over the prone Jordan. They cursed and kicked at the dying man and pushed his face into the ground.

"For pity's sake!" a woman wailed.

But there was no pity for young Pearse Jordan. It was a sickening scene.

Meanwhile, two other R.U.C. men searched the red Orion, and I heard one call out, "there's nothing in the car."

News reports later claimed that the car had been used to carry bomb-making materials. But it was clear, to those who were there, no guns, explosives, or other munitions were then found in the vehicle.

As the R.U.C. stepped away, a priest hurried over to where Jordan lay and knelt down to administer the Last Rites. I read in the morning paper, the priest was Father Eugene McArdle, from nearby St. John's parochial house.

After witnessing the calculated murder of the young I.R.A. man by Crown forces, I numbly walked back to the flat on Eglantine Avenue.

CHAPTER THIRTY-THREE
THE QUINNS AND SONNY BOYLE

On Saturday morning, Callaghan and I again boarded an Ulsterbus to take us down to Dublin, where we'd be spending the weekend with the family of Republican prisoner Terry Quinn. Then on Monday, we'd accompany Mrs. Quinn on a visit to Portlaoise Prison to see her husband.

It was a chilly, overcast afternoon, but the crowds of shoppers were thick along O'Connell Street. We made our way past Daniel O'Connell's monument and across the River Liffey to the southside of the city, to Dublin's famous Grafton Street.

The thoroughfare between Trinity College and St. Stephen's Green was a pedestrian street and was even more jam-packed with holiday shoppers. In less than a month it would be Christmas. Street musicians were out in force to entertain and earn a few bob.

A young guy with long hair and an even a longer green, white, and orange striped scarf played traditional Irish tunes on a fiddle. A little farther on a woman with equally long, flowing hair, in what looked like a white wedding dress, plucked at an enormous harp. Then we came to four South American Indians, wearing brightly colored ponchos, playing flutes and a guitar. The only woman among them wore a brown bowler hat – the kind seen on the native women of Bolivia. They were quite good, and we paused with a growing crowd to listen. We tossed into their plastic bucket a couple of punt coins before we moved on.

The bustling crowds on Grafton Street stepped around three young boys – maybe eight to ten years old – belting out an awful rendition of Elvis Presley's "You Ain't Nothing But A Hound Dog." An upside-down flat cap was on the ground by their feet with a few coins passersby had dropped in.

I thought to take a picture of them and took out my camera. But as I attempted to focus the lens, a little waif of a girl, perhaps seven or eight, large-eyed and elfin-like with a gaunt, pinched face and stringy blonde hair, appeared before me with a cup in her hand.

"Please sir, do yeh have any spare coins?"

I put a 50 pence coin into her cup.

"More please, sir, for a hamburger, sir."

I dug into my pocket and fished out my last 20 pence coin to give the little beggar girl.

When I looked back at the Elvis Presley wannabees, I saw they were being told to go home by a policeman. The eldest of them ran off a bit, turned and flashed the garda an outward-facing V sign with his fingers. An obscene gesture in Ireland, it was comparable to giving someone the middle finger in America.

"Away with youse!" roared the garda, as the two other boys scampered off. "You little bastards!"

After a good laugh at the spectacle, Callaghan and I went to take a city bus to the suburb of Tallaght, in the southwest of County Dublin.

Like so many other places in Ireland, it saw its origins as a monastic settlement, when the Emerald Isle was known as the land of saints and scholars. In the eighth century, Saint Máel Ruain founded a monastery at Tallaght.

But according to my guidebook, the place-name Tallaght was derived from the Gaelic *támh-leacht,* meaning "plague pit." What a cheery name for a place!

Nonetheless, the place grew over the centuries into a small, pleasant village, and in recent decades became part of the growing urban sprawl of Dublin City. From what I saw of Tallaght, from the bus window, it couldn't be called an attractive town, with street after street of ugly, modern housing estates.

"Come on, this is our stop," said Callaghan.

I followed him off the bus and we walked a short distance on a street lined with two-story, beige and brown stucco rowhouses, or terraced homes, built circa 1980, each with its own patch of green grass. Children ran and played in the street. We were in the Killinarden housing estate.

Callaghan turned in a path leading us to a house identical to all the others. A blue Ford Sierra was parked in the driveway and on the small lawn laid two kids' bikes and some scattered toys.

Mrs. Quinn welcomed us into her home. She was a small, mousy woman in her mid-thirties with short carrot-top hair and glasses. She wore a large white bathrobe and had well-worn slippers on her feet. After apologizing for her appearance, she hurried off to the kitchen to fix us some hot tea, remarking that the weather was cold and damp.

Callaghan and I were left standing in the empty living room. More toys were scattered on the floor, around a big, comfy sectional sofa surrounding a huge TV. On the wall hung a framed pre-partition map of Ireland and nearby was a mirror with a profile portrait of the 1916 leader Pádraic Pearse at its center. Under his picture were engraved the words of the martyred patriot: "You cannot conquer Ireland; you cannot extinguish the Irish passion for freedom. If our deed has not been sufficient to win freedom, then our children will win it by a better deed."

"Terry engraved that mirror himself in Portlaoise," said Callaghan.

"Me daddy made that," chirped a little girl, with bright carroty hair, who had entered the room.

"And what's your name, young lady?" I asked.

"I'm Lizzie," she replied, "but I'm not a young lady. I'm just five years of age."

"She'll be six in a fortnight," said her mother, returning from the kitchen with a tray loaded with floral teacups on saucers, a little creamer pitcher, a sugar bowl, and plates of finger tuna fish sandwiches.

We were both hungry as we hadn't eaten since leaving Belfast and our hostess soon brought us out another stack of finger sandwiches along with a plate of scones.

"Ah, that's great, Mrs. Quinn," I said. "Keep feeding us like this and you'll never get rid of us."

"Good God," she laughed, "call me Dolores! That's been me name a lot longer than Mrs. Quinn. Besides, *missus* makes me feel *soooo* bloody old!"

As Callaghan and I wolfed down the little sandwiches and scones, Dolores Quinn told us how she and her husband of fourteen years were true blue Dubs. Both were proud Northsiders. That is, they were born and reared on the rough northside of Dublin's River Liffey. They moved down to Tallaght a decade earlier when they were expecting their second child.

"Terry was workin' as a welder at the time. Back then I hadn't a clue about his involvement with the I.R.A. and I hadn't until the Special Branch came for him."

Officially, it was the Special Detective Unit, the main domestic security agency of the *An Garda Síochána,* that is, the national police force. They were commonly referred to as Special Branch, though, as they were under the British. The unit's primary purpose was to combat the I.R.A., and as Callaghan would say, suppress any Republican activity in the Irish Republic.

The door swung open, and the two Quinn brothers came running in. Dolores introduced me to the copper-haired boys. There was Derek, aged twelve, and pudgy, grinning Barry, aged nine.

Their mother went to freshen up and get dressed, as we were going out for drinks – or as Dolores put it, "out for a gargle" – with the Boyles, close friends and neighbors of the Quinns. Sonny Boyle was the son of Mrs. Boyle in Belfast.

"D'you want to see our pony?" asked Barry, enthusiastically.

"Not me," said Callaghan. "I've seen your pony more than a couple of times already."

Young Barry turned to me hopefully.

"Lead the way, boys!" I eagerly replied, with a wink at Callaghan. "I can't remember the last time I had a good look at a real Irish pony."

I was soon out behind the houses, in a grassy field with junk strewn around. Amid old tires and a rusting stove, were a bunch of kids leading by a rope a skinny, spotted gray pony with a long shaggy mane and tail.

"He's a Connemara pony," said Derek. "We got him from a Sligo man. Sure, Chancer – that's his name – was nothin' but skin and bones."

"Half dead, he was," added the freckled-faced boy, holding the rope around Chancer's neck and gently stroking his nose.

"We've been feedin' him and fattin' him up, so we have," said a cheerful Barry. "Soon Chancer will be strong enough to ride."

"He's a feckin' brilliant pony!" exclaimed a girl of about ten, in pigtails with two missing front teeth.

The freckled-faced boy ran, and the pony trotted behind him. The other kids ran after them, and I got talked into giving the little pigtailed girl a piggyback ride. Next, it was young Barry Quinn's turn, only he was nowhere as light as the girl. He was a fat boy and I strained under his weight as I ran with him on my back through the field.

"Giddy-up! giddy-up!" shouted Barry. "Hi-yo, Silver! Faster, faster!"

And faster I ran with Barry – until suddenly my foot slipped in a mound of shit and I fell to the ground with the boy. Neither of us were hurt but we found ourselves covered in the stuff, to the riotous laughter of Derek and the other kids.

It was getting dark, and I returned with the boys to the Quinn house for a wash-up and a change of clothes. Afterwards, I accompanied Callaghan and Dolores on the short walk around the corner to the Boyles.

A stout man of about forty, with a couple of days of gray stubble on his mug, asked us in. There was a tough and menacing look about him, despite his hair being styled in a comical Beatles-like bowl cut with bangs and his wearing a gaudy green and red Christmas sweater with prancing reindeer.

"I'm Sonny Boyle," he said, more as a statement than as a greeting.

Callaghan, he knew. I provided my name, and Sonny told me he knew who I was.

"Enough jawin' about, boys," declared Sonny's wife, Alice, "let's be off."

She was a heavyset woman with short, wavy black hair and red lipstick. Like her husband, she was from the Falls Road area of Belfast.

It was about a ten-minute walk to the local pub. There was a good-sized crowd, but we were able to get a table. The women immediately lit up cigarettes and Sonny called for drinks for us. Pints of Guinness with a Coke for Callaghan.

Sonny Boyle had spent a stint in Long Kesh due to his I.R.A. involvement in Belfast. After his release from prison, he said, he continued to face harassment from Crown forces and moved down to "the Free State" with his family.

In Tallaght, Sonny became a Sinn Féin party activist still fighting, as he put it, "for the reunification of Ireland and the establishment of a thirty-two county democratic socialist Republic through peaceful, political means, or…" He lowered his voice to a conspiratorial whisper, "or by any other fuckin' means."

Sonny smiled darkly as a barmaid set our pints down on the table. When she left, he brought his pint up to his lips and concluded, "and see the backs of the fuckin' Brits," before taking a generous swallow of the black stuff.

The women were puffing their cigarettes and excitedly chattering away about some television program that had them enthralled. While I drank my Guinness and Callaghan his Coke, Sonny indicated we should give an ear to the conversation at the next table.

We listened as two young men enthusiastically told their two female companions about how they regularly fired mortars at Brit patrols.

"We'd massacre whole bloody lorries full of 'em," said one.

"And any Brit soldiers still livin' ye'd hear cryin' for their mammies," said the other loudly, as they all howled with laughter.

It was quite the performance. The two guys were in their twenties and had Northern accents. But what they were saying, no I.R.A. man would ever say in a public place.

"Lads from Tyrone," said Sonny, in a low, amused voice. "Neither of them boyos was ever in the Ra. They're just spinnin' tales to impress a couple of local girls."

Sonny reached into his sweater and pulled out a green pack of Major cigarettes.

"Can't bloody blame 'em though" he added, lighting a smoke. "Who wouldn't want to be a rough, tough Provie – even if its only in one's overly fertile imagination. Isn't that right, Tim?"

Not a peep of a reply came out of Callaghan, as he was seemingly absorbed in the conversation at the next table. Sonny shrugged at me with a knowing smile, and I ordered us another round of pints.

"I've heard tell," he said, "ye're a pipe smoker."

"Yeah, I prefer a bowl of good tobacco over these," indicating the cigarette I held in my hand.

Sonny remarked he'd fancy a puff or two on the ould pipe himself if I had it handy and wouldn't mind. I took out the briar from my jacket pocket along with my tobacco pouch and packed a bowl full for him. As Sonny couldn't manage to get the pipe lit with his lighter, I fired it up and passed it back to him.

The women laughed as Sonny held the pipe between his teeth and tried to look sophisticated.

"Jaysus, Sonny," said his wife, "if ye only had the beard, they'd be takin' ye for Gerry Adams!"

We all laughed. The rough, tough Provie looked nothing like the tall, bearded, pipe smoking, bespectacled Sinn Féin president. Then Sonny took too long and hard of a draw from my pipe and began having a coughing fit, to the great amusement of the women. Half choking with his eyes streaming, he hastily shoved the pipe across the table at me.

"You best stick to the fags," chuckled Dolores.

"Aye, ye're fuckin' right, I will!"

No doubt about it, pipe smoking is an acquired taste, requiring some patience. As I got up to go to the loo, as the john was locally called, Alice Boyle was still cackling over her husband's discomfit.

A couple of guys exited the gents' room as I entered. I had my choice of the row of urinals on the wall and went to the one farthest from the door. No sooner had I begun to relieve myself, when a tall man in a suit entered and passed each urinal until he turned to use the one beside me. This was breaking an unspoken but universally practiced rule. Whenever possible a guy puts as much distance between himself and another guy when at a row of urinals. Unless he wasn't a normal, regular guy, meaning he was some sort of a pervert.

I recalled the time when I was about nineteen in the men's room at Manhattan's Penn Station, when a guy who came to stand at the urinal beside mine tried to make a grab at me. Fortunately, I was quicker and laid the perv out on the tiled floor before he ever touched me.

I took a quick glance over at the guy now standing next to me to see if he was eyeing me. He wasn't. Clean-cut in his early forties, in a tailored gray suit with shiny black shoes, he was softly whistling to himself. Then he stopped.

"You really ought to find yourself some better friends, Yank."

He said nothing more and departed before I could think of a response.

When I returned to our table, I related what happened in the loo. "That was Special Branch," said Sonny. "Britain's lackeys."

We were silent for a moment, letting the significance of my encounter sink in.

"I think it was Brendan Behan," commented Callaghan, "who called Dublin's Special Branch 'gombeen men lured down from the mountains of Kerry by the smell of fresh meat.'"

"Ah, aye…right, Tim," replied Sonny at length, with a strange look on his face.

"Are you sure, luv, that's just Coke you been drinkin' there?" teased Dolores, trying to hide the smile on her lips, as she lit another cigarette.

Out in the night air, as we walked back from the pub, the conversation wasn't about the Special Branch, or any possible connection they had to Callaghan's corrupt gombeen men, or even the Republican struggle for a free and united Ireland. One of the women had brought up a more immediate and urgent local concern.

"We got a war on drugs in Tallaght," declared Alice.

"Heroin was first introduced to Dublin by Larry Dunne in the late '70's," explained Dolores. "He's long been a notorious criminal here and became the country's first drug lord."

"A fuckin' toerag is what he is," spat Sonny. "The I.R.A. should have taken him out years ago."

"Well, they didn't," continued Dolores, "and Larry Dunne and his brothers became major heroin dealers. It spread from Dublin to the surroundin' suburbs by the early '80's, in areas where there was already high unemployment, crime, and anti-social behavior."

"When it rains, it pours," said Alice.

"And Tallaght," went on Dolores, "like so many communities, faced the scourge of heroin addiction. People were dyin' in our streets. And kids - just kids! - were becomin' heavy users of heroin. Holy Mother of God, who would've thought!"

"Often youngsters become drug pushers to support their own addiction," added Alice. "A boy of just thirteen years of age was caught sellin' bags of heroin for five pounds a day. Two of me nephews were junkies. One is now dead and the other in prison."

"Me own sister died with a needle in her arm," said Dolores. "The whole bloody area was saturated with heroin and the guards were doin' feckin' bugger-all about it."

"Peelers only act when it suits 'em," remarked Sonny.

"So, we organized as parents determined to save our kids and stamp out drugs," said Alice. "We called ourselves Concerned Parents Against Drugs and set out to stop dealers from operatin' in housing estates. We'd march as a group on the homes of known drug pushers, who were makin' money off of killin' our kids. Some of us, like Dolores and meself, were young mothers with weans in prams, and we'd chant with everyone else: 'Pushers beware. Addicts we care. Pusher, pusher, pusher! Out out out!'"

"And if the scum didn't get the message," said Sonny, "we'd put 'em out. We'd kick in their fuckin' doors, toss their furniture out in the garden, and run 'em out of the estates."

There were concerns for the safety of anti-drug activists when threats of retaliation began to be made by drug gangs. Then the local I.R.A. put out a warning: "Any drug dealer who interferes with any community activists or Concerned Parents Against Drugs will be severely dealt with."

The campaign didn't completely purge Tallaght of drug dealers, though, and the community was still plagued by heroin addiction.

"Three years ago," began Sonny, lighting a cigarette as we walked, "our fifteen-year-old daughter was raped on her way home from school, in the field just behind where we live."

His voice was filled with emotion. "A seventeen-year-old junkie done it. Me and Terry later got the heap of shite in the same field and fixed it that he'll never be makin' any babies."

I asked no questions and Sonny Boyle provided no further details. But I could well imagine him with Terry Quinn, holding down the badly beaten boy who raped his daughter, and Sonny putting a gun between his legs and pulling the trigger.

"Well, cheerio and goodnight!" said Alice, as she and Sonny continued on to their house and we turned to follow Dolores up the short path to her door.

When the Boyles were out of earshot, Dolores remarked how terribly they had suffered.

"And not just here, on account of what that bastard did to their daughter," she said. "A number of years ago, back when they were livin' in Belfast, their little son was run over and killed in the street by a British Army Land Rover. They believe it was deliberate."

Dolores had already prepared her sons' bunk beds upstairs for Callaghan and me and told the boys to sleep downstairs on the sectional sofa. We found Derek there wrapped in a blanket, a pillow under his head, and sound asleep. But his younger brother, Barry, was seated beside him, munching away at a big bowl of popcorn, and watching an old black and white movie on TV.

Dolores was annoyed he wasn't sleeping at that late hour and insisted that he immediately turn off the telly. Barry pleaded with his mother as only a nine-year-old could.

"Ah mam, let me just finish the oul film…it's almost over…we don't often have visitors…like it's a special occasion…maybe they wanna see it cause it's an American film, please mam…it's a classic, like."

Dolores relented. "Just be sure, Barry, the bloody thing's off once the film's over!"

"Oh, I will, mam," he answered, beaming.

I said I'd stay up and watch with him. As I sat down next to Barry on the sofa, he offered me some of his popcorn, with a big grin on his face. His battle won; Barry turned back to watching his World War II flick. I filled my pipe for a smoke, as a youthful Gregory Peck appeared on screen in a flight suit and a pilot's leather flying cap.

"Were you ever in the military?" asked Barry.

"Oh, aye," I replied, without thinking. "I was once a sailor."

"Is 'aye' how you say 'yes' in America?" he asked.

I realized my speech was picking up a few Irishisms, or rather Northern Irishisms, as "aye" is an example of a Scots word brought over to Ulster by the planters, and therefore not often heard in southern Ireland. But I told young Barry that "aye" was an old nautical term that I picked up in my navy days, "aye aye, sir," as we sailors put it.

"Me uncle is a soldier in the Irish Army," said Barry, "but we never see him anymore. Me da says he's a traitor cause he's a Free Stater in league with the Brits. Me da says the only legitimate army Ireland has is the I.R.A."

I couldn't tell the boy his father was wrong; however, I didn't want him to think his uncle was a traitor either.

"Sometimes, Barry, two men can be equally patriotic, but express the love they have for their country in different ways."

The movie ended and with the TV turned off, Barry stretched out on the sofa under his blanket to sleep with his brother, while I headed upstairs to join Callaghan.

I found my pal sitting up on the upper bunk scribbling away in his notebook.

"What'd you watch?" he asked, without looking up.

"*Twelve O'Clock High,* starring Gregory Peck."

"Did you know," Callaghan asked, after a few moments of silence, "that Gregory Peck was born in San Diego and his grandmother was an Ashe from County Kerry? She was related to Thomas Ashe - a leader in the 1916 Easter Rising - who died a martyr's death from being force-fed while on hunger strike."

I shook my head in disbelief. Callaghan had a one-track mind, which never strayed far from Ireland's noble cause and her heroes.

"No, I can honestly say, I've never made a study of Gregory Peck's pedigree."

CHAPTER THIRTY-FOUR
THE PATRIOT GAME

Come all ye young rebels, and list while I sing
For the love of one's country is a terrible thing
It banishes fear with the speed of a flame
And it makes us all part of the patriot game

My name is O'Hanlon, and I've just turned sixteen
My home is in Monaghan, where I was weaned
I learned all my life cruel England's to blame
So now I'm part of the patriot game

It's nearly two years since I wandered away
With the local battalion of the bold I.R.A.
I read of our heroes, and I wanted the same
To play out my part in the patriot game

The O'Hanlon in the song was young Fergal O'Hanlon, who died from his wounds, along with the celebrated I.R.A. leader Seán South (immortalized in a song of his own), following their flying column's attack on a R.U.C. barracks in a County Fermanagh village on New Year's Day 1957.

I always thought of Mr. O'Hanlon – that is, Tom O'Hanlon – who I knew as a boy, and also hailed from County Monaghan, whenever I heard "The Patriot Game," written by Dominic Behan, brother of the famous writer Brendan. But I began to associate the song too with Tim Callaghan, who so desperately wanted to play his own part in the Patriot Game.

That afternoon Callaghan and I walked over to see Sonny Boyle, as they had "some I.R.A. business" to discuss.

"So, Sonny's still an active volunteer?"

"He's higher up than that," replied Callaghan, in a tone suggesting I should be as impressed as he was. "Sonny's an I.R.A. commander."

He opened the door when we knocked and ushered us in. Still unshaven, Sonny wore another holiday-themed sweater with little Christmas trees and snowflakes. We entered a sparse room with a single couch, beside a coffee table stacked with piles of Sinn Féin pamphlets and *An Phoblacht/ Republican News* papers. I recalled Sonny worked at the local Sinn Féin office. The walls were mostly bare, except for an engraved mirror hanging on one wall commemorating the ten H-Block hunger strikers. I wondered if Terry Quinn made it in Portlaoise Prison.

In front of a TV set sat a boy of about fourteen in a gray tracksuit with blue stripes down the sides. Alice Boyle mentioned them having a son that age named Rory.

Sonny cast an eye in his direction and barked, "Up and out – now!"

The boy duly got up and headed upstairs. His father went and turned off the television.

"All his time spent in front of the bloody telly," he grumbled.

Sonny intended for us to talk there, but then decided it would be best to take the conversation outside.

"Bugs have been planted by the Special Branch in the homes of Republican activists," he explained once we were outside. "Yez must always mind what yez say and where yez say it."

We walked to the nearby field where the day before I ran with young Barry on my back and slipped in a mound of shit. There was no sign of the Connemara pony, Chancer, but a bunch of kids played in the distance around the old rusty stove.

Standing in the open chilly field, the I.R.A. commander scratched the gray stubble on his chin, lit a cigarette, and got down to business with Callaghan.

"Now, we're not seekin' any rocket launchers, AK-47s, Uzis, or Armalites," began Sonny. "Though if yez happen to have any of those handy, sure, we'd put 'em to bloody good use. But at the moment, we're havin' a tremendous problem gettin' our hands on small firearms, scanners, and even walkie-talkies."

Since the days of the Fenians, Irish Republicans have looked to foreign lands, especially to America, where so many of their countrymen had gone, for assistance with acquiring weapons and supplies for their armed struggle to wrench their native isle out of England's grasp.

In 1867, a sailing ship left New York bound for Ireland loaded down with guns and ammunition and manned by a crew of Irish-American veterans of the U.S. Civil War. They called their vessel *Erin's Hope,* as they hoped to help in the Fenian Rising in Ireland. But to their bitter disappointment, they failed in their mission. The British Navy prevented them from delivering their precious cargo to their waiting comrades on the Irish shore.

Over the next hundred years, many others tried to run guns into Ireland. Some were as equally unsuccessful as *Erin's Hope*. Sir Roger Casement immediately comes to mind. The Dublin-born British diplomat turned Irish patriot attempted to land thousands of rifles on the Kerry coast from a German ship in time for the 1916 Easter Rising. But the ship was captured, and her cargo of arms were scuttled. Casement, who followed by submarine, was arrested by the Royal Irish Constabulary when he landed and was later hanged in London.

Others were more fortunate. Another cache of German rifles was successfully smuggled into Howth harbor, near Dublin, in broad daylight on a private yacht and were used in the Easter Rising. The pleasure vessel belonged to the writer Erskine Childers, author of *The Riddle of the Sands,* and his American wife. Although born in England and raised in Ireland's County Wicklow as part of the Protestant Ascendancy, Childers became committed to the cause of Irish independence. During the Civil War, he took the anti-Treaty Republican side and was executed by the Free State government.

By the early 1970's, the Provisional Irish Republican Army had found a new ally in Gaddafi's Libya. The Arab North African state had become the sworn enemy of the Western world, especially the United States and her close ally, Britain. At the time, Colonel Gaddafi was the main Muslim sponsor of international terrorism. The ruthless Libyan dictator viewed the I.R.A. as a comrade-in-arms in his fight against British imperialism. I suppose it was a matter of "the enemy of my enemy is my friend."

Joe Cahill served as commander of the Provisional I.R.A. Belfast Brigade and became the I.R.A.'s chief of staff and was in charge of importing arms. He made visits to Tripoli, the Libyan capital, and met with Gaddafi.

In 1973, three Irish Navy ships intercepted a steamer called *The Claudia*, off the Waterford coast. Cahill was in the process of smuggling over five tons of weapons from Libya. All of which were promptly seized by Irish military authorities. One of the officers commented to Cahill that he must have felt it was hard luck that the cargo didn't get through.

"I said it was hard luck, all right," recalled the veteran Republican, a decade later in a newspaper interview. "But I told them the point is that the only time you know that we have hard luck is when you capture the stuff. They don't know about the successful trips that you have."

At his trial, Cahill declared from the dock: "All my life I have believed passionately in the freedom of my country. I believe it is the God-given right of the people of Ireland to determine their own destinies without foreign interference and, in pursuit of these aims and ideals, it is my proud privilege as a soldier of the Irish Republican Army, just as I believe it is the duty of every Irish person, to serve or assist the I.R.A. in driving the British occupation forces from our shores.

"If I am guilty of any crime, it is that I did not succeed in getting the contents of *The Claudia* into the hands of the freedom fighters in this country."

But Sonny Boyle wasn't suggesting that Callaghan boldly sail to Ireland on a ship laden with arms. What he was proposing was Callaghan send single handguns and whatever communication devices needed by the I.R.A. through the mail once he returned to America.

"First, ye'll need to obtain a private post office box under a false name."

"How's about Tadhg Fallon? asked an excited Callaghan. "My mother's people were Fallons from County Offaly. Maybe, Tadhg O'Fallon."

"Ah Jaysus, no!" replied Sonny, with a laugh. "Nothin' that Irish and nothin' that could ever be traced back to ye. Use a neutral soundin' English name."

Pausing to light another cigarette, he continued, "Like, when I contact ye, I'll be Rose – which as yez know, is me ma's name. I used to know a Derry man called Paddy English. Terrible quare name that, for an Irishman and a Republican. But I'll be callin' meself in all me correspondence with ye, Miss Rose English."

Somehow it was difficult to imagine Sonny – the menacing, rough, tough Provie with a hard mug in the need of a shave – as an English Rose.

"Now, what we need are proper code words," he said. "That way I can put pen to paper and place a wee order and ye in turn can tell us what to expect in yer next wee parcel."

"Harry for handgun," offered Callaghan.

"Aye, that'll work," said Sonny. "And Bill for bullets. Ye'd write out something like, 'Harry and Bill are on their way to visit dear ould Ireland.' Meanin' ye've sent us a short with bullets. Now, a walkie-talkie, we'll call Willie Thompson, and a scanner…em… Scanlon, Mrs. Scanlon."

"Got it all locked in here," answered Callaghan, tapping his forefinger to his flaming red head."

Sonny said he had to be off to meet his brother. After he left, Callaghan and I strolled around the near empty streets of Killinarden housing estate. We paused to watch a young boy playing with a small dog in a patch of grass in front of one of the beige stucco rowhouses.

"A few years ago," began Callaghan, "the top I.R.A. gunrunner in America was an old Irish guy in Brooklyn named George Harrison. He had been active since the Border Campaign in the 1950's and when the Troubles began in the Six Counties, Harrison became the I.R.A.'s main supplier of arms. This guy sent everything he could lay his hands on – handguns, Armalites, Bazookas. Over a period of thirty years, he shipped more than three thousand weapons and one million rounds of ammunition. Most of it left America from the Brooklyn docks. George Harrison had people leaving on ships who smuggled the stuff over to Ireland."

"Is that where John, Paul, and Ringo came in?" I asked.

"What are you, a smart-ass now? I'm serious here!"

"You always are, Callaghan."

My humorless, thin-skinned pal stormed off in a huff.

I was familiar, of course, with the gunrunner George Harrison's story, as it got a lot of coverage in *The Irish Echo* and other papers back in the early 1980's.

Born in a small village in County Mayo, in 1915, Harrison was from a Republican family. He was a small boy during the War of Independence, but he well remembered the night his parents' cottage was raided by the Black and Tans, and how he was roughly thrown into a corner for wearing a green sweater. At sixteen, he joined the local I.R.A., but the East Mayo Brigade never saw action.

While life was hard all across Ireland, it was a particular penance in the grinding poverty of the bleak and rock-strewn soil of the West. After crossing the Irish Sea to earn a few pounds to send home laboring on English farms, Harrison made the longer voyage across the Atlantic. He saw America as a place he could succeed and as a place, he said, where he "could do a lot for the Irish cause."

Harrison served in the U.S. Army in the Pacific during the Second World War, then returned to where he had settled in Brooklyn and found employment as a Brinks armored car guard. It was a job he held for thirty-six years. A lifelong bachelor, George Harrison joined several Irish-American socialist organizations in New York. Through one, he became close friends and comrades with another Irish immigrant and I.R.A. veteran, Liam Cotter, from County Kerry. Harrison got him a job as an armored car guard with Purolator Security Company.

Both men remained committed to seeing a united Irish Republic and believed militant physical force – opposed to electoral politics – was the best means to achieve this goal, and "to drive the Brits out, lock, stock and barrel." Together they became gunrunners extraordinaire.

Harrison got most of the weapons they sent to the I.R.A. from an old neighbor in Brooklyn, an Italian with connections to the Mafia, who operated a gun store just outside the city. From the early 1970's, Harrison and his arms network supplied the I.R.A. with between two to three hundred weapons a year. The weapons were quickly put to use in Ireland. Between 1970 and 1974, 285 British soldiers and members of the R.U.C. were killed, most were slain by the I.R.A. and many by the guns sent by Harrison and Cotter.

In 1976, Liam Cotter and another armed guard working for Purolator were ambushed by four gunmen when they arrived at a Times Square theater to pickup the weekend's receipts. Cotter and the other guard were shot dead.

Five years later, in 1981, sixty-six-year-old George Harrison was arrested, with four other Irishmen, including seventy-eight-year-old Michael Flannery, a founder of NORAID, and charged with arms-trafficking. The prosecutor called them terrorists committed to achieving the goal of a united Ireland through acts of violence. Harrison, described as their ringleader, said they "were not terrorists but patriots – Irish patriots and patriotic Americans as well." In their years in the United States, they had honorably served in the nation's military in World War II, Korea, and Vietnam. But they would never turn their backs on the land of their birth. To shorten the story, all five were acquitted.

As the verdict was read in the packed federal courthouse in downtown Brooklyn, one hundred supporters of the defendants erupted with thunderous cheers and applause.

"Up the Provos!" shouted George Harrison, the unrepentant Irish Republican.

American-born Irish have also played their part in the Patriot Game. Callaghan had closely followed the more recent case of the Boston Three, who were convicted in 1990 with assisting to develop surface-to-air missile technology for the I.R.A. to shoot down British Army helicopters in Northern Ireland. The Boston Three included two Americans and an Irishman.

Richard Johnson, a forty-one-year-old Connecticut native living in New Hampshire, was a highly trained electrical engineer for a major U.S. military contractor. His maternal grandparents were from Kerry and Cork, and he made his first trip to Ireland when in his twenties.

After striking up friendships with people who had I.R.A. connections, he became committed to the Irish Republican cause. He was reported as saying: "After being in the North of Ireland and seeing what was happening there, I was certainly sympathetic to people trying to defend themselves." Johnson was given a sentence of ten years and sent to a federal prison in Ray Brook, New York.

Christina Reid, a twenty-six-year-old Californian, had only recently graduated as an electrical engineer from San Francisco State University when she was arrested by F.B.I agents at her first engineering job. With Johnson, she shared an interest in Irish history, language, literature, and culture, and was fervently passionate about Irish freedom. Chris Reid was convicted of working with Johnson on I.R.A. projects and serving as a courier of electronic components for remote-control bombs that were sent to Northern Ireland. She was sentenced to three years and five months in a federal prison, which held female inmates, in California's Dublin – a city ironically named after the Irish capital, near San Francisco.

The Irishman was Martin Quigley, aged twenty-seven, from Dundalk, just south of the border with Northern Ireland. Before arriving in the United States in 1989, he spent six years as a computer specialist in Dublin. According to the F.B.I., Quigley was operating as an agent for the I.R.A. A search of his home in the Lehigh Valley region of Pennsylvania, turned up rockets in various stages of development, and technical data on rockets and British helicopters. Quigley was sentenced to eight years and sent to a federal prison in McKean County, Pennsylvania.

Callaghan had exchanged a few letters with Richard Johnson and Chris Reid.

The Boston Three was a high-profile case, as was George Harrison and his co-defendants', but there were so many lesser-known cases of Irish-Americans who played a part in the Patriot Game.

Among them was my Brooklyn-born cousin, Ronnie Dugan. He first visited Ireland on his honeymoon in the 1970's and spent time in the British-occupied North at the height of the Troubles. The trip left a deep impression on him and filled him with an intense pride in his Irish heritage. (He even toyed with the idea of assuming the Gaelic form of his surname, Ó Dubhagáin.)

Ronnie kept up with current events in Northern Ireland, even as he moved his family from New York to Colorado in 1981. That was the year ten Republican prisoners died on hunger strike in the H-Blocks of Long Kesh. As brave Irishmen sacrificed their lives for their principles and the I.R.A. continued their armed struggle for a free and united Ireland, it was hard for Ronnie to stand idly by.

My cousin knew an Irishman connected with the I.R.A. in Colorado, and together they attempted to raise money to purchase guns for the war against British forces. Unfortunately for them, their fundraising activities (which netted a paltry $200) involved a stolen ATM card that they used at an automated teller machine. Their photos were taken by surveillance camera and police arrested Ronnie and his accomplice in late 1983.

The Irishman was illegally in the United States and was already under investigation by the F.B.I. for gunrunning. But Ronnie at forty-six years old had no outstanding warrants and he was released on bail. He was placed on probation for three years and had to complete fifty hours of community service and pay the court a total of $690.

By 1988, Ronnie was stricken by Huntington's disease. Within three years, he was confined to a bed in a nursing home. My cousin remained proud of his attempt to strike a small blow against England for Irish freedom and spent his final days listening to sad Irish rebel songs on cassette tapes, as tears rolled down his cheeks. Ronnie Dugan died at the age of sixty-two.

Come all ye young rebels, and list while I sing
For the love of one's country is a terrible thing
It banishes fear with the speed of a flame
And it makes us all part of the patriot game

My name is Ronnie Dugan and
My true home is in Ireland, where I long to be...

CHAPTER THIRTY-FIVE
PORTLAOISE AND TERRY QUINN

On Monday morning, we piled into the Quinns' blue Ford Sierra for the short drive to the local Sinn Féin office to catch the bus to Portlaoise Prison. The kids were excited about our visit with their father, and Dolores allowed them to skip school for the day to accompany us. Callaghan crammed into the back seat with Derek, Barry, and little Lizzie, while I slid in the passenger seat beside Dolores.

"Smokers ride up front," she said, lighting a cigarette, as she started the engine. Without turning my head, I heard Callaghan roll down his back window to let out the smoke.

The Sinn Féin minibus that took us from Tallaght down to Portlaoise was filled with women and children. Again, I was seated beside Dolores, who puffed away at another cigarette. Looking out the bus window, I saw a field with a number of beat-up trailers and garbage strewn all around. There were kids running around and a few ponies could be seen.

"That's one of our tinker caravans," said Dolores. "They call 'em travellers now, y'know, but for me they'll always be tinkers."

"They're a bunch of feckin' knackers, if youse ask me," cut in a fat woman across the aisle.

"Well, God help 'em," said another woman. "They've a hard enough life."

The drive down to Portlaoise was about an hour. The maximum-security prison was situated on the town's Dublin Road. Built during the Georgian era and opened in 1830 as Maryborough Jail, it predated Belfast's Victorian Crumlin Road Jail by at least fifteen years. In 1929, it was renamed Portlaoise Prison, after the town.

We approached the entrance gate. Surrounded by a high fence, topped by billows of barbed wire, were the even higher, gray cut-stone walls of the prison. With its medieval-looking watchtowers, it resembled a grim Norman castle.

Callaghan turned around in the seat in front of us. "It was nearly twenty years ago," he remarked, "that nineteen Republican prisoners blew a hole through the gate here and escaped."

"I well remember it," said Dolores. "I was still in secondary school at the time. But it was all in the news. The prisoners overpowered the screws in the main cell block and climbed out onto a low roof and ran across the prison grounds. By the governor's residence they placed an explosive charge at a gate leadin' to the prison walls. Another charge was then set at an iron doorway and within seconds the men were outside. After a hundred-yard mad dash through the fields and bushes, the bold escapees reached Borris Road. There they commandeered cars and quickly disappeared."

The fat woman across from us, who overheard Dolores's account, began to sing.

> *There's nineteen men a-missing, and they didn't use the door.*
> *Just blew a little hole, where there wasn't one before.*
> *Now the army and the gardaí are searching high and low*
> *For the men from Portlaoise prison, who have vanished like the snow.*
>
> *On the eighteenth day of August, in the good year '74*
> *A blast occurred in Portlaoise town, that was heard through every door.*
> *And when the smoke and dust had cleared, there rose a mighty cheer,*
> *From those within who helped to plan the jailbreak of the year...*

The minibus stopped and there was a call for everyone to get out. Dolores and I followed Callaghan and the kids. We were subjected to the same search as at Long Kesh. Then we followed a guard through several heavy metal doors, each manned by its own guard, to a "visitors' cabin." In Portlaoise, unlike at Long Kesh, each prisoner had visits in a room of his own, furnished with a table, several chairs, and complete with its own guard, or screw, who generally sat in the corner reading a newspaper or magazine during the visit.

Terry Quinn was a well-built man of medium height in his midthirties. Clean-shaven with his balding, reddish-brown hair cut military short, he wore a crew-neck burgundy sweater and jeans. Callaghan and I were greeted with a firm handshake, before Terry hugged in turn his anxiously awaiting boys and giggling little daughter, then briefly embraced his wife.

Two years earlier, Terry Quinn was convicted of being part of the I.R.A. active service unit which attempted a bank heist armed with sawn-off shotguns and handguns. But after one of their comrades was shot in the ensuing gun battle with local gardaí, the other would-be bank robbers threw down their weapons and surrendered. Terry, who had previously served three years in Portlaoise for a firearms conviction, received a twelve-year prison sentence.

Funding for the armed struggle was very expensive and the I.R.A. was not averse to robbing the odd bank. After all, as the infamous Irish-American bank robber Willie Sutton once told a reporter who asked him why he robbed banks, "Because that's where the money is."

After talking with Derek and Barry about school and minding what their mother told them, Terry told me what brought him as a Dubliner into the armed struggle being waged in the North.

"As Tim here knows, I'm not from a Republican background. I'm from a typical, large workin'-class family from the northside of Dublin. Me father was a binman and we were too busy beatin' off poverty to give any thought to fightin' the Brits ninety miles away up in Belfast.

"We're still proudly workin'-class. But mostly tradesmen now. I've got one brother who's a plumber, another who's a plasterer, two others employed as house painters, and our sister's married to a window installer. Meself, I'm a welder by trade. As James Connolly said, 'Rise with yer class, not out of it.'

"Although our parents had no strong political views," he continued, with little Lizzie dangling from his knee, "we always had the basic belief that Ireland belonged to the Irish. And Ireland is one nation, not two, and shouldn't be divided. And that's as far as me thinkin' went for many years. I had never ventured into the Six Counties, and I'm ashamed to say I gave that corner of the country very little thought.

"Of course, like everybody else in Dublin, I had heard of Bloody Sunday and how the Brits harassed and shot dead our people in the Six Counties and the Loyalists there were slaughterin' any Catholic they could lay their hands on, claimin' they were all I.R.A.

"But what changed it for me was the hunger strike of '81. You can say the scales fell from me eyes. All Ireland took notice then what was happenin' in the H-Blocks. Here were young Irishmen from workin'-class families, like me own, who were prepared to starve themselves to death in a non-violent protest over the British lie that Irishmen and women fightin' against British oppression in Ireland were nothin' but common criminals. One after another, they willingly gave up their lives to be recognized as political prisoners, or prisoners of war.

"Now lots of Dubs don't give two damns about anything that has to do with our people in the Six Counties…"

"If you can believe it," interrupted Dolores, "some of 'em think it's an entirely different country up there."

"I was born in, and am a citizen of, the so-called Republic of Ireland," said Terry Quinn. "But this is a sham republic. This partitioned twenty-six county state is not the all-Ireland thirty-two county sovereign independent Republic proclaimed in the 1916 Proclamation and ratified by the First Dáil Éireann in 1919. It's not the Irish Republic so many have fought and died for – and are still fightin' and dyin' for."

"That was what the Civil War about, right Da?" asked Barry.

"That's right, son," answered Terry, with a proud smile.

"And instead of a genuine Republic," said Derek, "we got the Free State."

"As far as true Republicans are concerned," replied Terry, "'tis still the Free State."

Officially the Irish Free State ceased to exist when the Constitution of 1937 changed the name to Éire (or Ireland, in English). But the new state, like the Free State, remained within the British Commonwealth, symbolically subject to the king until 1949 when Éire left the Commonwealth and declared itself the Republic of Ireland.

Whatever the twenty-six county state called itself, though, there were those within it who denied its legitimacy and rightfully felt their fellow Catholic Nationalists in the North had been abandoned in a hostile, artificially created six-county Orange statelet set up by the British with "a Protestant parliament for a Protestant people."

"However, youse didn't come here for a lesson in Irish history," said Terry, his blue eyes looking from me to Callaghan. "I think both you lads are well-versed enough in our country's history and got a good understandin' of Ireland's struggle for freedom."

"But you're living it," I remarked.

"True enough, Ed," he replied. "In the words of me fellow Dubliner Pádraic Pearse: 'As long as Ireland is unfree the only attitude for Irishmen and Irishwomen is an attitude of revolt.'

"At the end of the day," continued Terry, "I got involved to try to put a stop to the ongoin' massacre of innocent Irish people in the Six Counties and to alleviate their sufferin'. For eight hundred years the Brits have tried but they can never beat a risen people. Now they use the Loyalists to do their dirty work, to murder our people in the streets, instill fear, and bring Catholics to their knees. The people stand fast though.

"The I.R.A is there to defend 'em and fight the Brits and their supporters until the last British soldier leaves our country. Until then we will continue to fill the jails and if necessary, we will give our lives for this land we call Ireland."

"Tiocfaidh ár lá agus beir bua!" exclaimed Callaghan. "Our day will come with victory!"

Despite everything Terry Quinn said, he maintained he was not politically minded.

"I do find it sometimes difficult to understand comrades when they tell me what they hope to bring about when we have a British withdrawal.

"One of the lads in here was tryin' to explain it all to me again just yesterday. He says Sinn Féin's political and economic policy is to bring about a thirty-two county socialist Republic. What he means is that Sinn Féin would ensure that the workin'-class would be in control of the wealth that it creates. This would mean takin' control out of the hands of the multinationals and runnin' industry and agriculture as far as possible under the democratic control of the workers and small farmers.

"The current situation shows that neither capitalism nor the type of bureaucratic socialism that existed in the U.S.S.R. work. Mass unemployment and a '30's style depression are becomin' the hallmarks of the world economy. A small country like Ireland can only survive in cooperation with other countries, but first it must have political and economic sovereignty. We can't have the first so long as the Brits are here, and we can't have the second if the wealth of the country is controlled by a small minority. Those who create that wealth, the workin'-class must control it.

"Well, that's the way the fella told me it would be. I honestly don't think the people of Ireland would give power or control to Sinn Féiners followin' a British withdrawal. But I'm not one to follow politics keenly. I usually let the politicians do their line of work and I do mine.

"When I joined the movement ten years ago it was purely to get the Brits out of our country. I'm still of the same mind and I really don't have much interest in the economy or anything else."

Dolores lit what must have been her fourth cigarette. Terry didn't smoke and I recalled his wife mentioning that he had been a chain smoker but had recently quit. I restrained from lighting up for his sake.

The children looked bored until Terry began to ask after their pony. Their faces instantly brightened, and the boys enthusiastically told their father how Chancer was gaining weight and strength.

"It's good for 'em to have a pony of their own," said Terry, turning to Callaghan and me. "As a lad, I was quite keen on ponies. They weren't an unusual sight then in Dublin streets."

"Even though it's the capital of Ireland," explained Dolores, "when we were comin' up in the '60's and into the '70's, coal and milk were still delivered by horse-drawn carts. Dublin was like a mix between city and country at the time. Jaysus, would youse believe, people still kept hens in their back gardens then."

"A few even had pigs," recalled Terry.

"Ah, Dublin in the rare oul times," I said in my best brogue, referring to the song made popular by The Dubliners.

My attempt at an Irish accent brought a laugh out of Dolores and a smile from Terry.

"Whilst the horses do be most sorely missed," remarked Terry, "none miss what they left steamin' piles of in the city streets."

"Ed here was able to find a heap of it in Tallaght without ever needin' to step into a city street," said Dolores, trying to suppress her laughter.

The conversation then turned to our night out with the Boyles, and Terry told us how Sonny and his brother, Bumpy, were two of his greatest friends in Tallaght. He added that he heard about our visits in Belfast to their mother.

"Mrs. Boyle is a grand woman altogether," he declared.

Callaghan and I agreed.

"Thanks a million for comin' with Dolores and the kids," said Terry, standing up to shake our hands, as our visit was at an end. "It does be a great boost for us in here when we get visits from good lads like yerselves."

CHAPTER THIRTY-SIX
IN DUBLIN'S FAIR CITY

"What got him a moniker like Bumpy?" I asked Callaghan, who interrupted my morning shave in the Quinns' bathroom to tell me he was going to meet with Sonny Boyle and his brother Bumpy.

"Hell, if I know," replied Callaghan. "Maybe he got it from bumping guys heads together or maybe he just prefers it over Eugene."

"If you ask me, Bumpy sounds like something kids call the ten-year-old bully in the schoolyard."

"Well, Audubon, I'm not asking you!" snapped Callaghan, getting his green shamrock-covered knickers in a twist again, as he stomped off to let me to finish my shaving in peace.

While I had agreed to spend another day in Tallaght, so Callaghan could receive further instructions in the fine art of smuggling weapons from the brothers Boyle, I planned to spend my day strolling along the River Liffey and visiting a few of Dublin's great old pubs.

A forty-five-minute bus ride brought me to the city center of Dublin. I stepped out on the southside of the river and was once again making my way along Grafton Street through the hustle and bustle of holiday shoppers and tourists. I heard the distinctive nasal accents of my fellow

Americans. A young boy and his father in matching Chicago Cubs baseball caps called to a mother and her teenage daughter peering into a clothing store window. A well-dressed couple walked by arm in arm, having an animated conversation in Italian. I passed an old, blind man in a dark overcoat and cap sitting in a chair playing an accordion outside a shopfront.

Above trendy, contemporary ground floor shops and boutiques could be seen the third- and fourth-floor levels of magnificent Georgian, Victorian, and Edwardian buildings. I looked at the attractive Art Deco neo-Egyptian façade of Bewley's Oriental Café. It seemed to be a popular place, judging by the steady stream of customers entering its doors. Across from the coffee shop, a guy in sunglasses and a gray fedora played jazz on a saxophone – a bit of New Orleans in Dublin – as people stopped to listen and toss coins into his basket.

Nearby was a recently placed black bronze statue of Molly Malone of "cockles and mussels" fame with her fishmonger wheelbarrow. Her ample buxom nearly popping out of her extremely low-cut 17th century dress caused locals to call her "the tart with the cart." There was a group of young people gathered around poor Molly taking pictures and making lewd remarks. I walked on half-humming her well-known song.

> *In Dublin's fair city,*
> *Where the girls are so pretty,*
> *I first set my eyes on sweet Molly Malone,*
> *As she wheeled her wheel-barrow,*
> *Through streets broad and narrow,*
> *Crying "Cockles and mussels, alive, alive, oh!"*
>
> *"Alive, alive, oh,*
> *Alive, alive, oh"*
> *Crying, "Cockles and mussels, alive, alive, oh."*
>
> *She was a fishmonger,*
> *But sure 'twas no wonder,*
> *For so were her father and mother before,*
> *And they each wheeled their barrow,*
> *Through streets broad and narrow,*
> *Crying, "Cockles and mussels, alive, alive oh!"*

She died of a fever,
And no one could save her,
And that was the end of sweet Molly Malone.
Now her ghost wheels her barrow,
Through streets broad and narrow,
Crying, "Cockles and mussels, alive, alive oh!"

"Alive, alive, oh,
Alive, alive, oh"
Crying, "Cockles and mussels, alive, alive, oh."

I was soon walking on crowded Nassau Street, along the south side of Trinity College, which was surrounded by an old stone wall with wrought-iron railings. According to what I read in my guidebook, Ireland's oldest and most prestigious university, founded in 1592, was officially the College of the Holy and Undivided Trinity of Queen Elizabeth near Dublin, since it was established outside the then city walls in the buildings of the outlawed Catholic Augustinian Priory of All Hallows.

For much of its history, the renowned institution was the university of the Protestant Ascendancy. Among those who passed through its doors and studied in its halls were: Jonathan Swift, the satirist, essayist, political pamphleteer, poet, Dean of Dublin's Anglican St. Patrick's Cathedral, and author of *Gulliver's Travels;* George Berkeley, the 18th century Church of Ireland bishop and philosopher; Oliver Goldsmith, the poet, playwright and novelist, who wrote *The Vicar of Wakefield*, along with other popular works; Edmund Burke, the great statesman, Irish parliamentary orator, author, political theorist and philosopher, remembered for championing Catholic emancipation; Henry Grattan, the politician, lawyer, and another celebrated orator in the late 18th century Irish parliament, who boldly demanded Ireland be recognized as an independent nation, though remaining under the British Crown; Theobald Wolfe Tone, patriot and martyr, and father of Irish Republicanism, who declared, "To break the connection with England, the never-failing source of all our political evils, and to assert the independence of my country – these were my objects," and was a founding member of the United Irishmen and leader of the Rising of 1798; Robert Emmet, another beloved patriot and executed leader of the Dublin Rising of 1803; Thomas Moore, the Bard of Ireland, one of the first Catholics admitted to Trinity College, who went on to become a poet, writer and balladeer, best remembered for "The Minstrel Boy" and "The Last Rose of Summer"; Thomas Davis, the writer and chief organizer and poet of the Young Ireland movement of the 1840's, which sought to unite all creeds and classes into a powerful national movement, and penned the patriotic verses of "A Nation Once Again"; Bram Stoker, the novelist and creator of *Dracula;* Oscar Wilde, the poet, playwright and novelist, best remembered for *The Picture of Dorian Gray* and *The Importance of Being Earnest;* Sir Edward Carson, the Dublin-born Unionist politician, barrister and judge, still revered by Ulster Unionists; John Redmond, another Catholic, a barrister and member of British Parliament, who was a Nationalist leader of the moderate Irish Parliamentary Party, and as leader of the Nationalist Volunteers encouraged Irishmen to fight for Britain in the First World War in the hopes of obtaining limited self-government for Ireland within the United Kingdom; Douglas Hyde, the distinguished Gaelic scholar and writer, who founded the Gaelic League, a Nationalist organization to revive the Irish language and culture, and was the first president of the Republic of Ireland; J.M. Synge, the playwright, poet and writer, best known for *The Playboy of the Western World;* and Samuel Beckett, the playwright, novelist and poet, who wrote *Waiting for Godot,* along with other acclaimed works, and was awarded the Nobel Prize for Literature in 1969, and was a resident of Paris most of his adult life and wrote in both French and English.

Have I forgotten any notable alumni? Undoubtedly, I have, but included more than enough to illustrate the importance of Trinity College to Irish culture and politics.

Heading up Westmoreland Street, I passed a handsome four-story classical Art Deco building, with a clock and carved Corinthian columns, topped by a cupola, across from the redeveloped Educational Chambers, curtained in ugly, dark reflective glass. At the corner, on my left, was the narrow, four-story stone office building of Coal Distributors Limited, and I turned onto cobblestoned Fleet Street, on the outskirts of the Temple Bar district. Farther on were rundown old brick buildings defaced by graffiti. Despite the heavy foot traffic, a guy in a shabby overcoat and a head of disheveled hair stood with his back to passersby urinating against a building.

Then there was the beautiful and inviting Victorian-era Palace Bar. I crossed the narrow street and strolled past the 19th century copper-topped lamppost outside the pub. Stepping inside was like going back in time, with its dark wooden interior, high altar-style mahogany backbar with Romanesque arches and mirrors rising to the lofty ceiling, stocked with bottles of every spirit imaginable. Along the long bar counter were tall, mirrored mahogany partitions with triangular pediment tops, set at regular intervals for some privacy. Long and narrow, the Palace Bar was magnificently cozy.

There was a good-sized crowd. A lot of the bar's patrons were men in suits and ties, who had the appearance of being office workers or government officials on their lunch break.

Sliding onto a stool at the bar, beside an old gent smoking a cigar with a pint of Guinness set in front of him, I ordered the same when the bald bartender, with a bullet-shaped head, in a black tie and white shirt, asked me what I'd have.

He soon returned with a glorious pint of the creamy black stuff. "A pint a stout…fit for drinkin'," declared the grinning bartender.

I took a large, thirsty gulp, emptying half the pint. I couldn't have hoped for a more delicious experience.

"Nothin' quite like a Guinness in Dublin, is there lad?" remarked the still grinning barman. "There's no disputin' the black nectar is Ireland's national treasure."

"That it is," I agreed.

I turned on my barstool to have a better look around. Light came filtering through the stained-glass front window, illuminating the backbar and high-vaulted ceiling. On the walls hung pictures of the celebrated Irish writers and journalists who used to drink in the old public house. It had an enchanting ambience. I noticed there was not a TV in sight, and I remembered I once heard somewhere that real Irish pubs were for drinking and talking – not for staring at screens. The bartender interrupted my thoughts.

"'When I first came to Dublin in 1939, I thought the Palace was the most wonderful temple of art,' so said Patrick Kavanagh, the powerful poet and novelist from the stony gray soil of County Monaghan."

Putting a fresh pint before me, the bartender launched into his monologue for tourists as I lit a cigarette.

"The Palace Bar was established in 1823. In the 1940's, '50's, and '60's it became the go-to pub for writers and newsmen. The longtime editor of *The Irish Times,* Bertie Smyllie, drank here, as did all the renowned scribblers of the day. I mentioned Mr. Kavanagh, also the acclaimed Flann O'Brien – or Myles na gCopaleen, as he wrote his columns under in the *Times,* whose real name was Brian O'Nolan – was another noted imbiber here. He was once found tryin' to hide in the telephone box durin' a police raid for after hours drinkin'. Samuel Beckett was a patron of the Palace as well. Often enough Dublin's wild broth of a boy, Brendan Behan, would stroll in to bend his elbow and sing a ballad or two or recite a poem. Brendan called himself a drinker with writing problems. The poet Austin Clarke was also known to have knocked back a few here. Séamus Heaney, the bard from the Derry bogland, still regularly ducks into the Palace for an odd jar."

The bartender went to attend to other customers. Reaching for another cigarette, I glanced over at the cigar smoker beside me. The smiling old gent, in a navy-blue peacoat, had an impressive silver handlebar mustache and a twinkle in his gray eyes.

"Personally, I always preferred the great Scottish adventure writer Robert Louis Stevenson," he said.

"He's long been a favorite of mine too," I admitted.

I went to light my cigarette when the old fellow pulled a cigar from his pocket and laid it on the bar.

"Here, lad, have a man's smoke."

The cigar band read "Cohiba." It was a nice-sized dark *maduro,* direct from Havana, Cuba.

I thanked him and lit up. Savoring the smoke, I found its flavor satisfyingly strong and intense.

"Now, that's a smoke!" I exclaimed.

His smile widened and he took a puff on his cigar. I called the bartender over to get us a couple of double whiskeys, neat, along with two more pints of Guinness, to go with the high-class stogies.

"Whiskey is liquid sunshine," I happily remarked, lifting my tumbler of John Jameson. The popular quote was from the famous Dublin-born playwright George Bernard Shaw.

"Indeed, 'tis," replied my companion, clinking his glass to mine. "And God knows gray oul Ireland certainly needs all the sunshine she can get."

We introduced ourselves and I shook the hand of Jack Carney, a born and bred Dubliner, and as I soon learned a resident for the past twenty years of Western Samoa in the South Pacific.

"We were talkin' about the man who penned such literary classics as *Treasure Island* and *Kidnapped*," he continued. "Do you know where Stevenson was laid to rest?"

I wrongly guessed the Edinburgh native was buried in Scotland.

"He spent his final days on Upolu, one of the Samoan islands, where he was beloved by the people," old Jack Carney informed me.

"The Samoans called him *'Tusitala'* – teller of tales – and when he died at the age of forty-four, in 1894, hundreds of sorrowful Samoans accompanied him to his grave, carryin' his coffin on their shoulders in relays to bury him just below the summit of Mount Vaea, overlookin' his house near the village of Vailima and the sea beyond. I've been there myself a number of times. Stevenson's 'Requiem' is inscribed on his tomb."

> *Under the wide and starry sky,*
> *Dig the grave and let me lie.*
> *Glad did I live and gladly die,*
> *And I laid me down with a will.*
> *This be the verse you grave for me:*
> *Here he lies where he longed to be;*
> *Home is the sailor, home from sea,*
> *And the hunter home from the hill.*

Mr. Carney took a long draw on his cigar, finished off his whiskey, followed by a generous swallow of Guinness, then carefully wiped the stout from the lower edges of his silver handlebar mustache.

"You know," he said, "though Robert Louis Stevenson was a Scotsman, he loved his stout and had a supply of Guinness shipped to him in Samoa."

The old gent then shared his own story. He hailed from Dublin's old Liberties district, where Bold Robert Emmet led his short-lived rebellion and was hanged and beheaded on Thomas Street.

In the 18th and 19th centuries, prominent brewing and distilling families established themselves in the Liberties. Arthur Guinness built his huge brewery – the world's largest – at St. James's Gate in 1759. The celebrated distilleries of Jameson and Powers, among others, were also once located in the Liberties. In the Victorian era, the cityscape was packed with chimney stacks, malthouses, mills, and busy streets. But amid all the industrial prosperity, were the city's notorious slums where the poor lived in grinding poverty and horrendous housing conditions.

While parts of the ancient Liberties, dating back to the medieval period, were demolished by the mid-1800's, much remained of the working-class, quintessential heart of Ould Dublin town well into the 20th century, until almost all of the crumbling old tenements were finally torn down.

"Ah," said Mr. Carney, "the Liberties were a great place to be *from*." He emphasized the word "from."

At twenty-two years old, he became a seaman in the British merchant service and went around the world on various ships for more than two decades. I noticed the large gold coin he had on a chain around his neck. Having collected old and unusual coins since I was a boy, I asked him about it.

"It's a two-hundred-year-old Spanish doubloon," replied Mr. Carney. "I won it in a bloody marvelous hand of cards from an Argentine naval officer in a Buenos Aires bar, back in '61."

The silver-mustached Dubliner ended his long stint in the merchant service and bought a rundown hotel on a Samoan beach, fixed it up and added a bar. He soon acquired a native woman and in time she presented him with four daughters. Later her sister joined their household, in what the French would call a *ménage à trois,* and bore him yet another daughter.

"They've all got kids of their own now. But I've still got me two lovely oul missuses lookin' after me. And in Samoa, you can usually find me standin' behind my bar most days chattin' with the regulars and drinkin' cold bottles of piss. Jaysus, I'm in bloody heaven there, what more can a man ask for in life? I'm livin' the life most blokes only bleedin' dream of. I got sunshine and warmth, a couple of devoted women, a slew of grandkids, and an endless supply of cold piss!"

When I asked him what brought him back to Dublin, the old fellow chuckled, drained the last of his Guinness, and told me after drinking nothing but piss beer for the past thirty-eight years – since he left home in 1954 – he was desperate for a proper pint of the black stuff.

"The only thing better than a pint of Guinness, is two pints of Guinness," I remarked, and called for two more.

Setting our pints down on the bar, the bald, grinning bartender declared: "Now, to quote the prolific Flann O'Brien, 'When things go wrong and will not come right, though you do the best you can, when life looks black as the hour of night – a pint of plain is your only man.'"

"Right you are," replied old Jack Carney, with a smile and a twinkle in his eye. Then turning to me, he said, "My father used to work at the Guinness brewery. Himself and my dear mother are both long gone now. May they rest in peace. I've still two sisters here though. One's married to some pencil-necked, government paper-pusher, and is livin' in posh Donnybrook. The other's a nun in a convent."

We shared a parting glass of liquid sunshine before we parted, and the old gent gave me another one of his Cuban cigars to smoke later on. I thanked him and carefully placed it into the pocket of my corduroy jacket.

Before I caught a city bus back to Tallaght, I ducked into a little gift shop on O'Connell Street and bought Mary and Biddy a couple of stuffed leprechaun dolls in matching green suits and hats with red beards.

The author in a Dublin pub

The Grattan Bridge

Dublin's Four Courts

Robert Emmet memorial at St. Catherine's Church.

CHAPTER THIRTY-SEVEN
RETURN TO THE WAR ZONE

In the morning, Callaghan and I boarded a Bus Éireann for Belfast. Taking a window seat, I opened a discarded copy of the *Irish News* that I found at the bus terminal. War continued to wage in the Six Counties and across the Irish Sea. A bomb planted by the I.R.A. the previous morning exploded in a busy pedestrian shopping area in the center of Belfast.

The device was placed in the ground floor doorway of Contact Travel in a three-story building on Ann Street. A warning call was received at the office of the Standard Supply Company, on the floor above the travel agency, giving staff ten minutes to evacuate. The manager went to look for the bomb and located it at the bottom of the stairs. But the device detonated less than two minutes after the warning was made.

It was reported the blast caused a huge fireball which swept through the building. A man was engulfed in flames. There was utter panic. Ten office workers were stranded on the upper floors by a fire on the stairs. A woman who worked at a nearby shop was quoted as saying people at the windows were screaming and begging for help. Firemen rescued them using a turntable ladder and up to a dozen ambulances took the injured

– many of them women – to the City Hospital. A total of twenty-seven people were hurt. Fortunately, no one was killed.

Later *An Phoblacht/ Republican News* published a statement by the I.R.A. claiming responsibility for the bomb attack. It read as follows:

> *A number of our Volunteers left a Semtex explosive device in offices in Ann Street this morning, 1 December. The Volunteers set the device to detonate 25 minutes after it was planted. Simultaneously a Volunteer phoned the office concerned describing the device and its exact location.*
>
> *The female receptionist was warned that no one should interfere with the device. It would now appear that someone in the building tampered with the device after our Volunteer left the area.*
>
> *The attack was on commercial property and we regret any injuries caused to civilians in the vicinity.*

As the bus carried us along the motorway through lush green fields, towards County Meath, I continued to read the newspaper. Across the water, London police found a van packed with explosives on Tottenham Court Road, a major shopping district, after receiving warnings attributed to the I.R.A. Death and destruction was avoided when the device was defused by the city's bomb disposal squad.

I understood the I.R.A. viewed their armed struggle as a war of national liberation. But even in war there were basic rules – or at least there should be. The volunteers of the Provisional I.R.A. considered themselves soldiers, but soldiers should not intentionally direct attacks against civilians and other noncombatants. It's a humanitarian law enshrined in the Geneva Conventions: "Civilians are not to be subject to attack. This includes direct attacks on civilians and indiscriminate attacks against areas in which civilians are present."

I thought of the I.R.A. bombing in Enniskillen, five years before, and the many other atrocities committed in the name of Irish Republicanism. All the many innocent lives that were taken or destroyed in the Troubles. Although I agreed with the cause of a free and independent and united Ireland, I sometimes wondered if the end justified the means.

Silently passing the paper to Callaghan, I looked out the bus window and reflected on the Easter Rising of 1916. When the bloody week-long battle was over and the army of the newly formed Irish Republic was defeated, hundreds were dead and wounded, while Dublin's city center was left in smoking ruins. An official announcement was made that Republican leaders had surrendered. The proclamation issued by Commander in Chief Pádraic Pearse stated: "In order to prevent further slaughter of unarmed people, in hopes of saving the lives of our followers, who are surrounded and hopelessly outnumbered, the Provisional Government have agreed to unconditional surrender…"

Pádraic Pearse was a noble-hearted patriot and brave soldier, a schoolteacher and poet, an Irish language enthusiast and idealistic visionary.

I also viewed Republican prisoners Fergus Martin and Terry Quinn as brave men, true Irish patriots and soldiers devoted to a noble cause.

For the most part, I didn't believe the I.R.A. intentionally targeted civilians – unlike Loyalist paramilitaries and the British Army. I knew the I.R.A., however, could be very reckless and they often made horrific mistakes. Callaghan callously termed such mistakes "collateral damage," an unfortunate but inevitable byproduct of modern warfare. I couldn't accept that.

When we arrived at Great Victoria Street Bus Station, in Belfast, instead of heading directly back to the flat, we walked over to Ann Street to see for ourselves the destruction the bomb caused. Broken glass was still scattered on the ground. Inside the burnt-out building, workmen were tearing down what was left of an interior wall. Callaghan and I had nothing to say to one another as we made our way to Eglantine Avenue.

After dropping off our bags, Callaghan immediately left to see Sandra. As I was preparing to go out to the Mad Hatter's Coffee Shop for a bite to eat and to catch up on my travel journal writing, there was a knock on the door.

It was a lanky young man with shaggy blond hair. He sported a little gold hoop earring in one ear and his worn blue jeans and sweater were speckled with various colors of paint. Explaining he was a new upstairs neighbor, he presented me with a small parcel bearing my name.

The package was from Jim Nesbitt, a navy buddy from South Carolina. I couldn't help but notice that it had been torn half-open, revealing a box of White Owl cigars.

"Ah, y'know, 'twas like that when I came across it yesterday, set on the wee table by the main door," he quickly made clear. "I reckoned I ought to hold onto it for ye, y'know, for safe keepin' like."

"Thanks," I replied, turning the torn parcel over in my hands. "Looks like whoever teared into it didn't much care for cigars."

"Aye, so it would seem," he agreed with a smile. "But I'd certainly fancy one meself."

I removed the remaining brown paper from the package, opened the White Owl box, and handed my new neighbor a cigar.

"Could I also trouble ye for a cup of milk?" he asked.

Opening the kitchen fridge, I found no milk, but two bottles of Guinness stood invitingly side by side on the top shelf and I offered him one. He smiled from ear to ear.

"Now, that's somethin' I'd never turn down!"

I grabbed the other bottle for myself and asked him to have a seat at the card table, while I poured the stout into a couple of glasses. Guinness isn't some swill beer to be chugged down directly from a bottle or can but should always be drank properly from a glass.

My upstairs neighbor introduced himself as Alan Jenkins. A twenty-one-year-old university student at Queen's, he had just moved into the building over the weekend from Finaghy, a predominately Protestant, middle-class area of south Belfast. He dreamed to be an artist, a modern impressionist painter, an Irish Claude Monet, and he had already turned his flat into a studio with easels set up with canvases in the process of being painted.

Unwrapping the White Owl cigar, Alan lit it and blew a cloud of smoke up towards the ceiling. I thought of Callaghan and how much he'd hate the pungent smell of a cigar, even more than he did pipes and cigarettes. Yeah, someone puffing a stinky stogie in *his* flat would really piss him off. What the hell! I reached for a White Owl from the box, unwrapped it, and gleefully lit up too.

Alan was looking at Callaghan's poster of Jimmy Cagney, in his fedora and double-breasted suit, appearing every bit the 1930's gangster. He also noticed the church calendar with a picture of the Sacred Hearts of Jesus and Mary tacked to the wall.

"Me girlfriend's a Catholic from Andersonstown," he said. "She's from a fiercely Republican family. But, y'know, they don't care for me cause I kick with the other foot."

The local expression came from the older idiom of "digging with the other foot." The story goes that Ulster Protestant planters used spades with a short shaft topped by a T-shaped handle, while Irish Catholics used spades with straight, long shafts without handles. The difference in design, apparently, caused the user of the "Protestant spade" to dig with one foot and the user of the "Catholic spade" to dig with the other foot. There has been some disagreement over who dug with the right and who dug with the left, but whichever foot the other dug with, it was the "wrong" one. In time, Irishmen of both creeds inquiring about a new acquaintance, whose religion wasn't known, would ask, "What foot does he dig with?"

In recent years, with soccer being more popular than farming, especially in northern industrial cities like Belfast, "kick" replaced "dig."

Alan went on to say that while he considered himself politically "somewhat of a Unionist," he was more liberal in his views than the majority of his fellow Belfast Protestants. As he knocked his cigar ash into the ashtray I placed on the table, I saw the faded letters "UDA" – for Ulster Defence Association – tattooed across his knuckles. Alan saw me looking at his hand.

"Ah, y'know, I got that when I was young and foolish."

The university student and up-and-coming artist finished the last of his Guinness and related how he had an uncle among the eleven people killed in the I.R.A. bombing of Enniskillen.

"I was, like, sixteen years of age then. I wanted to join the U.D.A. and defend Ulster and combat I.R.A. terrorism."

Alan Jenkins explained his view soon changed.

"I came to see the U.D.A., the U.F.F., the U.V.F., and other Loyalist paramilitaries, as purely criminal organizations. All with their own bloody extortion rackets and drug dealin' and their indiscriminate acts of violence against innocent people. The fuckin' Provos, y'know, haven't a monopoly on terror. Aside from murderin' ordinary Catholics, our Prod thugs attack members of their own community, metin' out punishment beatings and shootings."

Alan said he received a punishment beating from local U.D.A. men for keeping company with a Catholic girl, prompting him to move away from his old neighborhood. His older brother also once had a Catholic girlfriend and was kneecapped by the U.D.A. (that is, he was shot through one or both his knees) for going outside the "Protestant tribe." His brother survived and moved to England.

A year earlier, a twenty-eight-year-old Catholic man was murdered by the U.F.F. – the Ulster Freedom Fighters – a cover name for the U.D.A. He had the Protestant-sounding name of William Johnston and was living with his Protestant girlfriend in a staunchly Loyalist area, off the Donegall Road, in south Belfast. Apparently, he tried to pass himself off as a Protestant and referred to himself as "Billy."

It was reported that Johnston had feared for his personal safety and slept fully clothed with his shoes on in case he needed to flee from an imminent attack.

According to his girlfriend, they were in bed when two masked U.F.F. men began kicking down the front door of the house. They shoved past her on the stairs to get at her boyfriend. She heard one shout at him: "You are a liar! You are Liam Johnston!" (Liam typically being used for William among Catholics.)

The sectarian assassins shot Johnston, and as he lay helpless on the floor, the muzzle of the gun was put into his mouth and the trigger was pulled again.

The coroner stated at the inquest that there was no evidence that the victim "was anything but a totally innocent man." His only "crime" was being the wrong religion.

Later in the evening, after Alan Jenkins went back up to his flat, I tuned into the news on the old McMurdo Silver radio. It was reported that day there were over forty bomb hoaxes in Belfast and nearby Lisburn.

Callaghan was in the kitchen, angrily cooking us meat and potatoes for dinner. We had a few words earlier when, despite opening the windows, enough of the cigar smoke lingered for him to get a whiff of it when he returned.

I turned my attention back to the radio. John Hume, the leader of the Social Democratic and Labour Party was being interviewed. The S.D.L.P. was the largest Nationalist political party in Northern Ireland. They advocated Irish reunification and the devolution of powers while Northern Ireland remained under British control. In contrast to Sinn Féin, the S.D.L.P. was completely opposed to the violence of the I.R.A. campaign. John Hume and his moderate Nationalists were despised by Republican supporters of the armed struggle.

Callaghan popped his redhead out from the kitchen. "There's those who say S.D.L.P. stands for the Stoop Down Low Party," he scornfully remarked. "Others call it the Semi-Detached Loyalist Party."

"What the hell you trying to say?" I asked, growing irritated.

"They're cowardly enablers of British misrule," he shot back.

I took a deep breath, before I began. "This has long been a divided land with deep and ugly hatreds going back hundreds of years, especially in this corner of it.

"John Hume seems to be genuinely interested in trying to bring peace to people divided by politics and religion. For anyone who cares about this country, I think its at least worthwhile listening to what he has to say. The S.D.L.P. seeks a constitutional joining of the two parts of Ireland. But even if the Brits leave, the Unionists, or Loyalists, won't be bombed into a united Ireland. Therefore, both sides would be wise to give the peacemakers an ear."

"Any true-born Irish patriot worth his salt," started Callaghan, before I interrupted him.

"*You* are a true-born Yank!" I exploded in anger. "You're from freaking Staten Island. Your parents are both New Yorkers. Don't forget where you're from, Timothy Callaghan. You're a damn narrowback – same as me! You weren't reared in the streets of Belfast, and you certainly never fought the Black and Tans in Cork."

Callaghan just glared at me with his fierce blue eyes, his eyebrows drawn hard together to form a V. His jaw was clenched tight, and the muscle twitched furiously in his cheek, as the red color in his face deepened. He suddenly turned and walked back into the kitchen. The hostility between us had become so thick you could cut it with a knife.

He returned with two plates of meat and potatoes and dropped one with a clatter on the table in front of me. I looked up into his enraged face.

"I wish I never invited you here!" he snapped.

Enough was enough. I got up to leave. As I walked to the door, Callaghan yelled after me.

"Fine, fuck off then, I'll just eat the whole goddamned dinner myself!"

Pulling on my jacket, I shouted back over my shoulder, before slamming the door. "Good, I hope you choke on it – you fanatical bastard!"

CHAPTER THIRTY-EIGHT
THE PARTY

I staggered back to the flat in the wee hours of the morning, after having tied one on at a nearby pub, and collapsed fully clothed on my bed. It was late morning when I finally got up. Callaghan was gone. But I found last night's dinner wrapped in tin foil in the fridge with a note on top: "Sorry I snapped at you. I was wrong. I'm going for a couple of days to Banbridge to meet Sandra's family. Your pal, T.C."

I reheated the meat and spuds in a frying pan and had it for breakfast along with a cup of Lyons tea, as I was out of coffee.

A registered letter arrived from my uncle Bob in Montreal. He enclosed a money order for £25, writing:

> *Hello, my dear Boy!*
>
> *I am sending you whatever I could spare in the hope that it may help you a little. Hell, I had wanted to help you a lot! You're doing what so many people only dream of doing. Traveling across the Atlantic, back to the Ould Sod, the land of so many of your ancestors!*
>
> *Things over here at a sort of stand still. I get up and go to work in the morning, I come home at night, and after supper, I start the fire in the basement and we watch T.V. and later on,*

we go to bed. Such is our humdrum daily life. It's like the desert sand, it's always the same colour, pretty much always the same horizon displays itself week in and week out. Hey! how's that for a boring letter.

Uncle Bob was sixty-five years old, married for over thirty years, and his children were grown and on their own. He was still working six days a week though, driving a taxi and delivering pharmaceutical drugs to patients, many of them elderly, living in the Quebec countryside. When I once lived for a year in Montreal, I'd sometimes go along with him.

Uncle Bob and I were two of a kind. We both dreamed of strange and distant lands; be it traveling to see the Aztec pyramids in Mexico, or the Great Wall of China, or the rolling hills and lush green glens of Ireland. But Uncle Bob spent his life scraping by to support his family, and his dreams of visiting such faraway places remained just pipe dreams.

I read something once to the effect of: "The world is filled with old people who were going to do something big in their lives but waited till it was safe. Now it's safe and they're sixty-five years old."

Although I also had a family to support, I was determined not to let my life slip by without fulfilling at least some of my travel dreams.

Taking a chair out into the hallway, I loaded up one of my trusty briar pipes for a smoke and opened my journal to write. But my mind drifted as the smoke carried my thoughts far away from the Troubles of Belfast.

I thought of a book I read called *The Longest Walk,* by George Meegan, in which the English author chronicled his six-year epic walk from the southern tip of South America to the Arctic Ocean at the northern top of Alaska. Meegan wrote, ever since he was a boy, his ambition had been a life of high adventure. He certainly accomplished this. After spending half a dozen years sailing the world's oceans with the British Merchant Navy, at the age of twenty-four, he began the longest unbroken journey ever completed on foot – 19,019 miles, between 1977 and 1983. What a fantastic adventure, I thought, smiling to myself, as I blew smoke rings in the empty hall.

Later in the afternoon, I went down to the post office on University Road, across from the Botanic Gardens, to mail off to Mary and Biddy the stuffed leprechaun dolls I bought them in Dublin for Christmas.

When I returned to Eglantine Avenue and was heading back up to our flat, I met Alan Jenkins coming down the stairs, wearing the same paint-speckled blue jeans and sweater from the day before. He told me he was in a bit of a fix because he was having some friends coming over for a party and had several easels set up in his flat with canvases being painted and more canvases stacked against the walls and tubes of paint scattered everywhere.

Since Callaghan would be away for the next couple of days with Sandra in Banbridge, I told the budding young artist he could bring his friends to our place.

They arrived after seven in the evening. Alan was in a fresh set of clothes – clean jeans and a neat lavender button-down shirt with bright yellow polka dots. His shaggy blond hair looked like it had just been combed and he sported his little gold hoop earring in one ear. By his side was his girlfriend, Deirdre, from the "fiercely Republican family" in Andersonstown. Slender and almost as tall as Alan, she was a long, dark-haired beauty, with pale skin and large, dangling earrings. Clad in skin-tight black jeans and a matching black top, she wore a small gold Celtic cross around her neck.

Behind them was a big, portly fellow with curly brown hair, glasses and a double chin, wearing a snug blue turtleneck sweater, with his arms wrapped around several cans of Harp Lager. He was Bartly, I was told. Beside him, cradling a few bottles of Smithwick's Ale and a bottle of some sort of peach liqueur, was Bartly's girlfriend Sharon. She was a short, thick girl with short ginger hair and wide hips in a too-tight miniskirt. Like Alan, they were in their early twenties and students at Queen's.

As Alan was introducing us, Denis Irwin, the super, showed up, smiling in his uniform white shirt and white trousers from his hospital orderly job, carrying bags of more booze. He placed a number of bottles of Bulmers cider and Guinness on the card table, where Alan's friends had already put their bottles and cans.

With only three folding chairs available, Bartly and Sharon immediately made themselves comfortable on Callaghan's bed. While Alan dashed upstairs to his flat for a bottle of Bushmills, he remembered having stashed away, I went to the kitchen and returned with a few glasses.

"Ah Jaysus, this is brilliant!" declared Deirdre, standing over the venerable McMurdo Silver and gently touching the polished walnut cabinet. "Like pure class, so 'tis."

She turned on the old deluxe radio. A slow waltz was playing. She switched the station and Glen Campbell was singing a "Rhinestone Cowboy." American country and western music was popular in Ireland and Deirdre began singing along.

Denis poured a bottle of Guinness into a glass for me and a cider for himself. Alan then returned with his Bushmills and poured Denis and me a good four fingers of whiskey each. We both downed it and Alan gave us another dose, along with a generous one for himself.

Rod Stewart was singing "Downtown Train" on the radio. Deirdre turned up the volume. Bartly and Sharon had both helped themselves to my White Owl cigars and were puffing away contentedly on Callaghan's bed. Deirdre, with a bottle of Smithwick's in hand, was smoking a cigarette. Well, why not? I asked myself. After all, my flatmate was away for a couple of days. I packed a pipe and lit up.

"I'm hopin' to get to Paris next year to visit the Louvre," Alan was telling Denis. "I want to see the Old Masters with me own eyes."

"Like yer man Rembrandt?" asked Denis.

"Oh, aye," replied the young artist. "And the later post-Impressionists, y'know, like Vincent van Gogh and Paul Gauguin. One day I hope to escape this fuckin' tortured land for good. Like the Bible sez somewhere, shake the dust of this place off me feet."

"Where would you want to go?" I asked, pouring myself another few fingers of Bushmills.

"Jaysus, maybe Tahiti, like oul Gauguin…and spend me days paintin' lovely, naked, brown-skinned girls."

"And get syphilis like yer man!" merrily added Deirdre, before taking a swig from the bottle of peach liqueur.

I had another shot of Bushmills and as all the Guinness was gone, I reached for a can of Harp, as Denis opened another bottle of Bulmers cider for himself.

On the radio were the Spinners, the vintage but ever-popular rhythm and blues group, singing their hit "Working My Way Back to You." Deirdre turned up the volume even louder. Splashing more whiskey into my glass, I watched Deirdre and Sharon dance together, holding one another's hands, as they enthusiastically sang along –

I'll keep working my way back to you, babe
With a burning love inside
Yeah, I'm working my way back to you, babe...

Relighting my pipe and taking a couple of draws, I got a noseful of something that wasn't the sweet aroma of my pipe tobacco, nor the distinctive smell of the cigar Bartly was smoking. No, the intense odor that filled my nostrils was something nasty and putrid. I stepped into the kitchen and found Alan smoking a joint. The young artist's face broke into a grin.

"Here, ye gotta try this," he said, offering me his doobie. "The best pure Moroccan hash to be had in Belfast."

"No thanks," I said. "None of that goddamn crap for me. I'll stick to good old-fashioned tobacco."

Denis called me to join him for a final shot from the near empty bottle of Bushmills. Just as we were lifting our glasses, with Pat Benatar belting out on the radio "You Better Run," a most unwelcome sight appeared in the doorway.

There was himself, red face in a twist, eyes blazing with a fierce anger, bared teeth clenched, and the muscle twitching in his cheek.

"I do believe yer flatmate has returned," said Bartly, in an amused tone, puffing at his cigar, as he continued to lay back on Callaghan's bed next to Sharon.

The color in Callaghan's face turned to a deep shade of purple, that made him look like an overly ripe plum about to explode. His mouth suddenly dropped open, and he yelled –

"Ouuut!! Get ouuuut!! Everybody get outta my flat – NOW!"

Someone turned off the radio and an uncomfortable silence descended on the room. Callaghan stomped over to the window and abruptly threw it open, to let out the cloud of smoke.

"Come on, the party's over," I said.

Everyone filed out the open door, picking up the last remaining cans of Harp and bottles of cider left on the table. Only Deirdre looked at Callaghan as she walked past him.

"Ye're an absolute bollocks!" she declared.

"It's his place, not mine," I told her, as she headed out the door. I overheard Denis on the stairs inviting everyone down to his flat.

I knew that Callaghan hated drinking and I had agreed not to smoke in his flat when I came.

"Sorry about that," I said, when we were alone. "Just thought since you'd be away in Banbridge for a couple of days. But, I know, it's your place."

Grabbing my pipe and what was left of my box of White Owls, I began to leave to rejoin the party in Denis's flat.

"The place will be yours after tomorrow," said Callaghan, in a low voice.

I turned to face him. All the anger had been drained out of him, and a terrible sadness filled his blue eyes.

"Won't you stay, Ed?" he asked, dropping into a chair.

"Yeah, sure," I answered, closing the door, and sitting across from him. "What happened?"

"My father had a heart attack," said Callaghan, his voice cracking with emotion. "He's dead. I'm flying back to New York tomorrow night."

"Jesus…er…I…I'm sorry," I stammered, taken aback.

Callaghan stood up and said he was going to take a shower. Over the water in the shower, I could hear him sobbing. I put the radio back on to give my friend some privacy.

A news update was being broadcast. It was reported that the I.R.A. was suspected of being behind two bomb explosions that morning in the center of Manchester, injuring over sixty people and damaging a number of buildings.

CHAPTER THIRTY-NINE
CALLAGHAN LEAVES

May the road rise to meet you.
May the wind be always at your back.
May the sun shine warm upon your face;
the rains fall soft upon your fields and
until we meet again,
may God hold you in the palm of His hand.

    Callaghan spent the morning withdrawing himself from Queen's University and packing his bags to go home. Although he had been in Ireland for more than a year, he neatly fit everything he had into his two suitcases. The books he couldn't fit in, he left behind for me.
    Later in the afternoon, we took a long walk together down the Lisburn Road, turning onto Stockman's Lane, passing Musgrave Park, and around the Kennedy Way roundabout, crossing the Andersonstown Road, and up to the Glen Road, where we turned. We walked by where I.R.A. Volunteer Pearse Jordan was gunned down by the R.U.C. a little more than a week before. Memorial flowers were attached to a nearby fence.
    As we walked through the Upper Falls, Callaghan said he wasn't planning to return to Ireland any time soon. He'd continue working towards his master's degree in New York.

"Does Sandra know yet?" I asked.

"I told her before we left Banbridge. Anyhow, it's been obvious for a while now we don't have a future together. We're just too different. You know, with our differences in religion and politics."

"Yeah, you both kick with different feet, as they put it here," I remarked.

"You could say that," replied Callaghan, with a sadness in his voice.

We eventually found ourselves in the Lower Falls. All the walking brought about a great thirst – at least for me. I suggested quenching it at the Sports Bar and Callaghan reluctantly accompanied me inside. Two old men in caps sat together at the bar and farther down sat two young toughs in leather jackets with tight-cropped hair.

We hopped onto a couple of stools at the bar. A pint of plain for myself and, as usual, a glass of Coke for my teetotaling pal. I pulled out of my jacket pocket my pipe and tobacco pouch. As I lit up and smoked, Callaghan picked up a copy of the *Daily Mail* left on the bar and read about the I.R.A. bombing in Manchester.

Halfway through my pint, the bar door swung open and in strolled two R.U.C. men with a helmeted British soldier, his automatic assault rifle gripped tightly in his hands at the ready. They made their way directly to the toilet in the back and pushed in the door. There was no one inside and they turned to leave but stopped where the pair of young toughs sat at the bar. One of them had muttered something as they passed.

"What was that?" demanded one of the R.U.C. men. When he got no reply, he was in the young man's face. "What did ye say, ye Fenian bastard?"

Still getting no answer, the R.U.C. man grabbed the young man by the throat, knocking over his drink. "What the fuck did ye say?!"

The guy in the leather jacket struggled and tried to pull away, until the soldier pressed his weapon to the side of his head. They smirked and sniggered at his discomfort, as his companion stared down helplessly at the bar. Then the R.U.C. man released his grip on his throat and the forces of the Crown departed.

Callaghan sat beside me, staring intensely straight ahead, his jaw set, and his cheek muscle working furiously.

"*Tiocfaidh ár lá!*" he said aloud, when the last of them had gone out the door.

"Yer fuckin' right!" shot back one of the leather-jacketed toughs at the end of the bar. "Our day *will* come. Up the Ra!"

On the way back to Eglantine Avenue, we stopped to pick up some fish and chips. The man at the takeout doused it with vinegar, wrapped up our dinners in newspaper, and we brought them back to the flat.

Callaghan looked so grim and cheerless as we ate at the card table. I tried to take his mind off his father's death by launching into an account of George Meegan's book, *The Longest Walk,* and my own hope of one day traversing the length of Latin America by train. Then, one day, even island hopping across the Pacific. Wouldn't that be a great adventure? "What do you think of seeing Samoa – the final resting place of Robert Louis Stevenson?"

"It isn't Ireland," he answered flatly. Alas, dear ould Ireland was Tim Callaghan's one and only love and from her he wouldn't stray.

"I'd like to spend some time in the Gaeltacht in the West though," he said at length.

"Like out in the Aran Islands?"

"Yeah, in the real, authentic picture-postcard Ireland. Whitewashed cottages with thatched roofs and red painted doors and lush green fields divided by low stone walls. Where only the Irish language can be heard."

Ah, the idyllic Erin of Callaghan's imagination!

"If all goes as planned," he continued, "I hope to return to the Emerald Isle in around two years."

Lifting my glass of water, I clinked it to Callaghan's and declared enthusiastically: "Then here's to us trodding the Ould Sod together once again, *a chara*! To the Aran Islands in 1995!"

But the truth was, I doubted that I'd be seeing my teetotaling, green sock-wearing, fanatical, Ireland-obsessed pal again. He was heading to New York, and I'd be returning to my family in San Diego. Planning to meet up in the Aran Islands one day just made our parting easier. For all our differences, Callaghan was still a valued friend and I'd miss him.

Mr. Kelly - who we met at the courthouse for the Casement Accused trial - came later that evening in his black taxi. He had Sandra with him to see Callaghan off. I greeted them and helped carry Callaghan's suitcases down to the street.

Pretty Sandra looked so brokenhearted as she tried to hide her eyes, swollen with tears, behind her straw-blonde hair. Callaghan kissed her on the forehead and dried her eyes with his handkerchief from his pocket, as they got into the back of the taxi. Callaghan glanced at me through the rolled-up window as Mr. Kelly pulled away from the curb, and I gave him a nod goodbye. So long, pal.

CHAPTER FORTY
CATHLEEN NÍ HOULIHAN & THE GIANT'S RING

In the morning, I set out to see the famous Giant's Ring. Ever since I read about it in my guidebook, I wanted to see it. Located on the outskirts of Belfast, the Neolithic monument was a nice hour-long leisurely walk south of the city, in County Down.

It was a cool and breezy day, but clear and bright. I began my journey on the Malone Road, passing the familiar Victorian red-brick buildings and St. Brigid's Church; and beyond that leafy affluent Protestant suburbs with large Victorian or Edwardian homes, and even bigger contemporary houses with spacious lawns, many of them millionaire mansions. But I wasn't admiring the surrounding architecture or even taking much notice of it.

My thoughts were of a one-act play that I saw in Dublin back in 1984. *Cathleen Ní Houlihan,* written at the turn of the 19th century by William Butler Yeats and Lady Gregory, was a story of Irish nationalism and the need for a blood sacrifice for Mother Ireland. The play was set in 1798, in the village of Killala, County Mayo, where a force of about one thousand French soldiers landed in an unsuccessful attempt to aid Irish patriots in their rising against the English.

Cathleen Ní Houlihan (Cathleen the daughter of Houlihan) is the female personification of Ireland. She appears to most as a weary, poor old woman wandering the roads.

The Old Woman, in the play, visited a cottage where the family was preparing for the wedding of the eldest son. The mother and father welcomed her and invited her in. Sitting with the family, she lamented the loss of her "four beautiful fields" (representing the four provinces: Ulster, Munster, Leinster, and Connacht), stolen by the strangers now living in her house. Even more mysteriously, she spoke of the many brave young men over the generations who died for the love of her. As the parents speculated on the identity of the Old Woman, their eldest son, Michael, was so utterly captivated by her tales of those who fought in battle for her, and won everlasting fame and glory, that he forgot about his upcoming wedding.

When the Old Woman departed their cottage, she was heard singing outside:

They shall be remembered for ever,
They shall be alive for ever,
They shall be speaking for ever,
The people shall hear them for ever.

Then there was the sound of cheering outside. Neighbors entered the cottage, and with them Michael's fiancée, Delia, and his younger brother, Patrick, a lad of twelve. The boy announced that there were ships in the bay, "The French are landing at Killala!"

Michael seemed to be under a spell and looked at his bride-to-be as if she were a stranger.

Patrick declared: "The boys are all hurrying down the hillside to join the French."

"Michael! Michael! You won't leave me!" begged Delia. "You won't join the French, and we going to be married!"

But Michael did not hear her.

Again, the Old Woman's voice could be heard outside: "They shall be speaking for ever, the people shall hear them for ever."

Michael left the crying Delia and rushed out the cottage door after the Old Woman. The father asked his younger son if he saw an old woman going down the path.

"I did not," replied Patrick, "but I saw a young girl, and she had the walk of a queen."

Yes, that play I saw on a Dublin stage made a lasting impression on me. Cathleen Ní Houlihan was Ireland and for those who fell under her enchantment she was no mere old woman, ragged and weary, but a powerful, ravishing young queen, to be honored and loved above all else. Callaghan had been so enchanted by Cathleen Ní Houilhan that he couldn't see the endearing charms of a real earthy beauty like Sandra Maginnis. As the Irish would say, more's the pity.

I turned off the Malone Road onto a smaller road, lined by plenty of green leafy trees, which a sign indicated would take me to Shaw's Bridge, over the River Lagan, for pedestrians and bicyclists. Initially, according to my guidebook, a wooden bridge was constructed in 1655 by a Captain Shaw to transport across the river the guns of Oliver Cromwell's army. The current picturesque five-arched, stone bridge was built in 1709. Adjacent to the old bridge was a new, concrete bridge of the same name, built in the 1970's for the motorized traffic of Northern Ireland's A55 road. Crossing the pedestrian bridge, the Malone Road became the Milltown Road.

I lit up a smoke as I walked across the bridge and turned onto Ballylesson Road. I was really out in the country now, tall trees and greenery all around me. There were signs directing me to the little mill village of Edenderry and the Giant's Ring. Soon, I was making my way down Ballynahatty Road in the townland of the same name.

Ballynahatty, from the Gaelic *Baile na hÁite Tí,* "townland of the house site," contained the Giant's Ring.

I stood by a large oak tree a few minutes just taking in the breathtaking site. Before me, with fields all around it, was a circular grassy enclosure, maybe two hundred yards in diameter, surrounded by an earthen bank twenty-odd feet wide and more than ten feet high. Within the center of the ring was a prehistoric dolmen of five huge upright stones supporting a large capstone. I walked out through the green grass to better examine it, as an old man in a cap strolled around atop the earthen rim with a black and white dog.

Although there was little information about the origin and usage of the ancient fortification, the immense amphitheater-like structure certainly served some ceremonial or ritual purpose in pre-Celtic Ireland.

Built nearly five thousand years ago, around 2700 to 3000 B.C., it predates the pyramids of Egypt and England's Stonehenge. The dolmen stones were the remains of a ruined passage tomb.

Dating from the New Stone Age, or Neolithic period, passage tombs are burial chambers with a narrow entrance passage covered by an earthen mound or large upright stones capped by a large flat horizontal stone. These latter stone "table" monuments are called dolmens.

Passage tombs are found all over Western Europe. One of the most extraordinary megalithic complexes is Newgrange in Ireland's Boyne Valley in County Meath. (I'd see it on another trip to Ireland, a few years later.) Although Newgrange was classified as a passage tomb, archaeologists consider it to be more of an ancient temple, a site of astrological significance and religious importance. Sort of like a pagan cathedral in its day.

The Giant's Ring must have been the same. I marveled at all that must have transpired there over the past five millenniums.

The Victorian travel writer J.B. Doyle described the site, in his 1854 *Tours in Ulster,* thus: "In the centre of this space there is a Druid altar... Few things were more calculated to awe the mind and to affect the imagination than this scene, when we contemplate it as a vast heathen temple, within the circuit of which many thousands may have assembled to witness the awful rites of their sanguinary religion; and where no objects could attract their attention from the priest, the huge altar stone, the human sacrifices and the glorious luminary [i.e., the sun] that formed the principal object of their adoration..."

While the monument was a memorial to the dead, like hundreds of others built during that period, many archaeologists believe the ancient religion of the earliest Neolithic inhabitants of Ireland was solar rather than death orientated.

What a fascinating place! I walked clockwise the circle of the ring. The old man with his dog was gone, replaced by two pretty college-age girls in trim tracksuits jogging around the perimeter. According to my guidebook, in the 18th century the Giant's Ring was used for horse racing. Six circuits made a two-mile race and spectators watched and cheered on top of the earthen ramparts.

On my way back to the city, I stopped at a quiet pub for a late lunch and a couple of jars of the black stuff.

The Giant's Ring, south of Belfast

CHAPTER FORTY-ONE
PADDY MURPHY

It began as a quiet, solitary Sunday. Like Callaghan, I decided to try to attend Mass at different churches to better acquaint myself with different parts of Belfast. That morning, I went to St. Malachy's Church on Alfred Street in the Markets district.

The city's third oldest Catholic church was built in 1844, in red brick in the ecclesiastical style of the Tudor period topped with pinkish octagonal turrets. Parishioners were just beginning to file in. I genuflected at the entrance of a back pew and sat down to take in the beautifully ornate surroundings. The interior of St. Malachy's was extravagantly decorated. Above the sanctuary's white marble high altar were three large paintings. The central one depicted Our Lord falling under the weight of the Cross. It was flanked by paintings of Our Lady of the Immaculate Conception and Saint Malachy himself, Ireland's 12th century archbishop of Armagh and first native-born saint to be officially canonized.

My gaze drifted to the white marble altar rails and the fancy pulpit with a canopy. The sanctuary had an intricate blue mosaic floor. I looked up and smiled at the highly detailed and rather whimsical fan vaulted ceiling. The Belfast solicitor and architectural historian Sir Charles Brett once wrote: "It is as though a wedding cake has been turned inside out, so creamy, lacy and frothy is the plasterwork." Mass was celebrated by a Father Corcoran.

No sooner had I arrived back at the flat on Eglantine Avenue, than Denis Irwin was at my door to deliver a package Mrs. Boyle and her son-in-law had dropped off for me. Wrapped up in brown paper, it was addressed, "To Ed from Terry." That would be Terry Quinn from Portlaoise Prison. I thanked Denis and after he left, I removed the paper wrapping.

Inside was a beautifully handcrafted mirror that Terry made. A map of Ireland was engraved on it with the coat of arms of each province: Ulster's Red Hand, Leinster's gold harp, Munster's three gold crowns, and Connacht's dimidiated black eagle and armored arm with a raised sword. In the lower right corner was engraved in old Gaelic script "Portlaoise Gaol." I gave the gift a place of honor above my writing desk when I returned home.

Meanwhile, I carefully placed the mirror on Callaghan's bed. Glancing around, there were a number of things he left behind. His black and white poster of Jimmy Cagney, in his fedora and double-breasted suit, remained up on the wall, and on the card table were a stack of books Callaghan gave me.

I spread them across the table, reading the titles: *Revolutionary in Ireland,* by Seán MacStiofáin, the onetime chief of staff of the Provisional I.R.A.; *I.R.A. Tactics and Targets: An Analysis of Tactical Aspects of the Armed Struggle 1969-1989,* by J. Bowyer Bell; *Britain's War Machine,* a booklet by Father Maurice Burke, a chaplain for the Irish Northern Aid Committee; *Ballymurphy and the Irish War,* by Ciarán de Baróid; *Hell or Connacht! The Cromwellian Colonisation of Ireland 1652-1660,* by Peter Berresford Ellis; *Paddy's Lament: Ireland 1846-1847, Prelude to Hatred,* by Thomas Gallagher, about the Great Potato Famine, which as the introduction stated added substance to Ireland's bitter, undying hatred for England; an old and yellowed copy of the *Selected Writings of James Connolly;* a thin volume of *Quotations from Pádraic Pearse;* and *A Pathway to Peace,* by Gerry Adams, the president of Sinn Féin and Member of Parliament for West Belfast. It was the beginnings of an Irish Republican library.

I picked up MacStiofáin's autobiography to skim through as I had a peaceful pipe smoke in bed. The day after Callaghan left, when I could finally smoke in the flat, I ran out of my preferred tobacco, a sweet peaches and cream blend, which I brought to Ireland with me. Therefore, I loaded my pipe with the Condor tobacco that I picked up at a newsagent's shop. Lighting up and taking a deep draw, I began to gag. The pungent blend tasted and smelled like soap! Luckily, I still had the cigar that Jack Carney of Samoa gave me in Dublin.

I was just contentedly blowing a few smoke rings when there was a hard knocking at the door. I knew it couldn't be Denis again. He had a gentle, timid knock. This knocker was bolder and more insistent.

The banging persisted and a male voice called out: "Tim Callaghan! Paddy Murphy here!"

Opening the door, I met a grinning, balding, fat middle-aged man with a ruddy face and merry blue eyes, wearing a rumpled, unzipped tan jacket over a wrinkled button-down shirt spilling out over faded baggy blue jeans. He stuck out his hand and I shook it.

"Ye'd not be Tim Callaghan though, would ye?" he asked before I could introduce myself. "I just got out of Magilligan yesterday."

Magilligan was a medium security prison located near the town of Limavady in County Derry.

Inviting him in, I explained I was a friend of Callaghan's. Paddy Murphy – who told me to call him Paddy - said that while he never actually met Callaghan, he heard he was a ginger and they had exchanged a few letters when he was in Magilligan. He also heard about me from our visit to Fergus Martin in Long Kesh.

"Ye'd be the Yank with the name of the German motorway," remarked Paddy, with a humorous twinkle in his eyes.

"The *Autobahn*? No, it's the French *Aw-duh-bon.* Ed Audubon."

"Like yer man who painted birds?"

"My illustrious ancestor."

I knew enough about Irish hospitality by now to offer him a cup of tea.

"Ah, that'd be grand, so it would," said my guest.

I went to the kitchen to heat up the kettle and took out the Lyons tea and put some Scottish shortbread biscuits onto a plate to go with it. When I returned, I found Paddy Murphy looking through the books on the card table.

"Better be careful readin' too much Irish history," he warned in jest. "Sure, 'tis a dangerous thing. Learnin' about all the sufferin' dear ould Ireland's gone through has driven many a young man to run off and join the I.R.A. Jaysus, it got poor oul Paddy here three years in Magilligan!"

Reaching into his jacket, he pulled out a neatly folded poster which he opened for me. *"SAOIRSE"* was printed in bold letters – the Gaelic word for "freedom" and the name of a Republican prisoners' group. "Release Political Prisoners Now," it read and had a drawing of a dove holding keys in its beak sitting on a barbed wire fence. He gave me the poster and I later tacked it on the wall by Jimmy Cagney, who often spent time in prison on the silver screen.

Seated at the table, sipping our cups of tea, fifty-two-year-old Paddy Murphy told me he lived in Ardoyne and was a plumber by trade. In the summer of 1989, the British Army and R.U.C. raided his home in Velsheda Park and seized a wheelie bin full of explosives to be used by the local I.R.A. unit in Ardoyne. Paddy was immediately arrested and brought to Castlereagh Interrogation Centre in east Belfast. It later came out that an informer in the ranks of the I.R.A. tipped off Crown forces about Paddy and received a reward of £50.

Before Paddy appeared in court, he was held in Crumlin Road Jail where he shared a cell with then twenty-one-year-old Fergus Martin. They had been longtime neighbors in Ardoyne and became close friends during their time in the Crum. The comrades in turn each had a non-jury Diplock trial. Fergus was sentenced to twelve years in the H-Blocks of Long Kesh, while Paddy was sent to Magilligan for three years.

I relit my cigar and said I regretted I didn't have another for him but told Paddy he could help himself to my pack of Players on the table.

"Ah, no thanks," he replied. "I don't smoke anymore. The bloody fags nearly killed me in Magilligan."

Smiling at the unintentional pun, I thought how many Americans would assume Paddy meant he was attacked and nearly killed by homosexuals while in prison.

I suggested we visit the Botanic Inn around the corner for something more than a cup of tea. When we stepped out into the street, it was raining and Paddy quipped: "Ah, fine Irish weather. Sure, it would be a grand country if only they could build a bloody roof over it!"

It was early enough in the afternoon when we entered the Bot that the place was still devoid of many customers. Over a couple of jars of

Guinness, I heard more about Paddy's life. Born in 1940, he spent his earliest years in a Belfast Catholic orphanage and grew up not knowing his real family. But unlike his fellow orphan Denis Irwin, Paddy was adopted from the orphanage as a "wee lad" by a childless couple in Ardoyne. His new parents lived long enough to give him their name before they both succumbed to tuberculosis. Patrick Joseph Murphy was a boy of eight when he was orphaned a second time. Another Ardoyne couple named Hopkins had pity and took him in and reared him along with their own children.

They gave Paddy a decent home. But even before the Troubles, working-class Ardoyne in the 1950's was marked by poverty and despair. Large numbers of men were unemployed, and their women were often forced to become the family breadwinners, laboring for low wages in the busy mills of Ardoyne. Mr. Hopkins, though, managed to eke out a living for his family doing carpentry work.

Paddy Murphy, like many young Irishmen of the time, sought to escape poverty by joining the British Army. Again, this was before the later Troubles when the vast majority of Irish Nationalists saw nothing wrong with donning a British Army uniform. Among other places, Paddy was stationed for some time in postwar Germany and claimed to still be able to hold his own in German. The army made him a cook.

He happily related how he once prepared for an officers' party three large trays.

"One had green peas, another had cut and cooked carrots, and in the middle, I placed a tray of creamy mashed spuds. 'Twas feckin' beautiful, so 'twas. Put side by side, bejaysus, the trays resembled Ireland's lovely tricolor flag – green, white, and orange. Sure, a few of the Brit officers even asked if I was not makin' a political statement."

But Paddy's career as a soldier cook in the British Army came to an end when he heard the news about Bloody Sunday in Derry, in late January 1972, when the same army he was serving in slaughtered fourteen unarmed civilians. It came on the heels of the Ballymurphy Massacre, six months earlier in Belfast, when British paratroopers shot dead eleven unarmed civilians.

"There I was servin' in the bloody British Army in Germany, feedin' the bastards, and back in Ireland they were murderin' our people!"

Paddy Murphy deserted and returned home. However, he didn't remain long in Belfast, in British occupied Ireland, but headed south to Dublin, the capital of the Republic. There he joined the Irish Army, which he called the Free State army, and was part of the United Nations Task Force in various emerging African countries during the 1970's.

Lowering his voice and casting a cautious glance around lest anyone should overhear him, Paddy continued: "So, the Provisional I.R.A. was actually the fourth army I served in - and the best of 'em!"

After a couple of more pints, we left the Botanic Inn. The rain had stopped, and Paddy led the way down the wet sidewalk along the Malone Road, towards the city center, onto the University Road and past Shaftesbury Square and onto Great Victoria Street.

A lifelong bachelor with no children, Paddy was self-educated and an avid reader with a keen interest in Irish history and left-wing politics. As a committed Republican socialist, his political activism went beyond "Get the Brits out" and the I.R.A.'s armed struggle. He saw Ireland's fight for freedom as one with oppressed people worldwide. But I must admit, as Paddy went on about how capitalism should be viewed as the larger enemy and the need to unite the workers of the world and the inevitability of class warfare, he sounded more like a Marxist or a communist.

"It is merely the socialism of Ireland's greatest labor leader and patriot James Connolly," maintained Paddy.

I knew that socialism had long been part of the Irish Republican tradition. Before James Connolly died the death of a Republican martyr, after being a leading participant in the Easter Rising of 1916, he was a Marxist and syndicalist theorist. Two decades before the Rising, he helped found the Irish Socialist Republican Party in Dublin.

Socialism and communism are closely related though. So, it came as no great surprise that while Paddy called himself a socialist, he had communist sympathies. But I was taken aback a bit to learn he had been a member of the Communist Party of Ireland.

As Paddy explained it, about twelve years earlier he got permission from the Provisional I.R.A.'s Belfast command to go undercover and join the Communist Party. Later, his membership proved useful. After that wheelie bin full of I.R.A. explosives was discovered in Paddy's house, his membership in the Marxist-Leninist party cast a doubt at his trial whether he was actually in the I.R.A. as it was well-known that the Communists in Ireland opposed the Provisionals and their armed campaign. But his membership in the Party ended when he was arrested and charged.

We walked up to Castle Street and turned onto Chapel Lane and Bank Street to enter Kelly's Cellars, a wonderfully old whitewashed public house. Opened in 1720, Paddy told me Henry Joy McCracken and the United Irishmen met in the historic pub to plan the 1798 Rising. McCracken was said to have once hidden behind the bar when British soldiers were searching for him.

Paddy was enthusiastically greeted by a middle-aged bartender with dark shoulder length hair and long gray sideburns, who asked when he got out of Magilligan. After they chatted a bit, I ordered us pints of Guinness and doubles of Bushmills. But when the bartender returned with our drinks, he refused to accept my money.

"Ye see," he explained, "Paddy's a friend of ours and any friend of Paddy's is a friend of ours. So put away yer money, lad."

Once the bartender went to attend to other patrons, Paddy lifted his Bushmills and clinked his glass with mine.

"Sláinte mhaith," he said. Good health.

"Sláinte agatsa," I responded. To your health as well.

He then uttered a few more words in Gaelic, which I didn't understand.

Paddy was a self-taught Gaelic speaker. He became fluent in the language of his ancestors by regularly visiting the Donegal Gaeltacht over the years. Although he left school at the age of fourteen, not only did he learn the Irish language, but he also managed to complete several college courses while in prison. Paddy was a poet too and had several of his poems published in Ireland and over in England.

We only parted company after the pub closed for the night. Paddy took a black taxi back to Ardoyne. *"Oíche mhaith, a chara!"* he called out from the window, as it drove off. Goodnight, my friend.

I lit up a cigarette and walked back through the city center to Eglantine Avenue.

Late the next morning, I received another visit from Paddy Murphy, and we continued where we left off the night before. My new jovial, communist-sympathizing, Republican friend wanted to drop by nearby Queen's University Bookshop to see if they carried a certain book on

Russian history. When Paddy was told by a clerk that they didn't have it, he made his way to the section on Irish politics and history.

He said he wanted to pick up a book for a friend and asked me what I'd recommend. I looked over the books on the shelves and saw *The Dirty War,* by Martin Dillon, which Fergus claimed was an excellent, unbiased account of the Troubles. Paddy removed a copy from the shelf. Then looking at a rack of pamphlets and booklets, he plucked out Wolfe Tone's *An Argument on Behalf of the Catholics of Ireland,* written in 1791, on the eve of the United Irishmen Rising. He asked me what I thought of Wolfe Tone.

"A great Irish patriot, of course," I replied.

"Oh, aye," agreed Paddy, "the *greatest.*"

After he paid, we stepped outside. Reaching into his jacket pocket, Paddy produced a pen, scribbled something inside Tone's pamphlet, and handed it to me along with the plastic bag containing the book.

"Happy Christmas to ye!" he exclaimed.

"Ah Paddy, you didn't need to do that."

He had written in the pamphlet, "To Éamon from Pádraig Ó Murchú."

"To Éamon?" I asked puzzled.

"Sure, both our names in their Irish forms."

From that moment on, I was rechristened Éamon, at least for Paddy Murphy – a.k.a. Pádraig Ó Murchú.

I accompanied Paddy to Ulster People's College, on a street off the Malone Road. He wanted to duck in to greet a friend of his who taught there. I was briefly introduced to the bespectacled Dr. Johnston Price, who appeared to be in his late thirties. I stood a bit off and didn't hang onto every word of their conversation, but I heard the professor mention about being with a party delegation to the Soviet Union.

"That was the Communist delegation," said Paddy once we were out walking towards the Malone Road. "Yer man's a member of the Party."

Paddy made a remark about Johnston Price being a Protestant communist.

"A Protestant communist?" I queried. "Is there such a thing, I thought they were all atheists?"

"Ah, there is in sectarian Ireland!" laughed Paddy. "Sure, 'tis like when the Irishman asked his new acquaintance, 'Are ye Catholic or are ye Protestant?' And gets the reply, 'Well, actually I'm an atheist.'

Yer Irishman then asks, 'Now, are ye a Catholic atheist or a Protestant atheist?' Ye'll bloody well have a religion here whether ye like it or not!"

Paddy led the way to the Ulster Museum, located in Botanic Gardens, beside Queen's University. At the park's entrance, we passed the weathered, green bronze statue of bearded Lord Kelvin, a renowned Belfast-born physicist, up on his pedestal.

The museum was in a mostly neoclassical stone building with columns, constructed in the 1920's. But part of the façade had been grotesquely altered in the early 1970's. The classical look of the large edifice was changed when modernist architects added on an ugly extension of huge, featureless, rectilinear concrete blocks, which seemed to collide with the older stately building.

Paddy spoke to a woman seated at a desk in the lobby, and she picked up a phone and made a call. We were soon met by another bespectacled scholar. Mr. Terry Bruton was a dignified looking man of about sixty. On the walk over to the museum, Paddy had told me his old comrade was also an esteemed member of the Communist Party of Ireland. Another Belfast Protestant, he had been involved in the Northern Ireland Civil Rights Association. According to Paddy, he "wanted to change things for the better."

Mr. Bruton warmly welcomed us and brought us to his office. I listened with interest as he explained his work as a scientific officer of vertebrates, responsible for the preparation of skins and bones. He had recently been involved in digging up the carcass of a very rare European beaked whale which had been stranded on the rocks of County Sligo's Ballysadare Bay and was buried by the county council in the interests of public health. He then spoke at length about the history of Ireland's ice age and the extinctions of various native animals – including the Irish elk with its tremendous antlers, the fierce gray wolf, and the penguin-like great auk. Mr. Bruton also discovered an early prehistoric settlement at Ballyvaston in County Down.

Paddy and I were taken on a tour of the back rooms of the museum, where the general public wasn't allowed. Mr. Bruton showed us collections of hundreds of stuffed birds, ducks, foxes, badgers, stoats, otters, and scores of other lifeless animals with glass eyes.

But what left the most lasting impression on me was when I chanced to stop at one of the museum's upper windows and was able to look down on the adjacent Friar's Bush Graveyard.

"It's the city's oldest Christian burial site," said Mr. Bruton, who stood beside me with Paddy, gazing down. "There are those who would claim that it goes back to Saint Patrick's time."

He told us about a curious stone found in Friar's Bush marked A.D. 485. While its antiquity was doubted by historians, the ancient burying ground seems to go back to the earliest Christian times, if not back to pagan days. As far as its link to Saint Patrick, who may have died circa 461, records from the early 17th century refer to the site as the *Capella de Kilpatrick,* that is the Chapel of the Church of Patrick. Earlier medieval records indicate a friary was once situated there.

When the Penal Laws were enacted in 1695, making it illegal for Catholics to practice their religion, the faithful in Belfast worshipped in the graveyard. A wandering friar came to clandestinely say Mass under the shelter of an old hawthorn tree or bush, which is how the cemetery came to be called Friar's Bush.

Paddy recited the first part of the poem "The Friar's Bush" by Belfast poet Joseph Campbell:

> *In penal times, as peasants tell,*
> *A friar came with book and bell*
> *To chaunt his Mass each Sabbath morn*
> *Beneath Srath-milis' trysting-thorn.*
>
> *He came in sun, he came in flood*
> *From* Ard-micNasca's *holy wood,*
> *Where Niall built his monastery*
> *To house the scripts of the* Clann-Aedha-buidhe.
>
> *The folk who deemed their fathers' faith*
> *More dear than life and laughed at death,*
> *Came thither every Sabbath morn*
> *To worship God beneath the thorn.*

There's a legend that the good friar was caught and hung from the same thorn tree under which he said Mass. But as Father Leo McKeown told the story in a 1934 historical society's journal, the unnamed priest was shot rather than hung.

"The story is that the friar, who is described as short in stature and having snow-white hair, was accustomed to row across the Lagan in his currach to say Mass at Friar's Bush. One Sunday in winter, with heavy snow falling, the arrangements were made as usual; a temporary altar of boards and canvas was erected under the whitethorn bush in the centre of the graveyard, and the small congregation remained waiting anxiously, speculating as to whether the old priest had got lost in some snowdrift or perhaps been arrested. He arrived, however, to the great joy of his congregation, said Mass, but just as he turned round to give the last blessing, he fell at the foot of the improvised altar, shot through the heart. Consternation and fear seized the worshippers who scattered in all directions, sure that the military had arrived. On their return they found the friar dead: he was buried where he fell, and a stone erected on the spot."

Another priest, Father Phelim O'Hamill, was arrested in the early 1700's and thrown into Belfast Jail, where he remained until he died.

By 1769, the harsh Penal Laws began to be relaxed and local Catholics no longer needed to attend Mass at the graveyard, which was then in the countryside, and started to worship at a "Mass-house" in Belfast town, until the first Catholic church was opened in 1784. But Friar's Bush continued as the Catholic burial ground, and in 1828 the Marquis of Donegall, the leading Protestant landlord of Belfast, donated another acre to enlarge it, and enclosed the cemetery with an eight-foot-high stone wall, and built at the entrance a double-sided Gothic-style gatehouse.

Locked gates and high walls around city cemeteries were necessary in the early 19th century with the rise of the "resurrectionists," or body-snatchers, who robbed freshly dug graves for corpses to sell to medical schools.

"*Two Acres of Irish History,* is what Dr. Phoenix aptly called his recently published booklet about Friar's Bush," said Mr. Bruton.

He pointed to a low, grassy mound, not far from the entrance. "That's Plaguey Hill. It was used as a cholera pit when a major epidemic spread from Europe to Belfast in 1832-33. Over four hundred cholera victims were buried there. The pit was reopened for more than five thousand additional bodies during the Famine years, in 1845-49, when the impoverished, starving, and destitute were dying of typhus and other diseases."

"God have mercy on their souls," said Paddy.

Along with the unnamed poor buried in mass graves were some of the leading citizens of the city with prominent tombstones. A number were newspaper editors and businessmen.

"Over there," pointed Mr. Bruton, "at the far wall, is the tomb of Kevin Buggy, the young editor of the Roman Catholic *Vindicator* newspaper. He was a Kilkenny man, only a year in Belfast when he died prematurely at aged twenty-seven in 1843."

"Yer man was also a great Republican," added Paddy.

"Aye, so he was," agreed Mr. Bruton.

In the front corner, by the cholera mound, was the canopied monument of Andrew Joseph McKenna, who launched his *Northern Star* newspaper in 1868. In the other corner, along the front wall, was another elaborate monument to Robert Read, who established Ireland's first penny newspaper, *The Belfast Morning News,* in 1855. Beside him was the grave of Bernard "Barney" Hughes, the master baker known for making a cheaper bread during the Famine. He was the first Catholic elected to Belfast Town Council; but after he died in 1878, future generations best remembered him for his famous "Barney's Bap" (bread).

Paddy recited the children's street rhyme: "Barney Hughes Bread, sticks to yer belly like lead. Not a bit a wonder, ye fart like thunder! Barney Hughes Bread."

Beneath the museum window was the grave of Father Jeremiah Ryan McAuley, who was an architect before he became a priest and died in 1873, aged forty-three.

"You see that Celtic cross there?" asked Mr. Bruton, pointing to a large monument. "It was erected as a memorial for Dr. Francis Joseph Wisely, of Belfast, who was with the Royal Army Medical Corps, in 1915, at the Dardanelles in Turkey, and was killed while attending to the sick and wounded under heavy fire. The doctor was laid to rest in the British military cemetery in Alexandria, Egypt."

Paddy was staring down at the burial ground thoughtfully. "Somewhere there's the grave of the Fenian John Griffith. He was with the Young Irelanders of 1848, before he joined the Fenians. Griffith spent two periods in Crumlin Road Jail, and in later years he and his wife had a newsagent's shop in Divis Street."

"Yes, Paddy," said a smiling Mr. Bruton, "we wouldn't want to forget the Fenians now, would we?"

When John Griffith died in 1892, Friar's Bush had already closed as a graveyard and only families with burial rights were entitled to inter their dead there. The old burying ground had long been overcrowded and was replaced in 1869 by Milltown as the main Catholic cemetery. The gates of Friar's Bush on Stranmillis Road were then locked – only to be opened for the extremely rare burial – and the high walls that surrounded the graveyard prevented the curious passerby from wandering through its overgrown grass and neglected graves.

Paddy and I thanked Mr. Bruton and bid him a good afternoon. We then left the Ulster Museum and made our way to Kelly's Cellars, off Castle Street, where we were so warmly welcomed the night before. Again, our drinks were on the house, and we drank our fill and had a couple of hot bowls of delicious stew for dinner. But as Paddy was leaving early in the morning to visit friends in Derry City, we called it a night before closing time.

CHAPTER FORTY-TWO
A SHAMROCK TATTOO

Oh, Paddy dear, and did ye hear the news that's goin' round?
The shamrock is by law forbid to grow on Irish ground!
No more Saint Patrick's Day we'll keep, his colour can't be seen
For there's a cruel law against the Wearin' o' the Green.

I met with Napper Tandy, and he took me by the hand
And he said, "How's poor ould Ireland and how does she stand?"
"She's the most distressful country that ever yet was seen
For they're hanging men and women there for the Wearin' o' the Green."

So if the colour we must wear be England's cruel red
Let it remind us of the blood that Irishmen have shed
And pull the shamrock from your hat, and throw it on the sod
But never fear, 'twill take root there, through underfoot 'tis trod.

The day's mail brought me a postcard with a big Union Jack on it. Although Callaghan didn't sign it, I immediately recognized his handwriting. He sent it from the airport in London when he was on his way to New York.

Dear Lord Edmond –

I'm having an absolutely marvelous time on the mainland here in London. I sent this postcard in recognition of all that you've done to further the aims of the British Empire – on which the sun will never set! The British people are especially grateful for your efforts in subduing those nasty Irish savages across the water.

Up the border between Eire and the U.K.!
God Save the Queen!
Your British friends.

It seemed my humorless pal acquired some wit once he departed Ireland's green shamrock shores.

I also received Christmas cards from my parents and sister, and from Pat Hamill in San Francisco. I was surprised to find four $50 bills in Pat's card. It was the $200 he borrowed from me more than two years before. The money couldn't have come at a better time, as my cash was beginning to dwindle. "Heard you were in Clady and Strabane," he wrote. "Look after yourself. Don't get too drunk! All the best & happy Christmas. Your friends – Pat, Karen, Christina & baby Elizabeth."

After grabbing a bite for lunch at the Mad Hatter Coffee Shop, down Eglantine Avenue, I went to the bank and exchanged Pat's $200 for British pounds, then took a stroll to the city center. The streets were buzzing with holiday shoppers loaded down with bags full of Christmas gifts.

As I approached Donegall Square with its prominent, green copper-domed City Hall in its center, I noticed on the sidewalk by the ornamental wrought iron fence a street preacher waving a Bible and a few of his followers holding placards. The red-faced preacher with slicked-back hair was shouting how the wages of sin were death and how the blood of Jesus Christ cleanses us from all sin. I read the slogans on the placards as I passed by. "Repent and Believe." "The Wicked Shall Be Turned Into Hell." "Thou Shalt Surely Die," read the sign held by one grim-looking woman. There was too, of course, the Protestant staple: "The Pope Is The Anti-Christ." And pacing back and forth was a tall old man, in an overcoat and tweed cap, wearing a sandwich board sign emblazoned with "The End Of The World Is Nigh."

Leaving this merry band of doomsdayers, I continued on past stately old Victorian buildings. Many were venerable banks and leading law firms. I had no particular destination in mind and turned randomly onto different streets lined with businesses in three- to four-story stone or brick buildings.

I stopped at the window of an antique shop to see the various bric-a-brac on display and decided to look inside out of curiosity. Making my way past framed black and white portraits of King George VI and a young Elizabeth II, polished wood tables covered with fancy teacups, small vases, and porcelain figurines, I paused to examine an old samurai sword hanging on a wall by a World War II Japanese Rising Sun flag.

Near a large grandfather clock was other military memorabilia. Uniforms hung on a rack and more swords were placed on a table along with a mix of British Army officers' caps and helmets from different countries. I picked up an Imperial German black helmet with a great spike on top and a large gold eagle on the front of it.

"If you are interested, I have more military collectables here," said an old gentleman in a Germanic accent, behind a long glass counter. He had a neat white mustache and wore a tie with a charcoal gray cardigan.

I walked over and saw an assortment of medals. The antique dealer pointed out a Victoria Cross, Britain's highest military award for valor, and a French Legion of Honour. Among others on display were several medals with the Nazi swastika. The showcase also had a German Luger pistol, but my attention drifted to several beautifully crafted, vintage silver and gold pocket watches. I had always wanted to sport a pocket watch.

"Most of zem are Sviss made," said the shop owner.

He told me he was originally from Switzerland and was a watchmaker by trade. He came to London after the war and to Belfast in the 1950's after he married an Irishwoman.

I continued to look at the items in the case as the old Swiss proprietor lit up a pipe. Beside an elaborate silver crucifix ornamented with colored gems, from 18th century Portugal, was an Irish penal cross from County Galway. Carved from a single piece of wood, about ten inches in length and about two and a half inches across, the penal cross included the figure of Christ. Above His head were the letters I.N.R.I., for the Latin inscription: *Iesus Nazarenus, Rex Iudaeorum* (Jesus of Nazareth, King of the Jews). Below His feet were a rooster and a pot, which the antique dealer explained, as he puffed on his pipe, was from the early legend relating to Judas the betrayer, when a roasting cock suddenly came to life and crowed, prophesying the Resurrection. On the back of the cross was etched the year 1721.

"Can you imagine vat zee man voze hands carved zat humble cross had vitnessed," he reflected, relighting his pipe. "Ze persecution he must have zuffered for his faith. Zee destruction of Cazolic churches in zis land. Zee creator of zis cross must have knelt in hidden glens amongst his coreligionists to hear Mass in zecret by outlawed und hunted priests. Arh! I am not a Cazolic, but I regard zis as a most zacred object."

Just then a bunch of schoolgirls entered the shop, laughing and excitedly chattering away, full of youthful exuberance. They looked to be maybe fourteen or fifteen years old, all attired in matching school uniforms of navy-blue blazers with their school crest, over gray V-neck sweaters and red and blue striped ties, and gray pleated skirts down to their calves.

I had been too long in sectarian Belfast because it immediately occurred to me that their uniforms indicated they attended a Protestant school. All schools, of course, were segregated by religion in Northern Ireland.

The antique dealer proudly introduced me to his granddaughter, a pretty blonde girl with a turned-up nose, as the other girls giggled. I wished them all a good afternoon as I left the shop.

I walked on through the bustling streets packed with businesses and shops. At the corner of Victoria Street and Queen's Square, I stopped to gaze up at the Albert Memorial Clock Tower. Standing more than 110 feet tall, the local landmark was Belfast's mini–Big Ben. The city's great timepiece was mentioned in my guidebook and Jonathan Bardon's *Belfast: An Illustrated History.* The sandstone tower was completed in 1869, in a blend of French and Italian Gothic styles, to commemorate Queen Victoria's husband, Prince Albert. In addition to a statue of the Prince Consort, the tower included ornately carved crowned lions, angels, gargoyles, and floral decorations.

From where I stood, I could see two of the clock's four faces. I read the bell, housed in the tower, weighed two tons, and could be heard from over eight miles away.

A year earlier the clock was damaged, along with dozens of buildings in the area, when an I.R.A. bomb exploded outside the nearby River House on High Street, headquarters of the Police Authority for Northern Ireland and a Tourist Board office.

I turned at the green titled building of the Transport & General Workers' Union and took Victoria Street to the corner of Waring Street, where the large, four-story red-brick Nambarrie Tea factory was situated. I made a left onto Waring, and after passing Bridge Street junction, and more shops and restaurants, found myself strolling along the narrower Rosemary Street.

Noticing an alleyway marked Winecellar Entry, I turned into it. Belfast's historic alleyways, called entries, date back to the 17th century when the town began to develop into a city. Winecellar Entry received its name in the early 19th century due to the number of winecellars that were located there. The alley I wandered down led to White's Tavern, established in 1630. The white three-story structure was rebuilt in 1790. It was Belfast's oldest tavern. A tavern in those early days, unlike a public house, provided food and lodging, as well as alcoholic drinks.

Inside the décor was typically old-time, cozy pub or tavern, with a long wood bar, an open fireplace, oak ceiling beams, and framed old pictures and whiskey mirrors on the walls. There was a good-sized crowd occupying the tables, and I took a seat at the bar.

I had a pint of Guinness with a bowl of beef stew, then another Guinness to wash it down along with a double Bushmills. A large, black-bearded man with long hair, in his early forties, sat down a couple of barstools over from me. He pulled off his denim jacket and placed it on the stool between us, revealing his thick arms covered in tattoos down to his wrists. He looked like a biker.

Having overheard my accent when I was talking to the bartender, he asked me where in America I was from.

"New York," I replied, "but I've been living for the past few years in California."

"Is that right, in what part of the Golden State?" he asked.

When I told him San Diego, he said he once lived in Northern California for five years. He was a Belfast man but had served sixteen years in the U.S. Army and saw two tours of duty in Vietnam.

I shook the extended hand of the big, bearded man and heard his name was David Bingham, though his friends called him "Skull." I learned he was a tattooist and our conversation naturally turned to the subject of tattoos. As a former sailor, I followed naval tradition and had a few tattoos myself.

Taking off my jacket, I rolled up my right shirt sleeve to show Skull the anchor tattoo I had on my outer forearm and the colorful downward swooping bird I had on the inside. My left forearm was bare. I had other tattoos, but I wasn't going to remove my shirt at the bar to show them off. On my chest, I had a butterfly tattoo. Over my heart was my wife Beth's name and on my upper right arm were my daughters Mary and Brigid's names. On my upper left arm was my first tattoo, a small green shamrock with "ERIN GO BRAGH" above it. I was just out of boot camp when I got it at one of the tattoo parlors along San Diego's Broadway. A sailor pal named Ron Reilly – who was proudly Chicago Irish – was with me and got the same. Beneath the little shamrock I later added a larger Celtic cross, in red and black ink.

When Skull suggested I ought to get a tattoo to commemorate my stay in Ireland, I agreed and accompanied him to his nearby parlor at Wellington Place. As we walked, he told me he operated one of the only two legal tattoo parlors in the city. The other was run over on the Shankill Road and did "mostly Loyalist tats," like Union Jacks and Red Hands of Ulster. While Skull seemed to come from a Protestant background, and admitted his father had a career in the British Army, he chose to steer away from what he called political tats.

Skull's parlor was being minded by his girlfriend Tracey, called "Dark" presumably due to her long jet-black hair. If Skull looked like a biker, she looked every bit like a biker chick. Slim and shapely, in her late twenties, her slender arms were heavily decorated with tattoos.

I glanced at the numerous drawings on the walls. There were a lot of Celtic and Gothic designs, crosses and Claddagh symbols, wizards, dragons, ghouls, and monsters. Skull said most of the artwork was his own and he recommended I get one of his Celtic knots. As attractive as the intricate knot patterns were, I knew what I wanted before I ever left the bar – another shamrock tattoo, only larger and on my bare left outer forearm.

Without further ado, Skull had me take a seat and soon set to work on my arm with an electrically vibrating needle, injecting ink into my skin. A black outline was drawn, about the size of a U.S. silver dollar, and green ink was then used to fill it in. He printed "IRELAND" above the shamrock, as I requested, and under a leaf put "92" for the year. The tattoo was expertly done and well worth the £20 Skull charged me for my permanent souvenir of Ireland.

The simple three-leaved clover is the very symbol of the Irish. The word "shamrock" is derived from the Gaelic *seamóg,* meaning "young clover," and it grows in abundance all over the green Emerald Isle. The diminutive plant was sacred to the ancient Druids because its leaves formed a triad, and three was a mystical number in their pagan religion. When Saint Patrick brought Christianity to the Irish, he used the shamrock to illustrate the concept of the Holy Trinity. With a crowd of potential converts gathered around him, good ould Saint Paddy stooped down and plucked a sprig from the sod and held it before them. Behold, one clover but three leaves. One God but three Persons – the Father, the Son, and the Holy Ghost.

In the late 18th century, the shamrock was adopted as an emblem of the Irish Volunteers, as the local militias were known, formed to defend Ireland against invasion from France and Spain. Many of the Volunteers, however, had Republican sympathies. The United Irishmen of the 1790's wore green uniforms and hat ribbons to match the color of the shamrock. It was a time in Ireland when a person risked death by hanging by wearing green or showing their patriotism by displaying a shamrock on their hat.

CHAPTER FORTY-THREE
WHISKEY YE'RE THE DEVIL

A grinning Paddy Murphy returned from Derry with a fistful of money. He said he collected on an old debt owed him. So, with Paddy's wad of banknotes and with what I had left of the money I received from Pat Hamill, we went on a spree, knocking back pints and whiskeys in half a dozen different pubs on Castle Street and its vicinity.

We started with Guinness and a couple of Black Bush whiskeys at The Hercules Bar at the corner of Castle Street and Chapel Lane. Lest I think the drinking establishment we were patronizing was named for the Greek and Roman demi-god of strength, Paddy informed me as we sat at the bar the place took its name from a long-demolished street named for one Sir Hercules Langford, a burgess in old Belfast.

"A hundred years ago, yer nearby thoroughfare of Royal Avenue was called Hercules Street. Before 'twas cleaned up and widened, the whole bloody street stank from butcher shops and slaughterhouses. A couple of hundred years before that, in the earliest days of Belfast town, 'twas but a wee lane, Hercules Lane, so 'twas."

With fresh pints and whiskeys set before us, Paddy continued, as I lit a cigarette.

"The Hercules Bar was founded in 1875 by Patrick McGlade. In 1972, as the Orangies were celebratin' their Glorious 12th of July, some Loyalist bastard hurled a feckin' bomb into the Hercules because it was frequented by Catholics. The blast destroyed everything in sight, leavin' sixty-five people wounded, three quite severely."

From the Hercules, we made the short walk to the Cheers Bar for a couple of more pints and doubles of Black Bush. The bartenders in all the places we went knew Paddy by name, as did so many of the people who came over to greet him, shake his hand, and pat him on the back.

"Jaysus! Paddy Murphy! They finally let ye out!" exclaimed an older man wearing a cap, as he grasped Paddy's hand.

"Ah Paddy, dear man, good to see ye again," said a buxom middle-aged woman, giving him a hug.

"Cheers, Paddy," I toasted, when she was gone, lifting my whiskey.

"*Sláinte mhaith,* Éamon," he happily replied, clinking my glass.

We spent very little of our money for drinks as people kept buying us rounds. As we dandered down to Kelly's Cellars, Paddy recalled how he didn't always have the price of a pint.

"Sure, I was once in that great frozen land of Canada, back in the winter of '66, and was ramblin' through Vancouver town without so much as a Canadian buck in me pocket, and me desperate something fierce for a creamy pint of stout. Then I chanced upon this bar with a big, lovely shamrock and a Mc or O name on it.

"I says to meself, surely Paddy from the good ould Emerald Isle would find a welcome here and some kind soul with a few drops of Irish blood flowin' through his veins would be good enough to stand me a pint. But just to be sure, I threw open the door, turned and shouted over me shoulder into the wind, loud enough for all within to hear me: 'Ye can fuck off, I'm proud to be an Irishman!' Sure, Paddy didn't need to pay for a single drink there *atoll.*"

Tending bar at Kelly's was the same gent with the long hair and long gray sideburns, and we again drank on the house. Over Guinness and doubles of Bushmills, Paddy continued to relate his misadventures while in the Great White North above the U.S.A.

"I even had the opportunity to experience Canadian justice at its bloody finest when I got arrested for relievin' meself when drunk in front of a Royal Bank of Canada. When I appeared before the oul judge, I found his name was Patrick Murphy too! Sure, he let me off scot-free – or rather Irish-free!"

We roared with laughter over this, as fresh pints of stout and whiskeys were set before us.

"Speakin' of names," continued Paddy, "did ye hear the one about the man who was stopped by a R.U.C. patrol? The peeler asks him for his name, but yer man says he can't give it. 'Why's that?' asks the peeler. 'Because if I give ye me name then ye'd have two names and I'd have none,' says yer man."

We left Kelly's Cellars and made the walk down the street, across Royal Avenue, and down to Winecellar Entry to White's Tavern, which took us from Belfast's oldest pub to its oldest tavern. Another couple of pints of the black stuff with whiskey chasers and we were back out in the cool night air. Drunk, but none the worst for it. We were in grand form – as the Irish would say. Suddenly Paddy burst out into song. The words weren't in English, but it certainly wasn't any traditional Irish song in Gaelic either.

¡Arriba, parias de la Tierra!
¡En pie, famélica legión!
Los proletarios gritan: Guerra!
Guerra hasta el fin de la opresión.

Although a far cry from how it would have been sung in old España, I could make out the gist of Paddy's Irish accented and broken Spanish. Living in San Diego, I spent enough time south of the U.S. border to pick up a good smattering of the language.

"'Tis the Spanish version of 'L'Internationale,'" explained Paddy. The anthem of worldwide communism. "Of course, there's many different versions of it," he added, and began loudly singing one in English.

Arise, ye workers from your slumber,
Arise, ye prisoners of want.
For reason in revolt now thunders...

Paddy continued for maybe a couple of more verses, but I was no longer listening to the communist propaganda. Young lovers with their arms around each other passed by us and smiled. We must have made quite the sight staggering along with Paddy's arm draped over my shoulder as he sang about the workers of the world uniting in a proletarian revolution against the bourgeoisie.

We turned off Waring Street and passed through a lane or two and came out onto another street. I wondered where we were and Paddy pointed to a sign that read, "Skipper Street."

"When Belfast was a seafarin' town," he said, "skippers of sailing ships lodged here."

We entered the Blackthorn Bar on Skipper Street and as we waited for the barman to pull our pints and pour our whiskeys, we focused our attention on the news report on the TV behind the bar. The Ulster Freedom Fighters had carried out seven incendiary bomb attacks on shops in Dublin and towns near the border. The Irish National Liberation Army had shot and wounded a man who worked for the Belfast City Council. The Irish Republican Army had planted three incendiary bombs at an industrial estate in Belfast and damaged three buildings. And following their long-term strategy of taking the war to England, the I.R.A. had bombed a shopping center in London's Wood Green district, injuring eleven people including a number of police officers. Thus, the war continued.

Paddy leaned closer to me to whisper, "At least our Provie boys got their licks in too."

Someone called out for a round of drinks, as I contemplated my tumbler of whiskey on the bar. I was a stout man more than a whiskey drinker. But I couldn't deny that night I was enjoying my fill of *uisce beatha* – that's Irish Gaelic for the "water of life" from which the word "whiskey" is derived. It's said the distilled spirit made from grain was invented in Ireland over a thousand years ago. Irish monks carried it to Scotland where their fellow Gaelic-speaking Celts called it *uisge beatha*. Centuries later, Scotch whisky (spelled without the "e") became more popular on a worldwide scale than the Irish variety.

Of course, America has her own proud whiskey-making tradition, inherited from the Scotch-Irish, with bourbons from Kentucky and Tennessee whiskeys. Canadians too have long had their own good selection of whiskies (unlike us Yanks, though, the Canucks use the

Scottish spelling of "whisky"). I heard tell even the Japanese had taken to distilling whiskey.

But when I drank whiskey, it was Irish I drank. I gave little thought, however, to the brand. Be it Jameson, Bushmills, Powers, Tullamore Dew, or Paddy's – they were all fine products of Irish distilleries. I couldn't at that point really distinguish the subtle differences between the various Irish whiskeys. Although that night I fancied myself an experienced whiskey connoisseur, as I detected the sweet, honeyed taste in the sharp yet smooth and mellow, triple-distilled Bushmills I was sipping. The Black Bush that I had earlier was darker in color; I heard from being matured in Spanish sherry casks and bourbon barrels. Velvety smooth, rich and a tad spicy, Black Bush had more malt and less grain, making it heavier and Scotch-like in character.

Both the standard Bushmills and Black Bush, of course, come from the Old Bushmills Distillery on County Antrim's north coast. Established in 1608, Bushmills holds the title of the world's oldest licensed whiskey distillery.

"Sufferin' Jaysus! Drink up, Éamon," said Paddy Murphy jovially, awakening me from my boozy reverie.

Two whiskey doubles were now before me on the bar along with another fresh pint of the black stuff. *Sláinte!*

I quickly knocked back the doubles and drained the pint, with a few precious drops of Guinness dribbling down my chin, before Paddy grabbed my arm and ushered me back out into the cold night air. I wasn't familiar with the darkened streets, but Paddy was, and he led the way. We threw our arms over one another's shoulders and marched soldier-like, after a few near stumbles. Paddy again burst out into song and this time I joined in as I well knew the words.

> *Now brave boys, we're on the march*
> *Off to Portugal and Spain*
> *Drums are beatin', banners flyin'*
> *The Devil at home will come tonight*
> *So it's go, fare thee well*
> *With a too da loo ra loo ra doo de da*
> *Me rikes fall too ra laddie-o*
> *There's whiskey in the jar*

Oh, whiskey ye're the devil
Ye're leadin' me astray
Over hills and mountains
And to Amerikay
Ye're sweetness from the Bleachner
And spunkier than tea
Oh whiskey, ye're me darlin' drunk or sober

The French are fightin' boldly
Men are dyin' hot and coldly
Give every man his flask of powder
His firelock on his shoulder
So its go, fare thee well
With a too da loo ra loo ra doo de da
Me rikes fall too ra laddie-o
There's whiskey in the jar

Oh, whiskey ye're the devil
Ye're leadin' me astray
Over hills and mountains
And to Amerikay
Ye're sweetness from the Bleachner
And spunkier than tea
Oh whiskey, ye're me darlin' drunk or sober

Says the ould wan do not wrong me
Don't take me daughter from me
For if ye do I will torment ye
When I'm dead me ghost will haunt ye
So it's go, fare thee well
With a too da loo ra loo ra doo de da
A too ra loo ra loo ra doo de da
Me rikes fall ra laddie-o
There's whiskey in the jar

The song dated back at least a couple of hundred years, but in the late 1950's the Clancy Brothers and Tommy Makem breathed new life into it and popularized the old song among lovers of Irish folk music around the world.

"Do ye know, Éamon, why the Clancy Brothers sing?" asked Paddy. "Because Tommy *Make 'em*," I answered.

We turned off the narrow, cobble-stoned street into the narrower cobbled entry of Commercial Court, where the Duke of York was located. Inside was a boisterous crowd. A quartet of American-style country singers were performing, complete with guitars and banjos, and donning cowboy hats and boots. Everywhere you looked on the pub's walls was crammed whiskey-branded and Guinness mirrors and other drinking memorabilia.

I sat at one of the tables just vacated as Paddy went over to the packed bar to order us drinks. He returned with doubles of Black Bush and soon the barman brought us our pints.

"Whilst the Duke is not yer oldest pub in Belfast," began Paddy, after a generous swallow of Guinness, "it's been here for a good long while and seen a bit of history. When Gerry Adams was just seventeen years of age, he pulled pints here. In '72, a couple of our boys were goin' to bomb the High Court and to avoid a security checkpoint ran up the entry just outside and the bloody bomb they were carrin' went off prematurely. The explosion flattened the pub. What ye see here is the rebuilt Duke."

A smiling middle-aged couple approached our table. The man had a full head of snow-white hair and a striped tie hung down over his potbellied stomach. The woman had salt and pepper hair and square wire-framed glasses and wore a neat blue dress for her night out with her hubby.

"Oh, Paddy luv, we didn't know ye were released," said the woman.

"Mind yez say nothin'," replied Paddy conspiratorially. "I just climbed over the wall this mornin'. Sure, they don't know I'm gone yet."

"Ah Jaysus, Paddy, ye're always the gas man!" chuckled the white-haired man.

I was introduced to the McCloskeys, and they bought us all a round of drinks before departing.

Paddy was standing at the bar talking with two young men he seemed to know. Before me were two fresh pints, a half finished one, and a couple of more tumblers of whiskey. My head was spinning as the four Irish guys in cowboy hats and boots sang, in faked American country accents, "The Two-Hundred-Year-Old Alcoholic," popularized by Liam Clancy and Tommy Makem.

When Paddy rejoined me at the table, he remarked that the young fellows I saw him chatting with were "active Republicans" from Ardoyne. I understood that to mean they were I.R.A. The barman then brought us over another round, courtesy of the volunteers at the bar. I looked over in their direction and one gave me a nod and I lifted my pint to him in a silent toast.

The music had stopped and suddenly the barman flickered the lights to indicate it was closing time. I quickly downed my three tumblers of whiskey and then needed to grip the edge of the table to steady myself. I could only manage a sip more of Guinness. But I still had two untouched pints in front of me. Not wanting to waste any of the black nectar, I carefully hid the two full pints under my jacket to smuggle them out of the pub. Sure, I'd surprise Paddy with a parting glass in the street.

Ever so slowly I walked, lest I spill any, to the door. Paddy was already outside wishing people a good night, a God bless, and a safe home. I intended to wait for the pub crowd to disperse before I'd unzip my jacket to reveal the pints I had taken to Paddy. But then he gave me a slap on the back.

"Well, we certainly had a bloody great time of it, didn't we?"

"That we did, Paddy," I replied, sadly looking down at my now wet trousers. Paddy's back slap sent half the Guinness out of each of the pints down my legs.

"Oh, Jaysus, Éamon! There was a perfectly good loo inside the pub," roared Paddy.

I opened my jacket and brought out the half empty pints. Still laughing, Paddy knocked back what was left in the pint I handed him, and I finished the remnants of the other.

"Good on ye, Éamon!"

Paddy then stepped into a black taxi along with a few others from the pub who were bound for Ardoyne. I was heading in the opposite direction and staggered off, jarred and legless, into the night with only a vague notion of my destination being Eglantine Avenue in south Belfast.

Oh, whiskey ye're the devil
Ye're leadin' me astray
Over hills and mountains
And to Amerikay
Ye're sweetness from the Bleachner
And spunkier than tea
Oh whiskey, ye're me darlin' drunk or sober

CHAPTER FORTY-FOUR
GERALDINE McKEEVER

"Oh, whiskey ye're the devil…ye're leadin' me astray…over hills and mountains…and to Amerikay." Only I wasn't in America. I was in Ireland, and it felt like all the hammers of hell were banging away at my head. I had an excruciating headache to say the very least. Opening my eyes, I found myself stretched out on a soft sofa, covered by a warm yellow wool blanket and under my head was a big fluffy pillow. Obviously, I wasn't in my flat and I tried to piece together the previous night's events.

I was drinking with Paddy Murphy at the Hercules Bar and Cheers and Kelly's, and where else? I needed to think. We made a stop at White's Tavern and then…then the Blackthorn, ending up at the Duke of York. I remembered walking out with pints, then the front of my trousers being soaked with Guinness. It was slowly coming back to me.

Paddy and I must have parted company sometime around 1:30 a.m. I wandered and staggered, aimlessly, through the dark and empty city streets, just struggling to put one foot in front of the other without stumbling and falling. Then I came to the flashing blue lights of a parked R.U.C. Land Rover at Shaftesbury Square. Nearby was a second Land Rover belonging to the British Army. It was a checkpoint. R.U.C. men and soldiers stood around their vehicles, some of them smoking cigarettes.

I was called over by a R.U.C. man with a closely clipped mustache, parted in the middle, who wanted to know where I was going at that "ungodly hour."

"Disgusting!" exclaimed another burly, clean-shaven constable, in a flak jacket and a peak cap too small for his large head, as I approached. "Ye pissed yerself, all over yer trousers."

"It's Guinness, actually," I remember saying.

"What's yer address?" demanded the other officer.

"2230 Dunlop Street," I duly answered.

"*Dunbar* Street, ye mean?"

"No, *Dunlop* Street," I insisted.

The mustached constable asked yet another R.U.C. man if he was familiar with a Dunlop Street in the city. He was not. As he called my address over a radio, I was told to produce my identification. I removed my California driver's license from my wallet and handed it to the constable. He shined his flashlight on it, smiled and shook his head.

"Dunlop Street in *San Diego, California*!" he called out to the other R.U.C. men. "Do ye not have a local address?"

It took a couple of moments for me to reorient myself and remember what country I was in.

"97 Eglantine Avenue," I finally said.

"Well, ye're goin' in the wrong bloody direction!" bawled the burly constable.

Redirected, I turned around and started walking unsteadily away from the city center. From that point things became a blank again. I must have kept walking, but I couldn't remember arriving back at Eglantine Avenue. In any case, I didn't end up face down in a cold, dirty puddle in the gutter. Instead, I was as snug as a bug in a rug, under a warm wool blanket on a comfy sofa. Somewhere.

I looked at the room around me. There were shelves with teddy bears, various other stuffed animals, and dolls. On a wall, hung a picture of the Blessed Virgin and a pastoral painting of horses grazing in a green field. On a corner table were a number of framed family photographs but I couldn't make out any of the people in them from where I was on the sofa. Across the room, bright sunlight came in through a window with lacy, peach-colored drapes. I glanced at my wristwatch; it was a quarter to eleven.

I sat up and saw my shoes had been removed and placed on the floor by the sofa. I heard the low clatter of pots or pans in the kitchen, and the sizzling of bacon or sausage.

Then my breakfast was brought into the room on a tray carried by a thin woman in a pink pastel sweater and slacks, with short light brown hair, thick glasses, and very pale skin. I recognized her as the quiet woman from the ground floor flat of my apartment building.

"Good mornin'," she greeted me, smiling awkwardly, and setting the tray down on a little stand in front of me. "If ye woke a bit later ye'd be havin' yer dinner instead of yer breakfast."

Thus, I met thirty-two-year-old Miss Geraldine McKeever. As I had the hearty meal she prepared for me of Irish sausages, scrambled eggs, fried potatoes, soda farls, and a cup of tea, I listened to how she found me sprawled out at the foot of her door.

"It was nearly four o'clock in the mornin', so 'twas, when I heard a terrible thud just outside me door and I opened it and found yerself – lookin' every bit the corpse lyin' there. Ye were quite the sight. Dead to the world. But I knew 'twas only dead drunk ye were. Sure, I tried to wake ye, and after a good long while I did, but ye were none too steady on yer feet, and I feared climbin' those stairs up to yer flat would be the death of ye, if ye fell, so I guided ye in here to sleep it off."

I had stopped eating as she related all this, in fact, stopped chewing in mid-mouthful. Feeling rightfully embarrassed, I stared down at my plate to avoid her wide pale blue eyes. I then swallowed and apologized for the trouble I caused her.

"G'wan and eat," said Geraldine McKeever, with another faint smile. "Ye're not the first man I've seen in such a state. Me da, when he was younger, used to come home tight sometimes and collapse on the sittin' room floor. Me mother and I would get him up and into bed."

She went to the kitchen and returned with a cup of tea for herself and a little floral teapot, from which she refilled my cup, before lighting a cigarette. I apologized again for having woke her in the wee hours of the morning.

"I don't sleep at night anyhow," she half-laughed uneasily. "I have insomnia amongst me other ailments."

I heard the nervousness in her voice and noticed how she kept fidgeting with her teacup. She removed another cigarette from her red and white box of Berkeley's and offered one to me. We smoked, drank tea, and talked. There seemed to be a deep sadness about her.

Geraldine McKeever was from north Belfast's Cliftonville Road area, near Ardoyne, and said she was one of nine children born into a Catholic working-class family. Her father was a house painter and plasterer. Growing up in the turbulent late 1960's and '70's, she witnessed enough of the violence of the Troubles to leave her permanently traumatized.

When Geraldine was a girl, her six-year-old cousin was run over by a British Army armored vehicle and killed. I remembered how the same happened to Sonny Boyle's little son. When she was in primary school three of her schoolmates and friends were shot dead by Loyalists. All were eight to nine-year-old Catholic girls.

As a teenager, she used to walk two of her young nieces to school along with one of their friends – the girls were seven to eight years old. One day, Geraldine stopped at a newsagent's shop to see if the latest copy of some celebrity gossip magazine had arrived. The girls remained outside, just in front of the shop. As she skimmed through the magazine, a British Army patrol passed by on the street. Suddenly, there were blasts of automatic weapons. The patrol was under attack, presumably by the local unit of the I.R.A. The soldiers returned fire. Then the gunfire stopped as quickly as it started. No British soldiers were hit, and it seemed no I.R.A. men had been wounded.

But two of the three little girls lay in pools of blood. One of Geraldine's nieces was seriously injured but survived. Their friend was killed instantly.

"I stood there in the street, screamin' and screamin', seein' all the blood oozin' from their wee bodies," said Geraldine, as her eyes filled with tears. She quickly blessed herself. "Sweet merciful Mother of God, I couldn't stop screamin' till they took me away."

She paused to pour us more tea and offer me another cigarette as she lit another one for herself.

"They say I had a mental breakdown," she continued. "The next few months were a blur for me anyhow, so they were. I was put in hospital for quite a while. They say I was suicidal and even tried to take meself out of me misery whilst in hospital. Me parents came with me brother, who's a priest, to remind me suicide was a mortal sin."

As Geraldine took another deep drag, slowly exhaling the smoke through her nose, I saw the multiple scars on her wrist. She noticed me looking and pulled her sweater sleeve further down to cover it.

"I tried a few times, without success," she said, smiling weakly.

"Thank God," I replied, disturbed that this gentle and kind-hearted but obviously damaged woman should want to end her life.

"I was diagnosed as manic-depressive. Me mother thought they'd commit me to Holywell Asylum, so she did, but they've care in the community now. So, I've a psychiatric social worker visitin' me each week to check in on me."

I spent the day talking and smoking with Geraldine McKeever. She confided that she had no friends, and her days were filled with a terrible loneliness. Then indicating the cigarette in her hand, she said, "There's a great comfort in these though."

As I sat sipping yet another cup of tea, I thought how Henry David Thoreau – the American naturalist, essayist, and philosopher – once wrote, "The mass of men lead lives of quiet desperation." Geraldine's life struck me as far worse than quiet desperation; it was tragic.

She told me she once considered being a nun and spent time in a convent as a novitiate in England. It was a nursing order that cared for the elderly in a home for the aged. But as much as Geraldine had sympathy for many of the old and infirm, she found the anti-Irish sentiments of others too much to bear.

"There was this one bedridden old Englishman who had been an officer in the army. As I fed him and wiped his arse for him, he called me a skinny Irish bitch and said I looked like a walkin' relic of the Potato Famine. The sisters told me to offer his insults up to our Lord as penance for me sins. But when the nasty oul sod spat in me face, I was done."

It was determined that Geraldine McKeever didn't have a religious vocation and she was sent back home to Belfast. Through the skills she learned from the nuns, though, she was able to find employment as a nurses' aide at an old age home. For a while, her life had a semblance of normalcy and stability. For a short time, she even had a boyfriend.

"He was from Cookstown in County Tyrone and was workin' in Belfast," she said, lighting another cigarette. "We were quite keen on each other. But when visitin' home, he went out drinkin' with his mates and crashed his car in some lonely country lane. The accident left him paralyzed from the neck down. God knows, I would've married him anyhow and have cared for him, only he wouldn't hear of it. He refused to see me again, sayin' he wasn't a proper man anymore."

Not long after that Geraldine was hospitalized again. When she was released, she didn't return to work. The responsibilities of a job and simply living life was too overwhelming for her.

"I've been three years idle now," she concluded. "Existin' more than livin', so."

I helped carry the tray with dishes and teacups into the kitchen. On the counter, beside salt and pepper shakers, I noticed a little statue of Saint Jude, the patron of hopeless cases.

"Me mother gave that to me," said Geraldine, with a slight smile. "She thought he's the saint for me. Sure, she was tryin' to tell me something."

It was already early evening and I asked Geraldine if she'd do me the honor of accompanying me to dinner. She readily agreed, happy to escape the confines of her cell-like flat, and I escorted her out to eat at a nice restaurant in the city center.

CHAPTER FORTY-FIVE
PADDY'S WEE TOUR OF ARDOYNE

On Sunday morning I went with Geraldine McKeever to Mass at nearby St. Brigid's Church on Derryvolgie Avenue. Afterwards we met Denis Irwin in the narthex, amid the crowd of departing parishioners, and exchanged a few words of greeting with him before we left the church. Geraldine was going to spend the day with her parents in Cliftonville and I planned to pay Paddy Murphy a visit up in Ardoyne. We agreed to share a taxi together to north Belfast.

Paddy had given me his address at 92 Velsheda Park. The taxi turned onto a street lined on either side with identical two-story gray rowhouses, each with its own little front yard and low brick walls, and dropped me off at his house. Opening the gate, I walked up the path. When I knocked, Paddy answered the door, his big mug unshaven, hair disheveled, and his wrinkled shirt hanging out of his baggy pants, but happy to see me.

"Ah, Éamon, if it isn't yerself," he greeted me with a smile.

Instead of asking me in, he grabbed his jacket off a hook by the door and threw it on as he stepped outside, shutting the door behind him.

"I'm hungry," said Paddy. "Let's get a bite to eat."

As we walked, he informed me that Velsheda Park – then overwhelmingly Catholic and Republican, like all of Ardoyne – was once a mixed street and actually had a Protestant majority.

"In the summer of '71 Loyalists burnt down this entire street, along with Farrington Gardens and Cranbrook Gardens. Two hundred houses were reduced to blackened shells. Many of the Prods before they left even torched their own homes to prevent them from bein' occupied by Catholic families seekin' refuge. The Loyalists then claimed they were burnt out by Taigs."

We entered O'Neill's Coffee Shop and Paddy bought us sandwiches and bowls of hot stew along with cups of coffee. Sitting at a table by the window, we watched two teenage girls, aged maybe fourteen or fifteen, at another table in an animated conversation jumping from boys to school to parents as they puffed cigarettes dramatically blowing smoke up towards the ceiling. After listening to the girls' excited chatter while we ate, Paddy got up and approached their table.

"Do yez not know smokin' will age yez?" he said, in mock seriousness. "Sure, look what the fags done to me – and I'm only twenty-one years of age!"

"G'wan with ye!" exclaimed one girl, as they both laughed at Paddy's antics.

There was a light drizzle when we stepped back out into the street, but the damp weather did nothing to dampen our spirits. As we walked along Paddy pointed out the street he was raised on and other significant places of his youth, along with places where various people were killed.

"The first woman victim of the Troubles in Ardoyne," began Paddy, "was actually a Protestant. Mrs. Sarah Worthington was a fifty-year-old widow with nine grown-up children and lived in Velsheda Park. As she prepared to leave with the two hundred other odd Protestant families fleeing the area as their fellow Loyalists attacked and the street was set ablaze, yer woman was shot dead in her own kitchen by a British soldier."

Brompton Park was lined with identical two-story red-brick rowhouses, with gates before little paved yards. A dark-haired girl with a pigtail, wearing a pink puffy jacket, passed us on roller skates.

"Ye must remember," reflected Paddy, "not every Prod is a Unionist and not every Unionist is a Loyalist. But even the worst of 'em, they're still Ireland's rotten Oranges. The most rabid Papist-hating, anti-Republican Orangeman fiercely wavin' his wee bloody Union Jack is still regarded as a Paddy or a Mick once he crosses the water over to John Bull's isle."

Paddy paused as a gray R.U.C. Land Rover slowly drove by us followed by two green British Army Land Rovers. He continued once the armored vehicles turned the corner and were out of sight.

"'Tis easy enough for Catholics, as well as even some committed Republicans, to be distracted and become sectarian in their outlook. But true Republicans understand our real enemy are the Brits. And by the Brits, I mean the British government and their agents – not ordinary British people."

As we made our way along Brompton Park, Paddy pointed to the entry where I.R.A. Volunteer Gerard McDade, aged twenty, was shot in the back by a British soldier in late 1971.

"Three years later," added Paddy, "his elder brother Jamesy was killed on active service in England when a bomb he was carryin' to blow up the Coventry telephone exchange exploded prematurely."

We turned onto Berwick Road and stopped at the Garden of Remembrance at the gable wall of a rowhouse; the same the two Seáns – Seán Moore and Seán Less – took me to see on my first visit to Ardoyne. Paddy stood silently looking over the many names of the local dead engraved on the black plaque, with its phoenix rising from the flames, mounted on the wall. Then the former soldier of Britain, the twenty-six county Irish state, the U.N. Task Force, and the Provisional I.R.A., with communist sympathies, bowed his head for a short prayer and blessed himself.

"I knew a lot of these people," he sadly remarked, "or knew their families. Aye, poor wee Ardoyne has suffered the brunt of the Troubles."

There were members of the I.R.A. and their youth wing Fianna Éireann listed, but most of the victims were civilians. Some according to Paddy who just happened to be in the wrong place at the wrong time and were killed by either the British Army or the I.R.A.

"When the I.R.A. took an innocent life," he said, "it usually was because the person got caught in the crossfire between our volunteers and Crown forces. Like in the case of Margaret McCorry. She was accidently shot and killed by the I.R.A. as they engaged a British Army convoy in the Crumlin Road. A lovely girl, she was but twenty years of age when she died. The family said she was engaged to be wed to a Yank."

Young Anthony McDowell was twelve years old and was in a car driven by his uncle when the British Army shot and fatally wounded the boy. Apparently, there had been shooting in the area and the uncle and his nephew drove into the crossfire on Ardoyne's Alliance Avenue.

Mrs. Martha Lavery, a sixty-seven-year-old grandmother living on Jamaica Street, was shot dead by a British Army bullet while sitting and watching TV with her son and grandchildren when a gun-battle started outside their house between the I.R.A. and the British Army.

But Paddy said the vast majority of the innocent lives lost in Ardoyne during the Troubles were taken by Loyalists simply because they were Catholics. He began reading out various names on the plaque and providing details about who they were and how they were murdered.

"Seán McConville, a lad of seventeen years, was walkin' home down the Crumlin Road when he was shot dead by Loyalists. Paddy O'Neill, twenty-three years of age, was out with his mates at Kelly's Cellars and was on his way home when he abducted, brutally beaten, and shot to death by the U.F.F. for no other reason than he was a Catholic. Gerry Gearon, aged twenty-two years, was a barman at McGlade's and one night he had the misfortunate of gettin' into a taxi with two men he didn't know – both members of the U.F.F. – and when they stepped out, they shot into the taxi killin' Gerry. Another purely sectarian attack.

"Hugh Martin, a fifty-six-year-old baker and devoted family man, who served in World War II with the British Army in North Africa, was captured by the Germans, and spent three years as a prisoner of war, was murdered in east Belfast, where he worked, by two U.V.F. gunmen just because he was a Catholic. Pat Crossan, thirty-four years of age, was a bus driver and a great man devoted to his family, community, and chapel. He ran regular trips to Lourdes. When Pat stopped his bus to pick up passengers on the Woodvale Road, two U.V.F. men shot him dead.

"Two years later, his younger brother Frankie was walkin' home late from Ardoyne to where he lived in west Belfast when he was abducted and brutally murdered by the notorious Shankill Butchers. His badly beaten and mutilated body, with his throat cut so deep his head was almost severed from his body, was found in an entry off the Shankill Road. Two members of the gang were actually caught and sentenced to life for the murder. One of the evil bastards said they just decided that night to 'pick up a Taig and do him in'. Frankie Crossan was only targeted because of his religion. He was a good man who never did anybody any harm and he did what he could to help others."

I was familiar with the vicious gang of Loyalists known as the Shankill Butchers from news reports, especially in Irish-American publications. Based in the Protestant Loyalist Shankill Road district, the small group of Ulster Volunteer Force members were called Butchers because they used butchering knives in their grisly handiwork. They could only be described as sadistic monsters in human form.

Their victims were mostly ordinary innocent Catholic civilians, not members of the I.R.A. - their sworn enemy - or necessarily Republican supporters of the armed struggle. But that made no difference to the violent U.V.F. murder gang with their fanatically blind hatred for all Catholics. As Paddy put it, for them "one Taig was the same as another."

The so-called "master butcher" was a psychopath named Lenny Murphy. Accompanied by three members of his gang, he'd drive in a black taxi through Catholic areas late at night hunting for a potential victim – usually a man walking home from a night out at the pub. The unfortunate man would be attacked, dragged into the taxi, savagely beaten and stabbed, and often driven to a darkened alley where the real torture of cutting and carving would be carried out.

One of the gang's most gruesome acts of butchery was their murder of Thomas Madden, an inoffensive middle-aged Catholic bachelor, who enjoyed a pint and went to Mass on Sundays. Employed as a security guard in a mill on the Crumlin Road, Madden was on his way to work his usual night shift when he was abducted by the Shankill Butchers. He was taken to a lock-up garage, stripped naked, hung upside down from a wooden beam, and slowly skinned alive.

During their reign of terror, from the 1970's into the early 1980's, the Shankill Butchers murdered countless Catholics (estimates range from fifteen to over thirty). They also killed several Protestants over personal disputes, and Protestants they had mistaken for Catholics. The gang's leader, Lenny Murphy, killed more people than any other mass murderer in Irish and British criminal history. In 1982, the I.R.A. finally executed Lenny Murphy in his own Shankill Road district.

The R.U.C. and British Army Land Rovers rumbled by again and stopped about a block up on the Berwick Road where three teenage boys were loitering by a brick wall. The vehicles then drove on and Paddy continued his painful litany of the dead of Ardoyne. Sometimes he paused at a particular name and his voice would crack with emotion.

"Charles Corbett was twenty-one years of age when he was killed along with fifty-six-year-old John Maguire as they delivered newspapers for the *Belfast Telegraph* in the Crumlin Road. Mr. Maguire's young son, Michael, was with 'em at the time.

"Their van was hijacked by three U.V.F. bastards. Charles and Mr. Maguire had hoods thrown over their heads and were forced into the back of the van, where they were shot dead. The young Maguire boy survived but was severely wounded. He later said, his father told him just before he was shot, 'God save ye'. Can ye imagine hearin' that as a young fella from yer da just before he was murdered? Sufferin' Jaysus.

"Ye see the name of Miss G. McKeown on the plaque? That would be Geraldine McKeown – the family called her Dena. The family were refugees due to sectarian intimidation when they came to live in a house in Mountainview Gardens. One of her brothers was in Crumlin Road Jail on remand for a political offense at the time.

"Two Loyalist gunmen came and rapped at the family's door and as fourteen-year-old Dena peeked through the venetian blinds to see who was there, they blasted away at the window at the wee girl...an innocent, lovely wee girl. She died in hospital two days later."

Paddy sniffled slightly and tried to steady his voice, "so many people, so many of our good and *dacent* people dead."

"C'mon, Paddy, let's go," I said, wanting to escape the dark cloud of sorrow that had come over us.

He looked away, down the empty road. "To be Irish is to know that in the end the world will break yer heart. Yer Irish-American politician Daniel Patrick Moynihan uttered those words after the assassination of President Kennedy."

As we walked up the Berwick Road and a black taxi drove by, I imagined how there must be similar memorials on the Shankill Road and Sandy Row to commemorate their dead. Many would have also been innocent Protestant civilians; mostly victims of I.R.A. bombs rather than directly targeted in sectarian gun attacks. But innocent lives lost all the same.

We turned down a side street, lined with more rowhouses, each with its own little gated paved yard. Four young girls, wearing brightly colored coats and wool hats with pom poms, were taking turns swinging around a lamppost from a rope tied from the top. They were merrily singing one of the popular old Belfast kids' songs.

Me Aunt Jane, she took me in,
She gave me tea out of her wee tin.
Half a penny bap with sugar on the top,
Three black lumps out of her wee shop.
Me Aunt Jane, she's awful smart,
She bakes wee rings in an apple tart.
And when Halloween comes around,
For next that tart I'm always found.
Me Aunt Jane has a bell on the door,
A white stone step and a clean swept floor.
Candy apples, hard green pears,
Conversation lozenges.

"Here girls!" called out Paddy, his jolly demeanor having returned, "can I have a wee swing too?"

The girls stopped and looked in our direction and giggled. One of them replied, "Ye're too old and *big*! Sure, ye'd break the rope!"

Paddy sighed and said, "Ah, to be a child again."

Farther down the street, two young boys were kicking a soccer ball against a gable wall. We turned into the yard of a brick rowhouse. Paddy told me he wanted to introduce me to the good woman who took him in as a boy and reared him up with her own.

Mrs. Hopkins was a kindly, white-haired, and bespectacled eighty-seven-year-old woman in a dark dress and a white sweater with little flowers on it. Her three sons had all long since married and immigrated to Australia. Only an unwed daughter remained living with her. Family photographs hung on the walls of the sitting room, along with the pictures typically found in Catholic homes of Mary's Immaculate Heart and the Sacred Heart of Jesus with a little red lamp set before it.

Tucked behind a group family portrait was a half rolled up Australian flag on a stick, showing just the white stars of the Southern Cross against a blue background. Paddy took it down and unrolled it, revealing, above the white Commonwealth Star, the Union Jack in the upper left corner.

"We like to keep that part hidden," he said, giving me a wink as he rerolled the flag to put it back behind the portrait.

Paddy and I sat together on the sofa while Mrs. Hopkins brought us from the kitchen tea and slices of lemon drizzle cake. As we ate, her spinster daughter, Christine, came into the room to greet us. A seemingly shy woman in her forties with dark hair and thick glasses, she didn't say more than a few words but frequently smiled at us. I had my camera with me and I snapped a couple of pictures of Paddy with them.

Paddy then took me to the Ardoyne Working Men's Club, which was locally known as "the League." Inside the small social and drinking establishment were just a couple of guys playing darts. Seating ourselves at the bar, the barman greeted us with jars of Guinness, and Paddy also called for doubles of Black Bush for us.

"The Land League Club, as this place was originally called," said Paddy, "dates back to 1878 and got its name from its association with the Belfast Branch of the Land League – founded by the great Charles Stewart Parnell and the one-armed Michael Davitt – which helped our poor tenant farmers to throw off the yoke of tyrannical landlords and their agents."

We were joined at the bar by a grizzly old man, with a long-withered face, a droopy gray mustache, and thick eyebrows, wearing a well-worn tweed cap and a blue and red Cleveland Indians jacket. Paddy said hello to him as the old guy lit up a cigarette, and the two briefly exchanged a few words. Paddy then bought us all a round of drinks.

"This here is Éamon from America," he said. "I'm givin' him a wee tour of Ardoyne. And this is Monk from Ardoyne."

The old fellow gave me a nod and mumbled something I didn't quite catch but ignored my extended hand. Pointing to the grinning red Indian mascot on his jacket, I asked if he was an American baseball fan.

"Arrah...I don't know nothin' about that, so," said Monk.

As he lit another cigarette and drank, I noticed his hands were badly gnarled and twitched every so often.

I ordered us a parting round of Guinness and Black Bush doubles. Monk's hand shook as he lit yet another cigarette, while the one he was smoking still burned in the ashtray on the bar, only half finished. Paddy and I left the League as Monk took a long, deep drag and slowly exhaled, staring straight ahead with a blank look on his old, wasted face.

Outside Paddy told me they were schoolboys together. That would mean Monk would only be Paddy's age of fifty-two. He could have passed for twenty years older.

"Why's he called Monk?" I asked, as we walked.

"Because he was once a Christian Brother," replied Paddy. "Long ago defrocked after he joined in the fight to drive the Brits from our shores and bring about a united thirty-two county socialist Irish Republic. When they interrogated him at Castlereagh, the bastards continuously tortured him, brutally beatin' him. They tied Monk to a chair and smashed his hands with a hammer, breakin' all the bones. He never gave up, though, the names of his comrades."

It was early in the evening when we arrived at the Golden Thread, but the bar was already packed. Paddy led us through the crowd and found us a spot at a table with a couple in their forties with whom he was acquainted. We shook hands and I sat down in a chair beside Paddy. He introduced them as simply Jim and Kate, "from County Armagh and now of Ardoyne." Jim had dark wavy hair, graying at the temples, and wore a rust-colored cardigan over a dress shirt. His wife, Kate, was a small woman with sandy hair styled in a pixie cut and had a silver Claddagh brooch pinned to her Aran sweater.

They were drinking Jameson with their pints and when Paddy called for doubles of Black Bush to go with our Guinness, Jim joked about us drinking "Proddy whiskey."

"Pure sectarianism," declared Paddy, "and outdated sectarianism at that. Sure, all the big distilleries here are now owned by the French."

Paddy began to tell us about a play he was writing about a black Ethiopian Jew who finds his way to sectarian Belfast and…

"A Jewish darkie?" interrupted Kate. "Where in the name of God, Paddy, do ye ever get such things?"

"Sure, haven't ye heard of the black American entertainer Sammy Davis Junior?" asked her husband.

"Yer man Davis didn't start out as a Jew though, he converted," said Paddy. "The Falashas are a proud and venerable people in Ethiopia who embraced the Jewish religion in the time of King Solomon of Israel, when their Queen of Sheba became one of his seven hundred wives."

"Mother of God, seven hundred wives!" exclaimed Kate.

"I got one and she's more than enough!" laughed Jim. "Me oul Trouble and Strife, I call her."

"No other woman would have him," replied Kate, lighting a cigarette.

"And I'd want no other," said Jim, giving his wife a cuddle.

I sprung for another round of drinks for everybody. Lifting his double Black Bush in a toast, Paddy declared: *"Sláinte na bhfear agus go maire na mná go deo."*

I glanced at Kate.

"Don't look at me," she said. "Sure, I understood *Sláinte* well enough but the rest of it's lost on me. I don't have any Irish."

"If I'm not mistaken," offered Jim, "it means, 'Health to the men and may the women live forever.'"

Paddy, his face red from drink, then launched into a long and impassioned speech in Gaelic that no one understood. But that didn't stop him.

"For all I know he could be reciting the entire Proclamation of 1916 in Irish," said Jim.

"Bloody man's drunk," laughed Kate.

When it was time to call it a night, a local black taxi was called to deliver me safely back to Eglantine Avenue. Kate and Jim wished me a goodnight, and Paddy reminded me to go straight back to my flat.

"Remember, Éamon, what I told ye about the Shankill Butchers. Not all the bastards have been killed yet. Y'know what happened to Mick Doherty, don't ye?"

Paddy proceeded to tell me, in a most serious tone. "Well, yer man was on his way home late one night after havin' a few jars, when out of the darkness an arm reached around his neck and put a big oul carving knife to yer man's throat, and he heard the age-old question in Belfast: 'Are ye Catholic or are ye Protestant?'

"Well, Mick Doherty didn't come up the effin' Lagan in a bubble and says to himself, now, if I say I'm a Protestant, Mack the Knife won't bloody well believe it, and if I say I'm a Catholic, well then, I'm surely done for. So, thinkin' quick he says, 'Neither one, I'm a Jew!'

"Now, yer man with the oul carving knife answers, 'Holy Mohammed, I must be the luckiest Arab in all of Ireland!'"

I burst out laughing. "Geez, Paddy, you oughta be up on stage! You're a riot."

It was sometime after midnight and I sat up in bed having a pipe smoke with a cup of coffee, as I jotted down the day's events into my travel journal. Mozart's overture to *The Magic Flute* was playing on the old McMurdo Silver radio. Earlier I had listened to the news.

Malachy Carey, a thirty-six-year-old Sinn Féin candidate and former I.R.A. man, died after being shot in the street by a U.F.F. gunman in the small town of Ballymoney, County Antrim, while he waited for his girlfriend to get off from work. Another thirty-six-year-old Catholic man, in Derry, died five days after being shot in both his legs by the I.R.A. as "punishment" for being a serial child-abuser and rapist. And in Belfast, an unidentified Loyalist paramilitary group carried out a rocket attack on an area of Crumlin Road Jail that was believed to hold Republican prisoners. No one was injured in the attack.

Paddy Murphy of Ardoyne

Ardoyne, Belfast

CHAPTER FORTY-SIX
THE GIANT'S RING REVISITED WITH GERALDINE

A couple of days passed since I took Paddy's wee tour of Ardoyne. I spent much of that time with Geraldine McKeever and Denis Irwin, when he wasn't working his orderly job at Royal Victoria Hospital. Not being much of a cook myself, I gladly accepted Geraldine's home cooked meals. After dinner in her flat, we'd watch whatever was on TV. One night we stayed up late to watch Clint Eastwood in the 1960's western *Hang 'em High*.

I was surprised to learn that Geraldine, born and bred in Belfast, had never seen the Giant's Ring and I offered to take her to see the city's most significant prehistoric monument. She excitedly agreed and said it would be like going on an adventure.

When I knocked on her door in the morning, Geraldine was all ready to go in her long purple puffy coat, a pink and white striped scarf around her neck, a white wool hat on her head, and matching white gloves. It was a beautiful but frigid morning, as we headed down the affluent Malone Road with its elegant and luxurious homes.

"They're like what ye'd see in a magazine," remarked Geraldine. "As a wee girl, I dreamt of livin' in a grand posh house like one of these, so I did."

Most of her eight siblings had moved away from the Troubles and poverty in Northern Ireland. Geraldine had a married sister in South Africa, another married sister across the water in Birmingham, and a sister and two brothers in Wales.

"Today was a hard day for me," she said, "as me sister in Cardiff was married yesterday. God knows, I ought to be happy for her but instead I feel even more sad and alone. Sure, now I'm the only unwed sister – the old maid of the family." She made a half-hearted laugh. "Even me brother, the one who's a priest, is well away. I used to be able to take the train straight down to Dublin to see him but now he's at a wee chapel in some wee town in County Leitrim."

We turned off the Malone Road and crossed old Shaw's Bridge, over the River Lagan. Most of the trees were now bare of their leaves. Although there was no snow on the ground yet, the grass was frosty and the air crisp. Wintertime had definitely arrived. As we approached the large circular enclosure of the Giant's Ring, I watched Geraldine's reaction.

"Oh my," she said, taking it in. "'Tis like a big fairy ring!"

"The Giant's Ring dates back almost five thousand years to pre-Celtic Ireland," I informed her, pleased to show off some of my knowledge of local history. Pointing to the dolmen at its center, I continued, "It's the entrance to a passage tomb. There's those who say it was once used as a Druid altar."

"It really looks quite like a giant fairy ring," replied Geraldine, smiling, and enjoying our outing.

As we walked on the frost covered grass within the huge circle, she went on: "A lot of country people, y'know, believe in the *Aes Sídhe* – 'the people of the mounds' – that is, the fairies. Also called the 'Good People,' so they'll do ye no harm. They're said to live underground in wee fairy forts and sometimes at night whole troops of 'em come out to dance in fairy rings and can't be seen by mere mortals unless they choose to be seen.

"Some hold they're the magical Tuatha Dé Danann – 'the people of the goddess Danu' – driven to live below the earth's surface when our Celtic ancestors, the Milesians, came by boats from Spain to invade Ireland.

"Others believe the fairies are fallen angels from after the great battle in heaven when Lucifer and his wicked minions were cast out by the Archangel Michael and sent down to the pits of hell.

"Those angels who hadn't actually rebelled against the Almighty, but hadn't sufficiently striven for Him either, were judged not worthy to remain in heaven nor bad enough for hell. Therefore, God in His mercy, asked them where in His universe they'd wish to spend their eternity. They answered, 'If heaven we must lose, let us spend our eternity in the delightfullest spot of all God's creation – the place that's nearest to heaven – send us to Ireland.' And here they are amongst us to this day!"

I lit a cigarette and tried hard not to smile too much. "Well Geraldine," I said, searching for the right words, "you certainly seem to know a lot about these little people."

"Aye, I do," replied Geraldine, as she too lit up a cigarette. "Me granny – God rest her – was a shanachie from the mountains of Donegal. A native Irish speaker, she passed down the oul stories and traditions. She came to Belfast as a young woman to work in the mills, same as me mother did before they closed them down.

"Me granny used to tell us tales about people who went missin' for days or more when they stepped into a fairy ring or got lost in the hills in a fairy mist. She had this one story about a neighbor in the Gweedore. The man's name was Dinny McGinley, and he was an oul bachelor farmer.

"One dark summer night," began Geraldine, "Dinny McGinley was comin' down through the gap, and he saw light comin' from the many windows of a castle he had never seen before. As he drew nigh, he heard shouts and laughter from people within. The door was wide open, and he chanced to enter. Dinny found himself in a big hall and he saw the king and queen of the fairies seated at the head of a long table with hundreds of people, all grandly dressed in old fashioned attire, eatin' and drinkin'. There were harpers and pipers playin' delightful old Irish airs. There were rich hangings on the walls and lamps blazing.

"The queen called out, 'Welcome, Mr. McGinley, welcome! Make room for Mr. McGinley at the table. Give Mr. McGinley a tumbler of punch. Sit down, Mr. McGinley, and make yerself welcome.' Dinny sat down and took a tumbler of punch. And just as he brought it up to his lips to taste it, he took notice of the man seated beside him. He was an old neighbor that was dead for twenty years. Says he to Dinny McGinley, 'For yer life, don't touch it nor sup.' Frightened by what the dead neighbor said, Dinny began to see how ghastly some of the fine people looked when they thought he was not minding them.

"Dinny's health was drunk to, and the queen pressed him to drink up. But he had the good sense to heed his old neighbor's advice, and he spilled the punch down between his coat and waistcoat. And that is what saved Dinny McGinley for he awoke the next morn smelling of punch upon the dewy grass in the very spot the fairy castle had stood."

"That's quite the yarn, Geraldine," I said, half-convinced she believed every word of it.

As we walked together around the perimeter of the circle, she began to hum a tune. Then she sang.

> *Up the airy mountain,*
> *Down the rushy glen,*
> *We daren't go a-hunting*
> *For fear of little men;*
> *Wee folk, good folk,*
> *Trooping all together;*
> *Green jacket, red cap,*
> *And white owl's feather!*
>
> *Down along the rocky shore*
> *Some make their home,*
> *They live on crispy pancakes*
> *Of yellow tide-foam;*
> *Some in the reeds*
> *Of the black mountain lake,*
> *With frogs for their watch-dogs,*
> *All night awake.*
>
> *High on the hill-top*
> *The old King sits;*
> *He is now so old and grey*
> *He's nigh lost his wits.*
> *With a bridge of white mist*

> *Columbkill he crosses,*
> *On his stately journeys*
> *From Slieveleague to Rosses;*
> *Or going up with music*
> *On cold starry nights*
> *To sup with the Queen*
> *Of the gay Northern Lights.*
>
> *They stole little Bridget*
> *For seven years long;*
> *When she came down again*
> *Her friends were all gone.*
> *They took her lightly back,*
> *Between the night and morrow,*
> *They thought that she was fast asleep,*
> *But she was dead with sorrow.*
> *They have kept her ever since*
> *Deep within the lake,*
> *On a bed of flag-leaves,*
> *Watching till she wake.*
>
> *By the craggy hill-side,*
> *Through the mosses bare,*
> *They have planted thorn-trees*
> *For pleasure here and there.*
> *If any man so daring*
> *As dig them up in spite,*
> *He shall find their sharpest thorns*
> *In his bed at night.*

The poem was called "The Fairies" and was by the 19th century poet and scholar William Allingham, who hailed from Ballyshannon in County Donegal.

CHAPTER FORTY-SEVEN
CAVE HILL

Following a filling breakfast at the Mad Hatter Coffee Shop and a quick glance at the *Irish News,* which reported that the I.R.A. exploded two small bombs in London and injured four people, I set out on my day's excursion. I wanted to hike again in the Belfast Hills before I returned home. It was a bitter cold morning, but with clear beautiful skies. I wore a thick sweater under my corduroy jacket, along with the cream-colored scarf that Geraldine had given me, and my gray wool gloves. In my back pocket, I carried a flask of whiskey to warm my insides.

I was bound for Cave Hill on the city's northern edge. It was a good nine mile walk there from Eglantine Avenue, going through the city center and up the Antrim Road. Across from St. Patrick's College, a Catholic secondary school for boys, I turned onto the residential Old Cavehill Road. Once I passed many fine, stately red-brick houses, a paved path led me just about halfway up the hillside.

I stared up at the craggy basalt summit. The outline formed a man's face looking heavenwards, and for the past two centuries or so had been known to locals as "Napoleon's Nose" as it supposedly resembled the profile of the famous French emperor. It was also thought to have inspired Jonathan Swift in writing his well-known novel *Gulliver's Travels,* as its shape appeared to be that of a sleeping giant.

The path turned and seemed to circle Cave Hill, not taking me to the top. So, I left the path and headed up the wooded hillside, over fallen trees and around bushes. The climb was a steep one and I often had to stop to catch my breath. It was nearly noon but still quite chilly. I took a swig from my flask. Using a branch I found as a walking stick, I tried to avoid slipping on the muddy leaves on the ground as I climbed higher.

Finally, I reached the top of Cave Hill. I stood there for some time, at a height of 1,200 feet above sea level, looking over the sprawling city of Belfast. Like "a radio with it's back ripped off," as Callaghan said when we were looking down from Black Mountain, quoting Craig Raine's poem, "Flying to Belfast." Standing on the peak, under a dark gray sky, the wind blew so fiercely that I had to struggle to remain upright. I felt exhilarated and invigorated and ran across the high grassy top like a kid. I was alone and as the powerful wind whipped at me, I wanted to let out a yell of triumph – so I did!

I pulled out my flask again and swallowed the last of the whiskey. With a great deal of difficulty, due to the gusty conditions, I lit a Player's cigarette and sat down on a large moss-covered rock. I reached into my jacket's inside pocket and took out the little notebook I had in which I jotted down some of the details I learned about Cave Hill from my guidebook.

There were actually five man-made caves at Cave Hill, carved out of the rock during the early Iron Age when iron was mined to make weapons, and later generations used the caves for shelter. The hill was originally known in Gaelic as *Beann Mhadagáin,* which means "the Hill of Madigan," and was anglicized as Ben Madigan. It was named for one of two Ulster kings, Matudán mac Muiredaig, who died in A.D. 857, or Matudán mac Áeda, who died in A.D. 950.

Cave Hill was the site of many forts. On the summit, the earthen walls of McArt's Fort could still be seen. The fortification was thought to be named for Brian McArt O'Neill, who took up arms against the English during the Nine Years' War (1593-1603) and was hanged by Crown forces in 1607.

Nearly two centuries later, it was at the hilltop fort that Wolfe Tone – the father of Irish Republicanism – stood with his comrades, and fellow radical Protestants, and looked down on Belfast, in the spring of 1795, and swore the oath as United Irishmen: "Never to desist in our efforts until we have subverted the authority of England over our country and asserted our independence."

In addition to Theobald Wolfe Tone, a Dublin barrister, the select group included Henry Joy McCracken, the manager of a cotton mill on the Falls Road, Samuel Neilson, the founder and editor of *The Northern Star,* the Belfast newspaper of the Society of United Irishmen, Robert Simms, the owner of a paper mill near Belfast, and Thomas Russell, the Cork man called "The Man from God knows where," who served as librarian of Belfast's oldest library and was the northern executive of the United Irishmen.

After the bloody Rising of 1798 was crushed, the fate of most of these Irish patriots was sealed. Tone was sentenced to be hanged but died in prison, either through being mortally wounded when being tortured by British soldiers, or, more likely, as the result of an attempt to slit his own throat. McCracken and later Russell died on the gallows. A few years after the failed rebellion, Neilson died in exile of yellow fever in Poughkeepsie, New York. Only Simms lived to a ripe old age and died peacefully at the age of eighty-two at his home in Belfast in 1843.

The gale force winds nearly blew me over as I tried to focus my Nikon N4004s on the city below. So, I laid down on my stomach on the moist grass at the edge of the cliff and tightly held onto my camera to take a few pictures, lest the wind snatch it away to go smashing down on the rocks below – a good hundred-foot drop.

Heading down the steep hillside, I came to one of the caves cut into the basalt rock and climbed up into it. Inside it was damp and the roof of the cave was about a head higher than I was; roughly it was about twenty feet wide and twenty feet deep. I lit another cigarette and took a picture from inside the cave looking out as a flock of birds flew by.

These caves were reputedly used by highwaymen in the 17th and 18th centuries as hideouts. Bold Ness O'Haughan was the most well-known in the region. The story goes that when Ness and his brothers witnessed their poor and aged parents being evicted by the local landlord and saw them manhandled and ill-treated by the bailiffs, a fight broke out in which one of the bailiffs was killed. With Ness at their head, the O'Haughan brothers were forced to go on the run as outlaws and became *rapparees,* or highwaymen. Like Tipperary's Éamonn an Chnoic, or Ned of the Hill, they robbed from the rich and often shared the loot they acquired with the poor. And, of course, there's also an old ballad for bold Ness.

> *'Tis of a famous highwayman a story I will tell,*
> *His name was Ness O'Haughan, in Ireland he did dwell.*
> *And on the Antrim Mountains he commenced his wild career,*
> *Where many a wealthy gentleman before him shook with fear...*

Our unfortunate hero was captured at last and brought to Carrickfergus Castle, on the north shore of Belfast Lough, where he was sentenced to die in 1720. At nearby Gallows Green, Ness O'Haughan was hanged, and his head cut off and put on a spike for all to see.

Climbing out of the ancient cave, I continued down the hillslope. As I took a muddy, moss-covered path, I was taken by surprise when a hedgehog or badger suddenly darted right in front of me, and I slipped and fell on my rear. I sat up on the ground, mud on my trousers, and burst out laughing. No wild woodland critter or a little mud could spoil the adventure of my day. I was as happy as a lark!

As I descended farther, the muddy path eventually turned back into a paved path that took me past Belfast Castle and its wooded estate. According to my guidebook, the large sandstone edifice, complete with towers and turrets, was built in the Scottish Baronial style in the late 19th century for the third Marquis of Donegall. I stopped and snapped a couple of pictures of the castle before I continued on my way back down to the Antrim Road.

It was still mid-afternoon, and I decided to grab some fish and chips over on the Falls Road and drop by to visit Mrs. Boyle.

When I knocked at her door on Harrogate Street, it was opened by a short, wiry fellow of about thirty, with a pug nose and a couple of broken off front teeth, wearing a red Manchester United football jersey. He was Mrs. Boyle's son-in-law, Joe Devine. I remembered that she told me everyone called her younger daughter Patricia's husband Little Joe, like Little Joe Cartwright from the 1960's western TV series *Bonanza*.

Little Joe Devine said Mrs. Boyle was away visiting her sons in Tallaght until after the New Year. But he was heading out and offered me a lift to my flat in his private, unmarked taxi.

As we approached the city center on Divis Street in his white Vauxhall Astra there was a lineup of cars. The R.U.C. and British Army had set up a security checkpoint and were stopping motorists and checking vehicles.

"Ye'd be wise to get out here," advised Little Joe. "Those bastards up ahead are none too fond of me and Yank or no Yank they'll liable to give ye a hard time."

I didn't need to be told a second time. Thanking him, I hopped out on Divis Street and briskly walked past the checkpoint and back to Eglantine Avenue as dusk began to fall.

CHAPTER FORTY-EIGHT
AS I ROVED OUT WITH PADDY

The waitress at the Mad Hatter poured me another cup of coffee as I finished my breakfast and read yesterday's *Irish News*. Sunday evening a Catholic father of four was shot dead in his home on the Upper Crumlin Road as he sat wrapping Christmas gifts with his five-year-old daughter on his knee. Two masked gunmen had burst into the family living room and shot Martin Lavery, aged forty, four times in the chest, just narrowly missing his youngest child. The U.V.F. claimed responsibility for the murder, stating he was an active member of the I.R.A. Lavery's family denied the claim. His brother was a former Sinn Féin councillor.

The news also reported in a separate incident, the I.R.A. exploded a bomb outside a central Belfast bank. There were no casualties, and damage from the blast was minor.

Walking back to my flat, I ran into good old Paddy Murphy coming down the street and invited him up for a cup of tea. He was most delighted when I suggested flavoring our tea with a splash of Bushmills. Under his arm, he had a brown paper bag containing a book he bought for me at a used bookshop.

The title read, *As I Roved Out: A Book of the North, Being a Series of Historical Sketches of Ulster and Old Belfast,* by Cathal O'Byrne. It was a 1982 hardcover edition, and I thanked Paddy for the gift, and he told me about the author.

"A superb storyteller in the shanachie tradition, O'Byrne was well-known as a poet, writer, local historian, and singer. A great patriot as well, he served in the Old I.R.A. After the Belfast pogroms of 1920-22, yer man went to America and worked as a freelance journalist and opened a bookshop there. He returned to Ireland after raising £100,000 on behalf of the White Cross Fund for the relief of the poor sufferin' Catholics of Belfast. Cathal O'Byrne was a devout Catholic and as a journalist he even interviewed the Pope. A lifelong bachelor, he lived with his sister in Cavendish Street, off the Falls Road."

Paddy went on to say that the book was a collection of articles O'Byrne wrote as a columnist for the *Irish News* about Belfast and its environs.

"First published when I was a young lad, 'twas the first book I read in its entirety."

After a couple of more teacups with whiskey, minus the tea, we were off on our rove out on Belfast town.

From the phone booth on Eglantine Avenue, Paddy called a taxi to take us up to north Belfast's Donegall Street for another of his guided tours. We rode past the Botanic Gardens and Queen's University and took Great Victoria Street through the city center, past the Europa Hotel and the Grand Opera House, continuing up Fisherwick Place. Then we turned onto Wellington Place, past the many stately old Georgian and Victorian stone and brick buildings and city hall, and onto Chichester Street and made a left onto Victoria Street, and past the Albert Memorial Clock Tower. We turned again at the corner of Waring Street, where the old red-brick Nambarrie Tea factory stood, and made a right onto Donegall Street. We drove by the imposing gray stone Romanesque-style Protestant St. Anne's Cathedral, and farther up the street we came to a stop in front of the equally imposing St. Patrick's Catholic Church.

As Paddy paid the taxi driver, I looked up at the magnificent neo-Gothic, red sandstone church dedicated to the patron saint of Ireland, with its big circular window and belltower and spire reaching to the sky.

"St. Pat's was the second Catholic chapel in Belfast," declared Paddy, standing beside me. "Only the splendid edifice ye're now gazing upon isn't the original, which opened its doors in 1815. That one was demolished, and this grand chapel was built in its place and was consecrated in 1877."

Above the entrance doors was a seven-foot-high statue of a bearded and mitered Saint Patrick, a staff in his left hand and his right hand raised in benediction.

"That, Éamon, was carved by the father of Pádraic Pearse, hero of the Easter Rising of 1916. A stonemason and monumental sculptor, James Pearse was an English convert to Catholicism. He carved the high altar here as well."

I removed my cap as we stepped inside the church. It was large enough to hold two thousand worshippers, but the pews were mostly empty as daily Mass was over. Only a small devout group, reciting the rosary, occupied a few pews up by the altar. Paddy remarked that his foster father, Tom Hopkins, had made many of the pews in the church, along with the huge wooden front doors we had just come through.

As we stood behind the pews, talking in hushed tones, we were approached by a white-haired old priest, who knew Paddy. After they exchanged pleasantries, he briefly introduced me to Father Martin Kelly. We didn't linger, though, and once outside the church Paddy told me that the priest held strong Republican sympathies.

After ducking into a nearby pub for a couple of jars of the black stuff, we made the ten-minute walk down to Corn Market.

From the corner of Lombard Street and High Street, we looked across at Corn Market. Despite its name, no corn was being sold there. It was a busy pedestrianized shopping street filled with stores, shops, restaurants and cafes, and three days before Christmas was thronged with holiday shoppers. It was like Belfast's own Grafton Street. Beneath a red-hooded bandstand was a white-bearded Santa Claus and several girls dressed as his sexy elves, in short green and red costumes with fishnet stockings, singing Christmas carols. Sitting on the pavement nearby were a collection of skinheads and punks, clad in leather and ripped denim jackets, smoking cigarettes.

"Here they hung the gallant Henry Joy McCracken," said Paddy. Commander of the United Irishmen army in Ulster, he was captured following their defeat at the Battle of Antrim by the British and publicly executed in July 1798.

As crowds loaded down with bags and packages and young children in tow passed us by, Paddy softly sang Tommy Makem's ballad.

> *An Ulster man I am proud to be*
> *From the Antrim glens I come*
> *And though I've labored by the sea*
> *I have followed fife and drum*
> *I have heard the martial tramp of men*
> *I've seen them fight and die*
> *Ah! Lads it's well I remember when*
> *I followed Henry Joy...*
>
> *It was for Ireland's cause we fought*
> *For home and sire, we bled*
> *'Though our numbers were few, our hearts were true*
> *And five to one lay dead*
> *And many a lassie mourned her lad*
> *And mother mourned her boy*
> *For youth was strong in the daring throng*
> *That followed Henry Joy*
>
> *In Belfast town, they built a tree*
> *And the redcoats mustered there*
> *I saw him come as the beat of a drum*
> *Rolled out in the barrack square*
> *He kissed his sister, went aloft*
> *And waved a last good-bye*
> *My God he died, I turned and I cried*
> *They have murdered Henry Joy*

"Even now, if ye squint a wee bit, Éamon, ye can almost see him led up the gallows steps to the waiting rope, surrounded by redcoat soldiers."

Paddy paused and continued, "Because of his family's high standin' in Belfast, offers were made to spare McCracken's life if he informed on his comrades. He refused to do so. Years later, his comrade-in-arms and fellow United Irishman Jemmy Hope said of him, 'when all our leaders deserted us, Henry Joy McCracken stood alone, faithful to the last. He led on the forlorn hope of the cause of Antrim... He died rather than prove a traitor to the cause.'"

Paddy pointed over to the large Dunnes Stores building and said that was where the Old Market House stood two hundred years ago, in front of which the gallows McCracken was hanged from was erected.

We made the short walk up High Street to Pottinger's Entry and turned in the alley to the Morning Star. A two-story emerald green Georgian-era public house, a golden winged lion sat proudly above a sturdy square pillar at its corner entrance. Inside was a beautiful, large horseshoe-shaped mahogany bar with polished brass fittings, and behind it stood a handsome young barman, smiling in a neat white shirt and black bowtie.

"What can I get yez, gents?"

We asked for a couple of bowls of stew and doubles of Black Bush and pints of plain to wash it down.

"There's some who claim McCracken's body was laid out on a table here to be waked after he was cut down from the gallows," said Paddy. "But this building only dates back to 1810, so it must've been in another one of the pubs then in Pottinger's Entry."

I lit a cigarette as we waited for our stew to arrive, and Paddy continued with his history of the establishment.

"The Morning Star was first built as a coaching stop for the Belfast to Dublin mail coaches. It got its name from the postal boys, as when they'd arrive here, as their first call of the day, the morning star still shone in the dark skies."

"There yez go, gents," said the cheery young barman, as he set big bowls of stew before us. "A good hearty feed for yez."

The thick hot stew was delicious with its cubes of mutton, chunky potatoes, sliced carrots, and a bit of parsley and onions mixed in. I watched Paddy enthusiastically dig into his bowl. After three or four heaping spoonfuls, he looked up at me with a grin.

"Great stuff. Proper pub grub in a proper pub."

I wholeheartedly agreed, helping myself to another mouthful. "A damn sight better tasting than any Big Mac," I remarked.

"Jaysus!" roared Paddy. "It can't even compare. God knows, those so-called hamburgers they serve up at McDonald's aren't even food. Absolute shite! I once wandered into that bloody new McDonald's and sufferin' Jaysus, I nearly gagged on yer imported American cuisine. No offense to ye, Éamon, ye being a Yank, but ye can keep yer feckin' McDonald's hamburgers and those skinny chips ye call French fries over in *Amerikay*."

I laughed with Paddy, and we had a couple of more pints of Guinness before we left.

As we dandered up High Street, Paddy explained that under our feet, beneath the pavement, ran the River Farset, a tributary of the River Lagan. The modern city of Belfast had sprung from the ancient sandy ford, where the tributary flowed into the latter river, and owed its growth and early prosperity to the Farset. As noted earlier, Belfast took its Gaelic name, *Béal Feirste,* from the mouth of the sandbank.

During the Industrial Revolution of the 1700's and early 1800's, the River Farset flowed beside the High Street docks. Along with the Lagan and its other tributaries, the Farset provided power for the textile mills, factories, and distilleries that made Belfast a great industrial city. But all this production and the accompanying growth of a dense population of laborers and their families soon turned the urban rivers into open cesspools of toxic waste and raw sewage, which included rotting animal carcasses. It was said at the time, the stench of Belfast would reach travelers' nostrils before their eyes ever saw the city. These unsanitary conditions became a public health concern as diseases like typhoid fever, dysentery, and cholera rapidly spread among the overcrowded population and especially devastated the poor.

"By the 19th century the town's commissioners were forced to take action," said Paddy. "The Farset, and rivers like the Blackstaff, were gradually covered over with streets. The foul smell's long gone, but the rivers still flow underground."

We made our way back down High Street and across Corn Market, through the crowds of holiday shoppers, and onto Castle Place and turned onto Donegall Place, at the corner of Castle Street.

"'Twas here in the summer of 1701," declared Paddy, "that Arthur Chichester, the third Earl of Donegall, encamped with his 35th Regiment of Foot."

Paddy Murphy's incredible knowledge of Belfast could have rivaled the local historian Cathal O'Byrne's.

"Did you read that in the book you gave me?" I asked.

"I was just a wee lad at the time," replied Paddy, "but I saw for meself the oul Earl and his regiment of redcoats with their muskets on this very spot."

He gave me a wink and pointed to an old, green bronze plaque at the entrance to the Anderson and McAuley department store which commemorated the third Earl of Donegall's formation of the 35th Regiment of Foot and their encampment there.

Paddy continued, "Chichester went on to accompany his regiment to Spain in 1704 to fight in the War of Spanish Succession, where he was killed in action. Sure, no loss that for dear ould Ireland."

Black taxis were lined up on Castle Street and before stepping into one to bring him home to Ardoyne, Paddy said he'd be away in Dublin for Christmas.

"But I'll be back in Belfast by New Year's to spend yer last few days in Ireland with ye."

After he rode off, I strolled into a Castle Street barbershop for a haircut for £2 and 50 pence. The smiling young barber, in a neat white shirt and black tie, who greeted me could have been the twin brother of the young barman at the Morning Star.

CHAPTER FORTY-NINE
THE ROUND TOWER OF ANTRIM

In my guidebook there was a photograph of the Round Tower of Antrim that I kept turning to. I was utterly captivated by this ancient tower and decided I had to see it before I left Ireland. I mentioned it to Geraldine McKeever and Denis Irwin. Neither of them had seen the Round Tower before and agreed to accompany me out to Antrim town. But Denis was called in to work an extra shift at his orderly job at Royal Victoria Hospital, so I made the trip with Geraldine.

On the morning of December 23rd, we boarded the train at Belfast's Botanic Station. It was a journey of less than an hour through little villages and towns of south County Antrim. We passed through Knockmore, Lisburn, Upper Ballinderry, Glenavy, and Crumlin to Antrim town, with plenty of patches of farmland and green fields in between, all covered with a light layer of frost.

I always loved traveling by train. I used to watch on TV, as a teenager, *Great Railway Journeys of the World,* produced by the B.B.C. and sometimes hosted by a pipe smoking Englishman. I recalled an episode where a train traveled from Bombay to Cochin, along the western coast of India, and another where the train went over the Andes Mountains from Lima, Peru, to La Paz in Bolivia. What wonderful journeys, I thought. One day. As Dr. Seuss said, "Oh, the places you'll go!"

I reached for my pipe. Smoking was already banned on trains in the U.S., and it wouldn't be long before Ireland and Britain would prohibit it as well. But that time hadn't yet come, and as Geraldine puffed one of her Berkeley cigarettes, I loaded up my pipe with Mellow Virginia tobacco for a relaxing smoke as I looked out the window as the Irish countryside passed by.

It was just after 9:30 a.m. when we arrived in Antrim town. The winter morning air was particularly cold, and we were both bundled up for it in our coats, scarves, gloves, and hats. As we left the train station, I offered Geraldine a swig of whiskey from my flask to warm her up and she took a small swallow and passed it back to me and I took a bigger swallow. A short walk down Steeple Road and across the frosty green grass of a park brought us to the Round Tower.

Over 90 feet tall, the medieval freestanding stone structure, covered by a conical top, was quite an impressive sight to behold. A week earlier I picked up some literature about the Round Tower from the Northern Ireland Tourist Board in Belfast.

The Round Tower of Antrim is the only remaining part of a Celtic Monastic settlement which occupied this site for 650 years. There is uncertainty as to the founder of the monastery – St. Comgall, St. Aedh and St. Durtract are variously suggested. The tower, built much later, probably in the 9th or early 10th century, marked a period in history when Viking raids were quite common. The monks would be warned of the approaching invader when a lookout stationed at the upper four windows (each facing the cardinal points of the compass), would sound a bell. The inhabitants of the monastery would take any precious objects from the church, climb into the high-set door of the tower by means of a ladder which was then pulled up behind them. There they would wait until the marauding Vikings had left.

The annals of the Four Masters record that the Aentrobh Monastic settlement was burned in 1147 and after that date the site appears to have been abandoned as a monastery. The local name of the Round Tower is "The Steeple" which was perhaps given by the Scottish and English settlers in the 17th century. It is one of only two surviving intact towers in Ulster. *The stone close to the Tower was moved to this position from a point close to Steeple House. The original purpose of the Bullaun Stones, which are found at Celtic Monastic sites, is unknown.*

We walked around the tall tower to see it from various angles and tried to imagine how it must have been when the monks lived there in the days of the Viking raiders. I took a number of pictures of the magnificent tower. As I snapped a few of Geraldine standing in front of it, we were approached by an old man in a gray overcoat and tweed cap walking a brown and white border collie. Geraldine bent down to pet the friendly dog and I asked the old gent if he knew anything about the huge stone by the tower. He said he lived in the area his entire life and told us the legend he heard as a boy.

Long ago a giant half as tall as the Round Tower itself came to destroy it. A dozen of the strongest monks lifted the huge stone and dropped it from the top of the tower onto the oul giant's head, killing him instantly. And to this day, the stone is there as a reminder of that long ago event.

Well, I suppose, the old man's story was as good as any other. But Geraldine was shivering from the cold and my own feet were freezing from standing too long in the frosty wet grass, so we bid the old fellow and his dog a good day and headed towards the town's center.

Along High Street were shops and businesses, and we ducked into a coffee shop to warm up with a couple of cups of joe and a smoke. Afterwards, we made our way to the Market Square to see the town's castle walls with its great barbican gatehouse.

Built around 1818, it was the main entrance into Antrim Castle. The gatehouse was designed in a neo-Tudor style complete with twin towers, and its upper floor was once used as a lodge by a gatekeeper who operated the heavy wooden studded gates. But the gates were open as we approached.

According to my guidebook, the castle walls dated back to the 17th century and surrounded Antrim Castle, built on the banks of the Six Mile Water by the wealthy English planter Sir Hugh Clotworthy and enlarged in 1662 by his son, John Clotworthy, 1st Viscount Massereene. This was the same Sir John Clotworthy who declared in the House of Commons, before the Rising of 1641 by native Irish Catholics, that the conversion of the Papists in Ireland was only to be effected by the Bible in one hand and the sword in the other. During the 1680's, the castle was raided by Jacobite General Richard Hamilton and his men who looted the Viscount's silver plate and other silverware and fine furniture.

The castle walls last saw action during the Battle of Antrim on June 7th, 1798, when the town was attacked by about 4,000 United Irishmen under the command of Henry Joy McCracken.

While the castle walls remained, Antrim Castle itself was no more. During a lavish Halloween ball in 1922, the grand house caught fire and was almost completely destroyed. Although there was evidence that pointed to arson by the I.R.A., the official verdict was never conclusive. Therefore, no insurance claim was ever paid out. The old Castle remained a ruin until it was demolished in 1970. The only remnants left standing were the gatehouse and a freestanding Italianate stair tower.

A paved road brought Geraldine and me to what we learned was the Clotworthy House. The attractive coach house and stable block with its Jacobean Revival style façade of coursed rubble basalt and Tardree granite dressings was built in the mid-19th century by the 10th Viscount Massereene. After Antrim Castle burned down, the Massereene family lived in the Clotworthy House, where the 12th Viscount died in the 1950's. The family seat then moved to England.

As we strolled the well-manicured grounds, we met up with the caretaker. A short, heavy-set man in his early fifties with wavy gray hair, he introduced himself as William Hutchinson. He said he had been caretaker there for the past eleven years and lived over in Ballymena. His broad, distinctive accent sounded almost Scottish.

Mr. Hutchinson walked for a while with us around the grounds and ornamental garden and told us more about the history of the place.

We heard from him the legend of Lady Marian and the Irish Wolfhound. Sir Hugh Clotworthy's young wife was accustomed to taking walks through the woods to the shore of Lough Neagh. Shortly after her marriage in 1607, as she stood at the water's edge one day, she was startled by the growl of a huge wolf behind her. As the ferocious beast prepared to spring at her from the thicket, the Viscount's wife fainted. At that very instance a large wolfhound appeared and attacked the wolf. A violent fight ensued between the animals. When Lady Marian recovered, the wolf was stretched out dead on the ground and lying beside her, licking her hand, was the Irish wolfhound. Her noble defender was badly injured, however, and Lady Marian had the dog brought back to Antrim Castle, where she tended to its wounds with great care. Once the animal had sufficiently healed, it disappeared.

Some years later, during a storm one night, the baying of a wolfhound could be heard. The Castle wardens hastily lit a beacon fire to see what was going on and saw the shadowy forms of their enemies gathering below. The faithful wolfhound had raised the alarm.

"Must've been a Protestant wolfhound," whispered Geraldine, out of earshot of the caretaker.

A single cannon blast from the Castle, he continued, was enough to repel the attack. By early morning's light, the occupants of the Castle saw a stone effigy of the wolfhound on the highest turret. Over the centuries, the statue had been moved around a few times, and Mr. Hutchinson pointed out to us where it currently was in the garden.

Along with the harp, the shamrock, the Celtic cross, and the round tower, the Irish wolfhound has been symbolic of Ireland since ancient times. The wolfhound figures in some of Erin's oldest sagas. The legendary hunter-warrior Fionn mac Cumhaill (often rendered as Finn MacCool in English) had his loyal hounds Bran and Sceólang.

Known through the ages for their nobility and integrity, the great Irish wolfhound was respected for its hunting prowess and strength. The fierce canines also became renowned as war dogs, and Irish warriors of old would go into battle with their hounds. The huge dogs could drag men off horseback and chariots. In the first centuries of the Christian era, Ireland exported wolfhounds to Imperial Rome. Saint Patrick was said to have escaped his boyhood enslavement in Ireland by hiding among a shipment of hounds bound for the Continent.

The caretaker showed us the private burial ground of the 12th Viscount Massereene and his daughter, Lady Diana, who died at only twenty-one years old in 1930. Their graves, surrounded by high hedges, were marked by two tall Celtic crosses. Here the caretaker left us, after we thanked him for his time and wished him a good day.

When we were alone, Geraldine asked me what he said his name was.

"William Hutchinson," I replied.

"With that Proddy name and that Ballymena accent on him, he's probably a good Orangeman," she remarked.

After lunch at the same coffee shop on High Street we were at earlier, we visited the nearby grounds of the almost 400-year-old Protestant All Saints Church of Ireland. The stone edifice erected in 1596, with its lofty tower and octagonal spire added later, according to my guidebook, was one of the oldest parish churches still in use and one of the finest examples of Gothic and Elizabethan architecture in Ireland.

Under the church windows on each side were leper squints, so the unfortunate outcasts could glimpse into the church, they weren't allowed to enter. It has also been suggested these holes might have been loopholes from which muskets could have been fired. In 1649, during the Cromwellian invasion of Ireland, All Saints Church was burned, along with most of the town, by the Scottish army of General Robert Monro, and wasn't repaired until 1720. Later, the churchyard was a strategic landmark during the Battle of Antrim in 1798 and the original church door was struck by musket balls several times in the fray.

When we tried to enter the church, we found the door locked and contented ourselves to wander around the old churchyard, reading various names on the aged and weathered gravestones. Geraldine commented on how people lived such short lives then and so many were children's graves.

We continued down the narrow street called Riverside, past rowhouses a hundred or more years old, and then to a small field where we found several dilapidated, abandoned cottages with broken windows. I poked my head into one without a door. Inside was a table with broken dishes and teacups on it, dirty clothes were scattered on the floor, a Sacred Heart picture hung crookedly on a wall, and a small fireplace had a black kettle above it. Geraldine thought tinkers may have once lived there.

We walked back the way we had come and then along the banks of the Six Mile Water. It was an interesting name, though I read the river was in fact closer to twenty-six miles long. An indirect tributary of the River Bann, via Lough Neagh, the waterway rises in the hills west of Larne and north of Carrickfergus and descends westward into the Lough.

The River Six Mile Water – known in Gaelic as *Abhainn na bhFiodh* (river of the wood) – was once called the River Ollar (river of the rushes). The story went it received its English name after the Normans built Carrickfergus Castle, in the 12th century, and they placed outposts along the Ollar. Norman soldiers calculated that they marched six miles when they forded the river at Ballyclare, County Antrim, and thereafter called it Six Mile Water.

I had been so absorbed in my own thoughts that I hadn't noticed Geraldine had been quiet for some time. I asked her what she was thinking.

"The wee village of Toome isn't too far from here," she said. "When I was in the convent, we had a Sister Magdalene from Toome. She was only a year older than I was and we were great chums, so we were."

"Toome, like in the song about Roddy McCorley?" I asked.

"Aye. I don't believe there's another."

I offered Geraldine my flask and she had a sip and handed it back to me. I then polished off the last of the whiskey. That tiny bit of spirits seemed to lift her spirits, and she began to sing "Roddy McCorley." Being well acquainted with the old ballad, I enthusiastically joined in.

> *See the fleet foot host of men,*
> *That speed with faces wan,*
> *From farmstead and from fishers' cot,*
> *Along the banks of Bann,*
> *They come with vengeance in their eyes.*
> *Too late, too late are they,*
> *For young Roddy McCorley goes to die*
> *On the bridge of Toome today.*
>
> *Up the narrow street he steps,*
> *Smiling, proud and young.*
> *About the hemp rope on his neck,*
> *The golden ringlets clung;*
> *There was never a tear in his blue eyes,*
> *Both sad and bright are they,*
> *For young Roddy McCorley goes to die*
> *On the bridge of Toome today.*

When he last stepped up that street,
His shining pike in hand,
Behind him marched in grim array
A stalwart, earnest band.
For Antrim town, for Antrim town,
He led them to the fray,
And young Roddy McCorley goes to die
On the bridge of Toome today.

There was never a one of all your dead
More bravely fell in fray
Than he who marches to his fate
On the bridge of Toome today.
True to the last, true to the last,
He treads the upwards way,
And young Roddy McCorley goes to die
On the bridge of Toome today.

We continued walking through the town and up the main Dublin Road until we came upon St. Comgall's Catholic Church, with a statue of the saint set high in a niche in its tall square tower. We entered the gate and went up the steps. This time we found the front doors of the church unlocked.

As we passed through the narthex, I took a free leaflet from a rack. There was no one inside the church except for an old woman in a kerchief kneeling at an altar to Saint Anthony. The church wasn't overly ornate, but beautiful in its simplicity. I sat in a pew beside Geraldine. As she knelt in prayer, I glanced at the leaflet about the church's patron.

Saint Comgall was a sixth century Irish saint who founded an abbey at Bangor in County Down. When the Vikings plundered his great monastery in 822, the relics of the holy abbot were transferred to Antrim. More than a thousand years later, in 1870, the current parish church was dedicated to Saint Comgall.

Geraldine had taken a rosary from her coat pocket and began to finger her beads. I got up to walk around the church and knelt down at an altar to the Blessed Virgin. Crossing myself, I said a prayer that Our

Lady would continue to watch over my wife, Beth, and our precious little daughters, Mary and Brigid, and that she'd bring me safely home to them.

When we left the church, we took Oriel Road, past middle-class homes with large front lawns, down to Steeple Road. Since we had nearly an hour before the 4:30 p.m. train for Belfast, we walked back to see the Round Tower one last time.

It had been a pleasant day and we both enjoyed our excursion. Geraldine cooked us a chicken dinner that evening in her flat and afterwards we watched TV. We saw *A Christmas Carol,* the original black and white classic starring the Scottish actor Alastair Sim.

Round Tower of Antrim

Antrim Town street

The author in Belfast, 1992

CHAPTER FIFTY
CHRISTMAS AT OLD ST. MARY'S

It was Christmas morning and as I walked through the cold, empty streets of downtown Belfast, I turned up my coat collar against the icy wind and tucked in my scarf. Geraldine had gone to spend Christmas with her parents in Cliftonville and Paddy Murphy was spending the holiday with friends in Dublin. At Shaftesbury Square, I passed two parked R.U.C. Land Rovers across from a British Army one. The news reported that the I.R.A. had called a three-day ceasefire for Christmas.

I wanted to attend the Mass celebrating the Nativity of Christ at Old St. Mary's, as the locals called Belfast's oldest Catholic church. Located off Castle Street, on Chapel Lane, I had passed by it on a number of occasions but hadn't yet stepped inside.

I was reading through Paddy's book, *As I Roved Out,* by Cathal O'Byrne, and there was a chapter dedicated to Old St. Mary's.

As mentioned earlier, during the Penal era Mass was said at Friar's Bush, then on the outskirts of Belfast town. Once the harsh Penal Laws were somewhat relaxed, later in the 18th century, it was possible to have Mass in the town itself. A disused shed behind the house of one John Kennedy, a cutler on Castle Street, was used as a "Mass-house." It was described as "old and damp and dirty" and needed to be approached through a very narrow alley appropriately called Squeeze Gut Entry.

When the right to purchase land was restored to Catholics, they decided that they should have a church of their own. The parish priest, Father Hugh O'Donnell, acquired a lease on a site in Crooked Lane (later renamed Chapel Lane) for the purpose of building a chapel.

Catholics were a poor minority in an overwhelmingly Protestant town. But as was previously noted, the enlightened Presbyterian and Anglican (Church of Ireland) populations took up a special collection and generously donated the money to build the first Catholic chapel in Belfast. Moreover, when Father O'Donnell arrived to say the first Mass in St. Mary's, on a Sunday morning in late May 1784, he was greeted by the First Belfast Company of the Irish Volunteers lining the chapel yard. "Presbyterian almost to a man," wrote Cathal O'Byrne, they provided a guard of honor and presented arms to the priest as he passed into the chapel.

At the time, there was genuine good will between the Protestants and Catholics of Belfast. One local Presbyterian congregation alone contributed £84 to the total building cost of £170 for the chapel, and the Anglican vicar of Belfast donated the mahogany pulpit still in use at St. Mary's.

The original chapel was a simple structure, said to resemble an old-fashioned Presbyterian meetinghouse. The architect added multiple crosses, though, to make it appear more Catholic. When the parish had more money by 1868, St. Mary's was enlarged and reconstructed in a Romanesque style. Later, in 1941, the city's mother church underwent further renovations, and again in the early 1980's more renovations were made.

Hidden from view of the casual passerby on the main street, Old St. Mary's was a red-brick building, with a large circular rose window with tracery, and a white statue of Our Lady in a niche high above the entrance doors. I followed parishioners, dressed in their holiday best, inside and found my way in the well-filled church to an empty space in a pew.

It was a beautiful Mass, and included many of the traditional Christmas carols – "O Come, All Ye Faithful," "The First Noel," etc. I sat behind a man and his wife with their two little children, a boy in a blue suit and a girl in a frilly red dress. They must have been near the same age as my little daughters. As I watched the kids squirm and fidget throughout the Mass, I thought of Mary and Biddy. Suddenly a lonesome sadness came over me and I yearned to be back with my family, especially that Christmas day. But with only ten days left in Ireland, I'd be home soon enough.

After Mass, I paused briefly in the garden outside the church at a Grotto to Our Lady of Lourdes. As I stepped into Chapel Lane, I lit a cigarette, and a small, middle-aged man with black-framed glasses, wearing a black overcoat and gray fedora hat, walked past me. I recognized him as Mr. McGowan, the father of the teenager Hughie who put me up for a night when he found me wandering *legless* around the Falls Road.

"Mr. McGowan!" I called out, and he stopped and turned. "Merry Christmas!"

"Well, bless me, if it isn't me Hughie's young American friend."

We shook hands and walked together in the direction of the Falls Road, where he lived on Cairns Street. When I asked Mr. McGowan why he went so far for Mass, he said that he usually went to St. Paul's but wanted to go his boyhood parish for Christmas.

"Sure, I was reared only a stone throw away from Old St. Mary's. I was an altar boy there back when the Mass was still in Latin and there was still a proper altar to serve at."

The Second Vatican Council in the 1960's introduced Mass in the vernacular around the world (in English-speaking countries that meant Mass in English), sending the age-old Latin Tridentine Mass into disuse and alienating many traditional-minded Catholics. But it was much more than about the change in language. For instance, priests were made to face the congregation – in imitation of Protestant ministers – rather than facing in the same direction as the people, as they had always done.

Mr. McGowan elaborated further. "In time, everything was Protestantized. What was done to Old St. Mary's by our own Catholic hierarchy – may God forgive 'em – was nothin' less than an act of vandalism. Back in '83, our two side altars were removed as well as the altar rails, and a platform was erected which looks like some pop group should be performin' on it. Worst of all, the wreckers later ripped out our lovely high altar, which was replaced by a plain wooden table. Many of us are still very angry and sickened about the whole thing."

As we made our way down Divis Street and over the Westlink, I asked Mr. McGowan about how Hughie was keeping.

"He's sound enough. Workin', so he is, though still mixed up with those Sinn Féiners," the father replied, disapprovingly.

Mr. McGowan was going to pay his sister a visit, so we parted company near where Divis became the Lower Falls Road.

"God see ye safe home to America, son," he called after me.

I continued walking on my own when suddenly a white Vauxhall Astra pulled up alongside me.

"Hey Yank, happy Christmas!" said the driver cheerfully, through the lowered window. It was Mrs. Boyle's son-in-law, Little Joe Devine, in his private taxi. He offered me a ride and I climbed in, glad to be out of the cold.

Once inside the car, I got a better look at him and saw the left side of his face was badly bruised and discolored and his lip was split.

"What the hell happened to you?" I asked.

"Well," he answered grinning, "remember that checkpoint I had ye get out at a few days back? They had me pop the boot, and when I did and stepped back a wee bit for the peelers to look inside one of 'em asked me why I was steppin' away for. I told him so when the bomb goes off, I wouldn't get splattered by any of their blood and guts and whatever brain matter they had."

"That wasn't a very clever thing to say," I replied.

"I'd say it again," Little Joe shot back defiantly. "Piss on the bastards! They can beat me, but I ain't scared of the likes of 'em."

When we pulled in front of my place on Eglantine Avenue, I invited the bold wee man up for a drink. Once in my flat, I opened a new bottle of Bushmills and poured Little Joe and myself a fair amount.

"*Sláinte,*" I said, clinking his glass.

"*Nollaig shona duit,*" he replied.

"And Merry Christmas to you too."

I was well stocked with Guinness in the fridge, but Little Joe said unfortunately he couldn't linger. I understood. I once drove a cab when I first got out of the navy, and I knew Christmas was a big money-making day in the taxi business.

Later that afternoon, I went out to the phone booth on Eglantine Avenue to call Beth to wish her and the girls a Merry Christmas. I glanced at my watch and saw it was 3:30 p.m., so it would be 7:30 a.m. Christmas morning in San Diego.

Beth picked up the phone. She told me the girls were still asleep though. Mary had been asking if Santa would be bringing daddy home, and Biddy had the sniffles for the past couple of days and the night before had a slight temperature. Provided little Biddy felt better, she said, they'd go to Mass later that morning and then to her cousin Tessie's house for Christmas dinner.

That evening, my own Christmas dinner arrived with a visit from Geraldine. She brought me from her parents' table slices of roast turkey and spuds covered with gravy, which she reheated for me, and a couple of large pieces of Christmas cake with white icing. Then from a paper bag she pulled out a bottle of Longueville House Irish Apple Brandy.

"Something to wash it all down with," she said with a smile.

"Irish brandy? I never knew there was such a thing."

"It's from Cork, I believe. Someone bought it for me da, but he'll only drink Irish whiskey."

"What can I say, Geraldine? Thank you for everything."

"That's not all," she declared, reaching back into the bag, and handing me a book entitled *Ireland: A History,* by Robert Kee.

"I didn't have a chance to buy ye a gift," she explained. "So, I plucked this off me bookshelf. Me brother - the priest - gave it to me a few years back. You have such a great love of Ireland and her history that I want ye to have it. Happy Christmas!"

"I'll treasure it. But I've nothing to give you in return."

"Ah, Edmond, ye gave me the best gift of all, ye gave me yer friendship."

I gave Geraldine McKeever a quick hug in thanks and sat down to my delicious Christmas dinner.

CHAPTER FIFTY-ONE
THE GHOSTLY MASS AT FRIAR'S BUSH

After Geraldine went back to her flat for the night, I jotted down the day's events into my travel journal, as I continued to sample her Irish brandy, in between plenty of pourings of my Bushmills, and a good few bottles of Guinness. When my head became dizzy, I decided to take a walk, though the hour was close to midnight.

I had no particular destination in mind when I stepped out onto Eglantine Avenue and staggered towards the Malone Road, but the brisk night air sobered me up a bit. I paused to look at the dark and imposing Fisherwick Presbyterian Church, built in the prevailing ecclesiastical Gothic Revival style of the Victorian period, like so many of Belfast's churches.

My thoughts suddenly turned to that Halloween night on the Stranmillis Road. I could never quite get out of my mind the image of the girl with the porcelain face and large unblinking eyes, in her hooded cloak.

"For pity's sake, good sir…pray for me," she beseeched me.

And I had prayed for her.

I felt drawn to revisit the spot of that strange encounter. It was only a short five-minute walk up the Malone Road to where it arched round to

Stranmillis. As I passed the Ulster Museum, I glanced up in the general direction of the window from where I looked down on Friar's Bush Graveyard with Paddy and the museum's taxidermist, Mr. Bruton. I stood across from the cemetery's high stone wall, on the sidewalk by the old brick rowhouses, and anxiously smoked a cigarette. It was after midnight and the darkened road was deserted, like it was that night.

Stranmillis Road, located in the south Belfast district of the same name, was as ancient as the burying ground, and as Mr. O'Byrne told it in his book, *As I Roved Out,* was a rendering of the old Gaelic words *Sruthán millis,* "a sweet or pleasant stream," referring to the nearby River Lagan. But at that particular moment, I thought of none of that.

I stepped across the road to Friar's Bush and made my way along the eight-foot-high stone wall to the locked arched, double-sided Gothic style gatehouse. Still, no one was around, and I climbed over the gates; but fell as I dropped down. I laid on my back for a moment on the cold ground before getting up, unhurt, in the derelict graveyard.

Cautiously, moving slowly on the main grassy path, I tried to remember what Mr. Bruton had told me. To my immediate left was the cholera mound. "Plaguely Hill," he called it, and said over four hundred victims were buried there when the epidemic hit Belfast in the early 1830's, and a decade later during the devastating Famine years more than five thousand more bodies were cast into the reopened pit. Beyond this was an ornate Celtic cross, with a Sacred Heart carved in its center, erected in the memory of Dr. Francis Joseph Wisely, who was killed in the First World War.

There was no telling how many thousands upon thousands were buried in the just two acres of Friar's Bush. Many of the moss-covered gravestones were leaning over or broken. Old and eroded, most were difficult to read, especially by only the light of the moon. There were plenty of crumbling 19th century monuments to be seen, many topped by crosses or crucifixes. One tombstone had the face of Jesus carved into it. Another large monument had a harp surrounded by a profusion of shamrocks.

As I stepped over several empty beer bottles in the overgrown grass, a white cat quickly darted behind a tombstone, nearly scaring the bejaysus out of me.

All around the graveyard were tall, dark leafless trees and unkempt bushes. In the center was the venerable, twisted old thorn tree, under which faithful Catholics gathered in secret to hear Mass during Penal times. I read somewhere that hawthorn trees could live for four hundred years or more. That same tree served as gallows for an unnamed friar or was where he was shot to death. Either way, he died a holy martyr for the Faith.

Mr. Bruton said there was a mysterious stone by the thorn tree, which seemed to commemorate an earlier friar, implausibly inscribed: "This stone marks ye Friar's grave A.D. 485." Local historians believed it was probably placed there in the 19th century. I looked for the marker by the old tree but couldn't find it in the dark.

I began to feel very tired and all the alcohol I consumed had made me sleepy. A flat grave-slab, by an ivy-covered mausoleum, made the perfect place to lay on for a few minutes and rest. It was so peaceful and quiet, and I no longer felt the cold. I just remember looking up at the stars in the clear night sky.

I must have fallen asleep. I awoke to what sounded like the low chanting of prayers. The voice was in a language that was vaguely familiar, yet I couldn't understand it. Was I dreaming?

"Sanctus, Sanctus, Sanctus..." I distinctly heard in a slightly raised voice.

Instantly, I bolted upright on the grave-slab, as my heart raced, and fear shot through every fiber of my being. At least a hundred silent figures surrounded me! Huddled together on the ground…kneeling in prayer…all facing towards the old thorn tree, where a priest stood at a makeshift altar, his back turned, with two lit candles and a young altar boy at his side, offering the Holy Sacrifice of the Mass. Was I sleeping or awake and this all a hallucination?

As my heart continued to pound furiously in my chest, I stared transfixed at those figures closest to where I sat on the edge of the grave-slab. A handsome, well-built young man, with a square chin and a determined look, knelt on one knee, his strong hands clasped together on the other. His dark hair was pulled back and tied into a queue. He wore a white cravat around his neck, a long dark coat, and knee breeches with stockings. Kneeling beside him, leaning on a wooden staff, was an old man clenching a rosary. His long gray hair hung over his coat collar, and he too donned knee breeches with stockings. Nearby were women and young girls with dark hooded cloaks over their heads.

I was not among the living, but among the dead of long ago, whose spirits had returned to the place they worshipped when Mass was prohibited by law.

The ghostly congregation bowed their heads at the consecration. The priestly apparition genuflected and rose and elevated the Host with both hands above his head, his back turned towards his parishioners. He wore a red chasuble, for it was the feast of Saint Stephen, the first martyr of the Church. Again, the priest genuflected and rose, and lifted the chalice from the altar above his head.

I continued to observe everything in utter awe, but my earlier terror was gone. I was calm, almost at peace, as I drew comfort from the familiar rituals of my religion and began to feel a strange kinship with these visiting souls. They could have been my own Irish ancestors.

"Per ómnia sæcula sæculórum," said the priest aloud in Latin. World without end.

"Amen."

I joined the worshippers on my knees in the moist grass.

"Pater Noster, qui es in cælis: Sanctificétur nomen tuum: Advéniat regnum tuum..." Our Father, Who art in heaven, hallowed be Thy Name; Thy kingdom come...

In silence, various figures rose to approach the altar under the thorn tree to receive Holy Communion. I watched as they knelt before the priest to receive the Host on their tongues. Remaining where I was, instinctively I murmured a short prayer of spiritual communion.

I believed I was an invisible witness to the ghostly Mass, until the strapping young man nearest me turned, and his piercing pale blue eyes met mine and he nodded me a welcome.

"Ite, Missa est," concluded the priest. Go, the Mass is ended.

Then it was over. I had just sat back against a tombstone, when the worshippers, the priest, the makeshift altar, all vanished; and I was alone again in the derelict graveyard.

I departed Friar's Bush as I had entered it, over the gates. The cold and darkened streets were still empty. As I approached Eglantine Avenue, on the Malone Road, a gray R.U.C. Land Rover followed by a green British Army Land Rover sped past me, heading towards the city center. I was back in the Belfast of December 26th, 1992.

Friar's Bush Graveyard, Belfast

CHAPTER FIFTY-TWO
THE PARTING GLASS

Several days had passed since I picked up a pen to scribble into my travel journal. The I.R.A.'s ceasefire for Christmas had ended and the war continued. A couple of nights before, when I was seated in Geraldine's kitchen, chatting and having a cup of tea with her, we heard a loud explosion in the distance.

"That was yer Provos," remarked Geraldine.

The morning news reported authorities believed the I.R.A. had set off a 300-pound car bomb, at 11:14 p.m., in the parking lot of the Drumkeen Hotel in south Belfast's Castlereagh district, about two and a half miles from Eglantine Avenue. It was said that the blast could be heard up to ten miles away.

The hotel was extensively damaged, and windows of surrounding homes and nearby Forster Green Hospital were blown out by the blast. But fortunately, there were no casualties as the bombers called in a warning to evacuate the hotel just before the explosion occurred.

The following day the I.R.A. shot dead British soldier Stephen Waller, aged twenty-three, of the Royal Irish Regiment, in his home off the Cavehill Road in north Belfast.

It was the last day of 1992. Since neither Paddy Murphy nor I had a phone, I decided to venture up to Ardoyne to see if he was back yet from Dublin.

I took my usual hour-long route through the city center to the Crumlin Road, past the Mater Infirmorum Hospital, the jail and the courthouse, and made a right onto Flax Street, by the old, long-abandoned mill, to enter Ardoyne. I walked past the Shamrock Bar and a Séan Graham's betting shop at the junction of Flax and Ardoyne Avenue, and down several blocks of rowhouses to where Paddy lived on Velsheda Park.

When I arrived at Paddy's, he was just stepping out to meet a man at Kelly's Cellars and asked me to come along.

"Sure," he said, "we can knock back a few pints together."

Paddy had already called from a neighbor's phone for a black taxi, and it soon pulled up in front of the house. As the driver took the Oldpark Road down to the Crumlin Road, he said there had just been some shooting on Flax Street and the R.U.C. were all over the place.

We could feel the tension in the air as we entered Kelly's and saw a crowd gathered around the TV watching the news. There had been an attack on Séan Graham Bookmakers in Ardoyne. The same betting shop I had just walked past an hour earlier. A reporter said a three-man gang struck at 3:30 p.m. and tried to spray the bookie's with gunfire. Fifteen punters and two staff, one of them a woman, were inside at the time of the attack. Miraculously, no one was injured, unlike the massacres at James Murray's betting shop in November and at the other Séan Graham's on the Ormeau Road back in February. Apparently, this time the gunman's machine gun jammed.

"Thank Christ for that," declared a man standing beside me.

The reporter interviewed eyewitnesses who said that having failed to kill anyone in the betting shop, the gunmen opened fire indiscriminately as they made their escape. According to one, "The driver was still firing all round the place as he drove down Flax Street. He was like a madman; he was going to kill anybody on the street."

Later in a statement issued to a local newsroom, the Ulster Freedom Fighters claimed its men were responsible for the attack but that "sheer luck prevented us from completing our task."

The Loyalist paramilitary group added, "our active service units across Ulster are now fully armed and equipped to intensify and widen our campaign in 1993 to a ferocity never imagined."

The man that Paddy planned to meet at Kelly's didn't show, so after three pints a piece we were on our way. Which was just as well because I was getting very short on cash and didn't feel right about Paddy having to foot the entire bill, though I knew he wouldn't have given it a second thought. As Paddy said on more than one occasion, "what's a little money between friends."

As we made our way down Castle Street, I went to light a cigarette but found I didn't have my lighter with me. Paddy reached into his pocket and handed me a lighter.

"I picked that up in Dublin for ye." The white plastic lighter had an Irish tricolor flag with "Onwards to Victory" on one side and on the other a raised fist wrapped in barbed wire.

"So ye won't forget our Republican P.O.W.s behind the wire," he said.

I invited Paddy to my flat for dinner. But I didn't have much to offer him other than one of my frozen TV dinners, which had become my main fare except when Geraldine brought me over a home cooked meal. We had a couple of bottles Guinness as we waited for our macaroni and cheese with mashed potatoes and peas, in their divided aluminum trays, to be heated up in the oven. More stout to wash it down made it taste more palatable than it was.

Geraldine knocked on the door and I invited her in. She usually wore slacks but had on a pretty blue dress with a white lace collar. She had been to the beauty parlor and her light brown hair was styled in a pixie cut. Despite her thick glasses, she looked quite attractive.

I introduced Geraldine to Paddy, and he immediately rose from his chair, came over, bowed, and comically got down on one knee and kissed her hand.

"'Tis indeed an honor and a pleasure to make yer acquaintance, Miss McKeever. Éamon here told me about ye."

Geraldine stood there blushing, her outstretched hand in Paddy's, not knowing how to react to his antics.

"Paddy, can't you see you're embarrassing the girl!" I said, trying to come to her rescue, amid my own laughter.

Recovering somewhat, she managed to say, "And ye're the Paddy Murphy from Ardoyne."

"In the flesh, dear lady," he replied, still in a jovial tone, getting to his feet.

Geraldine asked us to join her down in Denis Irwin's flat for a little New Year's Eve get-together. I grabbed what was left of my Bushmills, so as not to come empty handed, and Paddy brought an armful of Guinness from my fridge.

Denis greeted us at the door. He too was dressed for the occasion, in a brown and red argyle sweater vest, crisp white shirt, and a brown tie. He had a table set up with pint glasses and tumblers for whiskey, a bottle of Jameson beside a bottle of Black Bush, and there were Bulmers and Strongbow ciders, along with stacks of finger sandwiches on a platter, and a big bowl of potato chips. Denis told us there was also plenty of more Guinness and Harp in the fridge that we could help ourselves to.

As Paddy ate a couple of the little sandwiches, Denis handed me a tumbler and I poured my Bushmills into it and some into a tumbler for him. Denis asked if I wanted any ice cubes in mine.

"I heard ye Yanks are quite keen on ice in yer whiskey."

"No thanks," I replied, "I just drink mine neat."

"Sure, Éamon is an honorary Irishman," said Paddy, with a wink at me.

Geraldine was over at Denis's stereo console looking through his record collection. Not finding anything to her liking, she said she was going to fetch a few albums from her flat.

Just then we were joined by the lanky, blond shaggy-haired university student and aspiring artist from upstairs. Alan Jenkins turned up in a deep purple button-down shirt and carrying a bottle of Smirnoff vodka.

When I asked him how he'd been, Alan said he was leaving for Paris in a fortnight.

"I already bought me ticket. I want to finally see the Louvre and then spend some time in Brittany, where Gauguin, y'know, found much of his inspiration to paint."

"What about yer girlfriend," inquired Denis.

"Och, Deirdre is history. I'm a free man once more."

Noticing my tumbler was empty, Alan offered me some of his vodka. But I politely declined, telling him when I was drinking liquor and Irish whiskey was available, I'd stick to that.

"What did I tell yez?" said an amused Paddy. "Yer man's more Irish than the Irish themselves." He poured himself a tumbler full of Black Bush, then refilled mine.

"Cheers, boys," said Denis, and we all clinked glasses.

I knew Paddy must have seen the faded UDA letters tattooed across Alan's knuckles and knew which foot he kicked with and where his political loyalties likely were, but he chose to ignore it. Perhaps Paddy contributed it to his misguided youth. After all, no hardened U.D.A. man would be drinking with a roomful of Taigs.

Hey, girl, whatcha doin' down there?
Dancin' alone every night
While I live right above you...

Geraldine had on one of her records of Tony Orlando and Dawn and was happily swaying to the music, as she sipped a glass of cider.

Knock three times
On the ceiling if you want me...

"What was the name of the German bank robber?" asked Paddy. "Hans Up!" he answered. We all laughed. "What about the Spaniard in the Spanish fire brigade?" he asked. "José!" We laughed again and refilled our glasses.

Geraldine was getting noticeably tipsy and was singing along with ABBA, the Swedish pop group from the 1970's and early '80's.

"Looks like it's gonna be golden oldies tonight," remarked Alan.

"Knowing me, knowing you, ah ha..." sang Geraldine, as she turned up the volume on the stereo.

Denis went around refilling glasses with whiskey, and vodka for Alan, and bottles of beer were being taken from the fridge, as our talk grew louder and our laughter more frequent.

Ooh...you can dance
You can jive
Having the time of your life...

Geraldine was now enthusiastically dancing to ABBA's "Dancing Queen."

"Will one of ye gents not come over and dance with me?" she called out.

As none of the guys made a move to join her, I went to give her a swirl. It had been sometime since the discos of my teenage years, but I still remembered a lot of the old moves.

"Jaysus," exclaimed Paddy, "if it isn't Johnny Travolta. 'Tis a grand wee party now, isn't it?"

Paddy was soon up with Geraldine, his fat belly shaking as he attempted to dance around with her. Next came Denis, who held her by the hand and awkwardly placed his other arm around of slender waist and led her in a sort of ballroom dance. Alan too took his turn and danced a few steps with Geraldine, a cigarette dangling from his lips.

Gloria Gaynor was belting out her hit "I Will Survive" when someone shouted, "Happy New Year!" It was 1993. Geraldine went over and gave Denis a peck on the cheek. Then she made the rounds and each of us received a quick kiss from her. More drinks were poured to toast the New Year.

"Please God, the New Year will be a good one," declared Geraldine, raising her glass.

Denis put on a Chieftains record and Irish jigs and reels filled the room. To our delight, Geraldine performed a traditional step dance.

"I learnt that as a wee girl," she said, after taking a seat.

Paddy lifted his tumbler of whiskey: "May those that love us, love us. And those that don't love us, may God turn their hearts. And if He doesn't turn their hearts, may He turn their ankles, so we'll know them by their limping. *Go mbeirimid beo ar an am seo arís.*"

After we all drank to that, Alan asked what the words in Irish meant.

"May we be alive at this same time again next year," answered Paddy.

I reached over to shake the big man's hand and said with feeling, "God bless you, Paddy."

It was already the small hours of the morning, and we sat having a last glass of stout before calling it a night. A Clancy Brothers and Tommy Makem record was playing, and we all joined in "The Parting Glass."

Of all the money that e'er I spent
I've spent it in good company
And all the harm that ever I did

Alas it was to none but me
And all I've done for want of wit
To memory now I can't recall
So fill to me the parting glass
Good night and joy be with you all
If I had money enough to spend
And leisure to sit awhile
There is a fair maid in the town
That sorely has my heart beguiled

Her rosy cheeks and ruby lips
I own she has my heart enthralled
So fill to me the parting glass
Good night and joy be with you all
Oh, all the comrades that e'er I had
They're sorry for my going away
And all the sweethearts that e'er I had
They'd wish me one more day to stay
But since it falls unto my lot
That I should rise and you should not
I'll gently rise and softly call
Good night and joy be with you all

Paddy put it best, it was a grand wee party, and a New Year's that I'd always remember, for it was my parting glass on Irish shores among all my newfound friends.

When I returned alone to my flat, my pipe and tobacco pouch were on the card table where I had left them. Unzipping the little leather pouch for a bowlful of Mellow Virginia, I found inside a folded ten-pound Northern Ireland banknote and two one-pound coins. Despite my state of inebriation, I remembered seeing Paddy open it when I was preparing dinner. He said he just wanted to take a wee sniff of the aromatic tobacco. But Paddy knew I was short on funds, and when I wasn't looking, had thoughtfully slipped the tenner and coins into the pouch. A friend in need is a friend indeed.

My last few days in Belfast were spent walking around the now familiar streets and revisiting parts of the city, and of course in the company of my new friends.

On Saturday, I wandered up the Lower Falls Road and chanced to stop at a frame and picture shop where sketches of street scenes, by the local artist Thomas Clarke, were on display. The proprietor said the drawings were of old Belfast before the Troubles.

I picked up one in a frame, which was labelled Albert Street and showed Brendan Murphy's Pub.

"Sadly, that bar's long gone," said the proprietor, "like the ould Pound Loney itself after the redevelopment in the '60's."

An area off the Lower Falls, which included Pound Street, the Pound Loney (as the little lane was locally called) ran off Divis Street to Durham Street and ended at the side of Barrack Street's old animal pound, hence its name.

I bought the drawing of Brendan Murphy's Pub for £3, and another unframed print labelled Mary Street, with quaint old rowhouses, for a pound. Once located off the Lower Falls, it too had long ago disappeared, demolished in the name of progress. I later put "Mary Street" in a frame and hung it by my little daughter Mary's bed in the girls' room.

With my artwork wrapped up in brown paper under my arm, I continued up the Falls Road. After stopping at a florist shop and buying a bouquet of flowers, I made my way to Harrogate Street to give them to Mrs. Boyle and bid her a farewell.

Once again, I was warmly received, and a bowl of hot and delicious stew was set in front of me. Before I left, Mrs. Boyle presented me with a belated Christmas gift of three pairs of black thermal socks.

"Sure, ye can never have too many stockings," she said, with a motherly smile.

Then at the door, she gave me a hug and stuck £2 into my coat pocket, "just cigarette money, so."

"Thank you, Mrs. Boyle, you've been most kind."

"Wisht! Now mind yerself and safe home to ye."

On the way back to Eglantine Avenue, I ducked into another florist and bought another bouquet for Geraldine. That evening I had dinner with her and Denis in her flat.

Sunday was my last full day in Belfast. After attending Mass at St. Patrick's Church on Donegall Street, I went to see Paddy. Instead of my usual route into Ardoyne by Flax Street, I took the Oldpark Road, due to the recent Loyalist attack at the betting shop on Flax Street.

Paddy took me to have lunch with him at the home of friends of his in Ardoyne. Although they shared his surname, he explained, the Murphy family weren't related to him.

I was introduced to Mick Murphy, a thin, balding man with a brush-like mustache in his late forties, his wife, Maureen, and their two daughters, aged ten and nine. The elder one, Denise, was dark-haired like her mother and the younger girl, Louise, was blonde.

Over lunch of meat and potatoes, Paddy returned to the subject of their shared surname.

"One could almost say there are as many Murphys in Ireland as there are spuds."

Both the girls giggled.

Then Paddy related how he and Mick, along with another Murphy, one Dan of Strabane, were once stopped by a R.U.C. patrol.

"When we were asked our names, we all gave Murphy. The peeler asked if we were brothers and we said we weren't. He then asked if we were cousins and we said we weren't. The bloody peeler thought we were having him on."

The table full of Murphys all roared with laughter.

After we had eaten, Mick brought Paddy and me upstairs to show us the room he was renovating for the girls. As they talked about rot in old drywall, I looked through the window's curtains. A British Army foot patrol was making its way down the alley below. Paddy stepped over to see what I was looking at and grabbed hold of my arm and pulled me away.

"Jaysus!" said an alarmed Paddy. "Stay away from the bloody window. The Brit bastards will shoot ye as soon as look at ye."

After a couple of parting shots of whiskey with the Murphy men, I thanked the family for their hospitality and waited outside with Paddy for the black taxi he called for me.

"Now Éamon, be sure to drop us a line every so often from America. And whatever ye do, until ye step onto that jet plane home, mind peeping through any curtains."

The taxi arrived and before I got in, Paddy gave me a firm handshake and a *"Slán go fóill."* Goodbye for now.

"Slán, a chara mhaith," I replied. Goodbye, my good friend.

As I packed my old navy seabag back at the flat, Alan Jenkins dropped by to take me out for a last final pint at the Botanic Inn. Afterwards, as we walked back up Eglantine Avenue, he removed from his coat pocket a black Guinness ashtray he swiped from the bar and handed it to me.

"Take it. They won't miss it and it'll be a wee little souvenir from Belfast for ye."

I accepted Alan's gift, smiling as I looked at the old ashtray with more than a few cigarette burns in it. As they say, it's the thought that counts.

My flight wouldn't be until the following morning at 7:10 a.m., but the first bus for the airport didn't leave Belfast until 6:30 a.m. It was more than an hour bus ride to the International Airport at Aldergrove, and the cost of taking a taxi direct was more than I had. So, I decided to take a taxi that night to the bus station, beside the Europa Hotel, and take the last bus at 9:30 p.m. out to the airport.

Again, I found myself standing outside and waiting for a taxi, this time in the company of Geraldine and Denis. My packed seabag lay near the curb. I had just opened it to squeeze in a can of Bulmers that Denis had given me to have as a nightcap at the airport. Beside the seabag was a duffle bag that I had recently bought to accommodate all the books I had acquired, and carefully rewrapped in brown paper next to it was Terry Quinn's map of Ireland mirror.

The night air was cold, and it began to drizzle. Denis wished me a safe trip and remarked that my wife and daughters would no doubt be overjoyed to finally have me home. Geraldine was silent but I could see her eyes were welling with tears behind her thick glasses. As the taxi pulled up, she pressed into my hand a couple of packs of her Berkeley cigarettes.

"For the long flight home," she said, and also handed me a little card in an envelope.

While Denis helped the driver load my bags into the trunk, I gave Geraldine a hug.

"Ye've been a dear friend to me, Edmond Audubon," she whispered, kissing my cheek. I promised to write her.

Turning to Denis, I shook his hand and told him to take good care of her.

As the taxi drove through the wet, darkened streets towards the city center and the bus station, I opened Geraldine's card. Inside was a little Saint Christopher medal, the patron saint of travelers, and in neat script she had written in the card: "Bon Voyage, dear Edmond. On your return to the U.S.A. think of me sometimes, as I will of you with the fondest of memories. Your friend, Geraldine"

It was nearly 11 p.m. when I arrived at the airport, and I made my way to the lounge to have a pint and relax. I had a long night ahead of me until my morning flight.

Fellow travelers were watching the news on a TV set behind the bar, as I slid onto a stool. A reporter was recounting the first sectarian murders of the new year to occur in Northern Ireland.

The Loyalist Ulster Volunteer Force had killed Patrick Shields, a fifty-one-year-old Catholic shopkeeper, and his twenty-year-old son, Diarmuid, in the rural townland of Lisnagleer, near Dungannon, County Tyrone. It was reported that they weren't a political family but had a deep interest in Irish music and Gaelic Football. When the U.V.F. burst into their two-story house and grocery shop, it was believed, they intended to massacre the entire family. However, Mrs. Shields was able to barricade herself along with a daughter and son in a downstairs room. Patrick and Diarmuid Shields couldn't get away in time and were both shot dead. Another son was seriously injured in the attack.

Reflecting on this latest tragedy, I had another pint of stout and left the lounge to find an empty row of seats to sleep on for the night.

As I stood on line the following morning to board my British Midlands flight to London's Heathrow Airport, I noticed among the waiting passengers a gray-haired gentleman sitting in a dark pinstriped suit, with a tan trench coat draped over the seat beside him. But it was the title of the book he held that caught my attention. He was reading Tolstoy's great Russian epic *War and Peace*. How befitting, I thought.

And so, I stepped onto the plane and departed the war zone of Belfast that Monday morning of January 4th, 1993.

CHAPTER FIFTY-THREE
FAR AWAY O'ER THE FOAM

A Yellow Cab taxi brought me from the airport in San Diego to our townhouse apartment on Dunlop Street. It was after 11 p.m. when I arrived, but Beth was anxiously waiting for me. I was like – in the words of Robert Louis Stevenson – "the sailor, home from the sea, and the hunter home from the hill."

The girls were long since asleep and Beth's parents too had retired for the night. My wife and I sat together in the downstairs living room until the small hours of the morning as I related to her all that happened in the nearly three months I'd been away; about all the fascinating people I met, the interesting places I traveled to around Ireland, all I saw there, and the numerous experiences I had. Beth commented that I should write a book about my Irish adventures. And, thirty years later, I did.

In the morning, I woke before Beth and made my way downstairs. My mother-in-law was already cooking me a hearty breakfast in the kitchen. I entered the living room where two-year-old Biddy sat watching morning cartoons. Her greeting was so simple and innocent, it was as if she had only seen me the night before. "Daddy, my button," she said, seeking my help in buttoning her shirt.

Mary, having awoken, came downstairs. Her angelic face looked up at me, surprised, and then my three-old-year daughter informed me: "Daddy, I wait and wait and wait for you!"

The girls both showed me the little stuffed leprechauns that I sent them for Christmas. When Beth joined us, I opened my still packed seabag and passed out other little gifts I brought them. At that moment, there was nowhere else in the world that I wanted to be than at home with my family.

But traveling was in my blood. Not only had I inherited a roaming disposition from my illustrious, four-times-great-grandfather John James Audubon – albeit his travels were in the pursuit of birds to draw – and his roving, seafaring father, who came from a long line of sailors, I had the wandering blood of the ancient Celts flowing through my veins. I was a wanderer by nature and dreamed of distant lands to explore. However, wherever I wandered, there was a special place in my heart for Ireland.

Three months later, I was driving my blue Ford Ranger pickup truck down a long, desolate stretch of highway. To my right was the crystalline blue of the vast Pacific, and on my left were barren hills and more than a hundred miles of desert. I was heading south along the coast of Mexico's Baja California peninsula, with no particular destination in mind, just to travel again.

I brought my trusty Nikon camera along and stopped to take some pictures of the spectacular landscape and panoramic views of the ocean. If I had more time, I would have made the thousand-mile journey down the peninsula to Cabo San Lucas and La Paz like I had two years before or driven again across Baja's mountainous and desert terrain with giant cacti to the Sea of Cortés. But I just had a couple of days off from work to take a short little excursion.

I left San Diego before dawn and crossed the Mexican border into the infamous, sprawling city of Tijuana, known for its streets packed with *cantinas,* nightclubs, and prostitutes, and took the scenic highway past the sandy beaches of Rosarito and the port town of Ensenada. The road then turned inland and went through some agricultural land. I drove through more barren hills and dusty little towns and was back on the empty coastline again.

I had driven a good two hundred miles and pulled over at a small roadside restaurant to get something to eat and down a couple of cold *cervezas*. What had started out as a pleasantly warm morning had become oppressively hot before noon. The sun blazed fiercely in the sky with an intensity unknown in Ireland. At least the outdoor restaurant had an awning that provided some shade.

Placing my wide-brimmed straw hat down on the bar and wiping the sweat from my brow, I greeted the proprietor.

"*Hola, señor.*" He was a big, brown-skinned Mexican with a thick, bushy mustache, like Pancho Villa.

"*¿Cómo estás, amigo?* What can I get you?" he asked, putting a cold bottle of Dos Equis beer in front of me.

Behind the bar, a small portable fan ran at full blast, beside a framed picture of Our Lady of Guadalupe. Along with several bottles of José Cuervo tequila, I saw a bottle of mezcal with its loathsome, bloated worm floating around on the bottom. I had a couple of enchiladas and tacos. Then another cold Dos Equis, as I had a pipe smoke and glanced at my map of Baja.

Stepping back out under the glaring, merciless sun, I got into my pickup and turned the air-conditioner on high and put on a cassette tape. I continued down the dusty, deserted Mexican highway, as the soft, smoothing brogue of Christy Moore transported me to a land of lush green fields and low stone walls, dotted by little whitewashed cottages with roofs of thatch. A cool breeze blew as I stood on a cliff overlooking the north Atlantic and heard the crashing of the waves on the rocks below.

> *You may travel far, far from your own native home,*
> *Far away o'er the mountains, far a-way o'er the foam,*
> *But of all the fine places that I've ever seen,*
> *Sure, there's none to compare with the cliffs of Dooneen.*

EPILOGUE

Two and a half months after I left Belfast, the Provisional I.R.A. detonated two bombs planted in trash cans at a shopping area in Warrington, England, on March 20, 1993. Two young boys, aged three and twelve, were killed. Another fifty-six people were injured in the explosion, some seriously. One young mother had to have her leg amputated and later died from cancer. The attack drew expressions of outrage from around the world, including across Ireland, and calls for peace.

On August 31, 1994, after months of secret talks with the British government, the I.R.A. stunned the world by announcing a ceasefire with "a complete cessation of military operations."

Then, on February 9, 1996, the I.R.A. ended the ceasefire when it detonated a powerful truck bomb in the Docklands area of London, killing two people and injuring more than a hundred others and devastating the area.

In July 1997, the I.R.A. declared a new ceasefire. That September, the British government met with Sinn Féin to negotiate in formal peace talks. On April 10, 1998, the Good Friday Agreement was signed by the British and Irish governments and most of the political parties in Northern Ireland, including Sinn Féin, on how the Six County state should be governed, with the goal of ending three decades of violence and bloodshed. Following a vote in both the Irish Republic and Northern Ireland, the referendum was passed in late May. The Good Friday Agreement, also known as the Belfast Agreement, created a new Northern Ireland Assembly with equal say among Unionists and Nationalists.

The terms of the Agreement allowed most Republican and Loyalist prisoners to be released.

But not all Republicans supported the Agreement. I.R.A. splinter groups calling themselves the Continuity I.R.A. and the Real I.R.A. rejected the Agreement.

On August 15, 1998, the Real I.R.A. perpetrated the deadliest attack in the conflict in Northern Ireland when it detonated a massive car bomb in the town of Omagh, County Tyrone, which left twenty-nine people dead and more than two hundred wounded. After the initial shock, there was an even greater outcry for peace.

On July 28, 2005, the Provisional I.R.A. formally announced an end to its armed struggle: "All I.R.A. units have been ordered to dump arms," stated the organization. "All volunteers have been instructed to assist the development of purely political and democratic programs through exclusively peaceful means. Volunteers must not engage in any other activities whatsoever."

After thirty-six years of conflict, leaving more than 3,600 people dead and more than 30,000 injured, Northern Ireland still exists as a political entity of the United Kingdom.

By 2007, Loyalist paramilitary groups such as the Ulster Volunteer Force and the Ulster Defence Association / Ulster Freedom Fighters had also ended their campaigns.

While most consider the long war finally over, dissident paramilitaries – Republican as well as Loyalist – continue to exist in Northern Ireland and to engage in sporadic acts of violence.

Timothy J. Callaghan (a pseudonym) obtained his master's degree in journalism and settled in New England, where he worked for a major news agency. He married an Irish-American woman who shared his passion for all things Irish.

Unfortunately, the differences we had in Ireland over the tactics employed by the I.R.A. and living on opposite coasts of the United

States, caused us to drift apart. The last I heard from Callaghan was when he sent me a series of newspaper articles he wrote about the terrorist attacks on September 11, 2001, on the Twin Towers of the World Trade Center in New York.

Fergus Martin (a pseudonym) was released from Long Kesh Prison in 1998, following the Good Friday Agreement. He had served seven years of a twelve-year sentence. After we met in Long Kesh, we corresponded until the time he was released.
His first wife had divorced him soon after he was sent to prison. After Fergus returned home to Ardoyne, he married a second time.
Although I hadn't heard from Fergus in nearly a decade, when I was in Belfast in 2006, I went to Ardoyne and paid him a visit. Fergus had suffered a lot in his thirty-eight years and had gone prematurely gray, but he appeared happy and content when I saw him with his family around him. His new wife had given him two children.

Terry Quinn (a pseudonym) was also released from Portlaoise Prison after the Good Friday Agreement. He had served eight years of a twelve-year sentence and returned home to his family in Tallaght. For a while, I exchanged holiday cards with the Quinns, but eventually lost touch with them.

Sonny Boyle (a pseudonym) was among the dissident Republicans who didn't support the Good Friday Agreement. It was reported in the late 1990's that Sonny had cut ties with Sinn Féin and been removed from his position in the Provisional I.R.A.'s southern command, and to avoid arrest he had fled to the European continent.

Patrick J. Murphy (his real name) wrote me periodically over the years. He shared his observations about the ongoing peace talks, misgivings about concessions being made by the Republican movement, and his views about the future of socialism in Ireland and throughout the world. Even though we differed ideologically, our bonds of friendship remained firm, and Paddy often reminded me that whenever I was in Ireland, I had a place to stay in Ardoyne.
In addition to being an Irish language enthusiast, Paddy had a keen interest in poetry, history, and literature, and we discussed in our letters

whatever books we were currently reading. I wrote him about my travels in Mexico and sent him a bottle of José Cuervo tequila and a few books from time to time, including William H. Prescott's classic *The History of the Conquest of Mexico* and John Steinbeck's *The Pearl,* a novella set in a village on the Baja California peninsula.

Paddy included in his letters some of his poems, which had been published in various poetry journals. It was through one of these journals that he was contacted by an Englishwoman named Anne, who admired his poetry. She came to visit him in Belfast. Just as a budding romance developed, they learned she had cancer. Her death left Paddy, in his own words, "completely shattered."

When I visited Fergus Martin in 2006, he brought me to the house Paddy was then living in on Jamaica Street in Ardoyne. We hadn't seen one another in fourteen years and the once jolly fat man had become frail and old. But Paddy's blue eyes were still bright, and he grinned broadly as he grasped my hand, as we stood in his front room, which was packed wall to wall with books on shelves and in towering stacks. His health had deteriorated, and I learned he suffered a number of strokes.

Patrick Joseph Murphy (a.k.a. Pádraig Ó Murchú) died at the age of seventy-one on November 17, 2011. May God rest him.

Geraldine McKeever (a pseudonym) became my devoted pen pal. I also wrote her about my trips to Mexico and we told one another about whatever books we were reading. Geraldine sent me Peadar O'Donnell's *Islanders,* a novel about fishermen living off the coast of Donegal, and various newspaper clippings she came across of stories that she thought would interest me.

Soon after I left Belfast, Geraldine moved from Eglantine Avenue into a flat nearby. But the change brought about another severe depression, and she was hospitalized again. Denis Irwin (a pseudonym) faithfully visited her and when she was discharged, they were married. I sent them a set of floral dishes with matching teacups as a wedding present and wished them the very best.

Geraldine and Denis soon put the Troubles of Belfast behind them and moved to Wales, where two of her brothers and a sister had already settled.

GLOSSARY

Aes Sídhe (Pron. ace shee): older Gaelic form of the modern Irish Gaelic *aos sí,* meaning "people of the mounds." A supernatural race in Celtic mythology, comparable to fairies or elves, said to live underground.

AK-47: Soviet assault rifle. The initials AK are for Avtomat Kalashnikova, Russian for "automatic Kalashnikov," and the number "47" refers to 1947, the year the rifle was first produced.

Amerikay: old-time Irish pronunciation of America.

An Phoblacht/ Republican News (Pron. ahn fob-lackt; English: the republic): weekly newspaper of the Irish Republican movement, published by the Sinn Féin party.

Armalites: assault and semi-automatic rifles manufactured by an American small arms company called ArmaLite. Their AR-15s and AR-18s were favorite weapons of the I.R.A.

Atoll: Irish pronunciation of "at all."

Aye: "yes" in Ulster English, from Scots English.

Bap: crusty bread roll that originates from Belfast.

Bazookas: shoulder-type rocket launchers, widely used by the U.S. Army, especially during World War II.

B-Specials: as the Ulster Special Constabulary were commonly called, was a quasi-military special police force in Northern Ireland. Formed in 1920, just before the partition of Ireland, they were overwhelmingly Protestant and Unionist, and were seen by the Catholic minority in Northern Ireland as a bigoted sectarian force. The B-Specials were disbanded in 1970 and replaced by the Ulster Defence Regiment.

Beidh ár lá againn (Pron. beh are la ah-ginn; English: we will have our day): popular Irish Republican slogan.

Bejaysus: see Jaysus.

Binman: garbage collector.

Black North: used to describe the North of Ireland, or Ulster, due to the majority presence of Protestants in the northern province. Sometimes said in a pejorative way, other times in a mildly mocking way. Black meaning evil or wicked.

Black stuff, The: good, strong pint of Guinness Stout.

Blitz: German bombing campaign against Britain during World War II. The term came from *blitzkrieg,* the German word meaning "lightning war."

Bloke: regular guy, an ordinary man.

Blootered: drunk.

Bob: shilling. Old shilling coins, in Britain and Ireland, were worth 12 pence.

Bodhrán (Pron. bow-rawn): traditional goatskin frame drum of the ancient Celts.

Bollocks: literally means testicles, but often used as a vulgar insult for one who is spitefully stubborn or mean-spirited, or generally despicable. Also, simply used as an expression of anger.

Boot: trunk of a car.

Bout ye: means "how are you?" Short for "what about you?"

Boyos: boys or lads, sometimes derogatory or patronizing.

Brilliant: fantastic or great, popular term among young people.

Brits: refers to the British people, but more specifically to the British Army stationed in Northern Ireland.

Brogue: English pronunciation of the Gaelic word *bróg,* meaning shoe, but also often referring to an Irish accent. It was once falsely suggested the term stemmed from the perception that the Irish spoke English so peculiarly that it was as if they did so "with a shoe in their mouths." But the term may have come from the Gaelic word *barróg,* meaning "a hold (on the tongue)," thus accent or speech impediment. Some Irish people may consider a *brogue* to describe their accent as offensive.

Bru, brew: mispronunciation of bureau, as in the welfare bureau. In Northern Ireland, the *bru,* also known as the dole, is a government unemployment benefit.

Bugger-all: very little or nothing.

Cantinas: Mexican bars or saloons.

Cara (Pron. kor-ah; English: friend): when addressing a person, the vocative is used, *a chara* (Pron. ah khor-ah; English: oh, friend). When referring to a person as a friend, the third person is used, *mo chara* (Pron. moh khor-ah; my friend). My good friend, *mo chara mhaith* (Pron. moh khor-ah wah).

Casey Kasem's Top Forty (or American Top Forty): a popular syndicated radio music program that played the top weekly rock-and-roll hits, hosted in the 1970's and 1980's by Casey Kasem.

Cathleen Ní Houlihan: female personification of Ireland.

Céad míle fáilte (Pron. kayd mee-leh fahl-cheh; English: a hundred thousand welcomes): traditional Irish greeting.

Céilí (Pron. kay-lee): social event at which there is Irish traditional music and dance.

Celtic cross: Christian cross featuring a nimbus or ring that emerged in the early Middle Ages in Celtic Ireland, Scotland, Wales, Cornwall in England, and Brittany in France.

Celts: ancestors of the native Irish, Scottish, Welsh, Cornish, and Bretons.

Cervezas: Spanish for beers.

Claddagh: Irish design originating in the village of Claddagh, County Galway, in the 17th century, of hands holding a crowned heart, most often used on a ring, which represents love, loyalty, and friendship.

Colleen: anglicization of the Gaelic word *cailín,* meaning a girl or young woman.

Connemara pony: a breed of pony originating in Connemara, a region in the West of Ireland.

Craigavon: James Craig or 1st Viscount Craigavon (1871-1940), Unionist politician who served as the first prime minster of Northern Ireland from 1921 to 1940.

Craythur (Pron. crate-her; from the Gaelic *créatúr*): means both creature and whiskey, as whiskey (anglicization of *uisce beatha;* English: water of life) can be said to give life and have a life of its own. "A drop of the craythur" is a popular expression.

Cromwell, Oliver (1599-1658): Lord Protector of the Commonwealth of England, Scotland, and Ireland after the execution of King Charles I. A Protestant religious fanatic, Cromwell led a ruthless campaign against the Catholics of Ireland.

Crum, The: short for Crumlin Road Jail, officially H.M. Prison Belfast.

Cumann na mBan (Pron. kum-an nah man; English: league of women): formed in 1914 as a women's auxiliary to the Irish Volunteers. The women's paramilitary organization later became part of the I.R.A.

Currach: small round boat traditionally used in Ireland, made of wickerwork covered with animal hides.

Da: diminutive for father.

Dacent: Irish pronunciation of decent.

Dáil Éireann (Pron. doil air-awn; English: assembly of Ireland): lower house of the parliament of the Republic of Ireland.

Dander: walk or stroll.

Dear: expensive.

Diplock trial: criminal courts in Northern Ireland for non-jury trials of specified serious crimes, often during the Troubles for political and terrorism-related cases.

Divil a one, The: not a single one, none. "Divil" being the Irish pronunciation for devil.

Doobie: marijuana cigarette.

Dr. Seuss: popular author and illustrator of children's books.

Dubs: short for Dubliners.

Éamon, Éamonn (Pron. ay-mon): Irish given name for Edmond.

Éamonn an Chnoic (Pron. ay-mon ahn kunik; English: Edmond of the Hill): popular song in Gaelic about Éamonn Ó Riain, a rapparee or outlaw, who became a local Robin Hood-like figure in the late 17th and early 18th centuries in County Tipperary.

Easter Rising: armed insurrection during Easter Week in 1916. Republicans proclaimed the establishment of an Irish Republic in Dublin and along with some 1,600 followers staged a rebellion against the British government in Ireland. The bloody week-long battle left hundreds dead and wounded and reduced much of the city center to rubble. Although the Rising failed, and its leaders were executed by the British, there were those of the opinion that it was more glorious than many a victory. For it showed the world – and the Irish themselves – that Ireland still had men and women willing to fight and die so that she may be a free and independent nation. The Easter Rising led to the War of Independence (1919-21) and subsequently to the partitioning of Ireland. Twenty-six of the country's thirty-two counties gained partial independence as the Irish Free State, later to be declared the Republic of Ireland. While the six counties in the northeast of the country remained under British control.

Eejit: Irish pronunciation of idiot.

Éire, Éirinn, Éireann & Erin: all mean Ireland. *Éire* (Pron. air-eh), the Gaelic name of the modern twenty-six county Republic of Ireland, evolved from the Old Gaelic word *Ériu,* the name of the ancient matron goddess of Ireland. *Éirinn* (Pron. air-in) is the dative case form and *Éireann* (Pron. air-awn) is the genitive case form. The anglicized form *Erin* became a popular poetic and romantic name for Ireland and is used as a female personification of the country.

Emerald Isle: Ireland has long been known as the Emerald Isle because of her rich, green fields.

Entry: alleyway in Belfast.

Erin go Bragh (Pron. erin go brah): anglicization of the Gaelic phrase *Éirinn go Brách* (Pron. air-in go brawk; English: Ireland forever). An ancient Irish battle-cry.

Fag: in addition to American slang for a homosexual, is British and Irish slang for a cigarette.

Fenian Brotherhood: secret revolutionary organization formed in America in 1858 by Irish Catholic immigrants, linked to the Irish

Republican Brotherhood (I.R.B.) in Ireland. Their name was derived from the ancient Fianna, the fierce band of warriors led by the legendary Fionn mac Cumhaill (anglicized as Finn MacCool). The Fenians gained powerful support in the Union army during the American Civil War (1861-65), and a number of Irish-Americans returned to Ireland to take part in the Fenian Rising of 1867. The word "Fenian" also became a derogatory term, particularly in Northern Ireland, for an Irish Catholic.

Fianna Éireann (Pron. fee-ah-nah air-awn; also written as Fianna na hÉireann and Na Fianna Éireann; English: warriors of Ireland): founded in 1902 in Belfast as a national youth organization, inspired by the British Boy Scouts. Became the youth wing of the I.R.A. An individual member is known as a *Fian*.

Flat: apartment; and a flatmate is a roommate.

Fortnight: period of two weeks.

Free Staters: those who supported the Anglo-Irish Treaty of 1921 that led to the creation of the Irish Free State. Republicans continue to use "Free Staters" as a term of derision for their political opponents in the Republic of Ireland.

Frog: derogatory term for the French.

Front room: older term, synonymous with living room.

Gaelic: derives from *Gaelige,* which is the word in Irish Gaelic for the language itself. With the rise of Irish nationalism in the early 20th century, it became customary in Ireland to call Gaelic simply Irish when speaking in English. But outside of Ireland, the Irish language is still generally referred to as Gaelic. This has especially been the case in America, which experienced large-scale Irish immigration in the 19th and early 20th centuries. Irish-Americans, often several generations removed from Ireland, have continued to call the language Gaelic as their Irish-born ancestors had.

Gaelic Athletic Association: founded in 1884, the organization primarily promotes Gaelic sports, but also the Irish language and culture.

Gaelic League: founded in 1893 as a social and cultural organization to promote the Irish language.

Gaelic Revival: late 19th century national revival of interest in the Irish language and culture, after Gaelic had died out as a spoken tongue except in isolated rural areas, as English had become the official and literary language of Ireland.

Gaeltacht (Pron. gail-tockt): regions of Ireland which are still largely Gaelic-speaking. These areas are mostly in the western counties of Donegal, Mayo, Galway, and Kerry, with smaller pockets in Cork and Waterford.

Gaol: older spelling of jail.

Gardaí (Pron. gar-dee; English: guardians, and often called guards): national police service in the Republic of Ireland; officially *An Garda Síochána* (Pron. ahn gar-dah shee-oh-cahn-ah; English: the guardian of the peace). An individual officer is known as a *garda*.

Gargle: alcoholic drink.

Gas: very funny situation or person.

Gent: short for gentleman.

Go mbeirimíd beo ar an am seo arís (Pron. go mer-ih-meed bee-oh er ahn am shuh areesh; English: may we be alive at this same time again next year): Irish blessing popular as a New Year's toast.

Gob: mouth; derived from the Gaelic word for beak.

Gombeen men (from the Gaelic *gaimbín*, meaning monetary interest): originally greedy usurers who lent money to small farmers and others of limited means at ruinous interest rates. Later extended to corrupt businessmen and politicians looking to make quick profits at the expense of others.

Great pond: other side of the Atlantic Ocean, as in "across the great pond."

Guinness: founded in 1759 in Dublin, the dark, dry stout beer has long been Ireland's national drink. Although actually a very dark shade of ruby, Guinness appears black in color, so it's sometimes referred to as "the black stuff." Also, called "a pint of plain," from when the noted author and humorist Flann O'Brien declared, "a pint of plain is your only man."

G'wan: for "go on" or "go away with you." Used to express polite disbelief.

Hard man: equivalent to the American tough guy.

Having someone on: means joking with someone.

H-Blocks of Long Kesh: officially H.M. Prison Maze, where the majority of paramilitary prisoners in Northern Ireland were held during the Troubles. Called the H-Blocks because of the uniform "H" shaped plan of each cellular block. Commonly called Long Kesh from the days in the early 1970's when a disused R.A.F. airfield, located in the small village of Long Kesh, was turned into the Long Kesh Detention Centre.

Heckler and Koch: German-made firearm. Northern Ireland's R.U.C. were issued Heckler and Koch MP5 submachine guns.

Hood: short for hoodlum.

Hoof, hoofing: to go on foot.

Hun: disparaging term for the Germans during World War I, when the German Empire was compared by the British to the ancient Huns who ravaged many regions under Attila. It then became a derogatory term for the British themselves in Ireland as the English people are largely descended from the Germanic Anglo-Saxon tribes that settled in Britain.

Hurling: one of Ireland's native Gaelic games.

Irish Citizen Army: small paramilitary group of trained union volunteers organized in 1913 to defend striking workers in Dublin against employers using the police to attack them. In 1916, it played a prominent role in the Easter Rising under the leadership of James Connolly.

Irish Echo, The: weekly Irish-American newspaper based in New York.

Irish Free State: created in 1922 with dominion status under the British Crown. It comprised twenty-six of the thirty-two counties of Ireland. In 1937, the state took the name "Ireland," or in the Irish language, *Éire* (Pron. air-eh).

Irish National Liberation Army (I.N.L.A.): see under Irish Republican Army (I.R.A.).

Irish Northern Aid Committee (NORAID): Irish-American fundraising organization founded in New York after the start of the Troubles in Northern Ireland in 1969, which supported a pro-Irish Republican lobby in the United States and offered financial assistance to Republican families in Ireland, especially the families of Republican prisoners. NORAID was also known to have raised money for the illegal Provisional I.R.A.

Irish People, The: NORAID's weekly newspaper based in New York.

Irish Republican Army (I.R.A.), (Gaelic: Óglaigh na hÉireann; Pron. og-luh nah air-awn; English: Volunteers of Ireland): underground army fighting for an independent Ireland since 1919. Split in 1969 into the Official I.R.A. and the Provisional I.R.A. The Officials adopted a communist ideology and sought a proletarian revolution. They declared a truce in 1972. Former members of the Officials went into constitutional left-wing politics or joined the Irish National Liberation Army (I.N.L.A.), a small Marxist-Leninist Republican paramilitary group founded in 1974. The dominant Provisional branch of the I.R.A., allied with the socialist Sinn Féin party, maintained traditional Republican goals of an independent, united thirty-two county state, by forcing the British government to leave Northern Ireland by political violence or negotiation. The Provos, often known simply as the I.R.A., also saw themselves as defenders of the Catholic working-class minority from Loyalist sectarian attacks. A member of the I.R.A. was known as a volunteer, *óglach* in Gaelic.

Irish Republican Brotherhood (I.R.B.): forerunner of the I.R.A., founded in 1858 in Dublin, was a secret, oath-bound revolutionary organization dedicated to overthrowing British rule by force in Ireland and establishing an Irish Republic.

Irish Volunteers (Gaelic: Óglaigh na hÉireann; Pron. og-luh nah air-awn): militia founded in 1913 in Dublin. The Volunteers fought for Irish independence in the Easter Rising of 1916 with the Irish Citizen Army and joined together to become the Irish Republican Army.

Jar: another word for a pint glass of beer; from which the term "jarred" comes, meaning drunk.

Jaysus: Irish pronunciation of Jesus. Used as a mild expletive and an alternative to Jesus to avoid blasphemously taking the Lord's name in vain. Also, bejaysus for "by Jesus."

Jerries: German soldiers, especially during World War II.

John Bull: personification of England, as Cathleen Ní Houlihan is the personification of Ireland.

John, Paul, and Ringo: three members of The Beatles, the hugely popular English rock band of the 1960's. The fourth member was named George Harrison.

Joint: marijuana cigarette.

Knackers: derogatory term for tinkers, or Irish travellers, meaning low class.

Knickers: women's underwear.

Langer: multi-purpose Cork slang word for an annoying or contemptible person (usually male), a fool or an idiot. Also, used for drunk and the male organ.

Legless: drunk.

Leprechauns: magical, mischievous, elf-like little men in Irish folklore, clad in green coats and green hats. Legend has it, leprechauns know the whereabouts of pots of gold.

Liam (Pron. lee-um): Irish given name for William.

Lifted: arrested.

Limey: American slang for British.

Loo: lavatory or toilet.

Lorries: trucks.

Loyalists: Protestant Unionists who staunchly believe Northern Ireland should remain a part of the United Kingdom and often advocated violence to remain in the union.

Luftwaffe: German air force.

Mack the Knife: cheery pop song from the 1950's about a murderer.

M.P.: Member of Parliament of the United Kingdom.

Narrowback: disparaging term Irish immigrants used for American-born Irish, because many of the immigrants worked hard laboring jobs that required strength and muscle, while Irish-Americans often worked better jobs that didn't require as much physical labor.

Nationalists: support an independent and reunited Ireland achieved by non-violent, political means. They are usually Catholics in Northern Ireland.

Navvies: laborers employed in hard physical work, often building roads or canals.

Nollaig shona duit (Pron. null-eg hunna ditch; English: happy Christmas to you).

NORAID: see Irish Northern Aid Committee.

Normans: were Vikings (also called Norsemen or Northmen) who in the 10th and 11th centuries settled in northwestern France, in the region which became known as Normandy. The Normans conquered England in 1066, and invaded Ireland a hundred years later in 1169.

Northern Ireland: while the Irish Free State gained partial independence in 1922 after the country was partitioned, and later became the Republic of Ireland, six counties in the northeast, within the province of Ulster, remained firmly under the British Crown as part of the United Kingdom. Republicans and many Nationalists refused to accept the legitimacy of the political entity of Northern Ireland and continued to call it "the north of Ireland" or "the North" or simply "the Six Counties." Loyalists and Unionists, on the other hand, often refer to Northern Ireland as Ulster, though only six of Ulster's nine counties comprise the British statelet. (The six counties are Antrim, Armagh, Derry, Down, Fermanagh, and Tyrone; the three Ulster counties in the Republic of Ireland are Cavan, Donegal, and Monaghan.) Northern Ireland's capital and largest city is Belfast.

Och (Pron. okh): Gaelic equivalent of "Oh!" An exclamation to express a range of emotions, typically surprise, disapproval, regret, etc.

Ochone (Pron. okh-own; from the Gaelic *ochóin*): expression of sorrow or regret.

Óglaigh na hÉireann: see Irish Republican Army (I.R.A.).

Oiche mhaith (Pron. ee-ha wah; English: good night).

O'Donnell, Peadar (1893-1986): prominent Irish Republican and socialist activist, politician, and writer.

On the wagon: abstaining from drinking alcohol.

Orange Order (or the Loyal Orange Association; its members known as Orangemen): Protestant Unionist fraternal organization based in Northern Ireland, where it was founded in County Armagh in 1795 to maintain the Protestant Ascendancy in Ireland. It was named for William of Orange, the Protestant Dutchman who seized the throne of England from Catholic King James II in the Protestant "Glorious Revolution" of 1688. The Order claims to defend Protestant civil and religious liberties, but critics have accused it of being explicitly anti-Catholic. The tradition of Orangemen triumphantly parading, in bowler hats and orange sashes, with drums and flute bands, through Catholic neighborhoods has long heightened sectarian tensions and provoked violent clashes.

Oul, ould: Irish pronunciations of old.

Ould Sod: affectionate reference to Ireland as a homeland, or country of origin, among Irish immigrants and their descendants.

Pádraic, Pádraig (Pron. pawd-rick): Irish given name for Patrick. My friend Paddy Murphy's name in Gaelic was Pádraig Ó Murchú (Pron. oh-mur-khoo).

Papists: disparaging term for Catholics, i.e., followers of the pope.

Peelers: in England police officers have been affectionately called "bobbies," from a diminutive derivative of the name of the 19th century founder of the London Metropolitan Police, Sir Robert Peel. But first Peel organized the countrywide Constabulary of Ireland in 1822, when he served there as chief secretary. His police force in Ireland were called – with considerably less affection – "peelers," as they're still known in Northern Ireland. Peel's Irish constabulary became the Royal Irish Constabulary in 1867, after suppressing the Fenian Rising.

Pioneers: The Pioneer Total Abstinence Association of the Sacred Heart, founded in 1898, is a Catholic organization for teetotalers based in Ireland.

Piss, Pissed: vulgar slang for urine or urinate, "piss" is also used for cheap beer. While in American slang it additionally means angry, in British and Irish slang "pissed" means drunk.

Planters: Protestant settlers of Ulster in the 17th century from the Lowlands of Scotland and northern England. The Plantation of Ulster was an organized colonization of the province to forcibly remove native Gaelic-speaking Irish Catholics from their ancestral lands and settle, or "plant," those lands with English-speaking Protestants who were loyal to King James I.

Poleaxed: drunk.

Prams: baby carriages.

Prods: derogatory term for Protestants. Also, Proddys.

Provie, Provo: short for the Provisional Irish Republican Army.

Pub: short for public house. Establishments licensed to serve alcoholic drinks and often food. Owners or managers are called publicans or landlords.

Punters: bettors or gamblers.

Quare: Irish pronunciation of queer, meaning strange or unusual. Also, can substitute for very, really, or extremely.

Queue up: means to "line up."

Quid: British pound sterling. Equal to 100 pence.

Ra: short for the I.R.A.

R.A.F. (Royal Air Force): British air force.

Rapparees: Irish irregular foot soldiers in the Williamite War (1688-91), who fought on the Catholic Jacobite side, armed with a weapon that in Gaelic was called a *rápaire,* a short pike. During and after the war, many rapparees turned to banditry.

Republic of Ireland, or Éire (Pron. air-eh): former Irish Free State, consisting of twenty-six of Ireland's thirty-two counties, was officially declared a Republic in 1949. As in the case of Northern Ireland, Republicans have denied the legitimacy of the Irish Republic and often continued to call it "the Free State" or "the twenty-six counties." The Republic of Ireland's capital and largest city is Dublin.

Republicans: support a reunited Ireland free from British rule, and during the Troubles generally accepted the use of violence as necessary to achieve this. They also tend to support the radical politics of Sinn Féin, whose objective is to establish a socialist Irish Republic. Most Republicans in Northern Ireland come from Catholic backgrounds.

Royal Irish Regiment (R.I.R.): British Army regiment formed in 1992 with the amalgamation of the Ulster Defence Regiment and the Royal Irish Rangers.

Royal Ulster Constabulary (R.U.C.): formed in 1922 after the creation of Northern Ireland. Formerly the Royal Irish Constabulary (R.I.C.) before Ireland was partitioned. The heavily militarized Northern Irish police force was almost entirely Protestant and as an extension of the British Crown was a target of the I.R.A. In 2001, the R.U.C. was replaced by the civilian Police Service of Northern Ireland (P.S.N.I.).

Royal Vic: colloquial abbreviation of Royal Victoria Hospital, Belfast's largest hospital.

Sacked: to be dismissed or discharged from a job.

Sanctus, Sanctus, Sanctus: from the traditional Latin Tridentine Mass (*Sanctus* is Latin for holy).

Saoirse (Pron. sur-shuh; English: freedom).

Saxon: used as a synonym for the English, as the English are largely descended from the Germanic Anglo-Saxon tribes that invaded the lower half of Britain in the fifth and sixth centuries A.D.

Screw: prison slang for guard or warder.

Séamus (Pron. shay-mus): Irish given name for James.

Seán (Pron. shawn): Irish given name for John.

Semtex: general-purpose plastic explosive.

Shanachie: anglicization of the Gaelic word *seanchaí* (Pron. shan-nuh-kee). Traditional Gaelic storyteller.

Shankill Butchers: violent Loyalist murder gang that was active between 1975-82 in Belfast. They were notorious for torturing and murdering random or suspected Catholics. Often the victims' throats were hacked with a butcher's knife.

Short: a handgun.

Siobhán (Pron. she-vawn): Irish given name for Joan.

Sinn Féin (Pron. shin fayn; English: ourselves alone): founded in 1905, originally as an Irish Nationalist political party, advocating passive resistance to British rule, such as the withholding of taxes, establishing an Irish ruling council and independent local courts, it became increasingly Republican. After the 1916 Easter Rising, the party became committed to the establishment of an Irish Republic. During the Troubles, Sinn Féin was the political wing of the Provisional I.R.A. Active both in the Republic of Ireland and Northern Ireland, Sinn Féin is a Republican, democratic socialist and left-wing party.

Slag: tease someone in a friendly manner.

Sláinte (Pron. slawn-cheh; English: health): Irish drinking toast. Also, *Sláinte mhaith* (Pron. slawn-cheh wah; English: good health), and *Sláinte agatsa* (Pron. slawn-cheh ah-gut-sah; English: to your health as well).

Slán leat (Pron. slawn lat; English: goodbye or farewell). Less formal, *Slán* (bye). Also, *Slán go fóill* (Pron. slawn go foyle; English: goodbye for now).

Social Democratic and Labour Party (S.D.L.P.): main constitutional Nationalist political party in Northern Ireland. Founded in 1970 by various Nationalist, civil-rights, and moderate left-wing activists, the S.D.L.P. has called for Irish reunification and an end to the British presence in Ireland, though rejects the use of violence to achieve this. It's largely supported by the Catholic middle-class.

Sod: vulgar slang for an annoying or unpleasant person, usually a man. Originally short for sodomite, a homosexual.

Special Air Service (S.A.S.): elite force of the British Army, organized and trained for special operations, surveillance, and counterterrorism.

Special Branch: main domestic security agency of the *An Garda Síochána*, the national police service in the Republic of Ireland. It's the state's primary anti-terrorism and counter-espionage investigative unit. Officially the Special Detective Unit, they are still commonly referred to as Special Branch as they were under the British. Note, there was also a R.U.C Special Branch in Northern Ireland during the Troubles.

Spuds: potatoes. Spud comes from the Gaelic *spád*, the word for spade.

Squaddies: British soldiers.

Stick: to be criticized, often unfairly or for something that is not one's fault. Such as, in "receiving a bit of stick," i.e., criticism.

Stormont: suburb of east Belfast and the location of the Northern Ireland Parliament Buildings, the seat of British rule in Northern Ireland.

Strongbow: nickname of Richard de Clare, 2nd Earl of Pembroke, who led the Anglo-Norman invasion of Ireland in 1169.

Taigs: derogatory term applied to Catholics. "Taig" is a misspelling of the Irish given name Tadhg (Pron. teig). Similarly, the common nicknames of Paddy and Mick have been used as pejoratives for Irish Catholics.

Tan War (or the Black and Tan War): another term for the Irish War of Independence (1919-21), as many of the British soldiers wore improvised uniforms which were a mixture of the dark green (that appeared black) of the Royal Irish Constabulary and the khaki of the British Army.

Taoiseach (Pron. tee-shack; English: chief or leader): prime minister of the Republic of Ireland. The *taoiseach* is the head of the government, while the president (*Uachtarán na hÉireann*) is the head of state.

Tay: Irish pronunciation of tea.

Teetotaler: person who never drinks alcohol.

Tight: drunk.

Tinkers: like Gypsies, are a nomadic itinerant people, roaming from place to place. But unlike Gypsies, who trace their origin to the Indian subcontinent, tinkers are ethnically Irish. They are thought to date back to the upheaval of the Cromwellian period, during the mid-1600's, when they became unsettled and wanderers of the Irish roads and byways. They became known as tinkers as they were itinerant tinsmiths, fixing pots and pans. But in recent decades, the term came to be considered by some a pejorative and was replaced by "travellers."

Tiocfaidh ár lá (Pron. chucky are la; English: our day will come): popular Irish Republican slogan. Also, *Tiocfaidh ár lá agus beir bua* (Pron. chucky are la ah-gus bear bew-ah; English: our day will come with victory).

Toerag: worthless, contemptible, or despicable person. The term originated from the strips of cloth that beggars wrapped around their feet or toes as a substitute for socks.

Tricolor flag: national flag of the Republic of Ireland, with three equal vertical bands of green, white, and orange. Green represents Catholics and the Republican cause. Orange represents Protestants and is associated with Protestant William of Orange, who defeated the deposed Catholic King James II in 1690. White signifies the hope for peace between them.

Troubles, The: euphemism for the three-decade long conflict in Northern Ireland.

Turf: peat. An accumulation of partially decayed vegetation or organic matter removed from bogs and burned as an alternative to firewood in Irish homes.

Uisce beatha (Pron. ish-ka ba-ha; English: water of life): the Irish Gaelic term from which the word "whiskey" is derived. Note, in Scottish Gaelic it's spelled *uisge beatha.*

Ulster Defence Association (U.D.A.): formed in 1971, was the largest and most violent of the Protestant Loyalist paramilitary groups during the Troubles. The majority of their victims were Catholic civilians, killed at random, in what the organization called retaliation for I.R.A. attacks on Protestants. In spite of their ruthless history, the U.D.A. long remained a legal organization, and claimed responsibility for most of their sectarian killings under the cover name of the illegal Ulster Freedom Fighters (U.F.F.), so that the U.D.A. wouldn't be held accountable. It was not until 1992 that the British government proscribed the U.D.A. as a terrorist organization.

Ulster Defence Regiment (U.D.R.): locally recruited, almost exclusively Protestant, regiment of the British Army that replaced the B-Specials in 1970. The Loyalist militia earned a reputation for anti-Catholic bigotry and had links with illegal Loyalist paramilitaries. A number of U.D.R. soldiers were convicted of involvement in sectarian killings of Catholics. In 1992 the regiment was merged with the Royal Irish Rangers to form the Royal Irish Regiment.

Ulster Freedom Fighters (U.F.F.): Loyalist murder squad. Cover name used by the Ulster Defence Association when it killed random Catholic civilians and assassinated known Republicans. (See U.D.A. above.)

Ulster Scots: descendants of Lowland Scottish Protestant settlers (called planters) who arrived in Ulster in the 17th century. In America, they are generally called Scotch-Irish.

Ulster Volunteer Force (U.V.F.): originally formed in 1912 as a Protestant Loyalist militia, with powerful British and Unionist support, to oppose Home Rule (the campaign for self-government for Ireland within the United Kingdom, 1870 – ca. 1921). The U.V.F. reemerged in 1966, just before the Troubles officially began, as a violent Loyalist paramilitary organization. Their stated goal was to combat Irish Republicanism and maintain Northern Ireland's status as part of the United Kingdom. The U.V.F. attacked and assassinated known Republicans and Nationalists, but the vast majority of their victims were random Catholic civilians. The British government proscribed the U.V.F. in 1975.

Union Jack: national flag of the United Kingdom.

Unionists: believe Northern Ireland should remain a part of the United Kingdom and are usually Protestants.

United Irishmen, Society of: founded in 1791 in Belfast by radical Protestants, they embraced Irishmen of every class and religious persuasion. In Belfast, the membership was Presbyterian and mostly middle-class. The Society in Dublin, divided between Protestant and Catholic, was likewise mostly middle-class but included members of the gentry and aristocracy. They initially sought to reform the government of Ireland on principles of civil, political, and religious liberty. However, disappointment in their aspirations of constitutional reforms, combined with a growing radicalism inspired by the American and French Revolutions, along with Irish patriotism, set them on the path to insurrection. When British authorities suppressed the Society, it reorganized as an underground movement which sought to break Ireland's connection with England and gain Irish independence. Although the short-lived 1798 United Irishmen Rebellion was crushed militarily, and its leaders put to death, it inspired future generations, like the later 1916 Easter Rising, to envision Ireland free and "A Nation Once Again."

Uzis: Israeli-made submachine guns.

Villa, Pancho: Mexican revolutionary, guerrilla leader, and bandit during the early 1900's.

Wean (Pron. ween): small child in Ulster English, truncation of "wee one," from Scots English.

Wee: small in Ulster English. Another word imported from Scotland. Sometimes put in front of words just to make them sound friendlier.

Wheelie bin: garbage can with wheels.

Whisht: hush. An exclamation used among the Irish to demand silence, such as "keep one's whisht," meaning "to hold one's tongue".

Ye, Yez, Youse: all mean "you" in the singular or plural. *Ye* is a remnant of older English still heard in Ireland. *Ye* is widely used to denote the second person pronoun and can be singular or plural. However, the plural can be rendered as *yez* or *youse,* often depending on what part of the country one is in.

Young Ireland Movement: Nationalist political and cultural movement in the 1840's dedicated to repealing the 1801 Act of Union between Great Britain and Ireland. A branch of Young Irelanders formed the Irish Confederation to free Ireland of British rule by direct action and in 1848 attempted a failed insurrection.

www.ingramcontent.com/pod-product-compliance
Lightning Source LLC
Chambersburg PA
CBHW060449170426
43199CB00011B/1137